EDUCATIONAL PSYCHOLOGY 98/99

Thirteenth Edition

Editors

Kathleen M. Cauley
Virginia Commonwealth University

Kathleen M. Cauley received her Ph.D. in educational studies/human development from the University of Delaware in 1985. Her research interests center on applying cognitive developmental research to school learning. Currently, she is studying children's mathematical understanding in classrooms that are implementing the National Council of Teachers of Mathematics Standards for Mathematics.

Fredric Linder
Virginia Commonwealth University

Fredric Linder received an A.B. in American civilization from the University of Miami, Florida, an M.A. in psychology from the New School for Social Research, and a Ph.D. in educational psychology from the State University of New York at Buffalo. His research and publications focus on the values, locus of control, and cognitive learning styles of students.

James H. McMillan
Virginia Commonwealth University

James H. McMillan received his bachelor's degree from Albion College in 1970, his M.A. from Michigan State University in 1972, and his Ph.D. from Northwestern University in 1976. He has reviewed and written extensively on many topics in educational psychology. His current interests are classroom assessment and school report cards.

A Library of Information from the Public Press

Dushkin/McGraw·Hill
Sluice Dock, Guilford, Connecticut 06437

Visit us on the Internet—http://www.dushkin.com/

The Annual Editions Series

ANNUAL EDITIONS, including GLOBAL STUDIES, consist of over 70 volumes designed to provide the reader with convenient, low-cost access to a wide range of current, carefully selected articles from some of the most important magazines, newspapers, and journals published today. ANNUAL EDITIONS are updated on an annual basis through a continuous monitoring of over 300 periodical sources. All ANNUAL EDITIONS have a number of features that are designed to make them particularly useful, including topic guides, annotated tables of contents, unit overviews, and indexes. For the teacher using ANNUAL EDITIONS in the classroom, an Instructor's Resource Guide with test questions is available for each volume. GLOBAL STUDIES titles provide comprehensive background information and selected world press articles on the regions and countries of the world.

VOLUMES AVAILABLE

ANNUAL EDITIONS

Abnormal Psychology
Accounting
Adolescent Psychology
Aging
American Foreign Policy
American Government
American History, Pre-Civil War
American History, Post-Civil War
American Public Policy
Anthropology
Archaeology
Astronomy
Biopsychology
Business Ethics
Canadian Politics
Child Growth and Development
Comparative Politics
Computers in Education
Computers in Society
Criminal Justice
Criminology
Developing World
Deviant Behavior
Drugs, Society, and Behavior
Dying, Death, and Bereavement

Early Childhood Education
Economics
Educating Exceptional Children
Education
Educational Psychology
Environment
Geography
Geology
Global Issues
Health
Human Development
Human Resources
Human Sexuality
International Business
Macroeconomics
Management
Marketing
Marriage and Family
Mass Media
Microeconomics
Multicultural Education
Nutrition
Personal Growth and Behavior
Physical Anthropology
Psychology
Public Administration
Race and Ethnic Relations

Social Problems
Social Psychology
Sociology
State and Local Government
Teaching English as a Second
    Language
Urban Society
Violence and Terrorism
Western Civilization, Pre-Reformation
Western Civilization, Post-Reformation
Women's Health
World History, Pre-Modern
World History, Modern
World Politics

GLOBAL STUDIES

Africa
China
India and South Asia
Japan and the Pacific Rim
Latin America
Middle East
Russia, the Eurasian Republics, and
    Central/Eastern Europe
Western Europe

Cataloging in Publication Data
Main entry under title: Annual Editions: Educational Psychology. 1998/99.
        1. Educational psychology—Periodicals. 2. Teaching—Periodicals. I. Cauley, Kathleen M., *comp.*; Linder, Fredric, *comp.*; McMillan, James H., *comp.* II. Title: Educational psychology.
ISBN 0–697–41284–9   370.15'05   82–640517   ISSN 0731–1141

Thirteenth Edition

Cover image © 1998 PhotoDisc, Inc.

Printed in the United States of America

Printed on Recycled Paper

Editors/Advisory Board

Members of the Advisory Board are instrumental in the final selection of articles for each edition of ANNUAL EDITIONS. Their review of articles for content, level, currentness, and appropriateness provides critical direction to the editor and staff. We think that you will find their careful consideration well reflected in this volume.

EDITORS

Kathleen M. Cauley
Virginia Commonwealth University

Fredric Linder
Virginia Commonwealth University

James H. McMillan
Virginia Commonwealth University

ADVISORY BOARD

Roberta Ahlquist
San Jose State University

Thomas L. Bennett
Bowling Green State University

Robert G. Brown
Florida Atlantic University

Edward J. Caropreso
Clarion University

Victor I. Culver
Virginia Wesleyan College

Karen G. Duffy
SUNY at Geneseo

Godfrey Franklin
University of West Florida

Albert H. Gardner
University of Maryland, College Park

William L. Goodwin
University of Colorado, Denver

William M. Gray
University of Toledo

Cheryl Greenberg
University of North Carolina Greensboro

Elaine C. Koffman
Northeastern Illinois University

Golam Mannan
Indiana University-Purdue University

Laura J. Massey
Montana State University

Donald H. Saklofske
University of Saskatchewan

Fred Schultz
University of Akron

Thomas J. Shuell
University of Buffalo

Sandra M. Stokes
University of Wisconsin, Green Bay

Harvey N. Switzky
Northern Illinois University

Lani M. Van Dusen
Utah State University

Staff

Ian A. Nielsen, Publisher

EDITORIAL STAFF

Roberta Monaco, Developmental Editor
Dorothy Fink, Associate Developmental Editor
Addie Raucci, Senior Administrative Editor
Cheryl Greenleaf, Permissions Editor
Deanna Herrschaft, Permissions Assistant
Diane Barker, Proofreader
Lisa Holmes-Doebrick, Program Coordinator

PRODUCTION STAFF

Brenda S. Filley, Production Manager
Charles Vitelli, Designer
Lara M. Johnson, Design/Advertising Coordinator
Shawn Callahan, Graphics
Laura Levine, Graphics
Mike Campbell, Graphics
Joseph Offredi, Graphics
Juliana Arbo, Typesetting Supervisor
Jane Jaegersen, Typesetter
Marie Lazauskas, Word Processor
Kathleen D'Amico, Word Processor
Larry Killian, Copier Coordinator

To the Reader

In publishing ANNUAL EDITIONS we recognize the enormous role played by the magazines, newspapers, and journals of the *public press* in providing current, first-rate educational information in a broad spectrum of interest areas. Many of these articles are appropriate for students, researchers, and professionals seeking accurate, current material to help bridge the gap between principles and theories and the real world. These articles, however, become more useful for study when those of lasting value are carefully *collected, organized, indexed,* and *reproduced* in a *low-cost format,* which provides easy and permanent access when the material is needed. That is the role played by ANNUAL EDITIONS. Under the direction of each volume's *academic editor,* who is an expert in the subject area, and with the guidance of an *Advisory Board,* each year we seek to provide in each ANNUAL EDITION a current, well-balanced, carefully selected collection of the best of the public press for your study and enjoyment. We think that you will find this volume useful, and we hope that you will take a moment to let us know what you think.

Educational psychology is an interdisciplinary subject that includes human development, learning, intelligence, motivation, assessment, instructional strategies, and classroom management. The articles in this volume give special attention to the application of this knowledge to teaching.

Annual Editions: Educational Psychology 98/99 is divided into six units, and an overview precedes each unit, which explains how the unit articles are related to the broader issues within educational psychology.

The first unit, *Perspectives on Teaching,* presents issues that are central to the teaching role. The articles' authors address the challenges of responding to calls for educational reform and the role of research in meeting those challenges.

The second unit entitled *Development,* is concerned with child and adolescent development. It covers the cognitive, social, and emotional components of development. The essays in this unit examine the developmental implications for teachers of early childhood programs, the social forces affecting children and adolescents, and the personal and social skills needed to cope with school learning and developmental tasks.

The third unit, regarding exceptional and culturally diverse students, focuses on the learning disabled, the gifted, and multicultural education. Diverse students require an individualized approach to education. The articles in this unit review the characteristics of these children and suggest programs and strategies to meet their needs.

In the fourth unit, *Learning and Instruction,* articles about theories of learning and instructional strategies are presented. The different views of learning, such as information processing, behaviorism, and constructivist learning, represent the accumulation of years of research on the way humans change in thinking or behavior due to experience. The principles generated by each approach have important implications for teaching. These implications are addressed in a section on instructional strategies, covering such topics as instructional methods, authentic instruction, computer-aided teaching, and learning styles.

The topic of motivation is perhaps one of the most important aspects of school learning. Effective teachers need to motivate their students both to learn and to behave responsibly. How to manage children and what forms of discipline to use are issues that concern parents as well as teachers and administrators. The articles in the fifth unit, *Motivation and Classroom Management,* present a variety of perspectives on motivating students and discuss approaches to managing student behavior.

The articles in the sixth unit review assessment approaches that can be used to diagnose learning and improve instruction. The focus is on grading practices and appropriate uses of standardized tests. Performance-based assessment is introduced as a promising new approach to classroom measurement.

A new feature that has been added to this edition are selected *World Wide Web* sites, which can be used to further explore the articles' topics. These sites are cross-referenced by number in the *topic guide.*

This thirteenth edition of *Annual Editions: Educational Psychology* has been revised so as to present articles that are current and useful. Your responses to the selection and organization of materials are appreciated. Please complete and return the postage-paid *article rating form* on the last page of the book.

Kathleen M. Cauley

Fredric Linder

James H. McMillan
Editors

Contents

The concepts in bold italics are developed in the article. For further expansion please refer to the Topic Guide and the Index.

UNIT 3

Exceptional and Culturally Diverse Students

Eight articles look at the problems and positive effects of educational programs for learning disabled, gifted, and culturally diverse children.

The concepts in bold italics are developed in the article. For further expansion please refer to the Topic Guide and the Index.

vi

The concepts in bold italics are developed in the article. For further expansion please refer to the Topic Guide and the Index.

UNIT 4

Learning and Instruction

Eleven selections explore the important types of student/teacher interaction.

The concepts in bold italics are developed in the article. For further expansion please refer to the Topic Guide and the Index.

UNIT 5

Motivation and Classroom Management

Seven selections discuss student control and motivation in the classroom.

The concepts in bold italics are developed in the article. For further expansion please refer to the Topic Guide and the Index.

ix

The concepts in bold italics are developed in the article. For further expansion please refer to the Topic Guide and the Index.

x

UNIT 6

Assessment

Five articles discuss the
implications of educational
measurement for the classroom
decision-making process and
for the teaching profession.

The concepts in bold italics are developed in the article. For further expansion please refer to the Topic Guide and the Index.

Topic Guide

This topic guide suggests how the selections in this book relate to topics of traditional concern to educational psychology students and professionals It is useful for locating interrelated articles for reading and research. The guide is arranged alphabetically according to topic. Articles may, of course, treat topics that do not appear in the topic guide. In turn, entries in the topic guide do not necessarily constitute a comprehensive listing of all the contents of each selection. **In addition, relevant Web sites, which are annotated on pages 4 and 5, are noted in bold italics under the topic articles.**

TOPIC AREA	TREATED IN	TOPIC AREA	TREATED IN
Action Research	3. Using Action Research to Assess Instruction *(6, 9, 11, 12, 25, 31, 32, 33, 34)*	Cognitive Development	5. New Brain Development Research 6. Moral Child *(1, 13, 16, 17, 21)*
Alternative Assessment	38. Taking Aim at Testing 39. What Happens between Assessments? 40. Practicing What We Preach in Designing Authentic Assessments *(31, 32, 33, 34)*	Cognitive Learning	19. Making Information Memorable 20. First Seven . . . and the Eighth 21. Styles of Thinking, Abilities, and Academic Performance 28. Blueprints for Learning *(18, 21, 22, 24, 25, 26)*
At-Risk Behavior	9. Developmental Tasks of Early Adolescence 10. Cooperative Learning in Middle and Secondary Schools 32. Using Motivational Theory with At-Risk Children *(6, 16, 17, 18, 20, 28, 30)*	Cognitive Maps	28. Blueprints for Learning *(21)*
		Computers in Education	29. Kids, Computers, and Constructivism *(7, 9, 10)*
		Constructivism	26. Caring Classroom's Academic Edge 29. Kids, Computers, and Constructivism *(25, 26, 27, 29)*
Authentic Assessment	38. Taking Aim at Testing 39. What Happens between Assessments? 40. Practicing What We Preach in Designing Authentic Assessments *(31, 32, 33, 34)*	Cooperative Learning	10. Cooperative Learning in Middle and Secondary Schools *(3, 5, 6, 9)*
Behaviorism	22. Rewards of Learning 23. Rewards Versus Learning 24. Sticking Up for Rewards 30. New Look at School Failure and School Success *(1, 16, 27, 28, 29, 30)*	Creativity	15. Creative Personality *(17, 18, 21)*
		Disabilities	11. Where to Educate Rachel Holland? 12. Holistic Approach to Attention Deficit Disorder *(17, 20)*
Child/Adolescent Development	5. New Brain Development Research 6. Moral Child 7. Early Childhood Programs That Work for Children from Economically Disadvantaged Families 8. Helping Children Become More Prosocial 9. Developmental Tasks of Early Adolescence *(1, 2, 13, 14, 15, 16)*	Discipline	35. Creating a Constructivist Classroom Atmosphere 36. Why Violence Prevention Programs Don't Work—and What Does *(13, 27, 28, 29)*
		Diverse Students	17. "All Kids Can Learn" 16. Goals and Track Record of Multicultural Education *(17, 18, 19, 20, 21)*
Classroom Climate	26. Caring Classroom's Academic Edge 27. Using the Learning Environment Inventory *(21, 22, 24, 25, 26)*	Early Childhood	5. New Brain Development Research 7. Early Childhood Programs That Work for Children from Economically Disadvantaged Families 8. Helping Children Become More Prosocial *(6, 7, 8, 9, 10, 11, 12, 14, 16, 17, 18, 19, 20, 21, 28, 29, 30)*
Classroom Management	33. How to Defuse Defiance, Threats, Challenges, Confrontations 34. Connecting Instruction and Management in a Student-Centered Classroom *(27, 28, 29, 30)*		

2

TOPIC AREA	TREATED IN	TOPIC AREA	TREATED IN
Educational Reform	4. Public's View of Public Schools 38. Taking Aim at Testing (6)	Performance Assessment	38. Taking Aim at Testing 39. What Happens between Assessments? 40. Practicing What We Preach in Designing Authentic Assessments (31, 32, 33, 34)
Emotional Development	5. New Brain Development Research (1, 2, 5)	Portfolio Assessment	38. Taking Aim at Testing (31, 32, 33, 34)
Family Structure	6. Moral Child 7. Early Childhood Programs That Work for Children from Economically Disadvantaged Families 9. Developmental Tasks of Early Adolescence (13, 14, 15, 16, 18, 19, 21, 23)	Positive Reinforcement/ Praise	22. Rewards of Learning 23. Rewards versus Learning 24. Sticking Up for Rewards (3, 5, 22, 24, 25, 26)
Gifted Children and Youth	13. Is It Acceleration or Simply Appropriate Instruction for Precocious Youth? 14. Meeting the Needs of Young Gifted Students (17, 21)	Self-Concept/Self	25. Tyranny of Self-Oriented Self-Esteem (1, 2)
		Social Development	8. Helping Children Become More Prosocial 26. Caring Classroom's Academic Edge (14, 16)
Grading	41. Grades: The Final Frontier in Assessment Reform (31, 32, 33, 34)	Standardized Tests	37. Challenges of Assessing Young Children Appropriately 38. Taking Aim at Testing (31, 32, 33, 34)
Humanistic Education	26. Caring Classroom's Academic Edge (21, 29)	Student Centered	32. Using Motivational Theory with At-Risk Children 34. Connecting Instruction and Management in a Student-Centered Classroom (17, 18, 21, 30)
Information Processing	19. Making Information Memorable (22, 24)		
Intelligence	20. First Seven . . . and the Eighth 21. Styles of Thinking, Abilities, and Academic Performance (22, 24, 25, 26)	Student/Teacher Relationships	2. How Novice Teachers Can Succeed with Adolescents 26. Caring Classroom's Academic Edge 27. Using the Learning Environment Inventory 30. New Look at School Failure and School Success 34. Connecting Instruction and Management in a Student-Centered Classroom (7, 10, 12, 24, 25, 27, 30)
Metacognition	28. Blueprints for Learning (21)		
Minority Students	16. Goals and Track Record of Multicultural Education (18, 19, 21)		
Moral Development	6. Moral Child (13, 15)	Teacher Beliefs	17. "All Kids Can Learn" (17, 18, 19, 20, 21)
Motivation	26. Caring Classroom's Academic Edge 30. New Look at School Failure and School Success 31. Motivating Underachievers 32. Using Motivational Theory with At-Risk Children (21, 27, 28, 29, 30)	Teacher's Role	1. Piece of Cake 2. How Novice Teachers Can Succeed with Adolescents (7, 8, 9, 11, 12)
		Technology	29. Kids, Computers, and Constructivism (7, 9, 10)
Multicultural Education	16. Goals and Track Record of Multicultural Education 18. Multiculturalism (18, 19, 21)	Thinking Skills	28. Blueprints for Learning (21)
Norms	38. Taking Aim at Testing (3, 5, 6, 31, 32, 33, 34)		

Selected World Wide Web Sites for
AE: Educational Psychology

All of these Web sites are hot-linked through the *Annual Editions* home page: *http://www.dushkin.com/annualeditions* (just click on this book's title). In addition, these sites are referenced by number and appear where relevant in the Topic Guide on the previous two pages.

Some Web sites are continually changing their structure and content, so the information listed may not always be available.

General Sources

1. American Psychological Association—*http://www.apa.org/psychnet/*—By exploring the APA's "PsychNET," you will be able to find links to an abundance of articles and other resources that are useful in the field of educational psychology.

2. Educational Resources Information Center—*http://www.aspensys. com/eric/index.html*—This invaluable site provides links to all ERIC sites: clearinghouses, support components, and publishers of ERIC materials. You can search the ERIC database, find out what is new, and ask questions about ERIC.

3. National Education Association—*http://www.nea.org/*—Something—and often quite a lot—about virtually every education-related topic can be accessed at or through this site of the 2.3-million-strong National Education Association.

4. National Parent Information Network/ERIC—*http://ericps.ed.uiuc. edu/npin/npinhome.html*—This is a clearinghouse of information on elementary and early childhood education as well as urban education. Browse through its links for information for parents and for people who work with parents.

5. U.S. Department of Education—*http://www.ed.gov/pubs/ TeachersGuide/*—Government goals, projects, grants, and other educational programs are listed here as well as many links to teacher services and resources.

Perspectives on Teaching

6. The Center for Innovation in Education—*http://www.educenter. org/*—This is the main page of the Center for Innovation in Education, self-described as a "not-for-profit, non-partisan research organization" focusing on K-12 education reform strategies. Click on its links for information about and varying perspectives on school privatization and other reform initiatives.

7. Classroom Connect—*http://www.classroom.net/*—This is a major Web site for K-12 teachers and students, with links to schools, teachers, and resources online. It includes discussion of the use of technology in the classroom.

8. Education World—*http://www.education-world.com/*—Education World provides a database of literally thousands of sites that can be searched by grade level, plus education news, lesson plans, and professional-development resources.

9. EdWeb/Andy Carvin—*http://edweb.cnidr.org/*—The purpose of Ed-Web is to explore the worlds of educational reform and information technology. Access educational resources around the world, learn about trends in education policy and information infrastructure development, examine success stories of computers in the classroom, and much more.

10. Goals 2000: A Progress Report—*http://www.ed.gov/pubs/goals/ progrpt/index.html*—Open this site to survey a progress report by the U.S. Department of Education on the Goals 2000 reform initiative. It provides a sense of the goals that educators are reaching for as they look toward the future.

11. PREPnet—*http://prep.net/*—This site contains Web sites for educators. It covers a wide range of topics dealing with K-12 resources and curricula. Its links will prove useful for examining issues ranging from school reform to teaching values.

12. Teacher Talk Forum—*http://education.indiana.edu/cas/tt/tthmpg. html*—Visit this site for access to a variety of articles discussing life in the classroom. Clicking on the various links will lead you to electronic lesson plans, covering a variety of topic areas, from Indiana University's Center for Adolescent Studies.

Development

13. Association for Moral Education—*http://www.wittenberg.edu/ame/*—AME is dedicated to fostering communication, cooperation, training, curriculum development, and research that links moral theory with educational practices. From here it is possible to connect to several sites on ethics, character building, and moral development.

14. Child Welfare League of America—*http://www.cwla.org/*—The CWLA is the United States' oldest and largest organization devoted entirely to the well-being of vulnerable children and their families. This site provides links to information about issues related to morality and values in education.

15. Ethics Updates/Lawrence Hinman—*http://ethics.acusd.edu/*—This is Professor Hinman's consummate learning tool. The site provides both simple concept definition and complex analysis of ethics, original treatises, and sophisticated search engine capability. Subject matter covers the gamut, from ethical theory to applied ethical venues. There are many opportunities for user input.

16. The National Academy for Child Development—*http://www.nacd. org/*—This international organization is dedicated to helping children and adults reach their full potential. Its home page presents links to various programs, research, and resources into such topics as ADD/ADHD.

Exceptional and Culturally Diverse Children

17. ERIC Clearinghouse on Disabilities and Gifted Education—*http:// www.cec.sped.org/gifted/gt-faqs.htm*—This page will give you access to information on identifying and teaching gifted children, attention deficit disorders, and other topics in gifted education.

18. Global SchoolNet Foundation—*http://www.gsn.org/*—Access this site for multicultural education information. The site includes news for teachers, students, and parents; as well as chat rooms, links to educational resources, programs, and contests and competitions.

19. Multicultural Publishing and Education Council—*http://www.mpec. org/*—This is the main page of the MPEC, a networking and support organization for independent publishers, authors, educators, and librarians fostering authentic multicultural books and materials. It has excellent links to a vast array of resources related to multicultural education.

20. National Attention Deficit Disorder Association—*http://www.add. org/*—This site, some of which is under construction, will lead you to information about ADD/ADHD. It has links to self-help and support groups, outlines behaviors and diagnostics, answers FAQs, and suggests books and other resources.

21. Scholastic/Kristen Nelson—*http://place.scholastic.com/instructor/ curriculum/smart.htm*—Open this page for Kristen Nelson's discussion of ways in which teachers can help to nurture children's multiple intelligences. She provides a useful bibliography and resources.

Learning and Instruction

22. Education Week on the Web—*http://www.edweek.org/*—At this *Education Week* page, you will be able to open archives, read special reports, keep up on current events, look at job opportunities, and access a variety of articles of relevance in educational psychology. A great deal of material is helpful in learning and instruction.

23. National Network for Family Resiliency—*http://www.nnfr.org/nnfr/*—This organization's starting page will lead you to a number of resource areas of interest in learning about resiliency, including General Family Resiliency, Violence Prevention, and Family Economics.

24. Online Internet Institute—*http://www.oii.org/*—A collaborative project among Internet-using educators, proponents of systemic reform, content-area experts, and teachers who desire professional growth, this site provides a learning environment for integrating the Internet into educators' individual teaching styles.

25. Teachers Helping Teachers—*http://www.pacificnet.net/~mandel/*—This site provides basic teaching tips, new teaching-methodology ideas, and forums for teachers to share their experiences. Download software and participate in chat sessions. It features educational resources on the Web, with new ones added each week.

26. The Teachers' Network—*http://www.teachnet.org/*—Bulletin boards, classroom projects, online forums, and Web mentors are featured on this site, as well as the book *Teachers' Guide to Cyberspace* and an online, 4-week course on how to use the Internet.

Motivation and Classroom Management

27. Canada's Schoolnet Staff Room—*http://www.schoolnet.ca/adm/ staff/*—Here is a resource and link site for anyone involved in education, including special-needs educators, teachers, parents, volunteers, and administrators.

28. Early Intervention Solutions—*http://www.earlyintervention.com/ library4.htm*—EIS presents this site to address concerns about child stress and reinforcement. It suggests ways to deal with negative behaviors that may result from stress and anxiety among children.

29. Kathy Schrock's Guide for Educators—*http://www.capecod.net/ schrockguide/*—This is a classified list of sites on the Internet found to be useful for enhancing curriculum and teacher professional growth. It is updated daily.

30. National Institute on the Education of At-Risk Students—*http:// www.ed.gov/offices/OERI/At-Risk/*—The At-Risk Institute supports a range of research and development activities designed to improve the education of students at risk of educational failure due to limited English proficiency, race, geographic location, or economic disadvantage. Access its work and links at this site.

Assessment

31. Awesome Library for Teachers—*http://www.neat-schoolhouse.org/ teacher.html*—Open this page for links and access to teacher information on everything from assessments to child development topics.

32. Carfax—*http://www.carfax.co.uk/subjeduc.htm*—Look through this extensive index for links to education publications such as *Journal of Beliefs and Values, Educational Philosophy and Theory,* and *Assessment in Education.* The site also provides links to articles and research that will prove helpful in assessment.

33. Phi Delta Kappa International—*http://www.pdkintl.org/home.htm*—This important organization publishes articles about all facets of education. By clicking on the links in this site, for example, you can check out the online archive of the journal, *Phi Delta Kappan,* which has resources such as articles having to do with assessment.

34. Washington (State) Commission on Student Learning—*http:// csl.wednet.edu/*—This Washington State CSL site is designed to provide access to information about the state's new academic standards, assessments, and accountability system, but it is useful to teachers from other areas as well. Many resources and Web links are included.

We highly recommend that you review our Web site for expanded information and our other product lines. We are continually updating and adding links to our Web site in order to offer you the most usable and useful information that will support and expand the value of your Annual Editions. You can reach us at: *http://www. dushkin.com/annualeditions/.*

Perspectives on Teaching

The teaching-learning process in school is enormously complex. Many factors influence pupil learning—such as family background, developmental level, prior knowledge, motivation, and, of course, effective teachers. Educational psychology investigates these factors to better understand and explain student learning. We begin our exploration of the teaching-learning process by considering the teaching role.

In the first article, Jeffrey Aceto describes the elementary teacher's role through the eyes of a first-time substitute teacher. He leaves his first day with a renewed admiration for the many talents required of full-time teachers. The next article, by Robin Gordon, describes aspects of the secondary teacher's role that many beginning teachers may overlook.

A less obvious aspect of the teaching role is the systematic effort to improve. In the third article, "Using Action Research to Assess Instruction," Carole Shulte Johnson and Inga Kromann-Kelly illustrate how teachers should conduct an action research project to improve the classroom learning environment. The authors describe five basic questions to guide the development of action research projects. The five questions determine (1) the question to answer in the study; (2) the data that are relevant; (3) how the data will be collected; (4) how the data will be analyzed; and (5) what implications can be drawn from the data. As the professional development schools envisioned by the Holmes partnership (a consortium of research universities and public schools) and others are established, teacher research may become a professional expectation.

Finally, educational reform and the public's view of our schools are examined. The article "The Public's View of Public School" provides insight into both community and teacher expectations for schools. Deborah Wadsworth argues that practices proposed by educational reformers like integration, heterogeneous grouping, and so on, are not valued by the public or by teachers.

Educational psychology is a resource for teachers that emphasizes disciplined inquiry, a systematic and objective analysis of information, and a scientific attitude toward decision making. The field provides information for decisions that are based on quantitative and qualitative studies of learning and teaching rather than on intuition, tradition, authority, or subjective feelings. It is our hope that this aspect of educational psychology is communicated throughout these readings, and that, as a student, you will adopt the analytic, probing attitude that is part of the discipline.

While educational psychologists have helped to establish a knowledge base about teaching and learning, the unpredictable, spontaneous, evolving nature of teaching suggests that the best they will ever do is to provide concepts and skills that teachers can adapt for use in their classrooms. The issues raised in these articles about the impact of the reform movement on teachers help us understand the teaching role and its demands. As you read articles in other chapters, consider the demands they place on the teaching role as well.

Looking Ahead: Challenge Questions

Describe several of the roles teachers are expected to perform.

As educational reform progresses, what new demands will it place on teachers?

How does research, either teacher research or formal educational research, improve teaching?

UNIT 1

A Piece of Cake

Mr. Aceto describes his first day as a substitute teacher in an elementary school. Would he do it again? Absolutely! Would he consider doing it for a living? Not a chance!

Jeffrey T. Aceto

JEFFREY T. ACETO is a civil engineer with DeLuca Hoffman Associates, Inc., consulting engineers, in South Portland, Me.

RECENTLY I found myself nearing 30 and an unemployed college graduate. So when a friend urged me to try substitute teaching, I thought, Why not? How could it possibly be difficult? I'm a mature, well-adjusted adult, and they'd only be little kids. Besides, the day would be a short seven hours. It would be a piece of cake!

Arriving at school on a crisp autumn morning, I find the scene reminiscent of my own youth. School buses unloading kids in colorful jackets who clutch homework, books, and lunch boxes. My own lunch is the sole content of my briefcase, and it occurs to me that after 20 years I've only traded my metal lunch box for a leather one.

The assistant principal greets me warmly and assures me the day will go smoothly. "Just follow your instructions, and everything will be fine," she says. Sure, I think. Piece of cake.

I find my classroom spotless and orderly, with clean chalkboards and the

Illustration by Brenda Grannan

desks and chairs lined up neatly. Student work and seasonal displays adorn the walls. A paper turkey with necktie feathers watches me warily from the back wall. Not a bad room, I think, although the teacher I'm replacing has spelled *calendar* wrong. That's a bad sign, I think, but I shrug it off.

The children begin to flood into the room. At least, I assume that these are my students. I realize that I'm largely at their mercy with regard to who is supposed to be where and when. As they shrug off their child-sized backpacks, they turn fresh little faces toward me. It is a scene a grandparent would love. At first they are reluctant to speak to me, but soon I am bombarded with questions and comments: "Where is Mrs. Smith? Are you Mr. Smith? How long will you be here?"

I can see the realization dawning on them that what they have here is a rare bird, indeed: a substitute teacher — and a man, to boot. This guy is fresh meat. The class quickly reaches a silent consensus: today is a good day for raising some hell.

"Just" follow the instructions, and everything will be okay, the assistant principal had said. Here, Christian, "just" go in there and take on those lions. Hail, Caesar, we who are about to die salute thee! Let the games begin. I confidently announce that it is time for math and ask them to take out their books. Immediately there is a flurry of activity that Federal Express would admire.

Have you ever tried to wrestle an octopus? One boy is fighting with another, and a girl is writing on the chalkboard. Someone has just gone out the door, and half a dozen girls are crooning over a troll catalogue.

Names are the first minor crisis. I have no idea who is who. I look up to the turkey for assistance, but its facial expression clearly says, "You're on your own, pal."

Great. Four years of college, and I've been reduced to babysitting on a large scale. My vocabulary for the day swiftly degenerates into versions of a few set phrases: Please sit down. Do your own work. Leave her alone. Raise your hand if you want to speak. Stay in line. I quickly discover that fact is stranger and more complicated than fiction; Schwarzenegger had it easy in *Kindergarten Cop*.

I find myself frantically scanning the instructions every five minutes or so. Are we doing what we're supposed to be doing? Is everyone in the right place? Are we falling behind or running ahead of the schedule? These instructions are my lifeline, and I tape them up — out of the students' reach — with great reverence.

An unbidden rush of thoughts cascades through my brain. Why did I wear a tie? It just gives them something to get a grip on. I've heard less noise at a University of Maine hockey game. Are fishing vessels lost at sea homing in on the roar emanating from this classroom? Are the other teachers shaking their heads in disgust at a rookie who can't control the students?

"Quiet, please" is like whistling in the wind. "Let's keep it quiet" has all the impact of a popgun on an elephant. It's time to go ballistic. "I need quiet right now or someone's going to the office!" That's better. Good job, Jeff, practice "teaching by terrorism." I'm not surprised that threats work — after all, I'm a little bit afraid of the office myself. But threats work for only about five minutes.

Soon, snack time arrives. Everything so far has been just a warm-up for the main event, as the little darlings go into a sugar-crazed frenzy. I see candy, donuts, chips, and soda; fruit, vegetables, and juice are scarcely to be found. What a great idea this is: fill them up with sugar-laden snacks; then ask them to sit quietly and read.

WE MOVE steadily through the day. There is a toothache, an earache, a nosebleed, a lost pair of glasses. Two of the worst offenders are dispatched to the office; one student has to take anti-nervousness drugs. I am assured by the veteran teachers that this qualifies as a typical day.

Recess duty is the longest 20 minutes of my life. Now I know how Custer felt. I'm surrounded by 200 little wingnuts running into, over, and through each other. "Suzie hit me!" "Johnny kissed me!" "I can't find my watch!" I resist the strong urge to seek a hiding place instead of the missing watch.

With the incessant din of children's sounds, I find myself yearning for adult companionship. I pass fellow teachers in the halls; as if we're members of a secret society, we salute one another with weary, harried looks.

The teachers' lounge has all the warmth of an unemployment office. The chairs are wooden, hard, and too heavy for most of us to move by ourselves. The teachers share the room with mimeograph machines and cast-off office equipment. Ragged notices from the union compete for bulletin board space with news of bake sales and Tupperware parties. Talk in the lounge revolves around kids with head lice, kids who aren't toilet trained, abused kids, and kids who, it is conjectured, need psychological evaluation. I've felt more relaxed during dental surgery.

The children are the centerpiece of this confusing circus, of course, and no one can spend even one day with them without encountering a few special moments. A girl whom I coax through a reading passage breaks into a broad smile when I tell her she did a great job. A few children who are clearly ignored by their parents and starved for attention give me big hugs at the end of the day. I notice a chubby, plain girl who is ignored by the rest of the children. She reads aloud a story she has written. "Once-upon-a-time stories are stories of beautiful places where you will never go," she reads. It's the saddest thing I've ever heard; she's 8 years old, and already she's decided that she can never go to beautiful places.

I realize that this teaching stuff is more than babysitting. Trying to encourage youngsters like her is truly an important, even noble, cause.

"You're the best teacher in the world! Are you coming back tomorrow?" All day long they've been running through the halls, talking out in class, and using the restricted art supplies. They're pulling fast ones on me, but it doesn't matter. My sole goal is to end the day with the same number of warm, breathing bodies with which it began.

The end of the day arrives at last. A bus number is garbled over the intercom, there's a final rush to the door, and, suddenly, the quiet and stillness are deafening. The room looks as if it has been visited by a division of Patton's tanks. Desks and chairs are strewn about; the wastebaskets are overflowing. The carpeted floor is a collage of paper, candy wrappers, crayons, a half-eaten donut, an escaped earring, and one blue sock. That last item troubles me a bit. The turkey droops from the wall and appears to be laughing at me. One of the paper decorations hanging from the ceiling suddenly comes unglued and drifts to the floor.

It's time to put the day into perspective, I think. This was a class of "normal" kids. I didn't have those with fetal alcohol syndrome or those who have been abused. Everything was in my favor. There will be janitors to clean up after us, and there were other teachers to take charge of music, physical education, library, and special needs. I had a detailed plan and a schedule of what to do. The buses ran on time, and no gangs stalked the halls. I didn't have to deal with any parents or committees. And yet I feel as if I have just run a marathon.

The insignificant events of this, my first day in elementary education, are just a sampling of business as usual. I am now doubly impressed by the commitment and talents required of full-time teachers. I no longer condemn Mrs. Smith for her spelling error. I'm so tired that I have trouble finding my car after just one brief, seven-hour day.

Would I do it again? Absolutely. Piece of cake. Would I consider doing this for a living? Not a chance!

How Novice Teachers Can Succeed with Adolescents

**Beginning secondary teachers need more than knowledge of
content and teaching strategies. Insight into adolescent culture
is critical to success in managing a classroom.**

Robin L. Gordon

A student teacher was having serious problems managing the behavior of her 10th grade math students. When her students were not working well in their collaborative learning groups, she'd often ask them, "Can't we all just get along?" She could not understand why the students laughed when she used this phrase. The students, of course, immediately recognized it as Rodney King's plea during the 1992 Los Angeles uprising. The line was later incorporated into a song, displayed on T-shirts, and chanted by students. One of her students remarked to this confused teacher, "It just cracks me up when you say that!" Nevertheless, she did not comprehend the impact of what she was saying until her university observer explained.

This incident illustrates the need for beginning teachers to understand two critical teaching behaviors: social insight and what has been called "withitness." Such awareness can be the critical element in establishing an effective learning environment.

Social Insight

Waller asserted that teachers must learn "an elusive something which it is difficult to put between the covers of a book or to work up into a lecture. That elusive something is social insight" (1967, p. 1). Social insight can be described as an understanding of what is taking place in the classroom. That sounds rather simplistic at first. Yet, to accomplish this effectively, the teacher must have a sense of the students' culture as well as an understanding of student behavior.

Hall (1981) examined eight elements of culture that he defined generally as (1) verbal language, (2) nonverbal communication, (3) culture in general, (4) world view, (5) behavioral style, (6) values, (7) methods of reasoning, and (8) cultural and ethnic identification. Pennington adds a few more characteristics of culture: beliefs/values, sense of time, religion, and social relationships/communication networks (1985, pp. 30–39). Bennett notes that we often define culture as what shapes our thoughts and behavior. In line with this, multicultural education often concerns the development of multiple standards for perceiving, believing, doing, and evaluating (1990, p. 47).

These notions represent a sample of what some believe constitutes culture. The characteristics illustrate the fact that adolescent culture goes beyond ethnic or linguistic differences. Adolescents' speech patterns, popular music, styles of dress, favorite movies, and preferred places for recreation may either transcend or incorporate the political, religious, and social causes deemed important by adults. The requisite attribute is that adolescent culture belongs solely to the adolescent. Social insight is a vehicle that teachers can use to glimpse the meanings of the adolescent cultural milieu.

When a teacher lacks social insight, communication with students may be less effective, resulting in classroom management problems. In the case of the student teacher mentioned above, the students knew that their insults would not be understood. Their daily

 From *Educational Leadership,* April 1997, pp. 56-58. © 1997 by the Association for Supervision and Curriculum Development. All rights reserved. Reprinted by permission.

behavior continued to disintegrate, and after six weeks the student teacher's assignment had to be terminated.

Helping preservice or beginning teachers develop social insight remains a critical challenge for the teacher educator. Although it might at first appear to be relatively insignificant when compared to the myriad learning and teaching theories new teachers must master, adolescent social development should be of paramount concern if for no other reason than its relationship to managing a classroom effectively. Assuming the lesson is appealing, teachers whom adolescents perceive as successful socially seem to experience less difficulty capturing the interest of their students. Their classrooms run more smoothly. The teacher educator will find it difficult to help the student teacher who lacks this "understanding of the social situation of the

more than one disturbance at a time and do so quickly. Beginning teachers too often focus on one disruption and miss the start of another. Students become adept at knowing when the teacher's attention is elsewhere and they may use the time for social interaction— chatting, flirting, making faces. Experienced teachers know this, address the behavior, and engender a modicum of respect by having "eyes in the back of their head."

Secondary students are particularly critical of any teacher who does not display social insight. The student teacher is especially fair game for the spunky adolescent and is a likely target of a certain degree of disdain and criticism. Thus, in a matter of days, the student teacher who lacks social insight and withitness can be reduced to emotional Jell-O.

A second anecdote involves a

A final example is more encouraging. A student teacher was discussing a particularly complex topic in genetics with a 10th grade ESL (English as a Second Language) class. The students were struggling with the content but were focused intently on the student teacher. She radiated warmth and professionalism, and she used a popular video game as an example to help the students remember the structure of a gene. Everything about her, including her body language, verbal expression, and even eye contact, communicated sensitivity and empathy with her students. They recognized that she understood them; she had encountered the same feelings they were experiencing. The teacher was familiar with their culture, and this familiarity laid the groundwork for mutual respect. Students did not need to act out with her. Additionally, if any disruption occurred, she spotted it immediately and acted accordingly.

Effective teachers understand the many behaviors taking place in the classroom and how to react appropriately. They learn their students' names and behavior patterns quickly.

---

classroom and the need to adapt his or her personality to the needs of that milieu" (Waller 1967, p. 1).

"Withitness"
Kounin (1993) introduces the term "withitness" in his discussion of classroom management (Charles 1989, p. 28). Teachers who demonstrate withitness understand the many behaviors taking place in the classroom and how to react appropriately. Kounin identifies two behaviors in particular that communicate to students that their teacher is aware of the classroom. The first is knowing who is causing a disturbance. Some students are brilliant at fomenting small classroom arguments and then fading into obscurity. Effective teachers learn their students' names and behavior patterns quickly. Second, withit teachers can handle

student teacher who was attempting to teach algebra to an uninterested group of 10th grade students. Solving for unknowns was not high on their list of priorities that day. Their questions began to veer from the mathematical to the personal: "Why do you perspire so much?" "Why does your shirt hang out?" "Why do you wear bow ties?" "Do you know what you are doing?" This student teacher had lost control of his class and had no clue about how to relate to 15-year-olds. The lesson here is that a teacher may have a thorough grasp of content, but without social insight, he or she will be perceived as being out of touch with what is happening in the students' culture. This particular teacher exacerbated the problem by displaying a seeming lack of withitness. He may actually have been conscious of the students' insults but took no action.

Acquiring Cultural Information
One of the teacher educator's goals is to expedite the development of classroom management skills. Expanding Waller's discussion of social insight to include Kounin's notion of withitness provides a useful tool for learning such skills. The teacher not only becomes aware of student behavior but understands what is current and meaningful in students' lives. I like to refer to the result as academic biculturalism. The withit and socially insightful teacher uses cultural information effectively.

The question of how to develop social insight and withitness was posed to a group of secondary student teachers in their weekly seminar. The instructor's goal was twofold. First, she wanted students to realize that some of them might lack social insight by the very fact of their inability to address the question. Second, students who displayed social insight had the opportunity to share their knowledge with their peers.

The following list summarizes the strategies these student teachers used to ensure that they were in touch with their students' culture, thus facilitating

Megen O'Keefe, a student teacher in social studies at Hawthorne High School, shows confidence as she answers questions in the classroom.

their connection and rapport with students.

1. Expose yourself to adolescent culture. As painful as it may seem, watching MTV, listening to current music, and attending popular movies can help provide a connection to what is current in students' lives. This does not require teachers to participate in the latest fashions. For example, having an eyebrow pierced will not endear an adult to young people and can actually alienate them. Adolescents need to distinguish themselves from the adults who nurture them. Teachers can appreciate adolescent culture without embracing it as their own.

2. Affirm students' "weather." It can be helpful to express an understanding of why students have a high level of energy or are not interested in class on a particular day. For example, the school dance, Halloween, a lunch fight, or approaching vacations can all contribute to volatile student weather. Telling students it makes no difference that the prom is the next day is whistling in the wind.

3. Relate content to students' outside interests. Making abstract ideas more concrete by using examples that come from the students' adolescent world can be very effective. For example, in

one classroom, the teacher's explanation of why an oxygen atom attracts two hydrogen atoms did not seem relevant to Jesse; however, phrasing the concept in terms of the fact that two 7th grade girls were attracted to him hit closer to home. Teachers learn quickly that metaphors involving sex immediately pique adolescents' interest as long as the metaphors do not cross the invisible boundary of propriety.

4. Know your students. The secondary teacher has very little time to talk with students one-on-one, but it is important to find time for individual chitchat. Effective teachers use strategies such as greeting students at the door, referring to a student's interests in their lectures, or talking to students as they monitor classwork. Attending sporting events and school plays, reading the school paper, or being a club advisor are just a few ways teachers can connect with their students' educational and social loops.

5. Share your humanity with your students. Celebrate life with them. Successful teachers are not afraid to show their strengths and weaknesses to students in the proper context. The classroom is not a therapy group, but teachers can enjoy life along with their students.

Facilitating the beginning teacher's transition into the classroom is not a simple matter of presenting a list of do's and don'ts. As much as it may dismay the proponents of a technological model of teacher education, fledgling teachers can effectively process only a limited amount of information before facing students. New teachers enter the classroom armed with explicit class management plans, a firm belief about how students should act, and a strong grasp of content. However, if they cannot transport that arsenal of information and teacher tricks into the context of what is actually taking place in the classroom, their success will be hindered. Adding social insight and withitness to the arsenal makes it far more likely that the necessary connections will take place.

References

Bennett, C. (1990). *Comprehensive Multicultural Education: Theory and Practice.* 2nd ed. Boston: Allyn and Bacon.

Charles, C.M. (1989). *Building Classroom Discipline.* 3rd ed. New York: Longman.

Hall, E.T. (1981). *The Silent Language.* Garden City, N.Y.: Anchor Press.

Kounin, J.S. (November 1993). *Classrooms: Individuals or Behavior Setting.* Address sponsored by the Horizons of Knowledge Lecture Series, Indiana University, School of Education, Bloomington.

Pennington, D.L. (1985). "Intercultural Communication." In *Intercultural Communication: A Reader,* 4th ed., edited by L.A. Samovar and R.E. Porter. Belmont, Calif.: Wadsworth.

Waller, W.W. (1967). *The Sociology of Teaching.* New York: John Wiley and Sons.

Robin L. Gordon is Coordinator of Master of Arts of Teaching and Assistant Coordinator of Secondary Education at the School of Education, Loyola Marymount University, 7900 Loyola Blvd., Los Angeles, CA 90045.

Using Action Research To Assess Instruction

Carole Schulte Johnson and Inga Kromann-Kelly

Carole Schulte Johnson is a faculty member in the Department of Elementary and Secondary Education, at Washington State University, in Pullman, Washington. Inga Kromann-Kelly is a faculty member in the Department of Teaching and Learning, at Washington State University, in Pullman, Washington.

For years teachers have used self assessment as one way to improve the learning environment in their classrooms. Such assessment, however, tended to be of a private, nonsystematic nature and often was not clearly focused on a central question. Today more and more teachers are developing and experiencing an organized approach to classroom inquiry, known as action research, a concept which has evolved over the past several years. This approach entails stepping back from the immediate concern in order to gain a broader perspective on a problem; then collecting, analyzing, and interpreting data on the basis of a defined plan, and often sharing the results with professional colleagues.

Rather than formulating complex research procedures, perhaps best left to experts, we recommend beginning action research by answering these five basic questions: 1) What is the main question I am interested in pursuing? 2) What data are relevant? 3) What specific data will be collected, and how? 4) How will the data be analyzed? 5) What interpretations or implications can be drawn from the data?

THE QUESTION

Teachers often have several questions they wish to explore; however, in order to keep the research manageable you as a teacher embarking on action research need to decide your basic or most important question. Limited questions related to what you are doing in your classroom, such as "Are my students learning from this strategy?" or "What strategies do students use most successfully in perform-

ing some particular task?" work well for action research. For example, suppose we are interested in learning more about our students' attitude toward reading. We realize that various elements of the literacy program probably affect those attitudes so our basic question could be "How do the students feel about the different methods and materials used in the literacy program?"

COLLECTING DATA

Data can be gathered from transactions/interactions, products and cued or structured responses. Figure 1, while not all inclusive, suggests various sources of data within each category.

Triangulation of data (using at least three different data sources) is recommended. The value of using triangulation is in analyzing the question from several different viewpoints. For instance, one data set could be from each of the three categories on the chart or from two of the three categories. If only three data sources are used, it is recommended that no more than one cued or structured response source be included since these data usually are collected only at specific points of time, thus limiting the information to the context of those times.

When the different data sources are congruent, the acceptance of the results is strengthened. Conflicting data raise questions such as: Should other types of data sets have been used? Should some data sources carry more weight—for example, were the cued responses too structured or answered to please the teacher? Would it be valuable to refine or do additional research on this question?

We make decisions regarding the specific data to collect on the basis of its importance in seeking answers to the question and also the feasibility of collecting and analyzing it. In general, quantifiable data take less time to collect and analyze; however, meaningful data are not always readily quantifiable. While importance and feasibility are basic, other aspects are considered. Using excessive class, student and/or teacher time is avoided by collecting data from ongoing class activities such as journals and portfo-

	From Teacher	From Students
Figure 1 *Data Sources*		
Transactions/ Interactions	Field/observation/anecdotal notes	Video/audio tapes
	Video/audio tapes	
Products		Written products
		Artifacts
		Open-ended interviews
		Open-ended conferences
Cued/Structured Responses	Ratings	Tests
	Checklists	Questionnaires
	Tally of behaviors	Attitude measures
		Structured interviews
		Structured conferences
		Writing/work samples
		Checklists
		Ratings
		Logs

lios, the taping of class or small group activities as well as from brief cued or structured responses.

Unless individual conferences are part of the ongoing program and the data to be collected a normal part of the conferences, they may not be a feasible source of information. However, if a second person is available or only a small subset of students is involved, individual conferences become a possibility.

Another consideration is that students may tell teachers what they think the teacher wants to hear when cued or structured responses are obtained face-to-face. Responses on paper may be similarly biased, but such data-gathering instruments are generally viewed as providing a degree of anonymity.

When teacher observations are used, consideration is given to how structured and systematic they will be. Ways to provide structure include using a checklist of behaviors (e.g., answering, volunteering, getting out of seat) and keeping a tally of the number of times a behavior occurs, or by describing behavior at set time intervals. Audio/videotaping of an on-going class activity is an example of an unstructured observation. Systematic observations are made on a regular basis such as daily or weekly. The data can be taped; however, if teacher notes

are used, it is recommended they be written daily. Less systematic observations are those noted occasionally, when the teacher has time or when something strikes the teacher as important to note.

When writing notes, we need to remind ourselves that we see what we expect, so there is danger of bias. For example, as teachers, we know that certain of our students love to read while others do not. Thus, in examining attitudes, we are more inclined to note student behaviors which confirm what we already believe than those which conflict with our expectations.

Each source of data requires decisions on the part of the teacher. With materials such as journals, portfolios, or tapes, you decide what data to include and then structure the class or group so it can be collected. When a checklist or questionnaire is involved, you decide its content and how students (or teacher) will respond. Among the possibilities for such instruments are open ended questions or statements, items for the respondent to check off, or some type of rating system.

If you use a rating scale, you need to decide whether it will be an even numbered scale, thus avoiding a neutral position, or an odd numbered one which includes it. A two or three point scale is simpler for students in the primary grades; a five to seven point scale is common in upper grades and has the advantage of identifying subtle differences. Common terms for labeling points on a scale are *agree/disagree, like most/like least,* or 1 *(very low)* to 5 *(highest)*.

A simple format is helpful. Present the ratings at the top of the page; then list the items below with a blank for the number rating in front of each item. With instruments such as this, it is important to remind the students that you really want to know what they think so their opinions can be considered in making decisions about materials or procedures. From whom will student data be collected—the entire class, a small group or groups of students, individuals or some combination? For our research on student attitudes, we prefer information from the class rather than from selected representative students. The latter may well provide the spectrum of attitudes regarding reading, but not its strength related to specific methods or materials.

In examining student attitudes toward reading, the feelings of students constitute important and relevant data. To collect such information, we might use informal teacher observations, preferably collected on a regular basis, and student records of books and pages read daily and brief comments or reactions to what they have read. All of these items are easily obtained as a normal part of classroom activity.

Additionally, we would include a questionnaire asking students to rate what they think about each of the different literacy materials and activities used in the program. If many items are included, the questionnaire can be divided into several parts. Class discussion of the results would provide a useful source of additional information. Neither activity would take an inordinate amount of time and the findings could result in an improved curriculum. Our questionnaire requires limited teacher preparation time since it only involves developing a list of the materials and activities used, deciding their order as well as the kind of rating scale to use, and formatting the instrument.

ANALYZING AND INTERPRETING DATA

When analyzing data, teachers may want information about the class as a whole, about individual children, or about certain subgroups. Subgroups might include students at certain achievement levels, such as above grade level, at grade level, students with special needs, boys at different achievement levels, or girls at different ones. When data are kept for each student, teachers can decide at any time what individuals or subgroups they may wish to study.

Some of the data teachers gather are quantifiable and can be analyzed without the use of statistics. Under some circumstances, statistical analyses show significance with only small differences in raw data, and such results may not be particularly useful. For example, knowing the percent of the class rating an item *very low* or *highest* may be more important for your consideration in curriculum change. Again, it is the teacher who must interpret the data and decide what is meaningful. What do the results mean in your classroom? How do they answer your original question? Were they what you expected? Any surprises? What was successful or not successful?

Our questionnaire regarding student opinion about materials and activities can best be summarized with tables for the class and for each subgroup. We would list the materials and activities in a column with the ratings listed across the top. Then for each item, the percent choosing the rating is listed.

To interpret the tables, we would consider the class or group distribution across the continuum: Were responses concentrated at one end of the continuum? Were there gross differences such as a large group at each end of the continuum, or was there a fairly even distribution across it? If the distribution is mainly at one end, we would decide what percent of the class or group to consider significant in our decision making: it might be 40 percent, $1/3$, $1/4$ or whatever we feel is appropriate. For example, if 40 percent of students rate something *very low* while few or no students rate it *highest*, or the reverse, that clearly is important information.

Data which are not readily quantifiable, such as that from logs, journals, informal observations, conferences or tapes of class activities, are usually reviewed by teachers so they can pull out what appear to be trends, major ideas, or important elements related to the question at hand. If these data are collected over a period of time, or if the material is extensive, it will need to be reviewed periodically, and preferably over a time frame which allows for reflection. This is an important and valuable process because it often leads to further insights and refinements. In general, for non-quantified data, we would review all the categories and subcategories and draw conclusions related to the original question. The conclusions may be firm or tentative. In either case, it is important to consider whether data from other sources agree with it. Informal observations, anecdotal notes, and class discussion of results are used to confirm, disconfirm or raise questions about findings from the rest of the data.

In the case of our question about students' attitudes, we would review teacher observations and anecdotal notes as well as student logs for indication of feelings about reading, positive, negative, or general reactions indicating that students are or are not involved with their reading. While we would start with categories such as *positive* and *negative,* as the data collection grows we would expect subcategories to develop. For example, we might subcategorize aspects related to writing, to self-selected reading, to assigned reading, or to informational reading. Categories are flexible and can change as we continue to review the data. Which categories make sense and help answer the question? How do these data fit with the results of the questionnaire?

Finally, we would review the data as a whole. What is supported by all data sources? What is partially supported? Is anything not supported? What conclusions do you draw?

We piloted a questionnaire in a fourth grade class which used both trade books and children's literature. The results indicated that boys and girls were quite similar in their high and low ratings, as were the readers who were mature, on-grade level or special needs readers. However, when we looked at the groups of items rated *high* or *low,* we noticed those rated *low* tended to be the type of activities associated with the basal while those rated *high* were those traditionally considered enrichment activities. In terms of materials, with the exception of the special needs readers, all rated using literature books higher than using basals. The students in the class willingly informed us why they responded as they did. In general, the special needs readers felt they could handle the grade level basal but with literature books they had trouble keeping pace with others in their groups, and in some cases with the vocabulary as well.

Since there was nothing in teacher notes or student logs to contradict this, we would use literature books as the core of the literacy program, avoiding "basalizing" them by incorporating writing and enrichment activities similar to those suggested by Yopp and Yopp (1992). In selecting and gathering books related to themes or units, we would seek to include books special needs readers would feel successful in using. Then while implementing this program, we'd probably start a new action research project concentrating on the special needs readers.

CONSIDERATIONS FOR INVOLVEMENT IN ACTION RESEARCH

There are four important factors to consider in planning action research. First, action research requires additional planning time. However, useful and successful projects can be accomplished without consuming an inordinate amount of additional time. Second, action research is improved when teachers discuss the five questions with colleagues because the interaction provides a supportive environment which helps clarify and solidify thinking regarding the project. Sharing ideas and suggestions, whether for the same question or different ones, can be valuable. Colleagues not involved in action research also can provide helpful insights.

Third, teachers undertaking action research should be aware that expectations affect what we see and how we interpret data. Triangulation of data is helpful as are our awareness of this effect, discussion with others as the research evolves, and an effort on our part to be open to alternative explanations as well as to surprises in the data. Finally, teachers can use the results of action research in their classrooms. Action research can improve the teaching/learning process in classrooms by reinforcing, modifying and/or changing perceptions based solely on more informal techniques such as non-systematic observations.

REFERENCES

Yopp, R. H., & Yopp, H. K. (1992). *Literature-based reading activities.* Boston: Allyn and Bacon.

The Public's View of PUBLIC Schools

Educators will not advance the case for public schools if they dismiss the public's concerns or simply pay lip service to the notion of public engagement.

Deborah Wadsworth

During a Public Agenda focus group last year, a Seattle teacher emphatically said, "The school system isn't broken. Society is broken." That may well be true. Americans seem roiled by deep-seated anxieties about the direction of the country, and these anxieties are often mirrored in concerns about our public schools.

Prominent among these anxieties is the widely shared sense of economic insecurity, which continues even as the economy grows and unemployment moderates. At the same time, people see moral decay as pervasive in American culture—crime, greed, lack of responsibility, the breakdown of values. At the heart of this anxiety is a sense that those who work hard and play by the rules are no longer rewarded.

Finally, there is an increasing sense that many leaders—in government, business, law, and journalism as well as

education—are out of touch with the concerns of average Americans. As a result, confidence in all leadership groups has dropped dramatically over the last 15 to 20 years.

A Mirror of Society

For the past six years, Public Agenda—a nonprofit, nonpartisan research organization that focuses on public policy issues—has conducted a series of national surveys and hundreds of focus groups on public education and school reform. Our goal is to understand what the general public, and particular groups within the public—such as parents, teachers, school administrators, minority groups, and community

leaders—think about public education and reform.

What has emerged is a picture of an American public frustrated and angered by the state of public education. Some of the public's chief complaints about the schools reflect the societal themes mentioned above: youngsters graduating without minimal basic skills,

truants sporting diplomas alongside youngsters who worked hard, educators making jargon-laden announcements of yet another educational fad.

Americans may not follow employment trend data showing the stagnating wages of people without strong educational backgrounds, but they clearly understand the concept: Young people without skills don't get good jobs. People find this unsettling for any child; they find it terrifying for their own. As a participant in an Albuquerque focus group said, "I see an awful lot of kids graduating from high school, putting in applications at my place of work, and they can't even fill out the forms. But they've graduated. It's very disturbing."

At the same time, many Americans see schools as the mirror image of a moral decay that has infected society at large. Many fear the most poorly-behaved students get too much of the teacher's attention, while those who want to learn get the short end of the stick. As shown in the table in Figure 1, people clearly expect schools to teach academic subjects, but most Americans believe schools also have an obligation to reinforce some basic values. In our surveys, more than 80 percent of respondents have said it is "absolutely essential" for schools to teach good work habits such as being responsible, being on time, and being disciplined.

> **Unfortunately, as they learn about local reform agendas, community members hear little that addresses their concerns.**

Nearly 80 percent have said it is absolutely essential for schools to teach the value of hard work.

Out of Touch

The public's feeling that many experts and leadership groups are out of touch with the thinking of average people extends to education reformers. While

FIGURE 1

What Subjects Are Absolutely Essential to Teach?

Percentages Saying "Absolutely Essential"	Teachers	General Public	Black Teachers	Hispanic Teachers	White Teachers
Basic reading, writing, and math skills	98%	92%	99%	96%	99%
Good work habits such as being responsible, on time, and disciplined	90%	83%	94%	89%	90%
The value of hard work	83%	78%	83%	82%	83%
Values such as honesty and tolerance of others	82%	74%	88%	79%	82%
Habits of good citizenship such as voting and caring about the nation	77%	66%	82%	72%	77%
Curiosity and love of learning	76%	57%	75%	73%	77%
Computer skills and media technology	72%	80%	79%	77%	73%
American history and American geography	72%	63%	73%	68%	72%
Biology, chemistry, and physics	64%	59%	64%	61%	64%
How to deal with social problems like drugs and family breakdown	61%	64%	76%	71%	60%
Practical job skills for office or industry	55%	57%	74%	61%	54%
The history and geography of such places as Europe or Asia	41%	35%	42%	49%	41%
Advanced mathematics such as calculus	36%	37%	42%	40%	36%
Classic works from such writers as Shakespeare and Plato	24%	23%	28%	28%	24%
Modern American writers such as Steinbeck and Hemingway	23%	22%	29%	26%	23%
Sports and athletics	14%	23%	20%	20%	14%

From *Given the Circumstances: Teachers Talk About Public Education*. Data for the general public from *Assignment Incomplete* survey (1995).

well-meaning reformers may favor such practices as heterogeneous grouping, mainstreaming children with special educational needs, bilingual education, and creativity at the expense of the basics, many people find these approaches troubling.

In our focus groups across the country, participants routinely talked about school reforms. A father in Minneapolis, for example, related this concern about his 3rd grade son:

> He'd come home and we'd see his journals. He wasn't getting the basics. He would just ramble—no complete sentences, not even complete thoughts. Sure it's creative, and they should try to help him be creative, but students also need the structure.

The public is remarkably clear about what it wants from public schools. Americans from all walks of life, in every demographic group and in every part of the country, endorse the very same list of priorities—safe, orderly schools where all children learn, at a minimum, basic skills. In the public's mind, until these tasks are accomplished, schools should not focus their attention elsewhere. Unfortunately, as they learn about local reform agendas, community members hear little that addresses their concerns.

In today's highly competitive environment, it is difficult to find a corporation that does not respond to, or at least acknowledge, its customers' perceptions. The more frequent and normally more successful approach is to address the issue immediately. If the customer's perception is incorrect, one can make a forceful case for an alternate point of view. But at least the customer will know he has been heard. Many educators argue that the public's perception that schools are unsafe is faulty, that parents' fears arise from media hype. Keep in mind that the presence of metal detectors in even *one* school violates the public's sense of the sanctity of all schools.

The principal of a highly acclaimed New York City magnet school suggests one approach to truly listening to the

> ## Right or wrong, the public feels that schools are no longer "theirs," that schools have been captured by the teachers, reformers, unions—whomever.

"customer's" concerns. Every year he invites parents of prospective students to an open house. He introduces the teachers, and he and the teachers explain the curriculum and field parents' questions. He makes a point of announcing that he has yet to hear one question: "Is this school safe?" He reports that every time he poses this question himself, an almost visible sigh of relief fills the room: what many parents shrink from asking has been asked. The principal then invites parents to observe for themselves—to visit the school when they like, go anywhere on the premises they like, and talk with students and teachers.

Right or wrong, the public feels that schools are no longer "theirs," that they have been captured by the teachers, reformers, unions—whomever. So long as their concerns go unaddressed, public resistance will stiffen, ultimately leading citizens to abandon public education.

No "Dialogue of the Deaf"
This past year, Public Agenda has been conducting a series of town meetings about public schools and the strategies the public would support to improve them. In partnership with the Institute for Educational Leadership, we have brought together teachers, parents, residents without children, business people, school administrators, recent public school graduates, and community leaders. By the end of each evening, we hope to find agreement about certain general strategies—a basis for developing the trust that is necessary to take more specific and ambitious steps.

In helping to build such a consensus, education and reform leaders must avoid what Public Agenda's cofounder Daniel Yankelovich, calls "the dialogue of the deaf," that is, people paying lip service to communication without actually listening to one another. Unfortunately, the traditional approach to ordinary public engagement is classic public relations, a three-step process that begins with consciousness-raising and moves quickly to a presentation of "the facts." The assumption is that people will then fall in line and support the solutions that leaders—often after years of contention—have already agreed upon. This top-down approach only works when everyone defines the problem similarly. But in this skeptical age, when experts, leaders, and the media are all suspect, and fears over a lack of values and economic insecurity abound, such a simplistic approach is doomed to fail.

Public Agenda's strategy is based on a more realistic assumption: It is impossible to impose solutions on people when those solutions do not conform to their values. We further believe that no major change will occur quickly. You are better off inviting your different constituencies into the tent for an ongoing conversation. And this means engaging a broad constituency, not just "the usual suspects." It also requires something more than a one-shot meeting. People must be able to vent at first, but you must then help them move beyond criticism and hold them responsible for realistic solutions. And again, people must listen to one another.

Whose Schools Are They?
I would ask you, the educator, to set aside your professional identity for a moment and think of yourself instead as a parent, grandparent, taxpayer, or church leader in your community. You may well have watched neighbors and friends lose their jobs and health benefits. You probably have sat around the kitchen table and bemoaned the country's loss of values, and the chasm between your town and Washington politicians. On occasion, you may even have criticized the impenetrable jargon that often passes for communication among experts. Keep these perspectives in mind when you listen to the public's concerns about the schools.

> ## In today's highly competitive environment, it is difficult to find a corporation that does not respond to, or at least acknowledge, its customers' perceptions.

What will not advance the cause of public education is to dismiss the public's views out-of-hand or attempt to manipulate people by paying lip service to their ideas. The public's fears are fundamental; at their core are very real concerns about the future of the children they love.

Deborah Wadsworth is Executive Director, Public Agenda, 6 East 39th St., New York, NY 10016-0112.

Development

Childhood (Articles 5–8)
Adolescence (Articles 9 and 10)

The study of human development provides us with knowledge of how children and adolescents mature and learn within the family, community, and school environments. Educational psychology focuses on description and explanation of the developmental processes that make it possible for children to become intelligent and socially competent adults. Psychologists and educators are presently studying the idea that biology as well as the environment influence cognitive, personal, social, and emotional development and involve predictable patterns of behavior.

Jean Piaget's theory regarding the cognitive development of children and adolescents is perhaps the best known and most comprehensive. According to this theory, the perceptions and thoughts that young children have about the world are often quite different when compared to adolescents and adults. That is, children may think about moral and social issues in a unique way. Children need to acquire cognitive, moral, and social skills in order to interact effectively with parents, teachers, and peers. If human intelligence encompasses all of the above skills, then Piaget may have been correct in saying that human development is the child's intelligent adaptation to the environment.

Today the cognitive, moral, social, and emotional development of children takes place in a rapidly changing society. A child must develop positive conceptions of self within the family as well as at school in order to cope with changes and become a competent and socially responsible adult. In "New Brain Development Research—A Wonderful Window of Opportunity to Build Public Support for Early Childhood Education!" Julee Newberger dis-

cusses the importance of both nature and nurture in early development, while the articles "The Moral Child" and "Helping Children Become More Prosocial: Ideas for Classrooms, Families, Schools, and Communities" discuss the moral and social skills of children. The article by Frances Campbell and Karen Taylor describes early childhood intervention programs that work. Adolescence brings with it the ability to think abstractly and hypothetically and to see the world from many perspectives. Adolescents strive to achieve a sense of identity by questioning their beliefs and tentatively committing to self-chosen goals. Their ideas about the kinds of adults they want to become and the ideals they want to believe in sometimes lead to conflicts with parents and teachers. Adolescents are also sensitive about espoused adult values versus adult behavior. The articles in this unit discuss the cognitive, social, and emotional changes that confront adolescents and also suggest ways in which the family and school can help meet the needs of adolescents.

Looking Ahead: Challenge Questions

What early childhood programs have long-term benefits for economically disadvantaged children?

How can parents and teachers provide children and adolescents with experiences that promote their cognitive, moral, social, and emotional development?

Describe the developmental tasks adolescents face. What are the historical and cultural changes that may put some youth at risk?

What can adolescents tell us about their perceptions of caring?

New Brain Development Research—
A Wonderful Window of Opportunity
to Build Public Support for
Early Childhood Education!

Julee J. Newberger

More than 20 years of brain development research is finally making news. Articles have appeared recently in *Time* (see Nash 1997), *Working Mother* (see Jabs 1996), *The Chicago Tribune, Newsweek* (see Begley 1996), and *The Washington Post*. A special edition of *Newsweek* focusing on learning in the early years is on the newsstands this spring in conjunction with the April 28, ABC-TV special "I Am Your Child." Receiving unprecedented attention, they kick off a massive three-year campaign to engage the public. What is the significance of this new research on the brain, and what does it mean for early childhood professionals?

New brain-imaging technologies have enabled scientists to investigate how the brain develops and works. Stimulated in part by growing concern about the overall well-being of children in America, the findings affirm what many parents and caregivers have known for years: (1) good prenatal care, (2) warm and loving attachments between young children and adults, and (3) positive, age-appropriate stimulation from the time of birth really do make a difference in children's development for a lifetime.

In addition to giving us a glimpse of the complex activity that occurs in the brain during infancy, the new research tools have stimulated dialogue between scientists and educators. In June 1996 Families and Work Institute sponsored a conference, "Brain Development in Young Children: New Frontiers for Research, Policy, and Practice," at the University of Chicago (see Families and Work Institute 1996). Convening professionals from the media, human services, business, and public policy, the conference explored how knowledge about the brain can inform our efforts to make better beginnings for

Just as experts agree that we have only begun to understand the complexities of the growing brain, so we have only begun to bridge the gap between neuroscience and education. The question for early childhood professionals is, How can we take advantage of the public interest that these stories and events have sparked to build support for high-quality early childhood education?

children and families. One month later, a workshop sponsored by the Education Commission of the States and the Charles A. Dana Foundation brought together 74 neuroscientists, cognitive psychologists, and education researchers and practitioners to foster communication and bridge a "historical communications gap" (ECS 1996). Similar events have followed, such as President Clinton's White House Conference on Early Childhood Development and Learning on April 17, 1997.

Just as experts agree that we have only begun to understand the complexities of the growing brain, so we have only begun to bridge the gap between neuroscience and education. The question for early childhood professionals is, How can we take advantage of the public interest that these stories and events have sparked to build support for high-quality early childhood education?

Julee J. Newberger, M.F.A., is a communications specialist in the NAEYC public affairs division. She is the primary author of "Early Years Are Learning Years" news releases.

What we know about how children learn

Although the scientists of all varieties who have been researching biology-versus-environment issues for much of this century have long agreed that both are enormously important influences on growth and development, only about 20 years ago neuroscientists believed that the genes we are born with determine the structure of our brains. They held that this fixed structure determines the way we develop and interact with the world. But recent brain research, enabled by new technologies, disproves this notion. Heredity may determine the basic number of neurons (brain cells) children are born with, and their initial arrangement, but this is merely a framework. A child's environment has enormous impact on how the circuits of the brain will be laid. Nature and nurture together—not nature or nurture alone—determine the outcome of our lives.

Beginning even before birth, the kind of nourishment and care a child receives affects not only the "wiring" of her brain but also the qualities of her experiences beyond the first few years of life. Many parents and caregivers have understood intuitively that warm, everyday interaction—cuddling infants closely or singing to toddlers—actually helps prepare children for learning throughout life. More and more we begin to understand the biological reasons behind this.

When a child is born, the brain produces trillions more neurons and synapses (connections between the brain cells) than she will ultimately need. Positive interactions with caring adults stimulate a child's brain profoundly, causing synapses to grow and existing connections to be strengthened. Those synapses in a child's brain that are used tend to be-

© The Growth Program

Many parents and caregivers have understood intuitively that warm, everyday interaction—cuddling infants closely or singing to toddlers—actually helps prepare children for the learning they will do throughout life. More and more we begin to understand the biological reasons behind this.

come permanent fixtures; those that are not used tend to be eliminated. If a child receives little stimulation early on, synapses will not sprout or develop, and the brain will make fewer connections. Therefore, a child's experiences during the first few days, months, and years may be more decisive than scientists once believed.

We now know that during the early years the brain has the greatest capacity for change. Neural plasticity, the brain's ability to adapt with experience, confirms that early stimulation sets the stage for how children will continue to learn and interact with others throughout life.

Neural plasticity: The brain's ability to adapt

Particularly during the first three years of life, brain connections develop quickly in response to outside stimulation. A child's experiences—good or bad—influence the wiring of his brain and the connections in his nervous system. Thus, when we snuggle a baby or talk to him in a singsong, undulating rhythm, we are contributing to the growth of his brain. How do we know this?

Recent research examining one of the body's "stress-sensitive" systems demonstrates how outside experiences shape a child's developing brain (Gunnar et al. 1996). One stress-sensitive system in particular is activated when children are faced with physical or emotional trauma. Activation of this system produces a steroid hormone called *cortisol*. High levels of cortisol cause the death of brain cells and a reduction in connections between the cells in certain areas of the brain. Research in adults who have experienced chronic or intense activation of the system that produces cortisol shows shrinkage

Particularly during the first three years of life, brain connections develop quickly in response to outside stimulation. Thus, when we snuggle a baby or talk to him in a singsong, undulating rhythm, we are contributing to the growth of his brain.

of a certain brain region that is important in learning and memory. Clearly, a link exists between physical or emotional trauma and long-term impairments to learning and development.

But nature has provided a way of buffering the negative effects of these stress systems in the brain: strong attachments between children and their parents or caregivers. Studies measuring the levels of cortisol in children's saliva showed that those who received warm and responsive care were able to turn off this stress-sensitive response more quickly and efficiently. Babies with strong emotional bonds to their caregivers showed consistently lower levels of cortisol in their brains.

While positive, nurturing experiences can help brighten a child's future, negative experiences can do the opposite. Children who are emotionally neglected or abandoned early in life not only are more likely to have difficulty in learning but also may have more trouble experiencing empathy, attachment, and emotional expression in general. An excess of cortisol in the brain is linked to impaired cognitive ability and difficulty in responding appropriately or productively in stressful situations. Healthy relationships during the early years help children create a framework for interactions with others throughout life.

Windows of opportunity

Studies have increased our understanding of "windows of opportunity" or critical periods in children's lives when specific types of learning take place. For instance, scientists have determined that the neurons for vision begin sending messages back and forth rapidly at two to four months of age, peaking in intensity at eight months. It is no coincidence that babies begin to take notice of the world during this period. A well-known experiment conducted in the 1970s prompted research on the window of opportunity in development of vision in children. The original study demonstrated that sewing shut

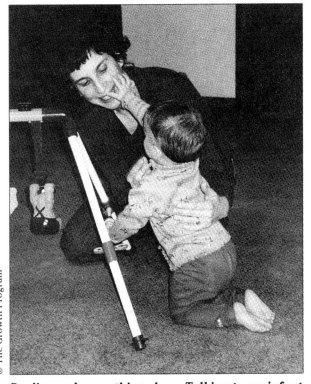

© The Growth Program

Studies make one thing clear: Talking to an infant increases the number of words she will recognize and eventually come to understand. She also will learn better when spoken to in brief phrases, preferably in singsong tones.

one eye of a newborn kitten caused the kitten's brain to be "rewired." Because no synapses were created in the brain to allow the kitten to see with the eye that had been closed, the kitten was blind in that eye even after scientists reopened it. The results could not be repeated in adult cats, whose brains were already wired for sight in both eyes. We now know that by the age of two these synapses in the human brain have matured as well. The window of opportunity for vision has already closed.

Scientists believe that language is acquired most easily during the first decade of life. Infants under six months respond with equal interest to the sounds of all languages, but they soon develop "perceptual maps" that direct them toward the sounds of the language they hear most frequently and away from the sounds of other languages. They start by forming connections for specific vowel sounds they hear repeatedly. The circuits in children's brains then become wired for those sounds that are significant in their own language, diminishing their ability to discern sounds that are not. As a result, the brains of babies in Japan, for example, begin to develop differently than those of babies in the United States. These perceptual maps eventually account for regional accents—and the increasing difficulty in acquiring new languages as we grow older.

Studies well-known to early childhood educators make one thing clear: Talking to an infant increases the number of words she will recognize and eventually come to understand. She also will learn better when spoken to in brief phrases, preferably in singsong tones. Researchers report that infants whose parents and caregivers frequently speak to them recognize far more words later on than do infants whose parents are less vocal or less engaged. An infant's repeated exposure to words clearly helps her brain build neural circuitry that will enable her to learn more words later on. For infants, individual attention and responsive, sensitive care-giving are critical for later language and intellectual development.

Children who are emotionally neglected or abandoned early in life not only are more likely to have difficulty in learning but also may have more trouble experiencing empathy, attachment, and emotional expression in general. An excess of cortisol in the brain is linked to impaired cognitive ability and difficulty in responding appropriately or productively in stressful situations.

Many reports on brain research point to the implications for the introduction of second-language learning during the early years (ECS 1996). We now know that if children are to learn to speak a second language like a native, they should be introduced to the language by age ten. Mastering an additional language is still possible after this point, but the window of opportunity for easy acquisition is gone.

Research does not suggest drilling children in alphabet songs from different languages or using flash cards to promote rote memorization of letters and numbers. Rather, it reinforces the principles of developmentally appropriate practice. Children learn any language best in the context of meaningful, day-to-day interactions with adults or other children who speak the language.

More windows of opportunity in children's learning may exist. Studies show that the most effective time to begin music lessons, for instance, is between the ages of three and ten. Few professional musicians began later in life. Music also seems to be linked to spatial orientation, so providing a child with the opportunity to play an instrument and using basic music education to spark her interest may do more than help her become musically inclined. With such knowledge, scientists and educators can work together to create the best plans for developing the whole child during the early years of life.

Implications for early care and education programs

Now that scientific research has reinforced what many already knew about early childhood education, what impact will this knowledge have on programs and centers across the country? We know that enriched home and school environments can help make the most of children's mental capacities. We also know that when we bring an understanding of child development to our interactions with children, we can meet their developmental needs more than just adequately. Parents and the general pub-

lic, having children's best interests in mind, may raise issues about early education practices. Here are some questions that are likely to arise.

1. Should new parents put off employment and stay at home?

The relationship between secure attachment and healthy brain development makes this a reasonable question, although working parents should not be blamed for any and every developmental obstacle their children encounter. At a time when 55% of women provide about half or more of their families' income, decisions as to whether parents should put off employment remain a personal, family matter (Families and Work Institute 1996). Research shows that the best scenario for children and families if child care is used involves high-quality parenting and access to high-quality, affordable child care and early education that enhances—not disrupts—attachments between parents and children. Flexible workplace policies can help accommodate and support modern family life.

2. Is it too late for children to develop cognitive skills after the early years?

While scientists have found that the early years may be even more important than anticipated, human development continues throughout the life span. It may not be as easy to acquire a second language at the age of fifty, but learning new skills is always possible. A meaningful context and the desire to develop new skills make learning more likely at any age.

The significance of this new research, according to Harry Chugani (1997) of Wayne State University, is for all of us to "be aware and take advantage of these critical periods nature has provided us with." Chugani says, "We must create innovations to make learning fun." Parents and educators should focus on ways to take advantage of windows of opportunity that remain open.

Research does not suggest drilling children in alphabet songs from different languages or using flash cards to promote rote memorization of letters and numbers. Rather, it reinforces the principles of developmentally appropriate practice. Children learn any language best in the context of meaningful, day-to-day interactions with adults or other children who speak the language.

3. To take advantage of the early years of learning, should I invest more in toys and new products for my child?

New developments in research may prompt manufacturers to market products that claim to make the most of children's learning potential. Remember that scientific evidence does not change the fundamental principles of developmentally appropriate practice. In fact, research supports the theory that learning must take place in a meaningful context and in an environment of love and support. A developing brain doesn't know the difference between an inexpensive set of measuring cups and a pricey set of stackables purchased at a toy store.

The key to fostering early childhood learning is understanding that there will be a range in the amount of stimulation children are comfortable with and can tolerate. Before children can move on to new skills, they must have time to practice and master those they have already learned. Parents or caregivers who push children too fast or too hard can do as much damage as those who do not challenge children at all. Chugani recommends, "Be rigorous, but be aware of early signs of overload" (1997). Continue to respect the child as a human being and use common sense in determining when he enjoys what he is learning and when he is resistant.

Bridging the gaps

The ECS workshop on neuroscience and education outlined the following conflicts between research and current education practice (ECS 1996):

• While we know that development of children's capacity to learn is crucial in the first few years of life, children during these years receive the least attention from the educational world.

• Interactive environments enhance development, but many children are in child care programs today with staff who are underpaid, lack training in early childhood and brain development, and may be responsible for too many children.

• Although some adverse effects can be reversed or prevented for much less than it costs to provide special services later on, our educational system waits for children to fall behind, then places them in special education programs at high costs to states.

In light of this research, shouldn't parents have more options to stay home with children during the years in which this critical learning takes place? Parental leave policies must be put on the table for discussion. And what about new welfare reform policies that push single mothers into the workforce without guaranteeing high-quality child care to promote children's optimum development and learning? The concerns raised and the dialogue generated at this workshop and other conferences may be timely in preventing more children from growing up without the benefit of the kind of education that early childhood professionals, utilizing years of research and practice, can provide.

Where we go from here

The Families and Work Institute conference on brain development offered the following recommendations for parents, caregivers, policymakers, and the public to institute policies and practices that improve the day-to-day experiences of all young children and families.

First, do no harm.

• Allow parents to fulfill their all-important role in providing and arranging sensitive, predictable care for their children.

Parents or caregivers who push children too fast or too hard can do as much damage as those who do not challenge children at all.

• Work to reform policies that prevent parents from forming strong, secure attachments with their infants in the first months of life.

• Mount intensive efforts to improve the quality of child care and early education so that families can be sure their young children's learning and emotional development are being fostered while parents are at work.

Prevention is best, but when a child needs help, intervene quickly and intensively.

• Ensure consistent and responsive care to help cushion children against the stresses of everyday life.

• Provide timely, intensive, sustained assistance to help children recover from serious trauma or overcome developmental problems.

Promote healthy development and learning for every child.

• Be aware that missed opportunities to promote healthy development may result later on in more expensive and less effective attempts at remediation.

• Support ongoing efforts to enhance the cognitive, emotional, and social development of children and adults in every phase of the life cycle.

Improve health and protection by providing health care coverage for expectant and new parents and their young children.

• Medical care, including preventive health screening, well-baby care, timely immunization, and attention to children's emotional and physical development, is cost-effective and provides a foundation for lifetime development.

Promote responsible parenthood by expanding proven approaches.

• Identify parent education and family support programs that promote the healthy development of children, improve the well-being of parents, and are cost-effective.

Safeguard children in early care and education from harm and promote their learning and development.

• Ensure that children will learn and thrive by improving the quality of early childhood programs and centers.

> While we know that development of children's capacity to learn is crucial in the first few years of life, children during these years receive the least attention from the educational world.

Enable communities to have the flexibility and resources they need to mobilize on behalf of young children and their families.

• Bring together leaders from business, media, community organizations, and religious institutions to develop goals and strategies for achieving the kind of community that supports all children and families.

*　　*　　*

Increased public awareness prompted by newsbreaking reports on brain research may represent a window of opportunity in the early childhood field. With plans to make further links between science and education, early childhood professionals and advocates may find increased support for our cause— public understanding and support for child care that guarantees proper nutrition, well-planned physical environments, and developmentally appropriate practices to ensure the most promising future for all young children and families. The window of opportunity is open and the time for action is now.

References

Begley, S. 1996. I am your child. *Newsweek*, 19 February, 55–61.

Chugari, H. 1997. Personal communication, 21 March.

ECS (Education Commission of the States). 1996. *Bridging the gap between neuroscience and education: Summary of the workshop co-sponsored by Education Commission of the States and the Charles A. Dana Foundation.* Denver: Author.

Families and Work Institute. 1996. Rethinking the brain: New insights into early development. Executive summary of the Conference on Brain Development in Young Children: New frontiers for Research, Policy, and Practice. University of Chicago, June.

Gunnar, M. R., L. Brodersen, K. Krueger, & R. Rigatuso. 1996. Dampening of behavioral and adrenocortical reactivity during early infancy: Normative changes and individual differences. *Child Development* 67 (3): 877–89.

Jabs, C. 1996. Your baby's brain power. *Working Mother*, November, 24–28.

Nash, M. 1997. Fertile Minds. *Time*, 3 February, 48–56.

THE MORAL CHILD

We're at ground zero in the culture wars: how to raise decent kids when traditional ties to church, school and community are badly frayed

Only in contemporary America could selecting a family anthology be considered a political act. On one cultural flank is famous Republican moralist William Bennett's bestselling *Book of Virtues,* a hefty collection of tales, fables and poems celebrating universal virtues such as courage, compassion and honesty. Side by side with the Bennett tome in many bookstores is Herbert Kohl and Colin Greer's *A Call to Character,* a similar assemblage of proverbs and stories organized around equally cherished values. No one could blame the casual browser for arbitrarily grabbing one or the other. But it's not a casual choice. These two volumes represent a fundamental and acrimonious division over what critics call the most pressing issue facing our nation today: how we should raise and instruct the next generation of American citizens.

The differences between the two volumes of moral instruction aren't even that subtle, once you're familiar with the vocabulary of America's culture war. Both agree on qualities of character like kindness and responsibility. But look deeper: Is unwavering patriotism more desirable than moral reasoning? Does discretion trump courage, or the other way around? Read the *Book of Virtues* to your children and they'll learn about valor from William Tell and Henry V at Agincourt. Read from *A Call to Character* and their moral instructors will be Arnold Lobel's decidedly unheroic but very human Frog and Toad. The former has sections devoted to work, faith and perseverance; the latter, playfulness, balance and adaptability. It's not just semantics or moral hairsplitting. These dueling miscellanies symbolize a much wider struggle for the hearts and minds of America's kids.

Beyond the hearth. Child rearing has always been filled with ambiguities. But while parents once riffled through their Dr. Spock and other how-to manuals for helpful perspectives on toilet training and fussy eaters, today the questions and concerns seem to have moved beyond the scope of child psychology and the familiar hearthside dilemmas. The issue for today's parents is how to raise decent kids in a complex and morally ambiguous world where traditional tethers to church, school and neighborhood are badly frayed. Capturing the heightened concerns of thousands of parents from around the country gathering at the Lincoln Memorial for this week's Stand for Children, one 41-year-old mother ob-

WIMP OR BULLY?

Your 5-year-old has been in a fistfight. Although another child was clearly the aggressor, your son dominated the older boy in the end. You experience mixed feelings: pride that your son is not a wimp, but concern about the escalating use of violence to resolve childhood disputes.

EXPERTS' VIEW

This is a common dilemma, experts say, and one that genuinely has two sides. Parents should always try first to teach a child that there are lots of ways to resolve conflict harmoniously and that reason and compromise are more effective than duking it out. Kids should also be taught that the distinction between wimp and aggressor is a false one. But if the choice is being a victim or not, children need to learn to stand up for themselves. Says psychologist William Damon: "Even young children can handle some complexity. You may not use the words 'justifiable self-defense,' but kids can grasp the idea."

serves about raising her teenage daughter: "It's not just dealing with chores and curfews. That stuff's easy. But what do you do when the values you believe in are being challenged every day at the high school, the mall, right around the corner in your own neighborhood?"

It is a sign of how high the stakes have risen that both first lady Hillary Rodham Clinton and former Vice President Dan Quayle weighed in this year with new books on proper moral child rearing. Both are motivated by fear that the moral confusion of today's youth could be deleterious to our democracy, which draws its sustenance and vitality from new generations of competent and responsible citizens. There's a sense of desperation in current writing about moral parenting, a sense that, as one psychologist puts it, improper child rearing has become a "public health problem" requiring urgent attention. Some lawmakers and public officials are even agitating for creation of a national public policy on the cultivation of private character.

The perceived threat to the commonwealth varies, of course, depending on one's political perspective. Critics on the right view moral relativity and indulgent parenting as the cause of today's moral confusion and call for the rediscovery of firmness, regimentation, deference and piety to counter our culture's decline. Those on the left are alarmed at what they see as a wave of simplistic nostalgia gaining force in the country: In their view, it is a bullying reformation designed to mold moral automatons incapable of genuine judgment or citizenship.

Morality's bedrock. The split is political, not scientific. Psychological understanding of moral development is actually quite sophisticated and consistent. For example, decades of research leave little doubt that empathy—the ability to assume another's point of view—develops naturally in the first years of life. Parents, of course, know this just from casual observation. Even infants show unmistakable signs of distress when another child is hurt or upset, and rudimentary forms of sympathy and helping—offering a toy to a distraught sibling, for example—can be observed in children as young as 1. Most psychologists who study empathy assume that the basic skill is biologically wired, probably created along with the bonds of trust that an infant forms with a caretaker, usually the mother. The task for parents is not so much a matter of teaching empathy as not quashing its natural flowering.

Building blocks. Empathy is the bedrock of human morality, the emotional skill required for the emergence of all other moral emotions—shame, guilt, pride

and so forth. Almost every form of moral behavior imaginable—from doing chores responsibly to sacrificing one's life for a cause—is inconceivable without it. Yet empathy is not enough. A second crucial building block of morality is self discipline, and psychologists have some solid evidence about how this moral "skill" is nurtured.

Most parents tend to adopt one of three general "styles" of interacting with their kids, each style a different combination of three basic factors: acceptance and warmth (vs. rejection), firmness (vs. leniency) and respect for autonomy (vs. control). How parents combine these traits sends very different messages to their children, which over time are "internalized" in such character traits as self-esteem, self-control, social competence and responsibility—or, of course, in the absence of those traits.

There is little doubt about what works and what doesn't. In fact, says Temple University child psychologist Laurence Steinberg, author of a new study called *Beyond the Classroom*, extensive research over many years shows that parents who are more accepting and warm, firmer about rules and discipline and more supportive of their child's individuality produce healthier kids: "No research has ever suggested that children fare better when their parents are aloof than when they are accepting, when their parents are lenient rather than firm, or when their parents are psychologically controlling, rather than supportive of their psychological autonomy."

Psychologists call this ideal parenting style "authoritative" parenting, a middle ground between "autocratic" and "permissive" parenting, both of which tend to produce untoward consequences for children in terms of both competence and integrity. The need to control children appears to be especially damaging to self-discipline. "Parents who are high in control," Steinberg says, "tend to value obedience over independence. They are likely to tell their children that young people should not question adults, that their opinions count less because they are children, and so on. Expressions of individuality are frowned upon in these families and equated with signs of disrespect."

The best con men, of course, combine self-discipline with a keen ability to read others' thoughts and feelings. Morality requires more—specifically, the ability to think about such things as justice and fairness and ultimately to act on those thoughts. According to the late psychologist Lawrence Kohlberg of Harvard Uni-

versity, people pass through six fairly inflexible "stages" or moral reasoning, beginning with a childlike calculation of self-interest and ending with the embodiment of abstract principles of justice. The ability to think logically about right and wrong, Kohlberg believed, was essential to the development of complete moral beings: Moral habits and emotions alone, he argued, were inadequate for dealing with novel moral dilemmas or when weighing one value against another, as people often must do in real life.

Moral identity. Psychologists emphasize the importance of young children's "internalizing" values, that is, absorbing standards that are then applied in different times, places or situations. In a recently published study called *Learning to Care*,

---

SHAME AND RIDICULE

Your 6-year-old's teacher punishes him by making him wear a dunce cap. That strikes you as archaic and severe, but the teacher insists a bit of shame helps teach old-fashioned manners.

EXPERTS VIEW

Psychologists no longer believe that shame and guilt are the stuff of neurosis. In fact, most now are convinced that morality cannot develop without these fundamental moral emotions. But public ridicule is more likely to produce humiliation and anger than healthy contrition. Parents should talk privately with the teacher to see if there are gentler and less demeaning ways to make misbehaving children feel shame.

Princeton sociologist Robert Wuthnow argues that teenagers basically need to go through a second experience of internalization if they are to become caring adults. Just as young children absorb and integrate a rudimentary understanding of kindness and caring from watching adult models, adolescents need to witness a more nuanced form of caring, to absorb "stories" of adult generosity and self-sacrifice. That way, they see that involvement is a real possibility in a world where so much caring has been institutionalized.

Similarly, a recent study suggests that people who have chosen lives of lifelong, passionate commitment have had more opportunities than most people to develop appropriate trust, courage and responsible imagination. There is no such thing as a "Gandhi pill," Lesley College Prof. Laurent Parks Daloz and his colleagues write in the new book *Common Fire,* but there are commonly shared experiences: a parent committed to a cause, service opportunities during adolescence, cross-cultural experiences, a rich mentoring experience in young adulthood. Often, the authors conclude, the committed differ from the rest of us only by having more of these experiences, and deeper ones.

Force of habit. Of course, cultural battles rarely reflect the complexity of human behavior, and the current debate about proper moral child rearing has a black-and-white quality. As Bennett writes in his introduction to the *Book of Virtues,* moral education involves "explicit instruction, exhortation, and training. Moral education *must* provide training in good habits." But critics charge that such preoccupation with drill and habit suggests a dark and cynical view of human nature as a bundle of unsavory instincts that need constant squelching and reining in. In theology, it's called original sin; in psychological terms, it's a "behaviorist" approach, conditioning responses — or habits — which eventually become automatic and no longer require the weighing of moral options. The opposing philosophy — drawing from the romanticism of Jean Jacques Rousseau, psychology's "human potential" movement and the "constructivist" movement in education — emphasizes the child's natural empathy and untapped potential for reasoning.

The Clinton and Quayle volumes show how simplistic psychology can make for unsophisticated public philosophy. There's no question that the first lady's *It Takes a Village* is informed by an overriding respect for children as essentially competent beings who need nurturance to blossom. But critics see Clinton's optimism as dewy eyed and unrealistic, too much akin to the self-esteem movement and a "child centered" parenting style that allows kids to become morally soft. Quayle's *The American Family,* by contrast, endorses control and punishment as "a way to shape behavior toward respect and obedience." He notes approvingly that the five healthy families he studied reject the counsel of "prominent child experts," including the well-document-

ed finding that spanking and other forms of physical coercion teach violence rather than values.

Quayle's analysis is only one of many calls to return to a time when children knew their proper place and society was not so disorderly. Perhaps the strongest prescription is *The Perversion of Autonomy* by psychiatrist Willard Gaylin and political theorist Bruce Jennings, both of New York's Hastings Center for Bioethics. The book is a gleeful celebration of the value of coercion. In the view of these authors, the manifest vulgarities of liberal society justify and demand a serious rollback of the civil rights era; for the good of society, it follows, children require early and decisive flattening.

There is little question that the worst of New Age gobbledygook makes the cultural left an easy target for attack. One parent tells the story of when her 6-year-old was caught stealing at school. She met with the teacher, hoping together they could come up with a strategy to make it clear that stealing was unacceptable. But the teacher's response astonished her: "We don't use the word *stealing* here," she said. "We call it *uncooperative behavior.*" Few defend such foolish excesses of the self-esteem movement. But progressives argue they are aberrations used to attack liberal parenting and pedagogy. It's naive to focus on examples of indulgence, they argue, when if anything our culture is a child-hating culture, with family policies to match.

Classroom politics. This same ideological tug of war can be observed in the nation's schools, specifically in battles over the so-called character education movement. Only a few years old, the movement is fairly diverse, in some schools involving a specific packaged curriculum and reading materials, in others more of a philosophy or administrative style. But the general idea has captured the attention of the White House and Congress, both of which are searching for an appropriate federal role in promoting basic decency. Lawmakers have lent their symbolic support by endorsing "National Character Counts Week." The Department of Education has funded a few pilot programs and will soon fund a few more. And next week, President Clinton will address a joint White House-congressional conference on character building, the third such meeting sponsored by this administration.

Many states have also created character education requirements, and by conservative estimate, hundreds of schools and districts have adopted strategies for addressing morals and civic virtue. Precisely because of the diversity of philosophies that fall under the rubric "char-

acter education," experts say, parents need to be aware of what the term means in their own child's classroom.

For example, some schools have adopted conservative models that tend to emphasize order, discipline and courage — what Boston University educator Kevin Ryan labels the "stern virtues," as opposed to "soft" or easy virtues like compassion and self-esteem. Such programs don't shy away from unfashionable ideas like social control and indoctrination, says University of Illinois sociologist Edward Wynne, a guiding light of this approach and coauthor, with Ryan, of *Reclaiming Our Schools.*

ORDER AND SQUALOR

Your 12-year-old daughter's bedroom is a pigsty. You worry that a disorderly room means a disorderly mind, but your husband says it's more important not to violate her personal space.

EXPERTS VIEW

Experts are divided. Some come down firmly on the side of orderliness as an important habit and a lesson in family obligation. They dismiss the personal space argument as New Age nonsense. Others do not consider it a moral issue at all but an aesthetic one. Even adults differ: Some don't bother to make their beds, while others are fastidious. It's an issue for negotiation, which is a life skill that teenagers should learn.

Wynne calls for a return to the "great tradition in education," that is, the transmission of "good doctrine" to the next generation. Because of the "human propensity for selfishness," Wynne encourages schools to use elaborate reward systems, including "ribbons, awards and other signs of moral merit." The model also emphasizes group sports and pep rallies as effective ways to elevate school spirit. Variations of this reward-and-discipline model emphasize drilling in a prescribed set of values, often focusing on a "virtue of the month." Programs based on the stern virtues also tend to emphasize institutional loyalty and submission of the individual to the larger community. Ryan points to Roxbury Latin, a 350-year-old private boys' school in Boston, as an example of this approach. The school subscribes to an unambiguous set of Judeo-Christian values—honesty, courtesy and respect for others, according to the catalog. It attempts to inculcate these values through a classical curriculum, through mandatory, sermonlike "halls" and

---

CODES AND CREATIVITY

Your son is dismissed from school because his pierced ear violates the dress code. You argue with the principal that the earring is a form of self-expression, but he insists societies need rules.

EXPERTS VIEW

Some psychologists consider it unconscionable to place a child in the center of a culture war. The most crucial issue, they argue, is for parents and other authority figures to present kids with a united moral front. But psychologist Michael Schulman disagrees: "It could be an opportunity for a valuable lesson in choosing life's battles: Is this an important one? If so, what's the most effective strategy for social change?"

---

through formal and casual interactions between teachers (called "masters") and students. No racial, ethnic or religious student organizations are permitted, in order to encourage loyalty to the larger school community. According to Headmaster F. Washington Jarvis, an Episcopal priest, Roxbury Latin's view of human nature is much like the Puritan founders': "mean, nasty, brutish, selfish, and capable of great cruelty and meanness. We have to hold a mirror up to the students and say, 'This is who you are. Stop it.'"

Roxbury Latin teaches kids to rein in their negative impulses not with harsh discipline, however, but with love and security of belonging. Displays of affection are encouraged, according to Jar-

vis, and kids are disciplined by being made to perform (and report) good deeds—a powerful form of behavior modification. Students are rebuked and criticized when they stray, but criticism is always followed by acts of caring and acceptance. Whenever a student is sent to Jarvis's office for discipline, the headmaster always asks as the boy leaves, "Do I love you?"

Ethical dilemmas. At the other end of the spectrum are character education programs that emphasize moral reasoning. These, too, vary a great deal, but most are derived at least loosely from the work of Kohlberg and other stage theorists. Strict Kohlbergian programs tend to be highly cognitive, with students reasoning through hypothetical moral dilemmas and often weighing conflicting values in order to arrive at judgments of right and wrong. A classic Kohlbergian dilemma, for example, asks whether it's right for a poor man to steal medicine to save his dying wife. Even young children tend to justify dishonesty in this situation, but only adults do so based on a firmly held principle of what's unchallengeably right. Kohlbergian programs are also much more likely to have kids grapple with controversial social dilemmas, since it's assumed that the same sort of moral logic is necessary for citizens to come to informed decisions on the issues of the day—whether gay lifestyles ought to be tolerated in the U.S. Navy, for example.

Variations in programs on strict moral reasoning are generally based on a kind of "constructivist" model of education, in which kids have to figure out for themselves, based on real experiences, what makes the other person feel better or worse, what rules make sense, who makes decisions. Kids actively struggle with issues and from the inside out "construct" a notion of what kind of moral person they want to be. (Advocates of moral reasoning are quick to distinguish this approach from "values clarification," a 1960s educational fad and a favorite whipping boy of conservative reformers. Values clarification consisted of a variety of exercises aimed at helping kids figure out what was most important to them, regardless of how selfish or cruel those "values" might be. It's rarely practiced today.)

The Hudson school system in Massachusetts is a good example of this constructivist approach. The program is specifically designed to enhance the moral skills of empathy and self-discipline. Beginning in kindergarten, students participate in role-playing exercises, a series of readings about ethical

dilemmas in history and a variety of community service programs that have every Hudson student, K through 12, actively engaged in helping others and the community. Environmental efforts are a big part of the program: Kindergartners, for instance, just completed a yearlong recycling project. The idea, according to Superintendent Sheldon Berman, is for children to understand altruism both as giving to the needy today and as self-sacrifice for future generations. By contrast, the conservative "Character Education Manifesto"

MEDIA AND MORES

You allow your kids to watch certain R-rated videos, but you can't preview each one. Your 13-year-old argues: "I'm not going to become an ax murderer just because I watch a movie, Dad."

EXPERTS' VIEW

It's true he won't become an ax murderer, but he might absorb some distorted lessons about uncaring sexuality—if you're not around to discuss the differences between fantasy and reality. It's OK to question and reject social codes like movie ratings, psychologists say, but if you do, you must substitute meaningful discussion of sex, violence and censorship.

---

states explicitly: "Character education is *not* about acquiring the right *views*," including "currently accepted attitudes about ecology."

Needless to say, these philosophical extremes look very different in practice. Parents who find one or the other more appealing will almost certainly have different beliefs about human behavior. But the best of such programs, regardless of ruling philosophy, share in one crucial belief: that making decent kids requires constant repetition and amplification of basic moral messages. Both Roxbury Latin and Hudson, for example, fashion themselves as "moral communities," where character education is woven into the basic fabric of the school and reflected in every aspect of the school day.

Community voices. This idea is consistent with the best of moral development theory. According to Brown University developmental psychologist William Damon, author of *Greater Expectations,* "Real learning is made up of a thousand small experiences in a thousand different relationships, where you see all the facets of courage, caring and respect." Virtue-of-the week programs will never work, Damon contends, because they lack moral dimension and trivialized moral behavior. Children can handle moral complexity, he says, and sense what's phony. "Kids need a sense of purpose, something to believe in. Morality is not about prohibitions, things to avoid, be afraid of or feel guilty about."

Building this sense of purpose is a task beyond the capacity of most families today. The crucial consistency of a moral message requires that kids hear it not only from their parents but from their neighbors, teachers, coach, the local policeman. Unfortunately, Damon says, few do. The culture has become so adversarial that the important figures in a child's life are more apt to be at one another's throats than presenting a unified moral front. Litigiousness has become so widespread that it even has a name, the "parents' rights movement." More than ever before, parents see themselves primarily as advocates for their children's rights, suing schools over every value conflict. In a New York case now making its way through the courts, for example, parents are suing because they object to the school district's community service requirement.

Moral ecology. The irony of postmodern parenting, writes sociologist David Popenoe in *Seedbeds of Virtue,* is that just when science has produced a reliable body of knowledge about what makes decent kids, the key elements are disintegrating: the two-parent family, the church, the neighborhood school and a safe, nurturing community. Popenoe and others advocate a much broader understanding of what it means to raise a moral child today—what communitarian legal theorist Mary Ann Glendon calls an "ecological approach" to child rearing, which views parents and family as just one of many interconnecting "seedbeds" that can contribute to a child's competency and character.

Hillary Clinton borrowed for her book title the folk wisdom, "It takes a village to raise a child." It's an idea that seems to be resonating across the political spectrum today, even in the midst of rough cultural strife. Damon, for example, ended his book with the inchoate notion of "youth charters," an idea that he says has taken on a life of its own in recent months. He has been invited into communities from Texas to New England to help concerned citizens identify shared values and develop plans for modeling and nurturing these values in newly conceived moral communities.

Americans are hungry for this kind of moral coherence, Damon says, and although they need help getting past their paralysis, it's remarkable how quickly they can reach consensus on a vision for their kids and community. He is optimistic about the future: "My great hope is that we can actually rebuild our communities in this country around our kids. That's one great thing about America: people love their kids. They've just lost the art of figuring out how to raise them."

SMOKE AND MIRRORS

Despite your own youthful experimentation with drugs, you're worried about your teenager's fascination with today's drug culture. He claims he's embracing the values of the '60s.

EXPERTS' VIEW

This comes up a lot, now that children of the '60s are raising their own teenagers. It's crucial to be honest, but it's also fair to explain the social context and the spirit in which drugs were being used at the time. And it's OK to say it was a mistake—it wasn't the key to nirvana. Most experts suggest focusing on health effects and illegality rather than making it a moral issue.

BY WRAY HERBERT WITH
MISSY DANIEL IN BOSTON

Early Childhood Programs
That Work for Children from
Economically Disadvantaged Families

Frances A. Campbell and Karen Taylor

T he demand for early child care continues to increase among economically disadvantaged families as welfare reform requires mothers receiving aid to return to school or work. This is both an opportunity and a challenge for early childhood professionals. The opportunity is to design quality programs in which children from low-income families can develop to their highest potential, but the number of children affected presents an enormous challenge. What sorts of programs will maximize children's chances of growing up physically and mentally healthy?

A survey of early childhood intervention programs provided for children from low-income families was undertaken to find ways in which children or parents derived benefits

© Francis Wardle

and to find how long the effects lasted. Only studies that permitted scientific comparison of outcomes among children who did and did not receive services were included.

The programs surveyed differed in their timing, their intensity, and their goals. The Mobile Unit for Child Health (Gutelius et al. 1972), the Prenatal Early Infancy Project (Olds 1988), and the Yale Child Welfare Program (Provence & Naylor 1983) began working with mothers before target children were born. Programs that began working with children in infancy were the Milwaukee Project (Garber 1988), the Syracuse University Family Development Research Program (Lally, Mangione, & Honig 1988), the Abecedarian Project (Ramey & Campbell 1991), Project CARE (Wasik et al. 1990), the Brookline Early Education Project (Pierson 1988), and the Infant Health and Development Project (HIDP 1990). The Houston Parent-Child Development Center (Johnson & Walker 1991) began working with families when target infants were one. The Harlem Study (Palmer 1983) contrasted outcomes in children provided short-term intervention either as two-year-olds or three-year-olds. The Verbal Interaction Project (Levenstein, O'Hara, & Madden 1983) provided a home-based language stimulation program for two- or three-year-olds. Other programs, such as the Perry Preschool Project (Beruetta-Clement et al. 1984), the Early Training Project (Gray, Ramsey, & Klaus 1982), the Chicago Child and Parent Center and Expansion Program (Reynolds 1994), and

Frances A. Campbell, *Ph.D., is a senior investigator and fellow at the Frank Porter Graham Child Development Center at the University of North Carolina. She is one of the principal investigators for the Abecedarian Project and the Head Start Transition Demonstration Project.*

Karen Taylor, *M.R.P., is the data coordinator for the North Carolina Head Start Transition Demonstration Project, which is designed to study the effects of providing Head Start-like services to low-income children during their first few years of public school. Karen works with both the program and evaluation staffs of the transition project.*

*This is one of a regular series of Research in Review columns. The column in this issue was invited by **Carol Seefeldt,** Ph.D., professor at the University of Maryland, College Park.*

From *Young Children,* May 1996, pp. 74-80. © 1996 by the National Association for the Education of Young Children. Reprinted by permission.

> ## Almost all programs, at their intervention end points, show cognitive benefits for children who participated in the program.

Head Start (McKey et al. 1985) began working with children in preschools beginning at age three or four. Four programs were clearly more intensive, in terms of duration of intervention, than the rest. These were the Syracuse University Family Development Program, which provided care for five years, the Milwaukee Project, in which children were involved from infancy through kindergarten (age six), and Project CARE and the Abecedarian study, whose maximal intervention was provided for children from infancy through age eight. (Other Abecedarian groups had either five or three years of intervention.)

Parent components were included in many programs because of the belief that early intervention would succeed only if parents became heavily involved and they themselves made major changes (Bronfenbrenner 1974). Several programs combined home visits with center-based child care. Some provided parents with opportunities for personal development, such as job training. Others used a home-visit model alone. A few had maternal and child health as their primary objective and used nurses as their visitors, while others had social workers to provide emotional support to parents.

Because children raised in low-income families are more likely to have academic and behavior problems in school (Connell 1994; Patterson, Kupersmidt, & Vaden 1990) and because preschool intellectual levels and early language development are so strongly associated with school success, almost all early childhood programs emphasized activities to enhance children's cognitive development. Some interventionists attempted to do this through direct teaching of children in child care centers or preschools. Others modeled interactive and teaching behaviors for parents with the expectation that parents would then teach their children.

All programs had end-point evaluations when intervention was terminated, but not all have long-term data on their participants. A few followed their samples into adolescence or even young adulthood. Program outcomes were examined in terms of cognitive/academic, socioemotional, and health benefits.

Cognitive/academic outcomes

Almost all programs, at their intervention end points, show cognitive benefits for children who participated in the program. However, early disillusionment with preschool intervention for children from low-income families came when a large-scale evaluation of Project Head Start (Cicirelli 1969) showed that mean IQs of Head Start children, after only three years in school, were not significantly different from those of children who had not participated. The study that delivered this bad news was attacked on methodological grounds, with many skeptics arguing that it did not fairly assess the benefits of Head Start. To provide a definitive investigation of the effects of preschool interventions for children from low-income families, a Consortium for Longitudinal Studies was formed in which 11 investigators followed up their participants to learn how long early benefits persisted (Lazar et al. 1982). Results pooled across all 11 programs showed that statistically significant IQ differences among intervention and control subjects were largely gone after three to four years in public school, and significant differences on academic tests of reading and mathematics were gone after five to six years. On the other hand, the consortium found important, lasting benefits in terms of fewer retentions in grade and fewer placements into special education for treated children.

The consortium results have been widely cited by both critics and proponents of early intervention as supportive of their own position. Focusing on the erosion of significant IQ and academic benefits, critics conclude that lasting, positive effects of early childhood programs have not been demonstrated. Some policymakers have labeled them ill-advised and wasteful. However, not all programs included in the consortium failed to find lasting IQ or academic benefits, and a number of early childhood studies carried out since those in the consortium also have found long-lasting IQ or academic gains. In general, the most enduring IQ benefits for children were associated with child-centered programs, such as the Milwaukee and Abecedarian studies, that began very early in the life span and provided many hours of educational exposure. On the other hand, participants in the Harlem study also showed long-term IQ gains with a much shorter period of participation that began no earlier than age two. Other preschool experiences that started at age three or four, such as those in the Early Training Project, Project Head Start, and the Perry Preschool study, reported significant IQ differences when their programs ended, but these differences eroded within a few years.

> To provide a definitive investigation of the effects of preschool interventions for children from low-income families, a Consortium for Longitudinal Studies was formed in which 11 investigators followed up their participants to learn how long early benefits persisted. The consortium found important, lasting benefits in terms of fewer retentions in grade and fewer placements into special education for treated children.

Socioemotional outcomes for children can be roughly grouped into three categories: behavioral adjustment, attitudes and attributions, and self-concept. Socioemotional outcomes for parents largely consisted of measures of maternal behaviors, such as affection and punitiveness.

Long-term (fifth grade or higher) academic test results or indices of school progress (retentions, placements, or graduation rates) are available for the Early Training Project, the Harlem study, the Perry Preschool Project, the Houston PCDC program, the Syracuse Family Development Program, the Milwaukee Project, and the Abecedarian study. Girls involved with the Syracuse study had higher grades than control girls in grades 7-8. Participants in the Early Training Project had fewer retentions or placements into special education, and girls who participated in this program were more likely to graduate from high school and more likely to return to school if they became teen mothers. Abecedarian subjects who received preschool services had significantly higher scores on tests of reading and math through age 15 and fewer retention and placements into special education. The Milwaukee study found no academic test-score differences after 10 years in school, but significant IQ differences persisted through age 14. All these programs contained child-centered components. The evidence thus shows that children from low-income families can derive significant and long-lasting cognitive and academic benefits from child-oriented preschool programs.

There are also reports of long-term positive effects on child IQ and academic performance from some of the more parent-oriented programs, but the evidence for long-term benefits is more mixed. Programs that emphasized parents as the mediators of treatment, such as the Mobile Unit for Child Health and the Brookline Early Edu-

cation Project, found significant child IQ or "language" benefits when their programs ended. The Verbal Interaction Project had mixed results; some, but not all, program variations resulted in significant gains for participating children. In contrast, the Family Education group from Project CARE and the Yale, Syracuse, and Houston programs did not find significant intervention/control IQ differences at their end points, although, as noted, Syracuse and Houston later found evidence of academic benefits, as also did some variations of the Verbal Interaction Project. Child IQ and academic benefits appear to have eroded quickly in the case of the Mobile Unit for Child Health (Gutelius et al. 1977).

The importance of providing young children with safer environments, better nutrition, and better dental and health care is obvious.

The evidence is also mixed on the value of continuing to provide intervention for graduates of preschool programs into public school. In their summary of findings from a Follow-Through project in a northern urban area, Seitz and colleagues (1983) found that Follow-Through children had higher IQs at the program end point than did children not in the program, and they earned higher scores on academic tests of math and general knowledge at the end of third grade. The findings through eighth grade showed that Follow-Through graduates continued to demonstrate modest positive effects. Their academic test scores declined less over the years than those of the controls, although there were some group and gender differences in this regard and positive effects were not found in all areas tested—there were none in reading, for example.

For children in the Abecedarian study, the effects of the school-age program were weaker than those of the preschool program. There was no evidence that having the three years of follow-up in the primary grades helped to maintain IQ gains even through age eight. The reading-score means through age 15 favor the group that had both preschool and school-age follow-through, but the difference between preschool graduates with and without the follow-through pro-

© Francis Wardle

gram was not significant by then. The preschool effect was even stronger for mathematics; by age 15 there was no longer an advantage associated with having had the school-age program in addition to preschool (Campbell & Ramey 1995).

Socioemotional outcomes

Socioemotional outcomes for children can be roughly grouped into three categories: behavioral adjustment, attitudes and attributions, and self-concept. Socioemotional outcomes for parents largely consisted of measures of maternal behaviors, such as affection and punitiveness.

An important socioemotional benefit associated with the Prenatal/Early Infancy Program was a reduction in child abuse and neglect within families of children who participated in the program. Parents involved with the Houston program were observed to be more affectionate and less punitive with their children, and mothers treated in the Verbal Interaction Program were observed to behave more positively toward their children than did control mothers.

Where follow-up data are available, it appears that intervention/control differences in socioemotional development have generally been short-term. Head Start researchers found strong positive effects on immediate behavioral adjustment in school, but this difference dropped sharply during the first year (McKey et al. 1985). Mothers of children in the Infant Health and Development program rated their three-year-olds lower on problem behaviors than did mothers of children who did not participate, but this difference was not found when the children were five (Brooks-Gunn et al. 1994). Kindergarten observers rated children served in the Brookline program significantly higher on "social adjustment" and "use of time," compared to controls, yet an effect was not seen by second grade. Children served in the Syracuse Family Development Program were rated as superior in socioemotional functioning in kindergarten, but by first grade they sought teacher attention in negative ways.

It would be interesting, however, to have more long-term follow-up on behavioral adjustment. A follow-up of

> **Many such children are born to young mothers who need to finish school. For them, and for all students who will eventually become parents, there is a lack of school curricula directed toward parenthood. For teenage parents, regular school curricula could be combined with child care and parent training at school sites, benefiting both parent and child.**

the Syracuse sample showed that girls who had participated in the program were more positive toward peers in adolescence. When participants in the Yale Child Welfare program were followed up after 10 years, boys who had participated in the program had better behavioral adjustment that did control boys (Seitz & Provence 1990). The Syracuse study found that program participants had fewer court records for delinquent acts, and the Perry Preschool Project found that program graduates had fewer arrests (Schweinhart & Weikart 1980).

Not all socioemotional differences associated with intervention were positive. The primary-grade teachers in the Milwaukee project described program graduates as less cooperative and less compliant than their controls. As noted, Syracuse program graduates displayed some negative behaviors toward teachers in first grade. Haskins (1985) found that primary-grade teachers rated children who had the Abecedarian preschool services higher on verbal and physical aggression than Abecedarian preschool controls.

As for attitudes, some investigators reported positive effects of early childhood programs on children's academic motivation and self-concepts. The Early Training Project, the Perry Preschool Project, and the Verbal Interaction Project found a significant difference in the proportion of program graduates who reported being proud of themselves for academic achievement, in contrast to

> **This brief survey of selected early childhood programs shows that providing appropriate and stimulating learning environments for young children of low-income families and supporting parents in their role benefit both parent and child. Many participants made higher academic test scores and better progress through school, as reflected in fewer retentions, fewer placements into special education, and high rates of graduation. Parents made positive changes in their own educational and employment levels and showed reductions in child abuse and neglect. Early childhood programs clearly do help overcome the barriers imposed by impoverishment.**

control subjects, but this finding was mainly true of younger program graduates—it was not true for groups aged 15–19 (Lazar et al. 1982). Schwein-hart and Weikart (1980) found that their program graduates placed a higher value on education at age 15. Meta-analysis of Head Start outcomes suggest immediate, small, positive effects on both self-esteem and academic motivation, but both dropped sharply after one year in school. Academic motivation, however, appeared to make a modest recovery during the third year. Abecedarian program graduates scored more like middle-class peers on achievement attributions in the primary years (Walden & Ramey 1983), but this effect did not persist into adolescence (Campbell 1995).

> **Those who are quick to discount the importance of early childhood programs have not suggested constructive alternatives.**

Health, dental, and nutritional benefits

The importance of providing young children with safer environments, better nutrition, and better dental and health care is obvious. The investigators of the Prenatal/ Early Infancy Project found a reduction in accidents and poison ingestions within homes of participating children. The better nutrition associated with Head Start resulted in both higher growth rates and higher serum levels of iron and other beneficial trace elements. There is not clear evidence of a lasting reduction in rates of illness for Head Start versus non-Head Start children, even though Head Start children had better rates of immunization. Head Start children had better dental care and more dental treatment than did non-Head Start children (McKey et al. 1985). These important outcomes are based on site-specific studies; the long-term consequences of these benefits are not known, but even if not sustained, they were clearly important in their own right at the time.

> **Politicians stress the importance of "family values" but are curiously silent on urging business leaders to provide family supports.**

Summary

This brief survey of selected early childhood programs shows that providing appropriate and stimulating learning environments for young children from low-income families and supporting parents in their role benefit both parent and child. Many of the surveyed programs demonstrated modest but long-lasting IQ gains, and participants in many programs made higher academic test scores and better progress through school, as reflected in fewer retentions, fewer placements into special education, and high rates of graduation. Parents made positive changes in their own educational and employment levels and showed reductions in child abuse and neglect. Early childhood programs clearly do help overcome the barriers imposed by impoverishment.

No one model emerges as clearly superior to another: positive benefits were found for limited interventions as well as for the most massive. The findings imply that cognitive gains are greater when intervention begins in very early childhood, but questions remain about the socioemotional effects of this practice. With more and more children needing early care, it is essential that such care be of the highest quality. Clearly, particular attention also should be paid to socioemotional factors. More research on how best to foster healthy emotional growth in young children is needed.

There are no easy answers on best practices for children from low-income families. Many such children are born to young mothers who need to finish school. For them, and for all students who will eventually become parents, there is a lack of school curricula directed toward parenthood. For teenage parents, regular school curricula could be combined with child care and parent training at school sites, benefiting both parent and child. However, it is difficult to fit yet another subject into a

> **Business and industry could do much more for families. If child care were provided at work sites, with work schedules flexible enough to allow parents—especially breast-feeding mothers—to visit infants during the day, both parent and child would greatly benefit. Management could provide parent education classes on site, with child care continuing through the instruction period. This would support parents in their role as nurturing caregivers as well as financial providers for their children. Further, primary health and dental care could be provided at work sites. Such coordination of services could greatly enhance the health and well-being of young children.**

The message for lawmakers is plain. If parents are to work, high-quality child care must be provided from the earliest years, and programs for young children will have to be greatly expanded. Early childhood professionals can help by urging their lawmakers to support quality programs for preschoolers. Low-income families could be supported through stipends for quality child care services. Schools and businesses should be given all possible incentives for providing child care and family supports. It does make a difference.

crowded school day, and only a few states mandate curricula for parenting. Schools where child care is available are almost nonexistent.

Business and industry could do much more for families. If child care were provided at work sites, with work schedules flexible enough to allow parents—especially breast-feeding mothers—to visit infants during the day, both parent and child would greatly benefit. Management could provide parent education classes on site, with child care continuing through the instruction period. This would support parents in their role as nurturing caregivers as well as financial providers for their children. Further, primary health and dental care could be provided at work sites. Such coordination of services could greatly enhance the health and well-being of young children.

Politicians stress the importance of "family values" but are curiously silent on urging business leaders to provide family supports. Tax incentives could be given to corporations that have family-enhancing benefit plans. Leaders in education, business, and industry will have to make a strong commitment to young children and their families for this to happen on a broad scale. Those who are quick to discount the importance of early childhood programs have not suggested constructive alternatives. Early childhood programs ultimately save taxpayer dollars in terms of reductions in the costs of education, welfare, and crime (Berrueta-Clement et al. 1984). These benefits are associated with child and family interventions provided in the preschool years. The message for lawmakers is plain. If parents are to work, high-quality child care must be provided from the earliest years, and programs for young children will have to be greatly expanded. Early childhood professionals can help by urging their lawmakers to support quality programs for preschoolers. Low-income families could be supported through stipends for quality child care services. Schools and businesses should be

© Francis Wardle

given all possible incentives for providing child care and family supports. It does make a difference.

References

Berrueta-Clement, J.R., L.J. Schweinhart, W.S. Barnett, A.S. Epstein, & D.P. Weikart. 1984. *Changed lives: The effects of the Perry Preschool Program on youths through age 19.* Monographs of the High/Scope Educational Research Foundation, no. 8. Ypsilanti, MI: High/Scope.

Bronfenbrenner, U. 1974. Is early intervention effective? *Day Care and Early Education* 44 (1): 12–18.

Brooks-Gunn, J., C.M. McCarton, P.H. Casey, M.C. McCormick, C.R. Bauer, J.C. Bernbaum, J. Tyson, M. Swanson, F.C. Bennett, D.T. Scott, J. Tonascia, & C.L. Meinert. 1994. Early intervention in low-birth-weight premature infants: Results through age 5 years in the Infant Health and Development Program. *Journal of the American Medical Association* 272 (16): 1257–62.

Early childhood programs ultimately save taxpayer dollars in terms of reductions in the costs of education, welfare, and crime.

Campbell, F.A. 1995. *The development of academic self-concept and its relationship to academic performance and self-esteem: A longitudinal study of African American students.* Paper presented at biennial meeting of Society for Research in Child Development, March, Indianapolis, IN.

Campbell, F.A., & C.T. Ramey. 1995. Cognitive and school outcomes for high-risk African American students at middle adolescence: Positive effects of early intervention. *American Educational Research Journal* 32 (4): 743–72.

Cicirelli, V.G. 1969. *The impact of Head Start: An evaluation of the effects of Head Start on children's cognitive and affective development, Vol. 1.* Athens: Westinghouse Learning Corp., Ohio University.

Connell, R.W. 1994. Poverty and education. *Harvard Educational Review* 64 (2): 125–49.

Garber, H.L. 1988. *The Milwaukee Project: Prevention of mental retardation in children at risk.* Washington, DC: American Association on Mental Retardation.

Gray, S.W., B.K. Ramsey, & R.A. Klaus. 1982. *From 3 to 20: The Early Training Project.* Baltimore: University Park.

Gutelius, M.F., A.D. Kirsch, S. MacDonald, M.R. Brooks, & T. McErlean. 1977. Controlled study of child health supervision: Behavioral results. *Pediatrics* 60 (3): 294–304.

Gutelius, M.F., A.D. Kirsch, S. MacDonald, M.R. Brooks, T. McErlean, & C. Newcomb. 1972. Promising results from a cognitive stimulation program in infancy: A preliminary report. *Clinical Pediatrics* 11 (10): 585–93.

Haskins, R. 1985. Public school aggression among children with varying daycare experience. *Child Development* 56 (3): 689–703.

Infant Health and Development Program. 1990. Enhancing the outcomes of low-birthweight, premature infants: A multisite, randomized trial. *Pediatrics* 263 (22): 3035–42.

Johnson, D.L., & T. Walker. 1991. A follow-up evaluation of the Houston Parent-Child Development Center: School performance. *Journal of Early Intervention* 15 (3): 226–36.

Lally, J.R., P.L. Mangione, & A.S. Honig. 1988. The Syracuse University Family Development Research Program: Long-range impact on an early intervention with low-income children and their families. In *Annual advances in applied developmental psychology, Vol. 3. Parent education as early childhood intervention: Emerging directions in theory, research, and practice,* eds. I.E. Sigel & D.R. Powell, 79–104. Norwood, NJ: Ablex.

Lazar, I., R. Darlington, H. Murray, J. Royce, & A. Snipper. 1982. *Lasting effects of early education: A report from the Consortium for Longitudinal Studies.* Monographs of the Society for Research in Child Development Vol. 47, No. 2–3, Serial No. 195.

Levinstein, P., J. O'Hara, & J. Madden. 1983. The mother-child home program of the Verbal Interaction Program. In *As the twig is bent: Lasting effects of preschool programs,* ed. Consortium for Longitudinal Studies, 237–64. Hillsdale, NJ: Lawrence Earlbaum.

McKey, R.H., L. Condelli, H. Ganson, B.J. Barrett, C. McConkey, & M.C.

Plantz. 1985. *The impact of Head Start on children, families, and communities.* Department of Health and Human Services Publication No. (OHDS) 90-31193. Washington, DC: U.S. Government Printing Office.

Olds, D. 1988. The Prenatal/Early Infancy Project. In *14 ounces of prevention: A casebook for practitioners,* eds. R.H. Price, E.L. Cowen, R.P. Lorion, & J. Ramon-McKay, 9–23. Washington, DC: American Psychological Association.

Palmer, F.H. 1983. The Harlem Study: Effects by type of training, age of training, and social class. In *As the twig is bent: Lasting effects of preschool programs,* ed. Consortium for Longitudinal Studies, 201–36. Hillsdale, NJ: Lawrence Earlbaum.

Patterson, C.J., J.B. Kupersmidt, & N.A. Vaden. 1990. Income level, gender, ethnicity, and household composition as predictors of children's school-based competence. *Child Development* 61 (2): 485–94.

Pierson, D.E. 1988. The Brookline Early Education Project. In *14 ounces of prevention: A casebook for practitioners,* eds. R.H. Price, E.L. Cowen, R.P. Lorion, & J. Ramon-McKay, 24–31. Washington, DC: American Psychological Association.

Provence, S., & A. Naylor. 1983. *Working with disadvantaged parents and their children.* New Haven, CT: Yale University Press.

Ramey, C.T., & F.A. Campbell. 1991. Poverty, early childhood education, and academic competence: The Abecedarian experiment. In *Children in poverty,* ed. A. Huston, 190–221. New York: Cambridge University Press.

Reynolds, A.J. 1994. Effects of a preschool plus follow-on intervention for children at risk. *Developmental Psychology* 30 (6): 787–804.

Schweinhart, L.J., & D.P. Weikart. 1980. *Young children grow up: The effects of the Perry Preschool Program on youth through age 15.* Monographs of the High Scope Educational Research Foundation, no. 7. Ypsilanti, MI: High/Scope.

Schweinhart, L.J., H.V. Barnes, & D.P. Weikart. 1993. *Significant benefits: The High/Scope Perry Preschool study through age 27.* Monographs of the High Scope Educational Research Foundation, no. 10. Ypsilanti, MI: High/Scope.

Seitz, V., & S. Provence. 1990. Caregiver-focused models of early intervention. In *Handbook of early childhood intervention,* eds. S. Meisels & J. Shonkoff, 400–27. New York: Cambridge University Press.

Seitz, V., N.H. Apfel, L.K. Rosenbaum, & E. Zigler. 1983. Long-term effects of projects Head Start and Follow-Through: The New Haven Project. In *As the twig is bent: Lasting effects of preschool programs,* ed. Consortium for Longitudinal Studies, 299–332. Hillsdale, NJ: Lawrence Earlbaum.

Walden, T., & C.T. Ramey. 1983. Locus of control and academic achievement: Results of a preschool intervention program. *Journal of Educational Psychology* 75 (3): 865–76.

Wasik, B.H., C.T. Ramey, D.M. Bryant, & J.J. Sparling. 1990. A longitudinal study of two early intervention strategies: Project CARE. *Child Development* 61 (6): 1682–96.

Helping Children Become More Prosocial:
Ideas for Classrooms, Families, Schools, and Communities

Alice S. Honig and Donna S. Wittmer

Alice Sterling Honig, Ph.D., professor of child development at Syracuse University in Syracuse, New York, was program director for the Family Development Research Program and has authored numerous books, including Parent Involvement in Early Childhood Education *and* Playtime Learning Games for Young Children. *She directs the annual Syracuse Quality Infant/Toddler Caregiving Workshop.*

Donna Sasse Wittmer, Ph.D., is assistant professor in early childhood education at the University of Colorado in Denver. She has had extensive experience directing, training in, and conducting research in early childhood care and education programs.

Part 1 of this review of strategies and techniques to enhance prosocial development focused on techniques that teachers and parents can use with individual children or small groups of children (see Wittmer & Honig, Encouraging Positive Social Development in Young Children, *Young Children* 49 [5]: 4–12). Part 2 offers suggestions for involving whole classrooms, entire school systems, parents, and communities in creating classroom and home climates for kindness, cooperation, generosity, and helpfulness.

Child-sensitive, high-quality care in classrooms promotes prosocial behaviors

If you thought so, you were right. Here is more information to back you up. Peaceful play and cooperation are more likely to occur when teachers set up developmentally appropriate classrooms (Bredekamp & Rosegrant 1992). Staff competence and years of teacher experience are signifi-

cant factors in ensuring such quality care. In one research study the more highly trained and stable the preschool staff were, the *lower* were teacher-rated and observed preschool aggression scores, despite children's varying histories of full-time or part-time nonparental care during infancy and toddlerhood (Park & Honig 1991). In another study 4-year-olds in a constructivist classroom, given many opportunities for choices and autonomous construction of attitudes, principles, and social problem-solving strategies, showed higher social-cognitive skills than their peers from another preschool program with whom they played board games (DeVries & Goncu 1990).

Children in strongly adult-directed preschool classrooms engage in less prosocial behavior than do children in classrooms that encourage more child-initiated learning and interactions (Huston-Stein, Friedrich-Cofer, & Susman 1977). In a longitudinal study of 19-year-olds who had attended either a highly adult-directed preschool or a program

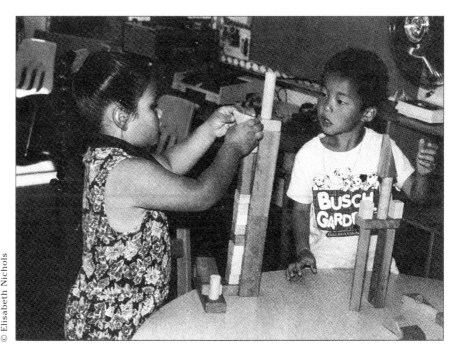

© Elisabeth Nichols

From *Young Children*, January 1996, pp. 62-70. © 1996 by the National Association for the Education of Young Children. Reprinted by permission.

that emphasized child initiations much more, the teenagers who had been in the latter program were more socially competent and had fewer juvenile delinquency convictions (Schweinhart, Weikart, & Larner 1986).

Howes and Stewart (1987) discovered that children who experience high-quality child care and supportive parents acquire the *ability to decode and regulate emotional signals in peer play.* Social sensitivity to others' cues and needs is a good predictor of positive peer relations. Unfortunately, the researchers also found that families who are the most stressed choose the lowest quality child care arrangements, are the most likely to change arrangements, and have children with the lowest levels of competence during social play with peers. A community resource-and-referral agency may be the best source of materials and information to help families recognize and choose high-quality child care and to inform parents about NAEYC accreditation.

Emphasize cooperation rather than competition

Every experienced preschool teacher surely wants young children to be prepared to succeed in their school learning careers. Competitive classrooms result in some children becoming tense, fearing failure, and becoming less motivated to persist at challenging tasks. In a cooperative-interaction classroom, the emphasis is on children working together to accomplish mutual goals (Aronson, Bridgeman, & Geffner 1978). Even toddlers can work together in cooperative play. For example, if each grasps the opposite end of a towel and both coordinate efforts, they can keep a beach ball bouncing on the towel.

Every child has an essential and unique contribution to make to class learning. One teaching tool has been called the "jigsaw technique" because the teacher provides each child with one piece of information about a lesson; then the children must work cooperatively with each other to learn all the material and information necessary for a complete presentation by the group (Aronson et al. 1978).

We have referred here only to a few studies emphasizing the positive outcomes of cooperative learning environments, but surely our readers have read about this in numerous books and articles in recent years!

Teach cooperative and conflict-resolution games and sports

Caregiver creativity in initiating group games and in devising conflict-resolution games promotes peace in the classroom (Kreidler 1984). New games and variations of traditional children's games and sports that encourage cooperation rather than competition facilitate prosocial interactions (Orlick 1982, 1985; Prutzman et al. 1988). When Musical Chairs is played so that each time a chair is taken away, the "leftover" child must find a lap to sit on rather than be forced out of the game, no child feels left out or a failure. Bos (1990) provides examples of such games. In Spider Swing one child sits on the lap of another, with legs hanging out the back of the swing. Bos calls games in which children play cooperatively together to create pleasure and fun "coaction." Why not try these and invent some of your own?

Of course, even more important than an occasional game is helping children live cooperatively in the classroom every day and resolve personal conflicts peaceably.

Set up classroom spaces and play materials to facilitate cooperative play

Arrangements of space and varieties of toys and learning materials affect whether children act more aggressively or cooperate more peacefully. A small, cluttered play area can lead to more tension and fights. A group seesaw, a tire-bouncer, or a nylon parachute encourage group cooperation because the children *need* each other to maximize their enjoyment.

In the research we reviewed, more prosocial responses were given by young children attending child care or nursery school programs when (1) a variety of age-appropriate materials were available and (2) space was arranged to accommodate groups of varying sizes (Holloway & Reichhart-Erickson 1988). Children who played with large hollow blocks and unit blocks in a large block area of their preschool learned and practiced positive social problem-solving skills rather than aggression (Rogers 1987). Yet, where preschoolers are crowded together in a narrow area with large blocks, there is greater pressure to use the blocks as missiles or pretend guns.

Classroom layout affects children's emotional security and sense of free choice in play. Combine your environmental design skills with your expertise in early childhood education to arrange class traffic patterns that maximize peaceful interactions. Think through the placement of clearly defined and well-supplied interest centers; provide unobstructed access to materials; give aesthetic attention to color and wall decorations; and decrease clutter. Arrange inviting spaces with soft cushions for children to nestle on when they need to calm down or rest when distressed.

Your executive space-planning skills can promote more comfortable feelings conducive to a more harmonious, cooperative classroom climate.

Use bibliotherapy: Incorporate children's literature to enhance empathy and caring in daily reading activities

A growing number of preschool and primary teachers do use bibliotherapy. If you do not, you may find this a good time to begin!

Choose children's literature for prosocial themes and characters that provide altruistic models. *Two Good Friends* (by Judy Delton) is the charming story of how two friends—Bear, who is messy but a fine cook, and Duck, who is tidy but a poor cook—care for each other lovingly and generously. Dr. Seuss's Horton the Elephant is that kind of prosocial character in the books *Horton Hears a Who* and *Horton Hatches an Egg*. So is the king's young page boy in Seuss's *The King's Stilts*. And so is *The Little Engine That Could*, as she chugs courageously up and over a very tall mountain to bring toys to boys and girls. Sucking his thumb vigorously, one little boy listened enraptured as his caregiver read the story of the brave little engine who did not want to disappoint the children. The child kept nodding his head and whispering to himself, "That was very nice of her! That was very nice of her!"

McMath (1989) suggests asking open-ended questions that help children think about and understand the motives and actions of storybook characters. When skilled adults read stories that feature altruistic characters, they promote children's ability to grasp socioemotional motivations and motivate children to imitate empathic and helpful responses (Dreikurs, Grunwald, & Pepper 1982). Many publishers, such as the Albert Whitman Company, provide children's books that adults can read to young children to help them cope with and find adaptive solutions to disturbing personal concerns, such as living with family alcoholism, parental divorce, or domestic violence.

Actively lead group discussions on prosocial interactions

Some teachers focus on developing supportive classroom communities. Discussion of social interactions within the group is usually a central part of the curriculum in this kind of classroom.

Sharing increases among preschool children whose teachers give them explanations as to *why* sharing is important and *how* to share (Barton & Osborne 1978). Some second-grade teachers daily set aside brief classroom time to encourage children to discuss specific incidents in which they and their classmates were helpful and kind with one another. After one month, prosocial interactions increased about twofold among these children, compared with a randomly assigned group of control children (Honig & Pollack 1990).

As a teacher, you have learned a great deal about the individual interests and talents of your children. During show-and-tell circle times you can extend group discussion to increase children's awareness of *distributive justice*—how goods and benefits are distributed justly among people with varying needs, temperaments, talents, and troubles. Lively discussions can center around what is "fair" or not so fair. Children between 4 and 8 years old are busy learning rules for games and rules for social relations, and they are often concerned about fairness and who gets advantages. Yet, preschoolers are capable of realizing, for example, that at meal and snack times, rigid equality in distributing food would not be the best plan if one child habitually comes to school without breakfast and is very hungry.

Young children often protest if there is not strict equality in distributing goodies. Many a teacher or parent has heard the protest, "That's not fair. He got more than me!" Through discussions, children can move from a position of belief in strict equality in treat or toy distribution toward awareness of the concepts of *equity and benevolence*—that is, the idea that the special needs of others must be taken into account (Damon 1977).

Talk about taking turns and about *different* ways each child gets some special time or privilege, although not exactly the same as another receives. These talks can be especially helpful for preschoolers who are distressed because Mama is now nursing a new baby and seemingly gives lots more time and attention to the tiny new stranger. Caregiver kindness lies not only in providing extra nurturing for that preschooler during this difficult time but also in assisting all the children to think through issues of neediness and fairness. As you help children to learn about "turn taking" through group discussions, you increase their understanding of fairness. Although in some families it may be a new baby's turn to get special attention, such as nursing, preschoolers now get other kinds of special attention from parents, such as a story reading at bedtime or a chance to help with cooking, a household repair job, or some other special activity in which a baby cannot participate.

Encourage social interaction between normally developing children and children with special needs

Teachers must initiate specific friendship-building strategies when atypical children in an inclusive classroom exhibit low-level prosocial skills. Activities to promote classroom friendship are available (Fox 1980; Smith 1982; Edwards 1986; Wolf 1986). Children with disabilities need your inventive interventions to learn how to make a friend, use positive and assertive techniques to enter a play group, and *sustain* friendly play bouts with peers (Honig & Thompson 1994). Promotion of specific friendship skills to enhance the social integration of typical and atypical children requires well-planned teacher strategies and initiatives. Prosocial interactions of children with disabilities may need a boost. Some typical preschoolers also may need a boost in their sensitivity to others' difficulties *and* competencies (Gresham 1981; Honig & McCarron 1990).

More than other children, a child with a disability may need help from classmates and the teacher or extra time to finish a project. If you are making preparations to create an inclusive classroom that integrates atypical and typical children, then class discussions about fairness become particularly urgent. Children will need to talk about and struggle with a new idea: strict equal apportionment according to work done may not be the kindest or most prosocial decision in special cases. If a child with cerebral palsy and marked difficulties in hand coordination finishes far fewer placemats than the other children in a class project, she or he has tried just as hard as the others and should receive the same share of any "profits" from the class craft sale.

Develop class and school projects that foster altruism

With the help of a caring teacher, children can think about and decide on a class project to help others (Solomon et al. 1988). Some classes prominently label and display a jar in which they put pennies to donate to hungry children or to families in need at holiday time. When the jar is full, children count the money and compose a joint class letter to the organization to which they are contributing. Other class projects can arise from children's suggestions during group discussion times about troubles that faraway or nearby children are having. Prosocial projects include cleaning up the schoolyard, writing as pen pals to children in troubled lands, collecting toys or food for individuals in need, and making friends with older people during visits to a home for the aged.

Your perceptive knowledge about individuals in the class is especially useful when you encourage each child to generate personal ideas for sharing kindness and caring in her or his own family. As a group, the children may decide to draw their own "helping coupons." Each child creates a gift book with large, hand-drawn coupons. Every coupon promises a helpful act to a parent or family member. Some of the coupons could be "reading my baby sister a story," "setting the table," "sorting socks from the laundry basket into pairs," "sharing my toy cars with my brother," and "brushing my teeth all by myself while Papa puts the baby to bed." Young children dictate their helpful offers for you to write down and then illustrate the coupons with signs and pictures that remind them of what sharing or caring action their coupon represents. Children generously give the coupons to family members as personal gifts—promises of help.

Encourage cooperative in-classroom activities that require several children's joint productive efforts. Ideas include drawing a group mural, building a large boat or space station with blocks and Tinkertoys, planning and producing a puppet show, and sewing a yarn picture that has been outlined on both sides of burlap.

Move very young children with peers to the next age group

Toddlers adjust more positively to movement from one group to a slightly older group in center care when they move with peers. Howes (1987) found that children who stayed in the same child care center with the same peer group increased their proportion of complementary and reciprocal peer play more than did children who changed peer groups within their center. Continuity of quality child care and continuity of peer group relationships are important in the development of a child's feelings of security and social competence. Consider security needs and friendship patterns rather than rigid age criteria in moving young children to a new classroom.

Arrange regular viewing of prosocial media and videogames

Viewing prosocial videos and television programs increases children's social contacts as well as fosters smiling, praising, hugging (Coates, Pusser, & Goodman 1976), sharing, cooperating, turn taking, positive verbal/physical contact (Forge & Phemister 1987), and willingness to help puppies in need (Poulds, Rubinstein, & Leibert 1975). Regular viewing of prosocial television, particularly *Mister Rogers' Neighborhood*, has resulted in higher levels of task persistence, rule obedience, and tolerance of delayed gratification. Children from low-socioeconomic families who watched this program daily showed increased cooperative play, nurturance, and verbalization of feelings (Friedrich & Stein 1973). In contrast, children who were exposed to aggressive videogames donated less to needy children than did children who played prosocial videogames (Chambers 1987).

Invite moral mentors to visit the class

Damon (1988) urges teachers actively to recruit and involve *moral mentors* in the classroom. Invite individuals who have contributed altruistically to better the lives of others in the community to come in and talk about their lives and experiences. Children may be eager to nominate someone in their own family to tell about how they help others. Perhaps Aunt Esther visits a nursing home and livens up senior citizens' days. Perhaps Uncle Irving outfitted the family station wagon with a ramp so he can take people in wheelchairs to weekend ball games. Children learn to reframe their ideas about community helpfulness and personal generosity toward others in trouble if a special guest—a high school swimming star who volunteers as a coach for children with physical impairments, for example—comes to visit and talks about her or his experiences helping others.

Work closely with families for prosocial programming

Families need to know that prosocial interactions are an integral curriculum component of your child care program. As a practicing professional, you use your prosocial skills to support and affirm family members of each child in your classroom. And, of course, you know how your close contact with parents provides you with insight and more sensitive understanding of each child. Parents also need you to share your concern for and emphasis on prosocial classroom activities and goals. During informal greetings at the beginning of the day or at end-of-day pickup times, you may want to affirm how special each parent's role is

in promoting care and concern for others at home (Barnett et al. 1980). Yarrow and colleagues (in Pines 1979) revealed that parents who exhibit tender concern when their very young children experience fright or upset and who firmly discourage aggressive actions to solve squabbles have children who show very early signs of concern and empathy for others' troubles. These personal examples of "baby altruism" persist into elementary school (Pines 1979).

In interviews 10 years after graduation from a program that emphasized caring and prosocial development in outreach with families as well as in high-quality group care, teenagers and their families reported that they felt more family support, closeness, and appreciation than did control youth. Compared with members of the control group, the adolescents also had far lower rates of juvenile delinquency (Lally, Mangione, & Honig 1988).

Establish a parent resource lending library

Interested parents will appreciate being able to browse through prosocial articles in your child care facility. For example, make available a copy of Kobak's (1979) brief article on how she embeds caring and awareness of positive social interactions in all classroom activities, dialogues, and projects. Her concept of a *caring quotient* (CQ) classroom emphasizes the importance of children learning positive social interaction skills as well as intellectual (IQ) skills. Social problem solving by a class must take into consideration that the child whose problem is being brainstormed has to feel that the class members *care* about him or her as they explore ways to resolve a problem, such as chronic truancy or a book borrowed from a teacher and never returned.

Convince parents of the importance of a specific focus on prosocial as well as cognitive curriculum through displays of brief, easy-to-read reports of research articles. The Abecedarian program provides powerful research findings (Finkelstein 1982). Children who had attended this infant and preschool program that emphasized cognitive development were 15 times more aggressive with kindergarten peers than a control group of children who had not been in child care or who had attended community child care. A prosocial curriculum was then instituted for future waves of children in the program; the difference in aggression between program children and their peers in kindergarten subsequently disappeared, according to later evaluations.

Promote a bias-free curriculum

A bias-free curriculum promotes more prosocial interactions among children despite multicultural differences in ethnicity, language, or family background (Derman-Sparks & the A.B.C. Task Force 1989). Emphasize how all children and adults feel better and get a fairer chance when others treat them courteously and kindly. Children who feel that others are *more,* rather than less, similar to themselves behave more prosocially toward them (Feshbach 1978). During class meeting times, children discover how much alike they are—in having special family members they feel close to, in enjoying a picnic or an outing with family, in playing with friends, and in wanting to feel safe, well-loved, and cared about.

Require responsibility: Encourage children to care for younger children and classmates who need extra help

Anthropologists, studying six different cultures, noted that when children help care for younger siblings and interact with a cross-age variety of children in social groups in nonschool settings, then children feel more responsible for the welfare of the group and gain more skills in nurturing (Whiting & Whiting 1975).

Children should be given responsibility, commensurate with their abilities, to care for and help teach younger children or children who may need extra personal help in the classroom. In a long-term study of at-risk infants born on the island of Kauai, children who carried out such caring actions of *required helpfulness* were more likely 32 years later to be positively socially functioning as family members and as community citizens (Werner 1986).

Become familiar with structured curriculum packages that promote prosocial development

Complete program packages are available with materials and specific ideas as well as activities for enhancing prosocial behaviors in the classroom. Shure's (1992) daily lesson plans give step-by-step techniques for teaching how the feelings or wishes of one child may be the same or different from those of another child and how to challenge children to think of the consequences of their behaviors and to think up alternatives to inappropriate or hurtful behaviors in solving their social problems. *Communicating to Make Friends* (Fox 1980) provides 18 weeks of planned activities to promote peer acceptance. Dinkmeyer and Dinkmeyer's *Developing Understanding of Self and Others* (1982) provides puppets, activity cards, charts, and audio-cassettes to promote children's awareness of others' feelings and social skills. The Abecedarian

program instituted *My Friends and Me* (Davis 1977) to promote more prosocial development.

Arrange Bessell and Palomares's (1973) Magic Circle lessons so that children, each day during a safe, nonjudgmental circle time, feel *secure enough to share* their stories, feelings, and memories about times they have had troubles with others, times when they have been helped by others, and times when they have been thoughtful and caring on behalf of others.

Commercial sources also provide some materials that directly support teacher attempts to introduce peace programs and conflict-resolution programs in their classrooms (e.g., Young People's Press, San Diego). Sunrise Books (Provo, Utah) is a commercial source of book and video materials for teachers and parents to promote positive discipline and conflict resolution. One book by Nelson (n.d.) features the use of class meetings, a technique that builds cooperation, communication, and problem solving so that classmates' mutual respect and accountability increase.

Watkins and Durant (1992) provide pre-K to second-grade teachers with specific classroom techniques for prevention of antisocial behaviors. They suggest the right times to *ignore* inappropriate behavior and specify other situations when the teacher must use *control*. Teachers are taught to look for signs that they may actually be rewarding socially inappropriate behavior by their responses. The use of subtle, nonverbal cues of dress, voice control, and body language are recommended in order to promote children's more positive behaviors.

Implement a comprehensive school-based prosocial program that emphasizes ethical teaching

John Gatto, a recipient of the

New York City Teacher of the Year award in 1990, admitted, "The children I teach are cruel to each other, they lack compassion for misfortune, they laugh at weakness, they have contempt for people whose need for help shows too plainly" (Wood 1991, 7).

Wood urges teachers to conceptualize a more ethical style of teaching that he calls " maternal teaching." He suggests that teachers develop a routine of morning meetings that involve greetings and cooperation, as in singing together. Children feel personally valued when they are greeted by name as they enter a school. Classes can create rules of courtesy for and with each other, and the rules should be prominently posted. Wood urges teachers to "figure out a way to teach recess and lunch . . . . When children come in from recess, the teacher often can spend another half hour of instructional time sorting out the hurt feelings and hurt bodies and hurt stories she wasn't even there to see or hear" (1991, 8). Children can be taught the power of "please" and "thank you." Role playing helps them become aware of how hurtful name-calling and verbal put-downs are. You, of course, are a powerful positive model of social courtesies as you listen to each child's ideas and give each a turn to talk at mealtime and grouptime. Help children feel all-school ownership. Flowers and tablecloths in school lunchrooms can be incentives for making lunchtime a friendly and positive experience.

Brown and Solomon (1983) have translated prosocial research for application throughout school systems. In the California Bay Area, they implemented a comprehensive program in several elementary schools to increase prosocial attitudes and behavior among the children and their families. In the program the following occur:

Suggested Books for Classroom Parents' Library

Bos, B. 1990. *Together we're better: Establishing a coactive learning environment.* Roseville, CA: Turn the Page Press.

Briggs, D. 1975. *Your child's self-esteem.* New York: Dolphin.

Crary, E. 1990. *Kids can cooperate: A practical guide to teaching problem solving.* Seattle, WA: Parenting Press.

Damon, W. 1988. *The moral child: Nurturing children's natural moral growth.* New York: Free Press.

Feshbach, N., & S. Feshbach. 1983. *Learning to care: Classroom activities for social and affective development.* Glenview, IL: Scott Foresman.

Finkelstein, N. 1982. Aggression: Is it stimulated by day care? *Young Children* 37 (6): 3–13.

Gordon, T. 1975. *Parent effectiveness training.* New York: Plume.

Honig, A. 1996. *Developmentally appropriate behavior guidance for infants and toddlers from birth to 3 years.* Little Rock, AR: Southern Early Childhood Association.

Kobak, D. 1970. Teaching young children to care. *Children Today* 8 (6–7): 34–35.

Orlick, T. 1985. *The second cooperative sports and games book.* New York: Pantheon.

Shure, M. 1994. *Raising a thinking child: Help your young child to resolve everyday conflicts and get along with others.* New York: Henry Holt.

Smith, C. 1993. *The peaceful classroom: 162 easy activities to teach preschoolers compassion and cooperation.* Mount Rainier, MD: Gryphon House.

Wolf, P., ed. 1986. *Connecting: Friendship in the lives of young children and their teachers.* Redmond, WA: Exchange Press.

Train older children as peer mediators

In some New York City schools and elsewhere in the United States, the Resolving Conflict Creatively Program (RCCP) trains fifth-graders as peer mediators to move to situations of social conflict, such as a playground fight, and help the participants resolve their problems. RCCP rules mandate that each child in a conflict be given a chance by the peer mediators to describe and explain the problem from her or his viewpoint and to try to agree on how to settle the problem. Peer mediators are trained in nonviolent and creative ways of dealing with social conflicts (RCCP, 163 Third Avenue # 239, New York, NY 10003).

Teachers of kindergarten and primary children may want to look into this. Think how much influence the "big kids" would have on *your* children!

1. Children from about age 6 onward, with adult supervision, take responsibility for caring for younger children.

2. Cooperative learning requires that children work with each other in learning teams within classes.

3. Children are involved in structured programs of helpful and useful activities, such as visiting the elderly or shut-ins, making toys for others, cleaning up or gardening in nearby parks and playgrounds.

4. Children of mixed ages engage in activities.

5. Children help with home chores on a regular basis with parental approval and cooperation.

6. Children regularly role-play situations in which they can experience feelings of being a victim *and* a helper.

7. The entire elementary school recognizes and rewards caring, helping, taking responsibility, and other prosocial behaviors, whether they occur at home or at school.

8. Children learn about prosocial adult models in films, television, and their own community. The children watch for such models in the news media and clip newspaper articles about prosocially acting persons. They also invite such models to tell their stories in class.

9. Empathy training includes children's exposure to examples of animals or children in distress, in real life or staged episodes. They hear adults comment on how to help someone in trouble, and they watch examples of helpfulness.

10. Continuity and total saturation in a school program create a climate that *communicates prosocial expectations and supports children's learning and enacting prosocial behaviors* both at home and in school.

Cherish the children: Create an atmosphere of affirmation through family/classroom/ community rituals

Loving rituals—such as a group greeting song that names and welcomes each child individually every morning, or leisurely and soothing backrubs given at naptime in a darkened room—establish a climate of caring in the child care classroom.

College students who scored high on an empathy scale remembered their parents as having been empathic and affectionate when the students were younger (Barnett et al. 1980). Egeland and Sroufe (1981), in a series of longitudinal research studies, reported devastating effects from the lack of early family cherishing of infants and young children. (Of course, therapists' offices and prisons are full of people who were not loved in their early years.)

A warm smile or an arm around the shoulder lets a child know he or she is valued and cared for. Encourage children to tell something special about their relationship to a particular child on that child's birthday. Write down these birthday stories in a personal book for each child. An attitude of affirmation creates an environment in which children feel safe, secure, accepted, and loved (Salkowski 1991). Special holiday celebration times, such as Thanksgiving, Abraham Lincoln's birthday, Father's Day, and Mother's Day, offer opportunities to create ritual class activities and to illustrate ceremonies and appropriate behaviors for expressing caring and thankfulness.

Teachers are bombarded with books and articles about the importance of developing positive self-esteem in each child and how to attempt to instill it. Many of these sources contain important and helpful ideas (see Honig & Witt-mer 1992).

Sometimes children come into care from such stressful situations that it is hard for them to control their own sadness and anger. One teacher uses a "Magic Feather Duster" to brush off troubles and upsets from children. A preschooler arriving in child care aggravated and upset announces, "Teacher, I think you better get the Magic Feather Duster to brush off all the 'bad vibes'!" After the teacher carefully and tenderly uses her magic duster, the child sighs, relaxes, and feels ready to enter into the atmosphere of a caring and peaceful classroom. Each teacher creates her or his own magic touches to help children feel secure, calm, and cooperative.

The more cherished a child is, the less likely he or she is to bully others *or* to be rejected by other children. The more nurturing parents and caregivers are—the more positive affection and responsive, empathic care they provide—the more positively children will relate in social interactions with teachers, caring adults, and peers and in cooooperating with classroom learning goals, as well.

References

Aronson, E., D. Bridgeman, & R. Geffner. 1978. Interdependent interactions and prosocial behavior. *Journal of Research and Development in Education* 12 (1): 16–27.

Aronson, E., C. Stephan, J. Sikes, N. Blaney, & M. Snapp. 1978. *The jigsaw classroom.* Beverly Hills, CA: Sage.

Barnett, M., J. Howard, L. King, & G. Dino. 1980. Empathy in young children: Relation to parents' empathy, affection, and emphasis on the feelings of others. *Developmental Psychology* 16: 243–44.

Barton, E.J., & J.G. Osborne. 1978. The development of classroom sharing by a teacher using positive practice. *Behavior Modification* 2: 231–51.

Bessell, H., & U. Palomares. 1973. *Methods in human development: Theory manual.* El Cajun, CA: Human Development Training Institute.

Bos, B. 1990. *Together we're better: Establishing a coactive learning environment.* Roseville, CA: Turn the Page Press.

Bredekamp, S., & T. Rosegrant, eds. 1992. *Reaching potentials: Appropriate curriculum and assessment for young children.* Vol. 1. Washington, DC: NAEYC.

Brown, D., & D. Solomon. 1983. A model for prosocial learning: An in-progress field study. In *The nature of prosocial development: Interdisciplinary theories and strategies,* ed. D.L. Bridgeman. New York: Academic.

Chambers, J. 1987. The effects of prosocial and aggressive videogames on children's donating and helping. *Journal of Genetic Psychology* 148: 499–505.

Coates, B., H. Pusser, & I. Goodman. 1976. The influence of "Sesame Street" and "Mr. Rogers' Neighborhood" on children's so-cial behavior in the preschool. *Child Development* 47: 138–44.

Damon, W. 1977. *The social world of the child.* San Francisco, CA: Jossey-Bass.

Damon, W. 1988. *The moral child: Nurturing children's natural moral growth.* New York: Free Press.

Davis, D.E. 1977. *My friends and me.* Circle Pines, MN: American Guidance Service.

Derman-Sparks, L., & the A.B.C. Task Force 1989. *Anti-bias curriculum: Tools for empowering young children.* Washington, DC: NAEYC.

DeVries, R., & A. Goncu. 1990. Interpersonal relations in four-year-old dyads from constructivist and Montessori programs. In *Optimizing early child care and education,* ed. A.S. Honig, 11–28. London: Gordon & Breach.

Dinkmeyer, D., & D. Dinkmeyer, Jr. 1982. *Developing understanding of self and others (Rev. DUSO-R).* Circle Pines, MN: American Guidance Service.

Dreikurs, R., B.B. Grunwald, & F.C. Pepper. 1982. *Maintaining sanity in the classroom: Classroom management techniques.* New York: Harper & Row.

Edwards, C.P. 1986. *Social and moral development in young children: Creative approaches for the classroom.* New York: Teachers College Press.

Egeland, B., & A. Sroufe. 1981. Developmental sequelae of maltreatment in infancy. *Directions for Child Development* 11: 77–92.

Feshbach, N. 1978. Studies of empathetic behavior in children. In *Progress in experimental personality research,* Vol. 8, ed. B. Maher, 1–47. New York: Academic Press.

Finkelstein, N. 1982. Aggression: Is it stimulated by day care? *Young Children* 37 (6): 3–13.

Forge, K.L., & S. Phemister. 1987. The effect of prosocial cartoons on preschool children. *Child Study Journal* 17: 83–88.

Fox, L. 1980. *Communicating to make friends.* Rolling Hills Estates, CA: B.L. Winch.

Friedrich, L.K., & A.H. Stein. 1973. *Aggressive and prosocial television programs and the natural behavior of preschool children.* Monographs of the Society for Research in Child Development, vol. 38, issue 4, no. 151. Chicago: University of Chicago Press.

Gresham, F. 1981. Social skills training with handicapped children: A review. *Review of Educational Research* 51: 139–76.

Holloway, S.D., & M. Reichhart-Erickson. 1988. The relationship of day care quality to children's free-play behavior and social problem-solving skills. *Early Childhood Research Quarterly* 3: 39–53.

Honig, A., & P. McCarron. 1990. Prosocial behaviors of handicapped and typical peers in an integrated preschool. In *Optimizing early child care and education,* ed. A.S. Honig. London: Gordon & Breach.

Honig, A., & B. Pollack. 1990. Effects of a brief intervention program to promote prosocial behaviors in young children. *Early Education and Development* 1: 438–44.

Honig, A.S., & A. Thompson. 1994. Helping toddlers with peer entry skills. *Zero to Three* 14 (5): 15–19.

Honig, A.S., & D.S. Wittmer. 1992. *Prosocial development in children: Caring, sharing, and cooperating: A bibliographic resource guide.* New York: Garland Press.

Howes, C. 1987. Social competence with peers in young children: Developmental sequences. *Developmental Review* 7: 252–72.

Howes, C., & P. Stewart. 1987. Child's play

with adults, toys, and peers: An examination of family and child care influences. *Developmental Psychology* 23 (8): 423–30.

Huston-Stein, A., L. Friedrich-Cofer, & E. Susman. 1977. The relation of classroom structure to social behavior, imaginative play, and self-regulation of economically disadvantaged children. *Child Development* 48: 908–16.

Kobak, D. 1979. Teaching children to care. *Children Today* 8 (6/7): 34–35.

Kreidler, W. 1984. *Creative conflict resolution.* Evanston, IL: Scott Foresman.

Lally, J.R., P. Mangione, & A.S. Honig. 1988. The Syracuse University Family Development Research Program: Long range impact of an early intervention with low-income children and their families. In *Parent education as early childhood intervention: Emerging directions in theory, research, and practice,* ed. D. Powell, 79–104. Norwood, NJ: Ablex.

McMath, J. 1989. Promoting prosocial behaviors through literature. *Day Care and Early Education* 17 (1): 25–27.

Nelson, J. n.d. *Positive discipline in the classroom featuring class meetings.* Provo, UT: Sunrise.

Orlick, T. 1982. *Winning through cooperation: Competitive insanity—cooperative alternatives.* Washington, DC: Acropolis.

Orlick, T. 1985. *The second cooperative sports and games book.* New York: Pantheon Press.

Park, K., & A. Honig. 1991. Infant child care patterns and later teacher ratings of preschool behaviors. *Early Child Development and Care* 68: 80–87.

Pines, M. 1979. Good samaritans at age two? *Psychology Today* 13: 66–77.

Poulds, R., E. Rubinstein, & R. Leibert. 1975. Positive social learning. *Journal of Communication* 25 (4): 90–97.

Prutzman, P., L. Sgern, M.L. Burger, & G. Bodenhamer. 1988. *The friendly classroom for a small planet: Children's creative response to conflict program.* Philadelphia: New Society.

Rogers, D. 1987. Fostering social development through block play. *Day Care and Early Education* 14 (3): 26–29.

Salkowski, C.J. 1991. Keeping the peace: Helping children resolve conflict through a problem-solving approach. *Montessori Life* (Spring): 31–37.

Schweinhart, L.J., D.P. Weikart, & M.B. Larner. 1986. Consequences of three curriculum models through age 15. *Early Childhood Research Quarterly* 1: 15–45.

Shure, M. 1992. *I can problem solve: An interpersonal cognitive problem-solving program.* Champaign, IL: Research Press.

Smith, C.A. 1982. *Promoting the social development of young children: Strategies and activities.* Palo Alto, CA: Mayfield.

Solomon, D., M.S. Watson, K.L. Delucci, E. Schaps, & V. Battistich. 1988. Enhancing children's prosocial behavior in the classroom. *American Educational Research Journal* 25 (4): 527–54.

Watkins, K.P., & L. Durant. 1992. *Complete early childhood behavior management guide.* West Nyack, NY: Center for Applied Research in Education.

Werner, E. 1986. Resilient children. In *Annual editions: Human development,* eds. H.E. Fitzgerald & M.G. Walraven. Sluice-Dock, CT: Dushkin.

Whiting, B., & J. Whiting. 1975. *Children of six cultures: A psychocultural analysis.* Cambridge, MA: Harvard University Press.

Wittmer, D., & A. Honig. 1994. Encouraging positive social development in young children, Part 1. *Young Children* 49 (5): 4–12.

Wolf, P., ed. 1986. *Connecting: Friendship in the lives of young children and their teachers.* Redmond,WA: Exchange Press.

Wood, C. 1991. Maternal teaching: Revolution of kindness. *Holistic Education Review* (Summer): 3–10.

Developmental Tasks of Early Adolescence: How Adult Awareness Can Reduce At-Risk Behavior

JUDITH L. IRVIN

Judith L. Irvin is an associate professor in the College of Education, Florida State University, Tallahassee. This article is drawn from her book, Reading and the Middle Level Student: Strategies to Enhance Learning *(Allyn and Bacon, 1997).*

At any inservice session for middle level educators, the first topic generally is "Characteristics of Young Adolescents," having to do with the physical, social, emotional, and intellectual growth and development of ten to fourteen year olds.

Although such information is important, it is somewhat incomplete. What needs to be explored in greater depth in those sessions—and by all middle level educators—are the developmental tasks of adolescence. A characteristic of early adolescents, for example, is defiance—not a pleasant trait. If looked at in broader terms, however, we see that defiance is a vehicle for the developmental task of personal autonomy.

Thus, although the developmental tasks of early adolescence more often than not are accompanied by obnoxious behaviors, it is how adults respond to those behaviors that can trigger a smooth or rocky transition into adulthood. And given that many "at risk" behaviors, such as drug and alcohol abuse and early sexual experiences, begin during early adolescence, it seems logical that success in developmental tasks and positive interactions with adults may reduce the need that some adolescents feel to engage in those behaviors.

In this article, I present a historical and cultural perspective of adolescence and discuss the developmental tasks at this period and the negative behaviors that can result from tackling those tasks. I believe that educators who understand the place of adolescence in history and society and who appreciate the behavior normally associated with the developmental tasks of that time in life will be in a good position to form positive relationships with young adolescents.

Background

Historical Perspectives

During the colonial days, the family formed the main social and economic unit of society; older children had an important and highly visible role in society and in the family. Young people were often farmed out to apprenticeships or boarding schools, and they generally functioned as adults at the tender age of fifteen or so (Modell and Goodman 1990).

In the next century, mass immigration and industrialization required keeping young people out of the labor force because of the need to provide sufficient employment for adult workers. Young people were obliged to remain in school for a longer period of time and were encouraged to attend college or vocational training beyond high school. That move had dire consequences for the teenager who, lacking an interest in formal education and biologically ready to assume a productive adult role in society, now was forced to continue in school or to become a "dropout" and face many negative consequences as a result. Thus prolonged formal schooling, together with a lack of adequate vocational training, appears to put non–college-bound young people at risk, as they are underprepared to assume a role in adult society.

Cultural Perspectives

Families, neighborhoods, economic conditions, and our historical era are all factors that influence a gracious or awkward transition into adulthood. Because adolescence is closely tied to the structure of and condition of adult society (Modell and Goodman 1990), many of the factors that put students at risk, in reality, reflect larger societal problems.

Family conditions, socioeconomic status, and ethnicity are all important factors in adolescent development (Feldman and Elliott 1990). Minority youth, in particular, have difficulty in school for two reasons. First, "minority youth are well aware of the values of the majority culture and its standards of performance, achievement, and beauty" (Spencer and Dornbusch 1990, 131). "Minorities whose cultural frames of reference are oppositional to the cultural frame of reference of American mainstream culture have greater difficulty crossing cultural boundaries at school to learn" (Ogbu 1992, 5). Second, the conflict between the majority culture and their own often creates tension for minority students working on the developmental task of identity.

The Myth of Storm and Stress

Perhaps because of the cumulative physical, social, and psychological changes experienced by young adolescents, adults have traditionally viewed early adolescence as a time of turbulence and disruption (Hill 1980). Recent information, however (Brooks-Gunn and Reiter 1990; Hauser and Bowlds 1990; Hillman 1991; Offer, Ostrov, and Howard 1989; Scales 1991; Steinberg 1990), clearly indicates that only a small percentage of students (less than 20 percent) exhibit signs of serious disturbance and need adult intervention. Although the changes experienced are stressful for most young people, Dorman and Lipsitz (1981) argued, adults should "distinguish between behavior that is distressing (annoying to others) and behavior that is disturbed (harmful to the young person exhibiting the behavior)" (4). When adults expect and reinforce irresponsible behavior, they may, indeed, exacerbate the occurrence.

Developmental Tasks

If most teenagers pass through adolescence relatively problem free, then why does such a negative stereotype of that age exist? It may be that parents and teachers see only the narrow picture of sometimes irritating behavior. "Even well-adjusted, intelligent, and reasonable adolescents do, on occasion, exhibit truly obnoxious behavior. . . . [T]hey are not like this all of the time, but probably all adolescents

behave this way some of the time. They can be exasperating, and adult reaction can lead to more serious problems" (Newman 1985, 636). Viewing young adolescent development from a broader perspective may help the adults who share their lives to accept, if not condone, the behaviors that result from working on the tasks before them.

Some of the most obvious developmental tasks are learning how to handle a more mature body, forming a sexual identity, continuing to progress with such abilities as reading and writing, and beginning to explore career options. Of course, developmental tasks begin in early childhood and continue through adulthood. Unique to early adolescence, however, are the new cognitive abilities of dealing with problems in more abstract ways and of considering multiple perspectives. Students are moving from the "concrete" stage (able to think logically about real experiences) to the "formal" stage (able to consider "what ifs," think reflectively, and reason abstractly). This intellectual change is gradual and may occur at different times for different students. They may even shift back and forth from the concrete to the abstract, although it is important to remember that not all young adolescents, not even all adults, achieve this capacity.

These new abilities for young adolescents represent "*potential* accomplishments rather than typical everyday thinking" (Keating 1990, 65). Most students begin the process at about age twelve and display formal thinking consistently at age fifteen or sixteen. Until that time, during early adolescence, students are practicing this new ability. Like any new skill, formal reasoning must be practiced repeatedly in a safe, encouraging environment.

Young adolescents are egocentric. But, the emerging formal thinker is, for the first time, able to consider the thoughts of others and perceive him- or herself as the object of attention of others; in fact, adolescents "assume themselves to be a focus of *most* other people's perspective *much* of the time" (Keating 1990, 71). "As adolescents develop the capacity to think about their own thoughts, they become acutely aware of themselves, their person, and ideas. As a result they become egocentric, self-conscious, and introspective" (Rice 1990, 183). As students become accustomed to that new ability, they outgrow the egocentrism so characteristic of early adolescence.

Cognitive growth and development regulate the success of the four other major developmental tasks that I will discuss here: (1) forming a personal identity or self-concept, (2) acquiring social skills and responsibility, (3) gaining personal autonomy, and (4) developing character and a set of values.

Personal Identity/Self-Concept

The development of a personal identity is not really possible until children move beyond concrete levels of thinking, enabling them to be self-conscious and introspective. The development of positive self-esteem takes reflection, introspection, comparisons with others, and a sensitivity to the opinions of other people. Those processes only become possible with the advent of formal thinking.

Self-esteem declines at age eleven and reaches a low point between twelve and thirteen (Brack, Orr, and Ingersoll 1988; Harter 1990). Students, especially girls, making the shift to large, impersonal junior high schools at grade seven seem to experience long-term negative effects on their self-esteem (Simmons and Blyth 1987), particularly because of the interruption of peer groups. "Schools that emphasize competition, social comparison, and ability self-assessment" can cause students' academic motivation and self-esteem to deteriorate (Wigfield and Eccles 1995).

Minority youth have an especially difficult time forming an identity because the values of their culture may clash with the values and standards of the dominant culture. Minority youth, however, who have successful role models and who can learn to negotiate a balance between the two value systems will develop self-esteem (Spencer and Dornbusch 1990).

In a thorough review of literature on self-esteem, Kohn (1994) questioned the value of programs designed to enhance self-esteem. Educators would do better to treat students with "respect [rather] than shower them with praise" (282) "When members of a class meet to make decisions and solve problems, they get the self-esteem building message that their voices count, they experience a sense of belonging to a community, and they hone their ability to reason and analyze" (279). A meaningful curriculum (Beane and Lipka 1986), a safe and intellectually challenging environment (Wigfield and Eccles 1995), and meaningful success experiences (Kohn 1994) lead to the long-lasting development of self-identity and positive self-esteem.

Social Skills

Socialization is an important developmental task. Savin-Williams and Berndt (1990) concluded that "students who have satisfying and harmonious friendships typically report positive self-esteem, a good understanding of other people's feelings, and relatively little loneliness" (288). Additionally, those students with harmonious friendships "tend to behave appropriately in school, are motivated to do well, and often receive high grades" (290). Adults often ridicule the time and intensity of phone conversations, frenzied note passing, and frequent broken hearts, but those interactions are "critical interpersonal bridges that move [adolescents] toward psychological growth and social maturity" (277).

A myth about the negative influence of peer groups has developed over the years. Recent research shows that young adolescents "do not routinely acquiesce to peer pressure. In fact, they are more likely to follow the advice of adults rather than peers in matters affecting their long-term future and they actually rely on their own judgment more often than that of either peers or parents" (Brown 1990, 174). Peer groups usually reinforce rather than contradict the values of parents. It is not surprising that young adolescents tend to form friendships similar to the relationships they have with their families. Brown (1990) further concluded that students "seek out the peer group best suited to

meeting their needs for emotional support and exploration or reaffirmation of their values and aspirations" (180).

Students do not select a crowd as much as they are thrust into one by virtue of their personalities, backgrounds, interests, and reputations among peers (Brown 1990). A peer group is a place for trying out roles and ideas and serves as a validation of one's value within a social unit beyond the family. Young adolescents need many opportunities to experience success in socially acceptable ways so that the peer group reinforces prosocial activities.

Autonomy

Another developmental task that sometimes leads to emotional trauma is a young adolescent's need to establish autonomy. The onset of adolescence is, no doubt, a time for major realignments in relationships with adults both at home and at school. Steinberg (1990) took a sociobiological perspective of "intergenerational conflict" (family fighting). He suggested that "bickering and squabbling at puberty is an atavism that ensures that adolescents will spend time away from the family of origin and mate outside the natal group" (269). Disagreement becomes a vehicle to inform parents about changing self-conceptions and expectations and an opportunity to shed the view that parents can do no wrong. Of course, this low-level conflict must begin with an already strong emotional bond between parents and

---

Although much young adolescent behavior appears rejecting, this is not the time for adults to alienate themselves from their children.

children. If relationships are not strong before puberty (and often stepchildren and stepparents have a particularly rough time), this fighting can become destructive.

We tend to treat young adolescents like children one minute, adults another. Their ambiguous status in society and their new powers of reasoning cause them frustration, which occasionally leads to their lashing out at adults. Although much young adolescent behavior appears rejecting, this is not the time for adults to alienate themselves from their children. Early separation from adults may result in an increased risk of susceptibly to negative peer influences and participation in unhealthy, even risky, behaviors.

Moral/Character Development

The development of character is intricately linked to socioemotional and cognitive growth. A new capacity for abstract thinking allows adolescents to ask the "what ifs"; social and emotional growth provide the context for the answers. "Character develops within a social web or environment" (Leming 1993, 69). Reference groups such as families, peer groups, and television are particularly important as students seek to understand their place in the world (Rice 1990). "Middle school students can be helped to think about who they are and who they want to be, to form identities as self-respecting, career minded persons" (Davis 1993, 32).

Young adolescents will acquire a value system with or without the help of parents and teachers. At a stage of development when students are emerging as reflective citizens, educators can help them to be consciously aware of constructive values, to think logically about consequences, to empathize with others, and to make personal commitments to constructive values and behavior (Davis 1993).

All young adolescents are "at risk" of not successfully completing developmental tasks and of bearing the emotional scars of inappropriate and negative interactions with adults. The socioeconomic condition of society partially shapes the experiences of youth, but societal norms and economic conditions change slowly.

Educators do, however, have control over their interactions with young adolescents. By understanding and appreciating the normal behaviors necessary to accomplish developmental tasks, they have the power to eliminate or at the very least reduce the "risk" for many young people.

REFERENCES

Beane, J. A., and R. P. Lipka. 1986. *Self-concept, self-esteem, and the curriculum.* New York: Teachers College Press.

Brack, C. J., D. P. Orr, and G. Ingersoll. 1988. Pubertal maturation and adolescent self-esteem. *Journal of Adolescent Health Care* 9: 280-85.

Brooks-Gunn, J., and E. O. Reiter. 1990. The role of pubertal processes. In *At the threshold: The developing adolescent*, edited by S. S. Feldman and G. R. Elliott, 16-53. Cambridge, Mass.: Harvard University Press.

Brown, B. B. 1990. Peer groups and peer cultures. In *At the threshold: The developing adolescent*, edited by S. S. Feldman and G. R. Elliott, 171-96. Cambridge, Mass.: Harvard University Press.

Davis, G. A. 1993. Creative teaching of moral thinking: Fostering awareness and commitment. *Middle School Journal* 24(4): 32-33.

Dorman, G., and J. Lipsitz. 1981. Early adolescent development. In *Middle grades assessment program, 4-8*, edited by G. Dorman. Carrboro, N.C.: Center for Early Adolescence.

Feldman, S. S., and G. R. Elliott. 1990. *At the threshold: The developing adolescent*. Cambridge, Mass.: Harvard University Press.

Harter, S. 1990. Self and identity development. In *At the threshold: The developing adolescent*, edited by S. S. Feldman and G. R. Elliott, 388-413. Cambridge, Mass.: Harvard University Press.

Hauser, S. T., and M. K. Bowlds. 1990. Stress, coping, and adaptation. In *At the threshold: The developing adolescent*, edited by S. S. Feldman and G. R. Elliott, 388-413. Cambridge, Mass.: Harvard University Press.

Hill, J. P. 1980. *Understanding early adolescence: A framework*. Carrboro, N.C.: Center for Early Adolescence.

Hillman, S. B. 1991. What developmental psychology has to say about early adolescence. *Middle School Journal* 23(1): 3-8.

Keating, D. P. 1990. Adolescent thinking. In *At the threshold: The developing adolescent*, edited by S. S. Feldman and G. R. Elliott, 54-90. Cambridge, Mass.: Harvard University Press.

Kohn, A. 1994. The truth about self-esteem. *Phi Delta Kappan* 76(4): 272-83.

Leming, J. S. 1993. Synthesis of research: In search of effective character education. *Educational Leadership* 51(3): 63-71.

Modell, J., and M. Goodman. 1990. Historical perspectives. In *At the threshold: The developing adolescent*, edited by S. S. Feldman, and G. R. Elliott, 93-122. Cambridge, Mass.: Harvard University Press.

Newman, J. 1985. Adolescents: Why they can be so obnoxious. *Adolescence* 10(79): 636-46.

Offer, D., E. H. Ostrov, and K. I. Howard. 1989. Adolescence: What is normal? *American Journal of Diseases of Children* 143: 731-36.

Ogbu, J. G. 1992. Understanding cultural diversity and learning. *Educational Researcher* 21(8): 5-14.

Rice, F. P. 1990. *Adolescent development: Relationships, and culture*. Boston: Allyn and Bacon.

Savin-Williams, R. C., and T. J. Berndt. 1990. Friendship and peer relations. In *At the threshold: The developing adolescent*, edited by S. S. Feldman and G. R. Elliott, 277-307. Cambridge, Mass.: Harvard University Press.

Scales, P. C. 1991. *A portrait of young adolescents in the 1990s*. Carrboro, N.C.: Center for Early Adolescence.

Simmons, R. G., and D. A. Blyth. 1987. *Moving into adolescence: The impact of pubertal change and school context*. Hawthorne, N.Y.: Aldine De Gruyter.

Spencer, M. B., and S. M. Dornbusch. 1990. Challenges in studying minority youth. In At the Threshold: The developing adolescent, edited by S. S. Feldman and G. R. Elliott, 123-46. Cambridge, Mass.: Harvard University Press.

Steinberg, L. 1990. Autonomy, conflict, and harmony in the family. In *At the threshold: The developing adolescent*, edited by S. S. Feldman, and G. R. Elliott, 255-76. Cambridge, Mass.: Harvard University Press.

Wigfield, A., and J. S. Eccles. 1995. Middle grades schooling and early adolescent development. *Journal of Early Adolescence* 15(1): 5-8.

Cooperative Learning in Middle and Secondary Schools

ROBERT E. SLAVIN

Adolescence is a time of great potential and great danger in human development. Characteristics of this developmental period have enormous importance for the design of instructional environments, especially those for at-risk learners. For example, adolescents are highly susceptible to peer norms. If those norms favor academic excellence, students will be motivated to achieve. However, it is far more common that adolescents' peer norms denigrate academic excellence and favor sports and social success. More ominously, adolescents' peer norms usually value independence from adult authority, which can lead adolescents into oppositional behavior—from skipping school to defying teachers to drug use or vandalism.

The structure of the traditional classroom is highly inconsistent with adolescent development and peer norms. Traditional classrooms expect students to work independently and to compete for good grades, teachers' approval, and recognition. Research has long shown that when socially interacting peers are placed in individual competition with each other, they discourage each other from working hard. In adult occupational settings, this is called a "work restriction norm" (Vroom 1964). In schools, students try to reduce each other's academic efforts (to make success easier for themselves) by calling hard workers "nerds," "geeks," or "teacher's pets." This is much in contrast to the situation in sports, where excellence is strongly valued by peer norms (Coleman 1961). The difference between sports and academics is primarily in the interpersonal consequences of success. In sports, one person's success helps the entire team to succeed. In academics, one person's success makes success for others more difficult.

Further, traditional schools treat adolescents as children, rarely giving them authority, responsibility, or even opportunities for active participation. In fact, adolescents crave responsibility and abhor playing a passive role. Little wonder, then, that so many of them seek responsibility, authority, active peer-oriented participation, and adult-like roles in antisocial arenas: delinquency (which among adolescents almost always involves groups or gangs), drug abuse, early sexual experimentation, early parenthood, and so on.

Cooperative learning—instructional programs in which students work in small groups to help one another master academic content—can be an ideal means of capitalizing on the developmental characteristics of adolescents in order to harness their peer orientation, enthusiasm, activity, and craving for independence within a safe structure. There are many forms of cooperative learning that are widely used at all levels of education. The particular forms developed and researched at Johns Hopkins University, called Student Team Learning (Slavin 1994), were strongly influenced by James Coleman's (1961) *Adolescent Society*, which contrasted adolescents' peer support for sports and social activities to their lack of support for academics and proposed that the cooperative dynamics of these peer-supported activities be embedded in daily classroom organization. The purpose of this article is to describe the cooperative learning programs that have been most extensively studied in grades 6–12 in middle, junior, and senior high schools and to summarize the outcomes of studies at this level.

Student Team Learning

Student Team Learning methods are cooperative learning techniques developed and researched at Johns Hopkins University. More than half of all experimental studies of practical cooperative learning methods involve Student Team Learning methods.

All cooperative learning methods share the idea that students work together to learn and are responsible for one

Robert E. Slavin is co-director of the Center for Research on the Education of Students Placed At Risk, Johns Hopkins University, Baltimore, Maryland. This article was written under funding from the Office of Educational Research and Improvement, U.S. Department of Education (No. OERI-R-117-40005). However, any opinions expressed are those of the author and do not necessarily represent OERI positions or policies.

another's learning as well as their own. In addition to the idea of cooperative work, Student Team Learning methods emphasize the use of team goals and team success that can only be achieved if all members of the team learn the objectives being taught. That is, in Student Team Learning the students' tasks are not to *do* something as a team but to *learn* something as a team.

Three concepts are central to all Student Team Learning methods:

1. *Team rewards.* Teams earn certificates or other awards if they achieve above a designated criterion. Grades are not given based on team performance, but in senior high schools students may sometimes qualify for as many as five bonus points (on a one-hundred-point scale) if their teams meet a high criterion of excellence. The teams are not in competition to earn scarce rewards; all (or none) of the teams may achieve the criterion in a given week.

2. *Individual accountability.* The team's success depends on the individual learning of all team members. This focuses the activity of the team members on tutoring one another and making sure that everyone on the team is ready for a quiz or other assessment that students will take without teammate help.

3. *Equal opportunities for success.* Students contribute to their teams by improving over their own past performance. This ensures that high, average, and low achievers are equally challenged to do their best, and the contributions of all team members will be valued.

Research on cooperative learning methods (summarized below) has indicated that team rewards and individual accountability are essential elements for producing basic skills achievement (Slavin 1995a). It is not enough to simply tell students to work together. They must have a reason to take one another's achievement seriously. Further, research indicates that if students are rewarded for doing better than they have in the past, they will be more motivated to achieve than if they are rewarded based on their performance in comparison to others, because rewards for improvement make success neither too difficult nor too easy for students to achieve.

Three principal Student Team Learning methods have been extensively developed and researched in secondary schools (grades 6–12): Student Teams–Achievement Divisions (STAD), Teams-Games-Tournament (TGT), and Cooperative Integrated Reading and Composition (CIRC), which is used in reading and writing instruction in grades 3–7.

Student Teams–Achievement Divisions (STAD)

In STAD (Slavin 1994), the teacher assigns students to four-member learning teams that are mixed in performance level, sex, and ethnicity. The teacher presents a lesson after which students work in their teams to make sure that all team members have mastered the lesson. All students then take individual quizzes on the material; they may not help one another on the quizzes.

Students' quiz scores are compared with their own past averages, and points are awarded based on the degree to which students can meet or exceed their own earlier performance. These points are then summed to form team scores, and teams that meet certain criteria may earn certificates or other recognition. The whole cycle of activities—from teacher presentation to team practice to quiz—usually takes three to five class periods.

STAD has been used in a wide variety of subjects, including mathematics, language arts, and social studies, and has been used from grade two through college. It is most appropriate for teaching well-defined objectives with single right answers, such as mathematical computations and applications, language usage and mechanics, geography and map skills, and science facts and concepts.

Teams-Games-Tournament (TGT)

Teams-Games-Tournament (DeVries and Slavin 1978; Slavin 1994) was the first of the Johns Hopkins cooperative learning methods. It uses the same teacher presentations and team work as in STAD, but it replaces the quizzes with weekly tournaments, in which students compete with members of other teams to contribute points to their team scores. Students compete at three-person "tournament tables" against others with similar past records in mathematics. A "bumping" procedure keeps the competition fair. The winner at each tournament table brings the same number of points to his or her team, regardless of which table it is; this means that low achievers (competing with other low achievers) and high achievers (competing with other high achievers) have equal opportunities for success. As in STAD, high-performing teams earn certificates or other forms of team recognition.

Cooperative Integrated Reading and Composition (CIRC)

CIRC is a comprehensive program for teaching reading and writing in the upper elementary and middle grades (Stevens, Madden, Slavin, and Farnish 1987). In CIRC, students are assigned to teams composed of pairs of students from different reading groups. While the teacher is working with one reading group, students in the other groups are working in their pairs on a series of cognitively engaging activities, including reading to one another, making predictions about how narrative stories will come out, summarizing stories to one another, writing responses to stories, and practicing spelling, decoding, and vocabulary. If the reading class is not divided into homogeneous reading groups, all students in the teams work with one another. Students work as a total team to master main idea and other comprehension skills. During language arts periods, students write drafts, revise and edit one another's work, and prepare for "publication" of team books.

In most CIRC activities, students follow a sequence of teacher instruction, team practice, team pre-assessments, and quiz. That is, students do not take the quiz until their teammates have determined that they are ready. Certificates are given to teams based on the average performance of all team members on all reading and writing activities.

Mostly found in elementary schools, CIRC is also used in the early middle grades and has been studied at that level by Stevens and Durkin (1992).

Other Cooperative Learning Methods

Jigsaw

Jigsaw was originally designed by Elliot Aronson and his colleagues (Aronson, Blaney, Stephan, Sikes, and Snapp 1978). In Aronson's Jigsaw method, students are assigned to six-member teams to work on academic material that has been broken down into sections. For example, a biography might be divided into early life, first accomplishments, major setbacks, later life, and impact on history. Each team member reads his or her section. Next, members of different teams who have studied the same sections meet in "expert groups" to discuss their sections. Then the students return to their teams and take turns teaching their teammates about their sections. Because the only way students can learn sections other than their own is to listen carefully to their teammates, they are motivated to support and show interest in one another's work.

Slavin (1994) developed a modification of Jigsaw and incorporated it in the Student Team Learning program. In this method, called Jigsaw II, students work in four- or five-member teams as in TGT and STAD. Instead of each student being assigned a unique section, all students read a common narrative, such as a book chapter, a short story, or a biography. However, each student receives a topic on which to become an expert. Students with the same topics meet in expert groups to discuss them, after which they return to their teams to teach what they have learned to their teammates. Then students take individual quizzes, which result in team scores based on the improvement score system of STAD. Teams that meet preset standards may earn certificates.

Learning Together

David and Roger Johnson at the University of Minnesota developed the Learning Together model of cooperative learning (Johnson and Johnson 1994). The methods they have researched involve students working in four- or five-member heterogeneous groups on assignment sheets. The groups hand in a single sheet and receive praise and rewards based on the group product. The model emphasizes the use of team-building activities before students begin working together and regular discussions within groups about how well group members are working together.

Group Investigation

Group Investigation, developed by Shlomo Sharan at the University of Tel Aviv (Sharan and Sharan 1992), is a general classroom organization plan in which students work in small groups using cooperative inquiry, group discussion, and cooperative planning and projects. In this method, students form their own two- to six-member groups. After choosing subtopics from a unit being studied by the entire class, the groups further break their subtopics into individual tasks, and carry out the activities necessary to prepare group reports. Each group then makes a presentation or display to communicate its findings to the entire class.

Research on Cooperative Learning

A recent review of research on cooperative learning (Slavin 1995a) identified fifty-two studies conducted over periods of at least four weeks in regular secondary schools (grades 6–12) that have measured effects on student achievement. These studies all compared effects of cooperative learning with effects of traditionally taught control groups on measures of the same objectives pursued in all classes. Teachers and classes were either randomly assigned to cooperative or control conditions, or they were matched on pretest achievement level and other factors.

Academic Achievement

Of these studies, thirty-three (63 percent) found significantly greater achievement in cooperative than in control classes. Sixteen (31 percent) found no differences, and in only three studies did a control group significantly out-perform the experimental group.

It should be noted, however, that the effects of cooperative learning vary considerably according to the particular methods used. Two elements must be present if cooperative learning is to be effective: *group goals* and *individual accountability* (Slavin 1983a, 1983b, 1995a). That is, groups must be working to achieve some goal or earn rewards or recognition, and the success of the group must depend on the individual learning of every group member. In studies of methods of this kind (e.g., STAD, TGT, CIRC), effects on achievement have been consistently positive; twenty-three out of thirty such studies (77 percent) found significantly positive achievement effects. In contrast, only ten of twenty-two secondary studies (45 percent) of cooperative methods lacking group goals and individual accountability found positive effects on student achievement, and three found higher scores in control groups.

Cooperative learning methods generally work equally well for all types of students. Although occasional studies find particular advantages for high or low achievers, boys or girls, and so on, the great majority find equal benefits for all types of students. Sometimes a concern is expressed that cooperative learning will hold back high achievers. The research provides absolutely no support for this claim; high achievers gain from cooperative learning (relative to high achievers in traditional classes) just as much as do low and average achievers (Slavin 1991).

Intergroup Relations

Social scientists have long advocated interethnic cooperation as a means of ensuring positive intergroup relations in desegregated settings. Contact theory (Allport 1954), the dominant theory of intergroup relations for many years, predicted that positive intergroup relations would rise from school desegregation if and only if students were involved in cooperative, equal-status interaction sanctioned by the school. Research on cooperative learning methods has borne out the predictions of contact theory. These techniques emphasize cooperative, equal-status interaction between students of different ethnic backgrounds sanctioned by the school (Slavin 1995b). In most of the research on intergroup relations, students were asked to list their best friends at the beginning of the study and again at the end.

High achievers gain from cooperative learning (relative to high achievers in traditional classes) just as much as do low and average achievers.

The number of friendship choices students made outside their own ethnic groups was the measure of intergroup relations. Positive effects on intergroup relations in secondary schools have been found for STAD, TGT, Jigsaw, Learning Together, and Group Investigation models (Slavin 1995a, 1995b).

Two of these studies, one on STAD (Slavin 1979) and one on Jigsaw II (Ziegler 1981), included follow-ups of intergroup friendships several months after the end of the studies. Both found that students who had been in cooperative learning classes still named significantly more friends outside their own ethnic groups than did students who had been in control classes. Two studies of Group Investigation (Sharan, Kussell, Hertz-Lazarowitz, Bejarano, Raviv, and Sharan 1984; Sharan and Shachar 1988) found that the improved attitudes and behaviors of students toward classmates of different ethnic backgrounds extended to classmates who had never been in the same groups.

Self-Esteem

Students in cooperative learning classes have been found to have more positive feelings about themselves than do students in traditional classes. These improvements in self-esteem have been found for TGT and STAD (Slavin 1995a) and for Jigsaw (Blaney, Stephan, Rosenfeld, Aronson, and Sikes 1977).

Other Outcomes

In addition to positive effects on achievement, intergroup relations, acceptance of mainstreamed students, and self-esteem, cooperative learning has been found to have positive effects on a variety of other important educational outcomes. These include liking of school, development of peer norms in favor of doing well academically, feelings of individual control over the student's own fate in school, and cooperativeness and altruism (see Slavin 1995a). TGT (DeVries and Slavin 1978) and STAD (Slavin 1995a; Janke 1978) have been found to have positive effects on students' time on-task. A study in the Kansas City schools found that when students who were at risk of becoming delinquent worked in cooperative groups in sixth grade they had better attendance, fewer contacts with the police, and higher behavioral ratings by teachers in seventh through eleventh grades than did control students (Hartley 1976). A year-long study of TGT and STAD in middle schools by Hawkins, Doueck, and Lishner (1988) found that low achievers who experienced cooperative learning had fewer suspensions and expulsions than did control students; they also gained more in educational aspirations and positive attitudes toward school.

Conclusion

Research on cooperative learning methods in secondary schools supports the usefulness of those methods for improving student achievement at a variety of grade levels and in many subjects and for improving intergroup relations and the self-esteem of students. Cooperative learning, especially when groups are rewarded based on the individual learning of all group members, is an instructional approach that is congruent with the developmental needs of adolescents. It gives adolescents a degree of independence and authority within their groups, and it creates a situation (as in sports) in which the progress of each group member contributes to the success of his or her peers. This creates peer norms favoring academic excellence, a strong motivator for adolescents. Cooperative learning is not a panacea for all of the problems of adolescence, but it can provide a means of harnessing the peer-oriented energies of adolescents for pro-social rather than antisocial activities, and for this reason alone it should be an important part of every middle and high school teacher's repertoire.

REFERENCES

Allport, G. *The nature of prejudice.* Cambridge, Mass.: Addison Wesley.
Aronson, E., N. Blaney, C. Stephan, J. Sikes, and M. Snapp. 1978. *The jigsaw classroom.* Beverly Hills, Calif.: Sage.
Blaney, N. T., S. Stephan, D. Rosenfeld, E. Aronson, and J. Sikes. 1977. Interdependence in the classroom: A field study. *Journal of Educational Psychology* 69(2): 121–28.
Coleman, J. S. 1961. *The adolescent society.* New York: Free Press of Glencoe.

DeVries, D. L., and R. E. Slavin. 1978. Teams-Games-Tournament (TGT): Review of ten classroom experiments. *Journal of Research and Development in Education* 12(1): 28–38.

Hartley, W. 1976. *Prevention outcomes of small group education with school children: An epidemiologic follow up of the Kansas City School Behavior Project.* Unpublished manuscript, University of Kansas Medical Center.

Hawkins, J. D., H. J. Doueck, and D. M. Lishner. 1988. Changing teacher practices in mainstream classroom to improve bonding and behavior of low achievers. *American Educational Research Journal* 25(1): 31–50.

Janke, R. 1978. *The Teams-Games-Tournament (TGT) method and the behavioral adjustment and academic achievement of emotionally impaired adolescents.* Paper presented at the annual convention of the American Educational Research Association, Toronto (April).

Johnson, D. W., and R. T. Johnson. 1994. *Learning together and alone.* 4th ed. Boston: Allyn and Bacon.

Sharan, S., P. Kussell, R. Hertz-Lazarowitz, Y. Bejarano, S. Raviv, and Y. Sharan. 1984. *Cooperative learning in the classroom: Research in desegregated schools.* Hillsdale, N.J.: Erlbaum.

Sharan, S., and C. Shachar. 1988. *Language and learning in the cooperative classroom.* New York: Springer.

Sharan, Y., and S. Sharan. 1992. *Group investigation: Expanding cooperative learning.* New York: Teacher's College Press.

Slavin, R. E. 1979. Effects of biracial learning teams on cross-racial friendships. *Journal of Educational Psychology* 71(3): 381–87.

———. 1983a. *Cooperative learning.* New York: Longman.

———. 1983b. When does cooperative learning increase student achievement? *Psychological Bulletin* 94(3): 429–45.

———. 1991. Are cooperative learning and untracking harmful to the gifted? *Educational Leadership* 48(6): 68–71.

———. 1994. *Using student team learning.* 4th ed. Baltimore: Johns Hopkins University, Center for Social Organization of Schools.

———. 1995a. *Cooperative learning: Theory, research, and practice.* 2nd ed. Boston: Allyn and Bacon.

———. 1995b. Cooperative learning and intergroup relations. In *Handbook of research on multicultural education,* edited by J. Banks. New York: Macmillan.

Stevens, R. J., and S. Durkin. 1992. *Using student team reading and student team writing in middle schools: Two evaluations.* Tech. Rep. No. 36. Baltimore: Johns Hopkins University, Center for Research on Effective Schooling for Disadvantaged Students.

Stevens, R. J., N. A. Madden, R. E. Slavin, and A. M. Farnish. 1987. Cooperative Integrated Reading and Composition: Two field experiments. *Reading Research Quarterly* 22(4): 433–54.

Vroom, V. H. 1964. *Work and motivation.* New York: Wiley.

Ziegler, S. 1981. The effectiveness of cooperative learning teams for increasing cross-ethnic friendship: Additional evidence. *Human Organization* 40(3): 264–68.

Exceptional and Culturally Diverse Students

Educationally Disabled (Articles 11 and 12)
Gifted and Talented (Articles 13–15)
Culturally and Academically Diverse (Articles 16–18)

The Equal Educational Opportunity Act for All Handicapped Children (Public Law 94-142) gives disabled children the right to an education in the least-restrictive environment, due process, and an individualized educational program that is specifically designed to meet their needs. Professionals and parents of exceptional children are responsible for developing and implementing an appropriate educational program for each child. The application of these ideas to classrooms across the nation at first caused great concern among educators and parents. Classroom teachers whose training did not prepare them for working with the exceptional child expressed negative attitudes about mainstreaming. Special resource teachers also expressed concern that mainstreaming would mitigate the effectiveness of special programs for the disabled and would force cuts in services. Parents feared that their children would not receive the special services they required because of governmental red tape and delays in proper diagnosis and placement.

It has been more than two decades since the implementation of P.L. 94-142, which was amended by the Individuals with Disabilities Education Act (IDEA) in 1991 that introduced the term "inclusion." Many of the above concerns have been studied by psychologists and educators, and their

findings have often influenced policy. For example, research has indicated that mainstreaming is more effective when regular classroom teachers and special resource teachers work cooperatively with disabled children.

The articles concerning the educationally disabled confront many of these issues. Todd DeMitchell and Georgia Kerns, in "Where to Educate Rachel Holland? Does Least Restrictive Environment Mean No Restrictions?" discuss a controversial case involving special education and IDEA. The next essay, by Thomas Armstrong, takes a new look at Attention Deficit Hyperactivity Disorder.

Other exceptional children are the gifted and talented. These children are rapid learners who can absorb, organize, and apply concepts more effectively than the average child. They often have IQs of 140 or more and are convergent thinkers (i.e., they give the correct answer to teacher or test questions). Convergent thinkers are usually models of good behavior and academic performance, and they respond to instruction easily; teachers generally value such children and often nominate them for gifted programs. There are other children, however, who do not score well on standardized tests of intelligence because their thinking is more divergent (i.e., they can imagine more than one answer to teacher or test questions). These gifted divergent thinkers may not respond to traditional instruction. They may become bored, respond to questions in unique and disturbing ways, and appear uncooperative and disruptive. Many teachers do not understand these unconventional thinkers and fail to identify them as gifted. In fact, such children are sometimes labeled as emotionally disturbed or mentally retarded because of the negative impressions they make on their teachers. Because of the differences between these types of students, a great deal of controversy surrounds programs for the gifted. Such programs should enhance the self-esteem of all gifted and talented children, motivate and challenge them, and help them realize their creative

potential. The three articles in the subsection on gifted children consider the characteristics of giftedness, and they explain how to identify gifted students and provide them with an appropriate education.

The third subsection of this unit concerns student diversity. Just as labeling may adversely affect the disabled child, it may also affect the child who comes from a minority ethnic background where the language and values are quite different from those of the mainstream culture. The term "disadvantaged" is often used to describe these children, but it is negative, stereotypical, and apt to result in a self-fulfilling prophecy whereby teachers perceive such children as incapable of learning. Teachers should provide academically and culturally diverse children with experiences that they might have missed in the restricted environment of their homes and neighborhoods. Rita Dunn, in "The Goals and Track Record of Multicultural Education," takes issue with some aspects of multicultural programs while other articles in this section address these individual differences and suggest strategies for teaching these diverse children.

Looking Ahead: Challenge Questions

What are some issues regarding the Public Law 94-142 provision called "least restrictive environment"? What are the pros and cons of mainstreaming?

Who are the gifted and talented? How can knowledge of their characteristics and learning needs help to provide them with an appropriate education?

What cultural differences exist in our society? How can teacher expectations affect the culturally or academically diverse child? How would multicultural education help teachers deal more effectively with these differences?

What are some of the criticisms concerning multicultural programs?

Where to Educate Rachel Holland?
Does Least Restrictive Environment Mean No Restrictions?

TODD DeMITCHELL and GEORGIA M. KERNS

W hat shall be taught? How shall it be taught? Who shall teach our children? Those three critical questions have long been a part of the discussion about the appropriate role of public education in our society. Since the rise of the "one best system" of public education, the questions have been the subject of much dialogue, debate, and policy making. During the last fifty years, a fourth question has been added to those three: *Where* shall the student be educated? Separate but equal schools, desegregated schools, neighborhood schools, special schools, and magnet schools have been some of the answers to that question.

In the past, that matter of where a child will be educated has been a civil rights issue. Recently, a new dimension of the issue has emerged—that is, whether to include students with disabilities in the regular class or to educate them in a more restricted environment. This question has divided the educational community as well as the broader community. As with other important questions, the debate has produced much heat and has seen the various antagonists turn to the courts for support of their positions.

Determining the appropriate educational environment for students with special education needs can be problematic. Consider the case of Rachel Holland, who has a tested IQ of 44. Rachel was born in 1982, and from 1985 to 1989, she attended a variety of special education programs in the Sacramento City School District in California. Dur-

ing these four years, Rachel spent approximately one hour a day in a regular classroom. Her parents constantly tried to convince the school district to increase the amount of time that Rachel spent in regular classrooms. In the fall of 1989, Rachel's parents requested that their daughter be placed full-time in a regular classroom for the 1989–1990 school year. The district rejected their request and instead offered a placement that divided Rachel's time between a regular education class for nonacademic subjects—art, music, lunch, and recess—and a special education class of children with disabilities for all academic subjects. This placement would have required that Rachel move six times a day between the two classes. Rachel's parents rejected the district's proposal and enrolled Rachel in a regular kindergarten class at Shalom School, a private school. Her parents decided to fight the Sacramento City School District's stance on what education was appropriate for Rachel. The odyssey of where to educate Rachel had now truly begun.

Appropriateness and Special Education

The issue of what constitutes an appropriate educational environment for a special education student is not unique to Rachel. How much to include or mainstream a special education student into a regular education classroom as part of a legal mandate is a matter that has received a lot of attention lately. The National Association of State School Boards of Education (1992) has endorsed full inclusion, as has the Council for Exceptional Children (1993). On the other hand, the Learning Disabilities Association of America (1993) has taken a stand against full inclusion, as has the National Joint Committee on Learning Disabilities (1993). The American Federation of

Todd DeMitchell is associate chair and an associate professor and Georgia M. Kerns is an assistant professor and program coordinator of special education—both in the Department of Education, University of New Hampshire, Durham.

From *The Clearing House*, January/February 1997, pp. 161-166. © 1997 by the Helen Dwight Reid Educational Foundation. Reprinted by permission of Heldref Publications, 1319 Eighteenth Street, NW, Washington, DC 20036-1802.

Teachers (Richardson 1994) has called for a moratorium on the placement of children with disabilities in regular classrooms.[1]

The matter of how to appropriately educate students who qualify for special education is of large consequence to education in general. In the 1991–1992 school year, 4,994,169 students received special education services in the regular classroom and via other service modalities. Almost three and one-half million of those students (69.3 percent) spent more than 40 percent of their instructional day in a general classroom while 25.1 percent, just over 1.2 million students, received services in a separate class for at least 60 percent of the day. Only 5.7 percent of the students received special education services in a separate school or other location (Ayers 1994).

Rachel Holland is and was one of these students who is entitled to special education services under the federal Individuals with Disabilities Education Act (IDEA). IDEA is predicated on the assumption that all children are capa-

---

"The mainstreaming issue imposes a difficult burden on the district court. Since Congress has chosen to impose that burden, however, the courts must do their best to fulfill their duty."

---

ble of benefiting from an education. The corollary is that all identified special education children can be educated. As the Rochester School District in New Hampshire found out in the *Timothy W.* (1989) case, a school district does not have the authority to withhold services if it deems a special education student is not capable of benefiting from an education. The court characterized IDEA as a "zero reject" of services for an identified student. In other words, any student who is entitled to special education services must receive an appropriate education. A school district may not impose a litmus test of whether it believes a child can benefit from services as a pre-condition for receiving educational services.

IDEA requires that a state that accepts federal IDEA funds must meet three basic requirements in order to comply with the law. First, it must provide a free appropriate public education (FAPE) to qualified students, and second, to the "maximum extent appropriate," a child with a disability must be educated in the least restrictive environment. This last requirement is often called the mainstreaming mandate. The underlying rationale for this mandate is found in the *Brown v. Board of Education* (1954) desegregation case, which embraced the concept that separate is not equal. A third principle of IDEA is that education is to be individualized and appropriate to the child's needs. This is usually

accomplished through the formulation of an individualized educational plan (IEP). All three of these components are important, but the one that has received the most attention lately, and maybe the least understood of the three, is the least restrictive environment (LRE) requirement. Because the issue of Rachel Holland's education turns on what the appropriate environment for Rachel is, we will explore this requirement in a little more depth.

Least Restrictive Environment: Case Law

The IDEA provides that each state must establish

> procedures to assure that, to the maximum extent appropriate, children with disabilities . . . are educated with children who are not disabled, and that special classes, separate schooling, or other removal of children with disabilities from the regular educational environment occurs only when the nature or severity of the disability is such that education in regular classes with the use of supplementary aids and services cannot be achieved satisfactorily. (20 U.S.C. 1412(5)(B))

Also, IDEA regulations require schools to educate children with disabilities together with children who do not have disabilities (34 C.F.R. Sect. 300.500). According to the regulations, when selecting the least restrictive environment, school authorities should give consideration to any potential harmful effect on the child or on the quality of services that he or she needs; consideration should also be given to any potential harmful effect on the education of the other students (34 C.F.R. Sect. 300.522).

The courts have likewise underscored the importance of the LRE mandate. For example, the Sixth Circuit Court of Appeals in *Roncker v. Walter* (1983) wrote, "We recognize that the mainstreaming issue imposes a difficult burden on the district court. Since Congress has chosen to impose that burden, however, the courts must do their best to fulfill their duty" (1063).

Prior to 1994, two LRE tests were devised by the federal circuit courts of appeal to ascertain if the defendant school district had met its burden of compliance under IDEA. The first LRE test was devised by the Sixth Circuit in *Roncker*, mentioned above. The test looked at three areas:

1. Comparison of educational benefits in the restricted setting with educational benefits in a regular setting
2. Degree to which the student will disrupt the regular classroom
3. Cost of the regular classroom placement

The *Roncker* test was adopted by the Eighth Circuit (*A. W. v. Northwest R-1 School District* (1987)) and the Fourth Circuit (*DeVries v. Fairfax County School Board* (1989)).

A second appellate LRE test was devised by the Fifth Circuit in *Daniel RR v. State Board of Education* (1989). In establishing a new test, the *Daniel RR* court wrote as follows:

> We respectfully decline to follow the Sixth Circuit's analysis. Certainly the *Roncker* test accounts for factors that are

important in any mainstreaming case. We believe, however, that the test necessitates too intrusive an inquiry into educational policy choice that Congress deliberately left to state and local officers. Whether a particular service feasibly can be provided in a regular or special educational setting is an administrative determination that state and local officials are far better qualified and situated than we are to make. (1046)

The court's reluctance to substitute its judgment on policy matters for that of professional educators is consistent with the Supreme Court's decision in *Board of Education v. Rowley* (1982). In that case, the High Court reminded the lower courts not to second-guess school leaders on matters relating to educational methodology.[2]

The Fifth Circuit in *Daniel RR* started its LRE inquiry by examining whether the school district had "taken steps to accommodate the handicapped child in regular education" (1048). The IDEA, according to the court, requires school districts to provide supplementary aids and services and to modify the regular education program when they mainstream children with disabilities. This is similar to the Supreme Court's FAPE decision in *Rowley*, in which the Court stated that an appropriate education is "personalized instruction with sufficient support services that will permit the child to benefit educationally from instruction" (203). Whether education in a regular classroom with the use of supplemental aids and services is appropriate for a given child involves the following three-part inquiry:

1. Will the child receive an educational benefit, both non-academic and academic, from the regular education placement?
2. What is the child's overall educational experience in the mainstreamed environment, balancing the benefits of regular and special education?
3. What effect does the special education child's presence have on the regular classroom environment and the education that the other students are receiving?

The Fourth, Fifth, Sixth, and Eighth Circuit Courts of Appeal have construed the least restrictive environment requirement of the IDEA as a presumption in favor of mainstreaming or educating children with disabilities in regular classrooms alongside their fellow students. For example, citing the *Daniel RR* test of the Fifth Circuit, the Third Circuit Court of Appeals in *Oberti v. Board of Education of Borough of Clementon School District* (1993) ruled that school districts have an obligation to consider placing students with disabilities in regular education classes with supplementary aids and services before they explore other alternatives. "The court stressed that in passing the IDEA, Congress recognized the fundamental right of students with disabilities to associate with nondisabled peers" (Osborne 1994, 548-49). Therefore, the starting place for any inquiry into what the appropriate least restrictive environment for a student is must be inclusion as a regular member of a regular education classroom; the inquiry can then move to the matter of a more restrictive environment if it is found that that environment is not appropriate.

This view is consistent with the Rehabilitation Act of 1973, which calls for placing a person with a disability in the regular education environment unless it is demonstrated that the education received in the regular classroom along with supplementary aids and services is inadequate. Thus, although the starting point for a least restrictive environment inquiry is the regular classroom, that does not mean that there can be no restrictions on what environment is appropriate for any given student. The decision as to whether a particular child should be educated in a regular classroom setting all of the time, part of the time, or none of the time is predicated on an inquiry into the needs and abilities of the child. The issue is not cast as the best academic setting possible for the student; rather, the presumption of the IDEA's least restrictive environment mandate in favor of mainstreaming is that the student receive a satisfactory education.

For example, in *Greer v. Rome City School District in Georgia* (1991), mainstreaming was emphasized over special education services.[3] This ruling allowed a nine-year-old student with Down's syndrome to be placed in a regular education kindergarten class rather than in the substantially separate special education class recommended by the school district. The court found that the student had made some progress in kindergarten with supplemental aids and services and was not disruptive. *Greer* also added "cost" to the *Daniel RR* test. The Eleventh Circuit in *Greer* stated that "[i]f the cost of educating a handicapped child in a regular classroom is so great that it would significantly impact upon the education of other children in the district, then education in a regular classroom is not appropriate" (697).

However, the LRE mandate does not require school districts to place students in their neighborhood schools, let alone in the regular classroom, in all situations. In *Barnett v. Fairfax County School Board* (1991), the Court of Appeals for the Fourth Circuit upheld a centralized program for high school students with hearing impairments, even though the parents of a student objected to busing their child several miles from home and requested that a similar program be established in the neighborhood school. The Tenth Circuit in *Murray by and through Murray v. Montrose County School District, RE-1J* (1995) held that a twelve year old with multiple disabilities was not entitled to an education in the neighborhood school because the child's needs could not be met in that setting. The court stated that while IDEA "clearly commands schools to include mainstreamed disabled children as much as possible, it says nothing about where, within a school district, that inclusion shall take place" (928-29). A federal district court in Colorado (*Urban v. Jefferson County School District, R-1* (1994)) reached a similar conclusion when it found that "the statutory preference for placement at a neighborhood school is only that—and it does not amount to a mandate" (1568).

Similarly, in Nebraska (*French v. Omaha Public Schools*) and in Pennsylvania (*Johnson v. Lancaster-Lebanon Intermediate Unit 13*) in 1991, two different federal district courts upheld the decision not to mainstream students who had profound hearing loss, severe language delays, and no meaningful communicative interaction with the hearing world. In those two cases, a more restricted environment more appropriately met the needs of the student than the less restrictive environment of the regular education classroom.

In *DeVries v. Fairfax County School Board* (1989), which adopted the *Roncker* test, the mother of a child with autism (who had depressed cognitive functioning, exhibited immature behavior, and needed a predictable environment) contested the school district's proposed placement in a vocational center. The mother wanted the child educated in the local public high school. The district court and the court of appeals found that the vocational center placement was appropriate because the student could not be educated satisfactorily, even with supplementary aids. The disparity

---

A hard-and-fast rule that all children will be mainstreamed irrespective of their needs and abilities . . . runs counter to the IDEA, judicial decisions, and good sense.

---

between the cognitive levels of the seventeen-year-old student and his non-disabled peers was so great that the court was concerned that the student would be simply "monitoring" the regular class.

From a different perspective, the Ninth Circuit in *Clyde K. and Sheila K. v. Puyallup School District* (1994) supported the transfer of a student with a special education designation from a regular classroom setting to a more self-contained setting. The student had Tourette's syndrome and attention-deficit/hyperactivity disorder. The behavior on his part that precipitated an emergency suspension and then placement in the restricted environment (a placement to which the parents initially agreed but one that they later rejected) included vulgar and profane comments, class disruptions, sexual harassment of female students, and the assault of a staff member and students.

The Case of Rachel Holland

We have briefly reviewed several court cases that found that the least restrictive environment for a student was one in which there were restrictions. What we have not looked at in depth is how that determination is made. For that part of the discussion, we return to the case of Rachel Holland to see how it was resolved. Should Rachel be educated in a special education classroom or should there be full inclusion?

The parents of Rachel Holland wanted Rachel to be educated full-time in a regular education classroom; the school district wanted her to be educated in a more restrictive environment. Rachel's parents appealed the Sacramento City School District's placement. Following a two-week hearing, the hearing officer, in a lengthy opinion dated August 15, 1990, found that the school district had failed to make an adequate effort to educate Rachel in a regular education class as required by the IDEA. The hearing officer found that Rachel had benefited from her year of kindergarten in a regular class at Shalom School, that Rachel was motivated to learn, and that she learned from imitation and modeling and thus would benefit from a regular education classroom setting with nondisabled peers. The hearing officer also found that Rachel would not be disruptive and that her IEP was consistent with the first-grade curriculum. The hearing officer ordered the district to place Rachel in a regular education classroom with appropriate support services, including a part-time special education consultant and a part-time classroom aide.

The school district appealed the decision of the hearing officer to the federal district court (*Sacramento City Unified School District v. Holland* (1992)). During the judicial proceedings, Rachel stayed put, completing first grade and half of second grade before the district court handed down its decision. The court fashioned a four-factor balancing test that was adapted from the *Daniel RR* test and the *Greer* addition of cost as a factor. The Rachel Holland court's four factors are (1) the educational benefits of placement in a regular class; (2) the nonacademic benefits of interaction with children who were not disabled; (3) the effect that Rachel had on the teacher and children in the regular class; and (4) the costs of mainstreaming Rachel. The school district lost and appealed the decision (*Sacramento City Unified School District v. Rachel H.* (1994)).

The court of appeals approved the district court's four-part test and adopted it and used it several months later in *Clyde K. and Sheila K. v. Puyallup School District* (1994) mentioned above. The court of appeals also accepted the findings of fact of the district court. The appellate court decided that the school district carried the burden of proof that its placement for Rachel provided mainstreaming to "the maximum extent appropriate."[4] Thus, the school district had to show that the four factors favored its preferred placement. The court found as to the first factor that, if a child's disabilities were so severe that he or she would receive little or no academic benefit from placement in a regular education class, then inclusion may not be appropriate. The experts for both sides provided conflicting evidence. The bulk of the evidence offered by the district related to Rachel's performance on achievement and aptitude tests. By contrast, Rachel's witnesses, who had observed her for extended periods of time in her classroom at Shalom School, testified that she had made significant academic strides there. The court, while acknowledging that the expert witnesses brought their own points of view to the case, gave great weight to the testimony of Rachel's second-grade teacher, Ms. Crone, who was characterized as experienced and skillful (and who was not a partisan to the controversy). Ms. Crone noted that Rachel was in many ways a typical second grader, eager to participate and very motivated. The district did not meet its burden of establishing that Rachel would not receive academic benefits in regular classes and failed to demonstrate that placement in special education classes would provide equal or greater educational benefit to Rachel.

The analysis of the second factor, nonacademic benefits to Rachel, centered on Rachel's attitude, her social communication skills, and her self-confidence. The school district's experts from the state's Diagnostic Center testified that Rachel was making little progress on her IEP goals and was isolated from her classmates. The school district's standardized testing techniques and results in this area were not persuasive to the court, however. The strongest evidence, according to the court, was Rachel's excitement about her class and her improved self-confidence. The district court concluded that the differing evaluations in large part reflected the predisposition of the evaluators. The testimonies of the classroom teacher and Rachel's mother were considered more credible by the district court.

The third factor, effect on the teacher and students, has two aspects. The first is whether there is a detriment to the other students because the child with the disability is disruptive, distracting, or unruly. There was no evidence that Rachel was a discipline problem at Shalom School; in fact, all parties agreed that Rachel was well-behaved. The second aspect is whether the child with special education needs would take up so much of the teacher's time that the other students would suffer from lack of attention. On this point, Rachel's second-grade teacher testified that Rachel's presence did not interfere with her ability to teach the other children in the class.

The fourth and last factor is cost. The court found that the school district had painted an exaggerated picture of what it would cost to educate Rachel in a regular classroom with appropriate services. For example, the district claimed that it would cost over $80,000 to provide schoolwide sensitivity training and another $29,000 for a full-time aide. Yet the district did not establish that such training was necessary. Further, much to the displeasure of the court, the district did not provide a cost comparison between placing Rachel in a special education class with a full-time teacher and two aides and the cost of placing her in a regular class with one part-time aide. The court found that the district did not offer any credible or persuasive evidence that educating Rachel in a regular classroom would be significantly more expensive than educating Rachel in a special classroom. The school district lost on all four factors of the test.

Conclusion

Where best to educate a child has emerged as one of the perennial questions of education. To include or not to include

is an important part of the question. It is a question that must be answered based on the individual needs and abilities of the child. We start from the proposition that the regular classroom is the appropriate setting; if through an analysis, such as Holland's four-factor analysis test, it is found to be inappropriate, then we must restrict the environment accordingly. A hard-and-fast rule that all children will be mainstreamed irrespective of their needs and abilities and the best interests of the other students without doing an analysis runs counter to the IDEA, judicial decisions, and good sense. Similarly, a rule that automatically places a student in a special restricted environment without an analysis is just as wrong. An appropriate analysis is crucial to meeting the needs of our students. The Holland analysis of educational benefit, noneducational benefit, effect on the teacher and other students, and cost is a fair and defensible test to use when we are deciding where best to educate a student.

NOTES

1. While much has been made of the difference between the terms *inclusion* and *mainstreaming*, we will not wade into that battle. The issue we are exploring here is that of determining a starting point for a special education student, regardless of what educators call it. McCarthy (1995) distinguished between the two terms as follows: "*inclusion* [consists of] bringing support services to the child rather than moving the child to a segregated setting to receive services" and *mainstreaming* means "integrating children with disabilities and nonhandicapped children for a portion of the day, usually at times when the regular education program does not have to be significantly modified to accommodate children with disabilities" (824). Yell (1995) asserted that while "mainstreaming refers to placement in regular education, LRE is a principle stating that students with disabilities are to be educated in settings as close to regular classes as appropriate for the child" (193, f.n. 7). Both terms refer to a special education student's receiving a meaningful education in a regular classroom with appropriate support services for as long as practical; therefore, we will use the terms interchangeably to avoid the definitional debate.

2. The Supreme Court in *Rowley* stated the following: "In assuring that the requirements of the Act have been met, courts must be careful to avoid imposing their view of preferable educational methods upon the States" (207).

3. The Eleventh Circuit Court of Appeals (950 F.2d 688 (11th Cir. 1991)) affirmed the judgment of the district court (762 F.Supp. 936 (N.D. Ga. 1990)), but withdrew its opinion (956 F.2d 1025 (11th Cir. 1992)) when the issue of jurisdiction arose. It reinstated its opinion (967 F.2d 470 (11th Cir. 1992)) supporting the district court except for Part 2 on jurisdiction, when the two parties signed a consent decree.

4. The court did not resolve the conflict of which party bears the burden of proof. The Third Circuit has held that the school district has the initial burden of justifying its placement decision at the administrative-hearing level and the trial level if the student challenges the placement (*Oberti v. Board of Education*, 995 F.2d 1204 (3rd Cir. 1993)). Also, the court in *Mavis and Mavis on behalf of Emily Mavis v. Sobol*, 839 F. Supp. 968 (N.D. N.Y. 1994) held that in mainstreaming cases, the burden is on the school district to establish compliance with the LRE mandate. Other courts of appeal have held that the burden of proof at the trial level rests with the party challenging the agency decision (*Roland M. v. Concord School Committee*, 910 F.2d 983 (1st Cir. 1990)). Either way, the school district in the Holland case carried the burden of proof, because the district was challenging the agency decision.

REFERENCES

A. W. v. Northwest R-1 School District, 813 F.2d 158 (8th Cir. 1987).
Ayers, G. E. 1994. Statistical profile of special education in the United

States, 1994. Supplement to *TEACHING Exceptional Children* 26(3): 1-4.

Barnett v. Fairfax County School Board, 927 F.2d 146 (4th Cir. 1991).

Board of Education v. Rowley, 458 U.S. 176 (1982).

Brown v. Board of Education, 47 U.S. 483 (1954).

Clyde K. and Sheila K. v. Puyallup School District, 35 F.3d 1396 (9th Cir. 1994).

Council for Exceptional Children. 1993. *Policy on Inclusive Schools and Community Settings.* Adopted by the Council for Exceptional Children Delegate Assembly, San Antonio (April).

Daniel RR v. State Board of Education, 874 F.2d 1036 (5th Cir. 1989).

DeVries v. Fairfax County School Board, 882 F.2d 876 (4th Cir. 1989).

French v. Omaha Public Schools, 766 F.Supp. 765 (D. Neb. 1991).

Greer v. Rome City School District, 950 F.2d 688 (11th Cir. 1991).

Johnson v. Lancaster-Lebanon Intermediate Unit 13, 757 F. Supp. 606 (E.D. Pa. 1991).

Learning Disabilities Association. 1993. Position paper on full inclusion of all students with learning disabilities in the regular education classroom. *Journal of Learning Disabilities* 26(9): 594.

McCarthy, M. M. 1995. Inclusion of children with disabilities: Is it required?" *95 Ed. Law Rep.* [823] (9 Feb).

Murray by and through Murray v. Montrose County School District, RE-1J, 51 F.3d 921 (10th Cir. 1995).

National Association of State Boards of Education. 1992. *Winners all: A call for inclusive schools.* Washington D.C. : National Association of State Boards of Education.

The National Joint Committee on Learning Disabilities. 1993. A reaction to full inclusion: A reaffirmation of the right of students with learning disabilities to a continuum of services. *Journal of Learning Disabilities* 26(9): 596.

Oberti v. Board of Education of Borough of Clementon School District, 995 F.2d 1204 (3rd Cir. 1993).

Osborne, A. G. Jr. 1994. The IDEA's least restrictive environment mandate: A new era. *88 Ed. Law Rep.* [541] (24 March).

Richardson, J. 1994. A.F.T. says poll shows many oppose 'inclusion'. *Education Week* (3 August): 14.

Roncker v. Walter, 700 F.2d 1058 (6th Cir. 1983).

Sacramento City Unified School District v. Holland, 786 F. Supp. 874 (E.D. Cal. 1992).

Sacramento City Unified School District v. Rachel H., 14 F.3d 1398 (9th Cir. 1994).

Timothy W. v. Rochester School District, 875 F.2d 954, cert. denied, 493 U.S. 983 (1989).

Urban v. Jefferson County School District, R-1, 870 F. Supp. 1558 (D. Colo. 1994).

Yell, M.L. 1995. Judicial review of least restrictive environment disputes under the IDEA. *Illinois School Law Quarterly* 15(4): 176-95.

A Holistic Approach to Attention Deficit Disorder

Thomas Armstrong

What do Winston Churchill and Florence Nightingale have in common? Both found inventive outlets for their boundless energy (also called *hyperactivity*). Here are some strategies for home and school that may help children labeled with ADHD to harness their talents and strengths.

Eight-year-old Billy, in the front row, will have nothing to do with my demonstration of new techniques for teaching spelling. During my visit to his elementary school classroom in upstate New York, Billy is out of his seat during most of the lesson.

When I ask the children to visualize their spelling words, however, I am amazed to see Billy return to his seat and remain perfectly still. Covering his eyes, Billy "looks" intently at his imaginary words—fascinated with the images in his mind!

Later on, I realize that something more important than a spelling lesson went on that afternoon: Billy was able to transform his external physical hyperactivity into internal mental motion—and, by internalizing his outer activity level, was able to gain control over it.

This incident occurred sometime ago but remains memorable to me. Why? Because it suggests that internal empowerment, rather than external control, is often the best way to help kids diagnosed as having ADHD (Attention Deficit Hyperactivity Disorder).

A Decidedly Unholistic Approach

Much of the work currently being undertaken in the field of ADHD looks at the issue from an external control perspective. The two interventions touted in almost all books and programs about ADHD are *medication* and *behavior modification*. While these approaches are often dramatically effective with kids labeled as having ADHD, both have troubling features that often receive scant attention.

When children receive medication, some researchers suggest that they may attribute their improved behaviors to the pills rather than to their own inner resources (Whalen and Henker 1980). Others may expect the medication to do all the work and thus neglect underlying issues that may be the true causes of a child's attention and/or behavior difficulties.

Behavior modification programs, which abound, seek to control children's behaviors through some combination of rewards, punishments, or response costs (the taking away of rewards). Some programs rely on token economy systems, while others use behavior charts, stickers, and even machines. For example, the Attention Training System sits on a child's desk and automatically awards a point every 60 seconds for on-task behavior.

 From *Educational Leadership*, February 1996, pp. 34-36. © 1996 by Thomas Armstrong. Reprinted by permission.

THOUSANDS OF STUDIES TELL US WHAT
these kids *can't* do, but few tell us what they *can* do and who they really are.

The teacher can also deduct points for bad behavior using a remote control. Students trade points for prizes and privileges.

Although behavior modification programs may influence children to change their behavior, they do it for the wrong reason—to get rewards. Such programs can discourage risk-taking, blunt creativity, decrease levels of intrinsic motivation, and even impair academic performance (Kohn 1993).

Looking at the Whole Child

What's needed is a new vision of educational interventions to reflect a deeper appreciation for the *whole child* based upon a *wellness* paradigm, rather than a deficit perspective rooted in a medical or *disease-based* model.

Most ADHD researchers and practitioners see children labeled with ADHD in terms of their deficits. Thousands of studies tell us what these kids *can't* do, but few tell us what they *can* do and who they really are. (One exception is Crammond 1994.) Where are the studies that tell us what these kids are interested in; what kinds of positive learning styles or combinations of intelligences they use successfully in the classroom; and what sorts of artistic, mechanical, scientific, dramatic, or personal contributions they can make to their schools and communities?

Such research is critical if we are going to develop sound classroom strategies that empower these kids. The above anecdote, for example, suggests that visualization may be a powerful tool. Parents and teachers tell me about cases of ADHD-labeled kids who are talented dancers, musicians, sculptors, and dramatists. The ADHD community needs to conduct research on the positive qualities of

these children and what these abilities could mean in contributing to their success in the classroom and in life. Recently, for example, a teacher told me of a child who'd had a terrible time in a traditional straight-rows-of-desks environment—but who was indistinguishable from his "normal" peers in hands-on, project-based classroom activities.

Some research suggests that kids with ADHD do better in environments that are active, self-paced, and hands-on (McGuinness 1985). Video games and computers are powerful learning tools for many of these kids. In fact, their high-speed behavior and thinking lend themselves quite well to such cutting-edge technologies as hypertext and multimedia (Armstrong 1995).

Alternative Avenues

While the ADHD worldview tacitly approves of a teacher-centered, worksheet- and textbook-driven model of education (almost all of its educational suggestions are based on this kind of classroom), current research suggests that all students benefit from project-based environments in which they actively construct new meanings based upon their existing knowledge of a subject.

We need to initiate a new field of study to help children with behavior and attention difficulties—one based upon their strengths rather than their deficits. Such a field would develop assessment strategies geared toward identifying their inner capabilities. Gardner's theory of multiple intelligences (Gardner 1983) is one possible framework for developing appropriate assessment instruments to help identify such abilities (a refreshing change from the behavior rating scales and artificial performance tests currently used to assess ADHD in children). We

must develop individualized educational plans (IEPs) that give more than lip service to a child's strengths and that solidly reflect, in their goals and objectives, that IEPs help the child achieve success.

Finally, interventions need to go beyond strategies such as smiley faces, points, and medications, and reflect a full sense of the child's true nature. Here are a few approaches for use at home and school that might help children identified as having ADHD.

- *Cognitive.* Use focusing and attention training techniques (for example, meditation and visualization), self-talk skills, biofeedback training, organizational strategies, attributional skills (including the ability to attribute success to personal effort), and higher-order problem solving.

- *Ecological.* Limit television and video games, provide appropriate spaces for learning, use music and art to calm or stimulate, find a child's best times of alertness, provide a balanced breakfast, and remove allergens from the diet.

- *Physical.* Emphasize a strong physical education program, martial arts training, use of physical touch and appropriate movement, outdoor activities, noncompetitive sports and games, and physical relaxation techniques.

- *Emotional.* Use self-esteem building strategies; provide positive role models and positive images of the future; employ values clarification; offer individual psychotherapy; and identify talents, strengths, and abilities.

- *Behavioral.* Use personal contracting; immediate feedback; natural and logical consequences; and consistent rules, routines, and transitions. Involve the child in a selection of strategies.

- *Social.* Stress effective communication skills, social skills, class meetings, family therapy, peer and cross-age tutoring, and cooperative learning.

- *Educational.* Use computers; hands-on learning; high-stimulation learning resources; expressive arts; creativity development; and multiple intelligences, whole language, and attention-grabbing activities.

This tentative list provides a far richer storehouse of interventions than the instructional strategies given in the ADHD literature—for example, seating the child next to the teacher, posting assignments on a child's desk, maintaining eye contact, and breaking up assignments into small chunks. Such a deficit-oriented perspective gives differential treatment to the "ADHD child." Most of the above strategies, by contrast, are good for *all* children. Thus, in an inclusive classroom, the child labeled ADHD can thrive with the same kinds of nourishing and stimulating activities as everyone else and be viewed in the same way as everyone else: as a unique human being.

The Creative Roots of ADHD

Because research has long suggested that many children labeled ADHD are actually *underaroused* (Ritalin provides enough medical stimulation to bring their nervous systems to an optimal level of arousal), a strength-based approach makes more sense than a deficit-based one (Zentall 1975). By providing these kids with high-stimulation learning environments grounded in what they enjoy and can succeed in, we're essentially providing them with a kind of educational psychostimulant that works as well as Ritalin but which is internally empowering rather than externally controlling.

Related Readings

- Crook, W. (1991). *Help for the Hyperactive Child.* Jackson, Tenn.: Professional Books.
- Hartmann, T. (1993). *Attention Deficit Disorder: A Different Perception.* Lancaster, Pa.:Underwood-Miller.
- Kurcinka, M. S. (1991). *Raising Your Spirited Child.* New York: HarperCollins.
- Reif, S. F. (1993). *How to Reach and Teach ADD/ADHD Children.* West Nyack, N.Y.: Center for Applied Research in Education.
- Taylor, J. F. (1990). *Helping Your Hyperactive Child.* Rocklin, Calif.: Prima Publishing.

Remember that a hyperactive child is an *active* child. These kids often possess great vitality—a valuable resource that society needs for its own renewal. Look at the great figures who transformed society, and you'll find that many of them had behavior problems or were hyperactive as children: Thomas Edison, Winston Churchill, Pablo Picasso, Nikola Tesla,[1] Charles Darwin, Florence Nightingale, and Friedreich Nietzsche (see Goertzel and Goertzel 1962). As educators, we can make a big difference in the lives of these kids if we stop getting bogged down in their deficits and start highlighting their strengths!

[1]Tesla, an electrician, invented the Tesla coil, the AC generator, and other innovations.

References

Armstrong, T. (1995). *The Myth of the ADD Child.* New York: Dutton.
Crammond, B. (1994). "Attention-Deficit Hyperactivity Disorder and Creativity: What Is the Connection?" *Journal of Creative Behavior* 28: 193–210.
Gardner, H. (1983). *Frames of Mind.* New York: Basic Books.
Goertzel, V., and M. G. Goertzel. (1962). *Cradles of Eminence.* Boston: Little, Brown.
Kohn, A. (1993). *Punished by Rewards.* Boston: Houghton Mifflin.
McGuinness, D. (1985). *When Children Don't Learn.* New York: Basic Books.
Whalen, C., and B. Henker. (1980). *Hyperactive Children: The Social Ecology of Identification and Treatment.* New York: Academic Press.
Zentall, S. (July 1975). "Optimal Stimulation as a Theoretical Basis of Hyperactivity." *American Journal of Orthopsychiatry* 45, 4: 549–563.

Thomas Armstrong is the author of seven books including *The Myth of the ADD Child: 50 Ways to Improve Your Child's Behavior and Attention Span without Drugs, Labels, or Coercion.* He can be reached at: P.O. Box 548, Cloverdale, CA 95425.

Is It Acceleration or Simply Appropriate Instruction for Precocious Youth?

John F. Feldhusen
Lanah Van Winkle
David A. Ehle

How do we arrange classroom learning experiences at a level, pace, and depth appropriate to individual students' levels of precocity and need?

How do we assess students' current levels of achievement and readiness for new material?

How do we arrange instructional conditions to place students with a teacher and curriculum material appropriate to their needs?

These questions are important to many teachers of students with special gifts and talents. Without such efforts, precocious students are often bored in school (Feldhusen & Kroll, 1991).

Robert Slavin (1990) stated the case well: "I would certainly be opposed to any plan that would `hold back' gifted children from achieving as much as they are able to accomplish" (p. 3). Yet, such is surely the school experience of many precocious youth much of the time (Westberg, Archambault, Dobyns, & Salvin, 1991). Slavin suggested that gifted programs "are most justifiable when the content of the special program represents true acceleration. Research generally does not find achievement benefits of enrichment programs" (p. 4).

We recently spoke with a junior high school student about the school reform movement. When we asked what she saw as the most serious problem with

American schools today, she responded, "They won't let us learn." We thought she misunderstood the question—but as she went on, her point was clear:

> What I mean is, they seem to think they have to keep us all together all the time. That means in the subjects I'm good at I can't learn more because I'm always waiting for others to catch up. I guess if I get too far ahead I'll be doing the next year's work, but I can't understand what's wrong with that if that's what I'm ready for.

For this student it seemed so simple, and she had clearly given it much thought while she was doing all that waiting. As we reflected on her words of wisdom, two ideas emerged: She seems to be calling for "acceleration" as it is often conceptualized; and yet, the underlying philosophy that her comments reveal is

not at all what we have traditionally called "acceleration."

Assessment Is Key

Effective teaching involves assessing each students' status in the curriculum sequence and posing new learning tasks slightly beyond the level already mastered (Feldhusen & Klausmeier, 1959). Good teachers have been addressing individual ability differences in this manner in their classrooms for years. In our traditional age-graded system, teachers carry a tremendous burden in planning to meet the needs of all students, one that will not lighten as long as we insist on equating "academic peer" and "age." Yet this effort becomes increasingly difficult when students vary markedly from the norm. If Julie has mastered concepts *A* and *B*, and our goal is to challenge her at a level slightly exceeding the level already mastered, does it not make sense that we should allow her to proceed to concept *C*?

What Is Acceleration?

Now comes that word—*acceleration*. Will we have to accelerate Julie before she can go on to concept *C*? Contrary to common perception, we do not have to *do* anything to Julie before she can learn advanced concepts. Julie is fine just being her own academic self, and we are here to serve her. There's nothing "accelerative" about meeting Julie's needs. If we do not meet her needs, in a sense we "decelerate" her: We hinder her learning. We agree with David Elkind (1988):

> Promotion of intellectually gifted children is simply another way of attempting to match the curriculum to the child's abilities, not to accelerate those abilities. Accordingly, the promotion of intellectually gifted children in no way contradicts the accepted view of . . . the negative effects of hurrying. Indeed, the positive effects of promoting intellectually gifted children provide additional evidence for the benefits of developmentally appropriate curricula. (p. 2)

Acceleration is a misnomer; the process is really one of bringing talented youth up to a level of instruction commensurate with their achievement levels and *readiness* so that they are properly challenged to learn the new material (Feldhusen, 1989).

Curricular Context of Acceleration

We often forget the traditional meaning of the words *acceleration* and *enrichment* when we apply them in education. Both "accelerated" and "enriched" only have meaning when used to compare two different states or situations. When we use acceleration and enrichment in the traditional educational sense, our usual reference point is the standard school curriculum. Jane is in *third* grade but is working on *fifth*-grade math; she is "accelerated" in math. Carl is planning an exploration of Mars; he is doing an "enrichment" activity in science. Adoption of a specific curriculum as a reference point, however, blurs the distinction between acceleration and enrichment. If Carl is in the second-grade enrichment program, but the space exploration ac-

tivity is done by all sixth-grade students, is he doing an enrichment activity, or has he been accelerated to the sixth-grade level? Most third-grade students are learning simple single-digit multiplication; if Jane is working on three-digit multiplication, is she not doing an enrichment activity in math?

The examples of both enrichment and acceleration programs that are typically given, demonstrate the lack of a precise meaning of these concepts and the importance of relating these terms to a curriculum. The most popular subject for acceleration is math, while language arts or social studies is usually the focus of enrichment programs. It is easier to identify math instruction as being accelerated, since most students learn math concepts in a fairly structured order. On the other hand, most language arts and social studies programs are referred to as enrichment programs. They are often seen as *extended* rather than *advanced* curriculum experiences.

A Call for New Terminology

Where does this leave us? We can either change conceptions of acceleration and enrichment to reflect their commonalities and relativism, or find new terminology to better reflect the concepts involved and

eliminate the confusion. Rather than talking about a program that is accelerated or enriched, why not talk about a program that focuses on *higher-level constructs*, greater appreciation of the underlying knowledge structure of a discipline, or mastery of a larger knowledge base in and associated with a field of study? These are the characteristics that differentiate an *expert* in a field from a *novice* (Johnson, Kochevar, & Zualkerman, 1992). This type of program could involve enrichment *and* acceleration; it transcends both terms to strike at the heart of the cognitive goals of gifted education. Such a program brings the content of the curriculum up to the level of the child.

If we accept the premise that gifted and talented students are precocious, doesn't it make sense to challenge them to move in the direction of more advanced learners? Coupled with strong services to meet the social and emotional needs of bright students, *a program to develop the leaders of tomorrow would result*. But what does all this mean in action in a school situation?

Providing Higher-Level Learning Opportunities

Practically, how do we go about bringing the content of the school up to the level

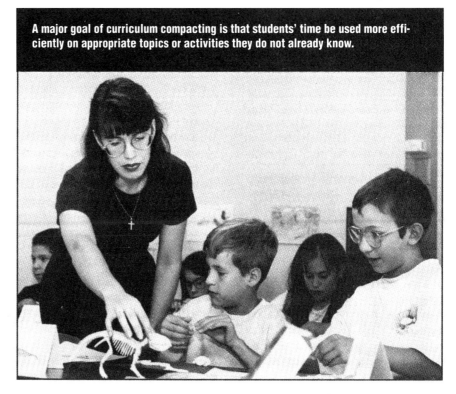

A major goal of curriculum compacting is that students' time be used more efficiently on appropriate topics or activities they do not already know.

The first step in the Diagnostic Testing followed by Prescriptive Instruction (DT-PI) model is to determine the students' current level of knowledge through appropriate tests.

of the child? First, we should not assume that a child does not know what we have not yet taught. A study by the Educational Products Information Exchange Institute (1980-81), a nonprofit educational consumer agency, revealed that 60% of the fourth graders in some of the school districts studied scored 80% or higher on a test of the content of their math texts *before* they had opened their books in September. Similar findings were reported for content tests on 4th- and 10th-grade science texts and 10th-grade social studies texts (Renzulli & Reis, 1986). Since textbooks have continued to drop in levels of difficulty over the past 10-15 years, one would not expect these percentages to be any lower today for our highly able students. We need a way to determine the exact level at which to begin appropriate instruction.

Diagnostic Testing-Prescriptive Instruction

Hoping to develop a teaching approach that would accommodate students' differing levels of knowledge as well as their rates of learning, Stanley (1978) originated the Diagnostic Testing followed by Prescriptive Instruction (DT-PI) model. Benbow (1986) developed the procedure further for use in educational programs for gifted youth. Described in simple terms, the DT-PI model has four steps:

1. Determine students' current level of knowledge through appropriate tests.

2. Identify areas of weakness by analyzing items missed on the tests.

3. Instruct the students in those areas of weakness and allow them to show mastery on a second form of the test.

4. Proceed to the next higher level and repeat Steps 1-3.

The DT-PI model of instruction has been the approach used in the Study of Mathematically Precocious Youth (SMPY) in the summer programs at The Johns Hopkins University since 1971. SMPY's longitudinal study has shown the effectiveness of such acceleration for talented youth. SMPY's most salient finding in working with 85,000 young gifted students over a 13-year period is that *school systems need far more curricular flexibility* (Benbow, 1986). Swiatek and Beubow (1991) have also conducted a 10-year follow-up of fast-paced mathematics classes and found higher achievement in classes using DT-PI methods.

Curriculum Compacting

Another technique that can be used to bring the content up to the level of the child is curriculum compacting (Reis, 1995), a system designed to adapt the regular curriculum to meet the needs of above-average students by either eliminating work that has been mastered pre-

viously or streamlining work that may be mastered at a pace commensurate with the student's ability. A major goal of curriculum compacting is that students' time be used more efficiently on appropriate topics or activities rather than completing tasks they already know. Both DP-TI and curriculum compacting strive for proficiency in the basic curriculum and then continue student learning at an appropriate level for which they are ready. The two approaches differ in that *curriculum compacting focuses on a challenging environment within the context of grade-level curriculum*, while the philosophy behind DP-TI is clearly to enable students to advance at their own pace through the scope and sequence of the curriculum.

The Bottom Line

Most teachers want their students to enjoy learning, to enjoy school, and most of all, to accomplish as much as they are capable. When their students are bored much of the school day, frustrated by repeating material they already know, and are not given the opportunity to accomplish nearly what they could, good teachers are troubled.

Each child has the right to learn new material commensurate with his or her ability and knowledge, even if other students who are ready for that material are 3 years older; age really makes no difference. If acceleration is not an accurate term, is there one? Although we are not at all convinced that we must have a word, there are some terms that appear more philosophically sound. In a recent review, Benbow (1991) made the following suggestions: "curricular flexibility," "flexible pacing," and "developmental placement."

The bottom line is that *our educational programs must respond to the abilities and readiness of individual children*. It is a sad irony that a student could say of those responsible for her education, "They won't let me learn." Let's try to loosen our dependence on the lingo of "acceleration" and "enrichment" and simply go about the business of meeting students' needs, whatever that may require. Curricular and instructional flexibility are the prerequisites. Adapting instruction to individual readiness and need is the answer.

One way to respond to the different abilities and readiness levels of individual students is through flexible curricula and instructional practices.

References

Benbow, C. P. (1986). SMPY's model for teaching mathematically precocious students. In J. S. Renzulli (Ed.), *Systems and models for developing programs for the gifted and talented* (pp. 1-26). Mansfield Center, CT: Creative Learning Press, Inc.

Benbow, C. P. (1991). Meeting the needs of gifted students through use of acceleration. In M. C. Wang, M. C. Reynolds, & H. J. Walberg (Eds.), *Handbook of special education: Research and practice: Vol. 4. Emerging Programs* (pp. 23-36). New York: Pergamon Press.

Educational Products Information Exchange Institute. (1980-81). *Educational research and development report*, 3, 4.

Elkind, D. (1988). Acceleration. *Young Children*, 43(4), 2.

Feldhusen, J. F. (1989). Synthesis of research on gifted youths. *Educational Leadership*, 46(6), 6-11.

Feldhusen, J. F., & Klausmeier, H. J. (1959). Achievement in counting and addition. *The Elementary School Journal*, 59, 388-393.

Feldhusen, J. F., & Kroll, M. D. (1991). Boredom or challenge for the academically talented. *Gifted Education International*, 7(2), 80-81.

Johnson, P. E., Kochevar, L. K., & Zualkerman, I. A. (1992). Expertise and fit: Aspects of cognition. In H. L. Pick, P. Van Den Broek, & D. C. Knill (Eds.), *Cognition: Conceptual and methodological issues* (pp. 305-331).

Washington, DC: American Psychological Association.

Reis, Sally M. (1995). *Curriculum compacting communicator, 28*(2), 1, 27-32. Mansfield Center, CT: Creative Learning Press, Inc.

Renzulli, J. S., & Reis, S. M. (1986). The enrichment triad/revolving door model: A schoolwide plan for the development of creative productivity. In J. S. Renzulli (Ed.), *Systems and models for developing programs for the gifted and talented* (pp. 216-266). Mansfield Center, CT: Creative Learning Press, Inc.

Swiatek, M. A., & Beubow, C. P. (1991). A ten-year longitudinal follow-up of participants in a fast-paced mathematics course. *Journal for Research in Mathematics Education, 22*, 138-150.

Slavin, R. E. (1990). Ability grouping, cooperative learning and the gifted. *Journal for the Education of the Gifted, 14*(1), 3-9.

Stanley, J. C. (1978). SMPY's DT-PI model: Diagnostic testing followed by prescriptive instruction. *Intellectually Talented Youth Bulletin, 4*(10), 7-8.

Westberg, K. L., Archambault, F. X., Dobyns, S. M., & Salvin, T. J. (1991). *The classroom practices observation study.* (Technical Report). Storrs, CT: The National Research Center on the Gifted and Talented.

John F. Feldhusen, *Director, Gifted Education Resource Institute;* **Lanah Van Winkle,** *Assistant Coordinator, Shared Information Services;* **David A. Ehle,** *Coordinator, Gifted Education Resource Institute, Summer Residential Programs, Purdue University, West Lafayette, Indiana.*

Address correspondence to John F. Feldhusen, Purdue University, 1446 Liberal Arts/Education Building, West Lafayette, IN 47907-1446 (e-mail: feldhuse@vm.cc.purdue.edu).

Meeting the Needs of Young Gifted Students

Karen Meador

Karen Meador is Assistant Professor, Department of Early Childhood, West Georgia College, Carrollton.

Kindergarten is a wonderful place for Jonathan, age 5, who exhibits knowledge beyond his years. He could already add and subtract single digit numbers before he arrived at Miss Kathryn's kindergarten classroom, and he continues to excel in math-related activities. Jonathan uses exceptional spatial abilities to plan and build intricate wooden block structures and make elaborate two-dimensional patterns with the shape blocks. Unlike some gifted children, Jonathan does not yet read; consequently, he needs the same language-rich environment as his peers. Miss Kathryn realistically appreciates Jonathan's exceptional mathematical abilities while simultaneously nurturing and guiding his social, emotional and cognitive needs. Jonathan is fortunate to be in a truly developmentally appropriate classroom.

Accolades are due Miss Kathryn and all early childhood educators who provide developmentally appropriate curricula. Early childhood classrooms that are both age-appropriate and individually appropriate (Bredekamp, 1987) eliminate much of the need for special outside classes for gifted children. This article focuses on the organization of early childhood classrooms, grades K-1, that strive to be individually appropriate for all students. The author writes from her perspective as a mother of two gifted children, a gifted education specialist and a regular classroom teacher. The article does not address the needs of the profoundly gifted who require services outside the regular classroom.

Developmentally Appropriate Practice

The position statement from the National Association for the Education of Young Children on developmentally appropriate practice (DAP) (Bredekamp, 1987) delineates two dimensions of the concept. The first is age appropriateness, which relates to curriculum and practice that "meet the needs of a particular age span" (Barbour, 1992, p. 148). Early childhood educators understand that "predictable changes occur in all domains of development—physical, emotional, social, and cognitive. . . . [and that this] provides a framework from which teachers prepare the learning environment and plan appropriate experiences" (Bredekamp, 1987, p. 3). Educators can anticipate the range of abilities based upon research and prior knowledge of what a specific age group can accomplish.

Planning family meals can serve as an analogy for this concept. Most of us shop and plan meals based upon the types of foods the family normally eats. We know that certain things (brussels sprouts, perhaps) will not appeal to the family and it is a waste of time and money to even offer these foods. Likewise, it is a waste of time and resources to teach algebra to kindergartners since it is beyond most 5-year-olds' cognitive range.

This analogy is challenged, however, by the second dimension of DAP, individual appropriateness. Children are unique and bring assorted experiences and needs to the classroom. "Both the curriculum and

From *Childhood Education*, Fall 1996, pp. 6-9. © 1996 by the Association for Childhood Education International, 17904 Georgia Avenue, Suite 215, Olney, MD. Reprinted by permission.

adults' interactions with children should be responsive to individual differences. . . . [While we should plan experiences that] match the child's developing abilities, . . . [we must also challenge] the child's interest and understanding" (Bredekamp, 1987, p. 2). Let us take another look at the family menu analogy. We know what our loved ones like to eat and what they will tolerate. If we never offer anything new on the menu, however, we will never know what else the family might enjoy. How do we determine whether or not a child likes carrot cake if we never serve it? It is unlikely that a child will say, "Hey, Mom, I'd really like to try some carrot cake to see if it's any good." Just as we need to offer a broader menu to determine individual tastes, so do we need to organize classrooms to accommodate needs that vary from the anticipated developmental range.

Characteristics of Young Gifted Children

Perhaps you have a Jonathan in your classroom or see other children whose characteristics differ from the norm. Identifying gifted students through formal procedures can yield valuable information about children's needs. Many schools, however, either do not begin indentification at the early childhood level, or the process takes many months to complete. Teachers can better prepare individually appropriate curriculum if they recognize characteristics of giftedness.

Remember that children can display giftedness in many ways. The following information on gifted children's traits can help, although it is by no means exhaustive. Gifted children often display the ability to learn rapidly, advanced ability in a specific domain such as math or reading, creativity, a long attention span when interested and verbal proficiency.

■ *The Ability To Learn Rapidly* (Saunders, 1986). High-ability students often require less help with new material and less practice to acquire a skill. A gifted student may be able to use spelling words introduced on Monday morning by Monday afternoon, for example. Sometimes, however, gifted students may resist learning a reasonably easy word such as "turtle," while quickly mastering a word they choose themselves, such as "anthropomorphics."

■ *Advanced Ability in a Specific Domain.* Gifted students may appear particularly advanced in a specific domain or subject. Some very young students, for example, display precocious reading ability— "an important and reasonably common gift" (Jackson, 1992, p. 199). Students who are gifted in other domains or who are highly creative may not have early reading ability. Gifted children who do not read early, however, often quickly catch up with the precocious readers.

Advanced ability in a specific domain signals talent that may not be apparent in other developmental areas. Some "young gifted children may exhibit uneven development" (Kitano, 1989, p. 60). The highly talented musical or math prodigy does not necessarily display precocious reading ability or advanced social skills. Both the student and the teacher may feel frustrated if their expectations are unrealistic—believing, for example, that gifted performance in a single area will translate to similar success in all areas.

■ *Creativity.* Clark (1988) calls creativity "the highest expression of giftedness" (p. 45), and others accept this as one type of giftedness (Davis & Rimm, 1994; Saunders, 1986). Creative students bring both excitement and challenge to a classroom. Their classroom talents are most easily recognized through art forms such as creative writing and drawing. These children's story characters and illustrations are often elaborate. Students also demonstrate creativity when they find unique solutions to problems or offer multiple reasons for a story character's actions. Their inappropriate drawings on spelling tests or math work, however, may be annoying.

Classroom observation uncovers conflicting characteristics of gifted children. Two examples of this follow.

■ *Long Attention Span/Short Attention Span.* A child who is excessively active and unable to sit still when uninterested may spend hours engrossed in a self-selected activity. A 1st-grader who cannot focus his attention during a 10-minute reading of a picture book and refuses to write more than a few words in his morning journal may be able to sit for hours making elaborately intricate drawings or models. A teacher may wonder if this is the same child who interrupted her insect lesson three times to describe various things he had read about spiders.

■ *Verbal Proficiency/Frustration.* The language-advanced child who "talks above the heads of his or her age peers" (Saunders, 1986, p. 22) frequently experiences difficulty during conversation and becomes exasperated during play when peers do not understand the game or the

Creative students bring both excitement and challenge to a classroom.

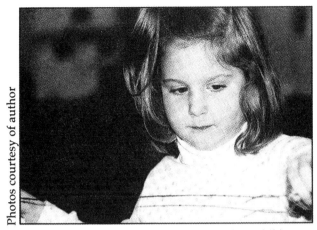
Photos courtesy of author

Open-ended problem-solving activities allow children to utilize varying strengths and abilities.

plan for adventure (Meador, 1993). At times, the child even becomes frustrated with parents. A child may plan elaborate adventures with multiple characters, instructing her mother about the part she should play and exactly what to say. An often preoccupied mother, however, may not remember what to say at the appointed time, leaving both parent and child frustrated.

No gifted child will exhibit all of the above characteristics. Furthermore, a classroom environment may not provide adequate opportunities for displaying talent. In order to uncover unique capabilities that may not fit into preexisting ideas about development, we must ask students challenging questions, offer them difficult tasks and permit exhibition of talent. Ben Ari and Rich (1992) discussed heterogeneously grouped classes, in which all children demonstrated significant progress. "The key to this success seems to be related to the school's ability to create conditions where meaningful learning activities are accessible to all children" (p. 350). We cannot discover a student's range of abilities without offering more difficult tasks, even though we would not expect all children to succeed. We have not explored each individual's full potential if the majority of the class can complete every task with relative ease.

Individually Appropriate Practice for All
Individually appropriate practice not only encourages students to reach their potential but also redirects many less desirable behaviors. Children gain self-confidence when they are intellectually challenged, encouraged, involved in self-selected tasks and when their social skills are facilitated through careful guidance. Individually appropriate curriculum that strives for "an optimal match between the child's cognitive level and task demands" (Kitano, 1989, p. 60) allows these conditions to occur.

It is not necessary to completely restructure programs to ensure individual appropriateness. Ongoing assessment of student progress and interests is already a part of many early childhood classrooms. Use this information to plan centers and large- and small-group activities. When evaluating individual students, consider the range of observable progress. Keep an eye out for students who no longer seem challenged by your curriculum, and devise opportunities for them to explore new "menus."

A centers approach (Meador, 1991) is a good place to begin. Expand and enrich preexisting centers by including alternative activities or second-tier activities that add greater depth.

SNACK CENTER ON INSECTS
(Appropriate for Beginning Kindergartners)
Original Activity: Create your own ant hill snack. 1) Use a plastic knife to spread peanut butter over a vanilla wafer. 2) Place three raisin "ants" on your ant hill. 3) Eat your treat.
Extended Activity: 1) Plan to make ant hills for five children. How many vanilla wafers and raisins do you need? 2) Explain your answer to the teacher.

This open-ended extension may appeal to all students since it provides for multiple means of finding answers. The manner in which the student calculates the supplies needed is indicative of his or her cognitive level. Students may simply draw a picture of five vanilla wafers with three raisins on each and count them, others may count on their fingers or use tokens and more advanced students may count by threes. Observing the students' cognitive processes provides additional information about ability, thus enabling teachers to plan other individually appropriate activities.

WRITING CENTER ACTIVITY INVOLVING *THE MYSTERIES OF HARRIS BURDICK* (VAN ALLSBURG, 1984)
(Appropriate for End of the Year 1st-Graders)
Original Activity: 1) Look at the picture (cover of *The Mysteries of Harris Burdick*, depicting people riding a vehicle with wheels and a sail on what appears to be a train track). 2) Write a story about where the train is going.
Alternative Activity: 1) Look at the picture. 2) Write a story about where the train has been and what caused it to be in this place. Tell why one person is wearing sailor's clothing.

While the first activity requires children to use imagination, the second also calls for critical thinking. A student could simply write about where the train has been, disregarding elements in the picture. Students show higher order thinking, however, when writing about how particular things in the picture evolved from earlier events.

Teachers can use their observations of students' responses to develop new individually appropriate centers with multiple levels of activities. Consider Kitano's (1989) multiple levels of activities:

1. Selecting and pasting precut figures of men, women, boys and girls to create a collage representing the child's family
2. Using a felt board to relate and illustrate a story about family members and how they are related
3. Drawing a family portrait, labeling the members by name, and writing or dictating a story about each member's role
4. Constructing a family tree. (Kitano, 1989, p. 61)

Children's interests, as well as their abilities, indicate which activities and centers are individually appropriate. Very young children may be able to recite lengthy dinosaur names and enthusiastically discuss intricate data about them. The children were able to learn this information because the topic excited them. All children should have opportunities to explore their passions. Gifted children seem to have an unusually strong appetite for information. Cohen (1989), for example, described a 3-year-old with a "consuming passion for volcanoes" (p. 8). The child spent an average of "one to two hours each day, focused on this interest over a span of about nine months" (p. 8).

Ultimately, individually appropriate curricula must create ample opportunities for children to have experiences in their "flow channel" (Csikszentmihalyi, 1990, p. 74). This channel balances between experiences that create boredom and those that create anxiety. Children attempting tasks that are too difficult may become anxious, while tasks that are too easy cause boredom. The flow channel experiences result when "tasks are of an appropriate level of difficulty for a child's current level of skill" (Kanevsky, 1992). Task complexity should increase as skill increases. This concept is important for *all* children, not just gifted ones.

Conclusion
Although this article is specifically intended to remind classroom educators of gifted children's needs, the con-

tent is about *all* children. Every child deserves a chance and should be challenged for optimal development. We must draw upon proven techniques from the field of gifted education to enhance learning for all children.

No easy formula for devising developmentally appropriate curriculum exists. No outside person can write a book of activities for your children, and the centers you prepare for one class may be inappropriate for the next. Educators continuously observe and question their students and try to "understand each child as a unique individual" (Winter, 1994/95, p. 92). They strive to facilitate the growth of each individual child and offer them challenging experiences. The key lies in providing a range of activities that allows students to display their full abilities. Let's remember to offer them carrot cake!

❖

References
Barbour, N. B. (1992). Early childhood gifted education: A collaborative perspective. *Journal for the Education of the Gifted, 15*(2), 145-162.

Ben Ari, R., & Rich, Y. (1992). Meeting the educational needs of all students in the heterogeneous class. In P. S. Klein & A. J. Tannenbaum (Eds.), *To be young and gifted* (pp. 348-378). Norwood, NJ: Ablex Publishing.

Bredekamp, S. (Ed.). (1987). *Developmentally appropriate practice in early childhood programs serving children from birth through age 8* (exp. ed.). Washington, DC: National Association for the Education of Young Children.

Clark, B. (1988). *Growing up gifted* (3rd ed.). Columbus, OH: Merrill Publishing.

Cohen, L. M. (1989). Understanding the interests and themes of the very young gifted child. *Gifted Child Today, 12*(4), 6-9.

Csikszentmihalyi, M. (1990). *Flow: The psychology of optimal experience.* New York: Harper Perennial.

Davis, G. A., & Rimm, S. B. (1994). *Education of the gifted and talented* (3rd ed.). Boston, MA: Allyn and Bacon.

Jackson, N. E. (1992). Precocious reading of English: Origins, structure, and predictive significance. In P. S. Klein & A. J. Tannenbaum (Eds.), *To be young and gifted* (pp. 171-203). Norwood, NJ: Ablex Publishing.

Kanevsky, L. (1992). The learning game. In P. S. Klein & A. J. Tannenbaum (Eds.), *To be young and gifted* (pp. 204-241). Norwood, NJ: Ablex Publishing.

Kitano, M. (1989). The K-3 teacher's role in recognizing and supporting young gifted children. *Young Children, 44*(3), 57-63.

Meador, K. (1991, November). *The centers approach to serving young gifted students.* Paper presented at the meeting of the National Association for Gifted Children, Kansas City, KS.

Meador, K. (1993). Parent to parent: Surviving early childhood with a creative child. *Gifted Child Today, 16*(2), 57-59.

Saunders, J. (1986). *Bringing out the best.* Minneapolis, MN: Free Spirit Publishing.

Winter, S. M. (1994/95). Diversity: A program for all children. *Childhood Education, 71*, 91-95.

Van Allsburg, C. (1984). *The mysteries of Harris Burdick.* Boston, MA: Houghton Mifflin.

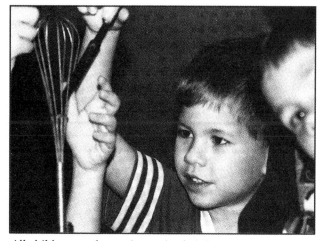

All children need experiences in their interest areas.

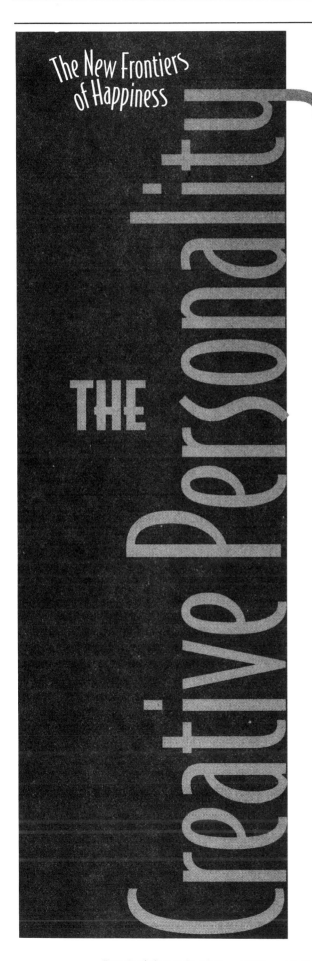

The New Frontiers of Happiness

THE

creative Personality

Of all human activities,
creativity comes closest to providing the
fulfillment we all hope to get in our lives.
Call it full-blast living.

By Mihaly Csikszentmihalyi

Creativity is a central source of meaning in our lives. Most of the things that are interesting, important, and human are the results of creativity. What makes us different from apes— our language, values, artistic expression, scientific understanding, and technology— is the result of individual ingenuity that was recognized, rewarded, and transmitted through learning.

When we're creative, we feel we are living more fully than during the rest of life. The excitement of the artist at the easel or the scientist in the lab comes close to the ideal fulfillment we all hope to get from life, and so rarely do. Perhaps only sex, sports, music, and religious ecstasy—even when these experiences remain fleeting and leave no trace—provide a profound sense of being part of an entity greater than ourselves. But creativity also leaves an outcome that adds to the richness and complexity of the future.

I have devoted 30 years of research to how creative people live and work, to make more understandable the mysterious process by which they come up with new ideas and new things. Creative individuals are remarkable for their ability to adapt to almost any situation and to make do with whatever is at hand to reach their goals. If I had to express in one word what makes their personalities different from others, it's complexity. They show tendencies of thought and action that in most people are segregated. They contain contradictory extremes; instead of being an "individual," each of them is a "multitude."

Here are the 10 antithetical traits often present in creative people that are integrated with each other in a dialéctical tension.

From *Psychology Today*, July/August 1996, pp. 36-40. Adapted from *Creativity: Flow and the Psychology of Discovery and Invention* by Mihaly Csikszentmihalyi. © 1996 by Mihaly Csikszentmihalyi. Reprinted by permission of HarperCollins Publishers, Inc.

1. Creative people have a great deal of physical energy, but they're also often quiet and at rest.

They work long hours, with great concentration, while projecting an aura of freshness and enthusiasm. This suggests a superior physical endowment, a genetic advantage. Yet it is surprising how often individuals who in their seventies and eighties exude energy and health remember childhoods plagued by illness. It seems that their energy is internally generated, due more to their focused minds than to the superiority of their genes.

This does not mean that creative people are hyperactive, always "on." In fact, they rest often and sleep a lot. The important thing is that they control their energy; it's not ruled by the calendar, the clock, an external schedule. When necessary, they can focus it like a laser beam; when not, creative types immediately recharge their batteries. They consider the rhythm of activity followed by idleness or reflection very important for the success of their work. This is not a biorhythm inherited with their genes; it was learned by trial and error as a strategy for achieving their goals.

One manifestation of energy is sexuality. Creative people are paradoxical in this respect also. They seem to have quite a strong dose of eros, or generalized libidinal energy, which some express directly into sexuality. At the same time, a certain spartan celibacy is also a part of their makeup; continence tends to accompany superior achievement. Without eros, it would be difficult to take life on with vigor; without restraint, the energy could easily dissipate.

2. Creative people tend to be smart yet naive at the same time.
How smart they actually are is open to question. It is probably true that what psychologists call the "g factor," meaning a core of general intelligence, is high among people who make important creative contributions.

The earliest longitudinal study of superior mental abilities, initiated at Stanford University by the psychologist Lewis Terman in 1921, shows rather conclusively that children with very high IQs do well in life, but after a certain point IQ does not seem to be correlated any longer with superior performance in real life. Later studies suggest that the cutoff point is around 120; it might be difficult to do creative work with a lower IQ, but an IQ beyond 120 does not necessarily imply higher creativity.

Another way of expressing this dialectic is the contrasting poles of wisdom and childishness. As Howard Gardner remarked in his study of the major creative geniuses of this century, a certain immaturity, both emotional and mental, can go hand in hand with deepest insights. Mozart comes immediately to mind.

Furthermore, people who bring about an acceptable novelty in a domain seem able to use well two opposite ways of thinking: the convergent and the divergent. Convergent thinking is measured by IQ tests, and it involves solving well-defined, rational problems that have one correct answer. Divergent thinking leads to no agreed-upon solution. It involves *fluency*, or the ability to generate a great quantity of ideas; *flexibility*, or the ability to switch from one perspective to another; and *originality* in picking unusual associations of ideas. These are the dimensions of thinking that most creativity tests measure and that most workshops try to enhance.

Yet there remains the nagging suspicion that at the highest levels of creative achievement the generation of novelty is not the main issue. People often claimed to have had only two or three good ideas in their entire career, but each idea was so generative that it kept them busy for a lifetime of testing, filling out, elaborating, and applying.

Divergent thinking is not much use without the ability to tell a good idea from a bad one, and this selectivity involves convergent thinking.

3. Creative people combine playfulness and discipline, or responsibility and irresponsibility.
There is no question that a playfully light attitude is typical of creative individuals. But this playfulness doesn't go very far without its antithesis, a quality of doggedness, endurance, perseverance.

Nina Holton, whose playfully wild germs of ideas are the genesis of her sculpture, is very firm about the importance of hard work: "Tell anybody you're a sculptor and they'll say, 'Oh, how exciting, how wonderful.' And I tend to say, 'What's so wonderful?' It's like being a mason, or a carpenter, half the time. But they don't wish to hear that because they really only imagine the first part, the exciting part. But, as Khrushchev once said, that doesn't fry pancakes, you see. That germ of an idea does not make a sculpture which stands up. It just sits there. So the next stage is the hard work. Can you really translate it into a piece of sculpture?"

Jacob Rabinow, an electrical engineer, uses an interesting mental technique to slow himself down when work on an invention requires more endurance than intuition: "When I have a job that takes a lot of effort, slowly, I pretend I'm in jail. If I'm in jail, time is of no consequence. In other words, if it takes a week to cut this, it'll take a week. What else have I got to do? I'm going to be here for twenty years. See? This is a kind of mental trick. Otherwise you say, 'My God, it's not working,' and then you make mistakes. My way, you say time is of absolutely no consequence."

Despite the carefree air that many creative people affect, most of them work late into the night and persist when less driven individuals would not. Vasari wrote in 1550 that when Renaissance painter Paolo Uccello was working out the laws of visual perspective, he would walk back and forth all night, muttering to himself: "What a beautiful thing is this perspective!" while his wife called him back to bed with no success.

4. Creative people alternate between imagination and fantasy, and a rooted sense of reality. Great art and great science involve a leap of imagination into a world that is different from the present. The rest of society often views these new ideas as fantasies without relevance to current reality. And they are right. But the whole point of art and science is to go beyond what we now consider real and create a new reality. At the same time, this "escape" is not into a never-never land. What makes a novel idea creative is that once we see it, sooner or later we recognize that, strange as it is, it is true.

Most of us assume that artists—musicians, writers, poets, painters—are strong on the fantasy side, whereas scientists, politicians, and businesspeople are realists. This may be true in terms of day-to-day routine activities. But when a person begins to work creatively, all bets are off.

5. Creative people tend to be both extroverted and introverted. We're usually one or the other, either preferring to be in the thick of crowds or sitting on the sidelines and observing the passing show. In fact, in current psychological research, extroversion and introversion are considered the most stable personality traits that differentiate people from each other and that can be reliably measured. Creative individuals, on the other hand, seem to exhibit both traits simultaneously.

6. Creative people are humble and proud at the same time. It is remarkable to meet a famous person who you expect to be arrogant or supercilious, only to encounter self-deprecation and shyness instead. Yet there are good reasons why this should be so. These individuals are well aware that they stand, in Newton's words, "on the shoulders of giants." Their respect for the area in which they work makes them aware of the long line of previous contributions to it, putting their own in perspective. They're also aware of the role that luck played in their own achievements. And they're usually so focused on future projects and current challenges that past accomplishments, no matter how outstanding, are no longer very interesting to them. At the same time, they know that in comparison with others, they have accomplished a great deal. And this knowledge provides a sense of security, even pride.

7. Creative people, to an extent, escape rigid gender role stereotyping. When tests of masculinity/femininity are given to young people, over and over one finds that creative and talented girls are more dominant and tough than other girls, and creative boys are more sensitive and less aggressive than their male peers.

This tendency toward androgyny is sometimes understood in purely sexual terms, and therefore it gets confused with homosexuality. But psychological androgyny is a much wider concept referring to a person's ability to be at the same time aggressive and nurturant, sensitive and rigid, dominant and submissive, regardless of gender. A psychologically androgynous person in effect doubles his or her repertoire of responses. Creative individuals are more likely to have not only the strengths of their own gender but those of the other one, too.

8. Creative people are both rebellious and conservative. It is impossible to be creative without having first internalized an area of culture. So it's difficult to see how a person can be creative without being both traditional and conservative and at the same time rebellious and iconoclastic. Being only traditional leaves an area unchanged; constantly taking chances without regard to what has been valued in the past rarely leads to novelty that is accepted as an improvement. The artist Eva Zeisel, who says that the folk tradition in which she works is "her home," nevertheless produces ceramics that were recognized by the Museum of Modern Art as masterpieces of contemporary design. This is what she says about innovation for its own sake:

"This idea to create something is not my aim. To be different is a negative motive, and no creative thought or created thing grows out of a negative impulse. A negative impulse is always frustrating. And to be different means 'not like this' and 'not like that.' And the 'not like'—that's why postmodernism, with the prefix of 'post,' couldn't work. No negative impulse can work, can produce any happy creation. Only a positive one."

But the willingness to take risks, to break with the safety of tradition, is also necessary. The economist George Stigler is very emphatic in this regard: "I'd say one of the most common failures of able people is a lack of nerve. They'll play safe games. In innovation, you have to play a less safe game, if it's going to be interesting. It's not predictable that it'll go well."

9. Most creative people are very passionate about their work, yet they can be extremely objective about it as well. Without the passion, we soon lose interest in a difficult task. Yet without being objective about it, our work is not very good and lacks credibility. Here is how the historian Natalie Davis puts it:

"I think it is very important to find a way to be detached from what you write, so that you can't be so identified with your work that you can't accept criticism and response, and that is the danger of having as much affect as I do. But I am aware of that and of when I think it is particularly important to detach oneself from the work, and that is something where age really does help."

10. Creative people's openness and sensitivity often exposes them to suffering and pain, yet also to a great deal of enjoyment. Most would agree with Rabinow's words: "Inventors have a low threshold of pain. Things bother them." A badly designed machine causes pain to an inventive engineer, just as the creative writer is hurt when reading bad prose.

Being alone at the forefront of a discipline also leaves you exposed and vulnerable. Eminence invites criticism and often vicious attacks. When an artist has invested years in making a sculpture, or a scientist in developing a theory, it is devastating if nobody cares.

Deep interest and involvement in obscure subjects often goes unrewarded, or even brings on ridicule. Divergent thinking is often perceived as deviant by the majority, and so the creative person may feel isolated and misunderstood.

Perhaps the most difficult thing for creative individuals to bear is the sense of loss and emptiness they experience when, for some reason, they cannot work. This is especially painful when a person feels his or her creativity drying out.

Yet when a person is working in the area of his or her expertise, worries and cares fall away, replaced by a sense of bliss. Perhaps the most important quality, the one that is most consistently present in all creative individuals, is the ability to enjoy the process of creation for its own sake. Without this trait, poets would give up striving for perfection and would write commercial jingles, economists would work for banks where they would earn at least twice as much as they do at universities, and physicists would stop doing basic research and join industrial laboratories where the conditions are better and the expectations more predictable.

Rita Dunn

The Goals and Track Record of Multicultural Education

Paying attention to the varied learning styles of all students will do more to accomplish the goals of multicultural education than misguided programs that often divide children.

*B*ecause multicultural education is a volatile political issue— one with articulate proponents and antagonists on both sides—the research on this topic needs to be examined objectively. Many practices that schools promote make little sense in terms of how multiculturally diverse students learn. Thus, we need to examine the data concerning how poor achievement has been reversed among culturally diverse students in many schools.

What Is Multicultural Education?

Multicultural education originated in the 1960s as a response to the long-standing policy of assimilating immigrants into the melting pot of our dominant American culture (Sobol 1990). Over the past three decades, it has expanded from an attempt to reflect the growing diversity in American classrooms to include curricular revisions that specifically address the academic needs of students. In recent years, it has been distorted by some into a movement that threatens to divide citizens along racial and cultural lines (Schlessinger 1991). Generally, multicultural education has focused on two broad goals: increasing academic achievement and promoting greater sensitivity to cultural differences in an attempt to reduce bias.

Increasing Academic Achievement

Efforts intended to increase the academic achievement of multicultural groups include programs that (1) focus on the research on culturally based learning styles as a step toward determining which teaching styles or methods to use with a particular group of students; (2)

emphasize bilingual or bicultural approaches; (3) build on the language and culture of African- or Hispanic-American students; and (4) emphasize math and science specifically for minority or female students (Banks 1994). Programs in each of these categories are problematic.

■ *Culturally based learning styles.* So long as such programs include reasonable provisions for language and cultural differences, they can help students make

Twenty percent of students in every culture are tactual learners—children who begin concentrating on new and difficult information by manipulating resources with their hands.

the transition into mainstream classes. In that sense, they may be considered similar to other compensatory programs that are not multicultural in their emphasis. As a researcher and advocate of learning styles, however, I would caution against attempting to identify or respond to so-called cultural learning styles. Researchers have clearly established that there is no

Photo courtesy of St. John's University's Center for the Study of Learning and Teaching Styles

Photo courtesy of the Lafayette Academy

At least 20 percent of all students in every culture are kinesthetic learners who cannot sit in their seats for very long; they learn by *doing* rather than by listening or reading.

single or dual learning style for the members of any cultural, national, racial, or religious group. A single learning style does not appear even within a family of four or five (Dunn and Griggs 1995).

■ *Bilingual or bicultural approaches.* Attention to cultural and language differences can be done appropriately or inappropriately. Bi- and trilingualism in our increasingly interdependent world are valuable for, and should be required of, all students. An emphasis on bilingualism for only non-English-speaking children denies English-speaking students skills required for successful interactions internationally. Today, many adults need to speak several languages fluently and to appreciate cultural similarities and differences to succeed in their work.

Another problem arises in those classrooms in which bilingual teachers speak English ungrammatically and haltingly. Such teachers provide a poor model for non-English-speaking chil-

dren, who may remain in bilingual programs for years, unable to make the transition into English-speaking classes. Ultimately, this impairs the ability of these children to move into well-paying professions and careers—the ultimate goal of most of their parents.

■ *Selective cultural programs.* Building on the language and culture of selected groups and not of others suggests bias and bigotry. Parents should teach their children to appreciate and respect their native cultures;

schools should teach children to appreciate and respect all cultures. If the need exists to expand attention to more cultures, let us do that. But let us stop promoting one culture over another with the inevitable result of dividing our children and diminishing their sense of belonging to the dominant culture that is uniquely American—intentionally a combination of the best of all its citizens.

■ *Minority- and gender-based grouping for math and science.* Emphasizing math and science specifically for minority or female students may be based on good intentions, but it ignores the fact that minority students and female students all learn differently from one another and differently from their counterparts —whether those be high- or low-achieving classmates. Providing resources and methods that help all students learn rapidly and well should be the focus for teaching math and science—and every other subject. Are there not males and majority students who fail those subjects? The answer is to change how those subjects are taught, not to isolate certain groups and teach them as though they all have the same style of learning.

Sensitizing Ourselves to Social Agendas

Some multicultural education programs are specifically designed to increase cultural and racial tolerance and reduce bias. These are intended to restructure and desegregate schools, increase contact among the races, and encourage minorities to become teachers; and they lean heavily on cooperative learning (Banks 1994). Sleeter and Grant (1993) describe these programs as emphasizing human relations, incorporating some compensatory goals and curricular revisions to emphasize positive contributions of ethnic and cultural groups, and using learning styles to enhance students' achievement and reduce racial tensions.

Some of these programs emphasize pluralism and cultural equity in American society as a whole, seeking to apply critical thinking skills to a critique of racism and sexism. Others emphasize multilingualism or examine issues from viewpoints other than those of the dominant culture.

In my judgment, these focuses are more political than educational or social. Critical thinking is a requirement for all—not a select few. In addition, whose thinking prevails in these programs, and what are their credentials? Being a minority member or having taken a course does not automatically make a person proficient in teaching minority or female students, or in critiquing social issues. Political debate is helpful to developing young minds; one-sided, preconceived viewpoints are not.

Curriculum and Multicultural Achievement

In the debate over New York's "Children of the Rainbow" curriculum, the ideas of multicultural education captured almost daily headlines. Opponents argued that curriculum change would not increase student achievement, whereas proponents insisted that culturally diverse students performed poorly in school because they could not relate to an American curriculum.

Drew, Dunn, and colleagues (1994) tested how well 38 Cajun students and 29 Louisiana Indian students, all poor achievers, could recall story content and vocabulary immediately and after a delay. Their recall differed significantly when they were instructed with (1) traditional versus multisensory instructional resources and (2) stories in which cultural relevance matched and mismatched students' identified cultural backgrounds. Each subject was presented with four story treatments

(two culturally sensitive and two dominant American) and tested for recall immediately afterward and again one week later. The findings for Cajun subjects indicated significant differences between instructional treatments, with greater recall in each multisensory instructional condition — Cultural-Immediate, Cultural-Delayed, American-Immediate, and American-Delayed. The main effect of instructional treatment for Louisiana Indian subjects was significant as well. Recall scores were even higher when they used multisensory materials for

> What determined whether students mastered the content was how the content was taught, not the content itself.

American stories. No significant main effect emerged for test interval with either group.

This study demonstrated that what determined whether students mastered the content was *how* the content was taught, not the content itself. The culturally sensitive curriculum did not produce significantly higher achievement for these two poorly achieving cultural groups; the methods that were used did.

Teaching Methods and Multicultural Achievement

Other studies of teaching methods revealed even more dramatic results. Before being taught with methods that responded to their learning styles, only 25 percent of special education high school students in a suburban New York school district had passed the required local examinations and state competency tests to receive diplomas. In the first year of the district's learning styles program (1987–88), that number

increased to 66 percent. During the second year, 91 percent of the district's special education students were successful, and in the third year, the results remained constant at 90 percent—with a greater ratio of "handicapped" students passing state competency exams than regular education students (Brunner and Majewski 1990).

Two North Carolina elementary principals reported similarly impressive gains as a result of their learning styles programs. In an impoverished, largely minority school, Andrews (1990) brought student scores that had consistently been in the 30th percentile on the California Achievement Tests to the 83rd percentile over a three-year period by responding to students' learning styles. Shortly thereafter, Stone (1992) showed highly tactual, learning disabled (LD) elementary school students how to learn with Flip Chutes, Electroboards, Task Cards, and Pic-A-Holes while seated informally in rooms where levels of light matched their style preferences. The children were encouraged to study either alone, with a classmate or two, or with their teacher—based on their learning style strengths. Within four months, those youngsters had achieved four months' reading gains on a standardized achievement test—better than they ever had done previously and as well as would have been expected of children achieving at normal levels.

Many professional journals have reported statistically higher scores on standardized achievement and attitude tests as a result of learning style teaching with underachieving and special education students (Dunn, Bruno, Sklar, Zenhausern, and Beaudry 1990; Dunn, Griggs, Olson, Gorman, and Beasley 1995; Klavas 1993; Lemmon 1985; Perrin 1990; Quinn 1993). Indeed, a four-year investigation by the U.S. Office of Education that included on-site visits, interviews, observations, and examinations of national test data concluded that the Dunn and

Dunn Learning Styles Model was one of only a few strategies that had had a positive effect on the achievement of special education students throughout the nation (Alberg, Cook, Fiore, Friend, and Sano 1992).

What Have We Learned?

Research documents that underachieving students —whether they are from other cultures or from the dominant U.S. culture—tend to learn differently from students who perform well in our schools (Dunn and Griggs 1995; Milgram, Dunn, and Price 1993). As indicated in the examples cited earlier, schools with diverse populations reversed academic failure when instruction was changed to complement the children's learning style strengths.

In our book, *Multiculturalism and Learning Style* (Dunn and Griggs 1995), my coauthor and I summarize research findings on each of the major cultural groups in the United States —African Americans, Asian Americans, European Americans, Hispanic Americans, and Native Americans. The research clearly shows that there is no such thing as a cultural group style. There are crosscultural and intracultural similarities and differences among all peoples. Those differences are enriching when understood and channeled positively.

Given this information, I believe it is unwise for schools with limited budgets to support multicultural education in addition to —and apart from — regular education. Instead, schools need to make their instructional delivery systems responsive to how diverse students learn (Dunn 1995).

Educational programs should not separate young children from one another. Any separation becomes increasingly divisive over time and is likely to produce the opposite of what multicultural education is intended to accomplish. Segregated children begin to feel different from and less able than the larger groups of children they see—but are apart from. These feelings can lead to emotional insecurity and a dislike of others.

The United States was founded as a nation intended to absorb people from many nations. Monocultural education in the guise of multicultural education offends the cornerstone of those intentions. The melting pot concept does not diminish one's heritage. It unites the strengths of many cultures into a single, stronger blend of culture to reflect the best of all.

References

Alberg, J., L. Cook, T. Fiore, M. Friend, and S. Sano. (1992). *Educational Approaches and Options for Integrating Students with Disabilities: A Decision Tool.* Triangle Park, N.C.: Research Triangle Institute.

Andrews, R.H. (July–September 1990). "The Development of a Learning Styles Program in a Low Socioeconomic, Underachieving North Carolina Elementary School." *Journal of Reading, Writing, and Learning Disabilities International* 6, 3: 307–314.

Banks, J.A. (1994). *An Introduction to Multicultural Education.* Boston: Allyn and Bacon.

Brunner, C. E., and W. S. Majewski (October 1990). "Mildly Handicapped Students Can Succeed with Learning Styles." *Educational Leadership* 48, 2: 21–23.

Drew, M., R. Dunn, P. Quinn, R. Sinatra, and J. Spiridakis. (1994). "Effects of Matching and Mismatching Minority Underachievers with Culturally Similar and Dissimilar Story Content and Learning Style and Traditional Instructional Practices." *Applied Educational Research Journal* 8, 2: 3–10.

Dunn, R., J. Bruno, R.I. Sklar, R. Zenhausern, and J. Beaudry. (May–June 1990). "Effects of Matching and Mismatching Minority Developmental College Students' Hemispheric Preferences on Mathematics Scores." *Journal of Educational Research* 83, 5: 283–288.

Dunn, R., S.A. Griggs, J. Olson, B. Gorman, and M. Beasley. (1995). "A Meta-Analytic Validation of the Dunn and Dunn Research Learning Styles Model." *Journal of Educational Research* 88, 6: 353–361.

Dunn, R. (1995). *Educating Diverse Learners: Strategies for Improving Current Classroom Practices.* Bloomington, Ind.: Phi Delta Kappa.

Dunn, R., and S.A. Griggs. (1995). *Multiculturalism and Learning Styles: Teaching and Counseling Adolescents.* Westport, Conn: Praeger Publishers, Inc.

Klavas, A. (1993). "In Greensboro, North Carolina: Learning Style Program Boosts Achievement and Test Scores." *The Clearing House* 67, 3: 149–151.

Lemmon, P. (1985). "A School Where Learning Styles Make a Difference." *Principal* 64, 4: 26–29.

Milgram, R. M., R. Dunn, and G.E. Price, eds. (1993). *Teaching and Counseling Gifted and Talented Adolescents: An International Learning Style Perspective.* Westport, Conn.: Praeger Publishers, Inc.

Perrin, J. (October 1990). "The Learning Styles Project for Potential Dropouts." *Educational Leadership* 48, 2: 23–24.

Quinn, R. (1993). "The New York State Compact for Learning and Learning Styles." *Learning Styles Network Newsletter* 15, 1: 1–2.

Schlessinger, A., Jr. (1991). "Report of the Social Studies Syllabus Review Committee: A Dissenting Opinion." In *One Nation, Many Peoples: A Declaration of Cultural Independence,* edited by New York State Social Studies Review and Development Committee. New York: Author.

Sleeter, C.E., and C.A. Grant. (1993). *Making Choices for Multicultural Education: Five Approaches to Race, Class, and Gender.* 2nd ed. New York: Merrill.

Sobol, T. (1990). "Understanding Diversity." *Educational Leadership* 48, 3: 27–30.

Stone, P. (November 1992). "How We Turned Around a Problem School." *Principal* 71, 2: 34–36.

Rita Dunn is Professor, Division of Administrative and Instructional Leadership, and Director, Center for the Study of Learning and Teaching Styles, St. John's University, Grand Central and Utopia Parkways, Jamaica, NY 11439. She is the author of 17 books, including ASCD's *How to Implement and Supervise Learning Style Programs* (1996).

"All Kids Can Learn": Masking Diversity in Middle School

CAROL ANN TOMLINSON

Carol Ann Tomlinson is an assistant professor of educational studies, Curry School of Education, The University of Virginia, Charlottesville.

In the Northwest Territories of Canada, the aboriginal peoples build giant figures roughly in the shape of a human by piling stone upon stone. The primitive-looking shapes, called *inukshuks*, serve a dual purpose. In the heavy snows and ice fogs, they serve as guides to people trying to find their way home. In better weather, they serve as decoys to fool bears and other prey. The inukshuk is placed near a location where a bear may go for food or water. Seeing the looming, human-like form, the bear believes it to be a man and turns away from the inukshuk toward a blind where a hunter hides, waiting for the bear to be frightened and to retreat in the hunter's direction. It is an interesting paradox that inukshuks serve as both guideposts and traps.

We build educational inukshuks too. We construct them to offer us guidance in making critical decisions. Sometimes, however, we become the bear, and the inukshuk becomes our trap. One example of guide-turned-snare is our current buzz-phrase, "All kids can learn." It is particularly pervasive in educational settings, such as middle schools, which promote "educational equity."

Like all clichés, this one reflects some reality. It is invoked as a way of telling teachers not to give up on students whom we might assume to be struggling, at risk, or remedial. The cliché is problematic, however, because rather than pointing middle school educators homeward, it lures us into the dangerous assumption that what benefits one child educationally is bound to benefit others in the same way. At a time in our educational history when middle school learners are more diverse, both culturally and academically, than at any other time in the past, it validates educational practices that mask the diversity. The real problem has never been so much that middle school teachers believe that some kids *can't* learn. The real problem is that, as middle school educators, we've

exhibited for decades a belief that all kids can learn the same things, in the same way, over the same time span.

Cases in Point: A Tale of Two Learners

Early in my career as a middle school teacher, I taught Golden and Jonathan during third period English. Eyes downcast and hand over his mouth, Golden whispered to me on the first day of school that he could not read. He was correct. At fifteen, he was a seventh grader who did not know the alphabet well and took a long time to grasp simple meanings, even when ideas were delivered orally or in pictures. He was a gentle boy, beautiful and persistent, and resilient in a quiet sort of way. I spent much of my time that year looking inside myself and learning from Golden how to teach reading to a fifteen-year-old and still have him feel fifteen. I was not trained to teach Golden, and I don't know that I did brilliantly with him academically, but I tried, and we cared for each other, and we both made progress in our learning.

Later that year, I discovered Jonathan. He'd been in the class all along—at the table with Golden, actually. It wasn't that I had been unaware of his physical presence. I knew he was there, interacted with him in the sort of way that's invited by the presence of 150 young bodies passing through the door each day. It was April when I discovered Jonathan's mental presence. It happened one day when Jonathan responded with a sigh to my query about whether anyone could explain what a symbol is in literature. He waited until it was clear no one else was going to answer. Then, sighing not with impatience so much as with resignation, Jonathan explained, "A symbol is a concrete representation of an abstract entity." He was right too. And it's as good a definition as I've ever read or heard. I wasn't trained to teach Jonathan either—or even to notice him. He made good grades. He was no trouble. I was grateful. In April, I discovered that my magical seventh-grade English class was as poorly suited to Jonathan as to Golden.

I concluded that year of teaching with my own two symbols clearly in mental view. They were concrete representations of the abstract reality that middle school stu-

From *The Clearing House*, January/February 1995, pp. 163-166. © 1995 by the Helen Dwight Reid Educational Foundation.
Reprinted by permission of Heldref Publications, 1319 Eighteenth Street, NW, Washington, DC 20036-1802.

dents differ immensely and that my previous notion of developing a single lesson plan that would reach them all was unrealistic. I always believed that both Jonathan and Golden could learn. Like most other teachers, I could not have continued to show up at school without that conviction. I would be a better teacher for Golden and Jonathan if I had the opportunity to teach them today, not because I have been a recent convert to believing "all kids can learn," but because I have spent a sizable portion of my career learning to respond to the reality that students have *different* learning needs.

Neglecting Golden

I have also spent a great deal of my career as a middle school educator being dismayed at our inability at this level to embrace Jonathan and Golden simultaneously and in ways appropriate for their individual needs. For at least a decade, students like Golden have drifted through junior high or middle school compensatory classes where they were taught to read in the same standard ways that proved unsuccessful during the previous year. As teachers, we weren't hostile to these students; we just accepted them as "limited." We understood little about how school must look to them. We certainly underestimated the impact of poverty and culturally different homes—or maybe we just didn't look outside the schoolhouse door often or long enough. Nature and nurture challenged Golden's learning, and a traditional, single lens view of students and schooling aggravated the problem.

Golden is not only a symbol for me as a teacher. He is a three-dimensional case for the urgency of addressing the needs of at-risk learners in American middle schools. Powerful cases for increasing attention to at-risk learners have been made by many sensitive and convincing writers (e.g., Kozol 1991; Freedman 1990; McLaren 1989). It is clear that schooling as it is typically structured still falls short of addressing the immense needs of many of America's young who are like Golden.

Points to Ponder on Golden's Behalf

Of course there is a need for educational improvement for at-risk learners, for "educational equity." The guidepost of equity becomes a trap, however, if we assume that equity for Golden means that all middle school students must learn the same things, in the same way, over the same time span. We need to think carefully about at least three propositions in Golden's behalf as we plan for his years in middle school:

Golden's educational challenges are real. Some students like Golden contend with specific physiological impairments in the intake or the processing of information. Many like him come to middle school lacking food or affection or security. Many come to middle school with communication patterns or views of time or ways of relating to peers and adults that differ in meaningful ways from those of the majority of educators who will

work with them. The list of challenges can be long and varied. Each item on the list can affect learning in powerful ways.

Ignoring Golden's differences is damaging. Traditional school practices seldom serve Golden well. Many educators make compelling arguments for movement away from traditional schooling for *all* children. The strengths of those arguments notwithstanding, many children have at least survived traditional schooling with functional skills in place. That has not often been the case for students like Golden. It may be that the ways in which we have most poorly served previous Goldens have stemmed from our assumptions that the culture that reflects the worldview of many children accurately reflects Golden's as well, and that the ways in which many children successfully take in and process information will yield success for Golden also. Those educators who have been triumphant with students like Golden have deeply understood the students' differences and have made powerful adjustments in their responses to those differences.

Most educational generalists are currently unprepared to respond appropriately to Golden's needs. Why can't Golden read at fifteen? How do we motivate him to try again for one more year? What if his peers reject schooling as well? What can we do to make his effort worth the risk? Why doesn't he follow directions that seem clear enough to other students? How do we contend with our curriculum when Golden can't read the basic vocabulary list in the rear of the text? What do we do if his anger causes him to boil over in the classroom? Why doesn't he look us in the eye when we talk with him? Why does he seem unconcerned at turning in assignments late? How do we keep him hopeful when we also operate in the tradition of keeping a gradebook? Our understandings of educational handicaps are shallow. Our understandings of cultural diversity are sparse. Our definitions of instruction are narrow. Our sense of fairness hangs on norms. We know how to teach groups better than individuals. In middle school, regular classroom teachers may (or may not) be prepared to work on Golden's self-concept. We currently know of little to do for his sense of self-efficacy.

Rejecting Jonathan

At least in our rhetoric, middle school education in recent years has embraced Golden. The irony is that, in doing so, we seem to feel it necessary to reject Jonathan.

I happened upon a colleague in an airport recently. She is an enthusiastic educator and an effective staff developer for teachers of middle school students. As we walked down a corridor, she said she had been puzzling about the tensions that exist between middle school and gifted education and that she had discussed it with a nationally known middle school educator and leader. "I think I understand now," she said. "In middle school, we are for the underdog. Gifted kids are so far ahead.

What we are interested in is making sure the other kids catch up. Gifted kids are just so privileged. They don't need us like at-risk learners do."

Another nationally respected educator with deep middle school roots said to me recently, "Gifted education just isn't interesting. It's not important."

In a recent issue of the *Washington Post* (Denny 1994), a staff editorialist called for the abolition of special programs for gifted learners, advocating that all students be exposed to "the same challenging curriculum."

Middle school students mirror our adult rejection of high-end achievement. In our schools, notes the president of the Educational Testing Service (Anrig 1992), we apply derogatory names to our brightest students. These days, they are *nerds* or *dweebs*. Students like Jonathan understand the messages. In a recent study, such adolescents indicated that they wanted to do well in school but not exceptionally well. To do too well is to be rejected by the "in crowd." To be perceived as "a brain" is to be banished.

Points to Ponder on Jonathan's Behalf

It is not acceptable for middle school educators to deny or dismiss students like Jonathan, any more than it is to turn our interest away from Golden. There are at least three propositions that middle school educators need to consider in determining a course of action for Jonathan and his tribe:

High-end talent is a reality. Some kids learn faster than others and with a greater depth of understanding. At twelve, Greg understood the physics of black holes and of time. Ray could discuss the imagery and symbolism of Poe. Theresa was more than conversant with calculus. These youngsters once again give evidence that while it is true that all kids can learn, they learn in different ways, at different rates, with differing facility and insight. Advanced talent is not everything, but it is real. It is an important human resource.

It is okay to have talent as a learner. It is not elitist to be an advanced learner any more than it is elitist to be taller than average or a better-than-average soccer player. It is the way some kids are. Middle schools need to be in the talent development business, eager to latch onto and develop talent whenever it surfaces—and to help it surface when it does not do so on its own. If middle school does not celebrate and extend the talent of high-end learners, it is at risk as an institution. No organization grows that does not accept the challenge of those of its members who push against its ceilings and cause them to rise.

Highly talented kids need teacher assistance in developing their potential. In part, the learning capacity of students like Golden is compromised by parents, neighborhoods, teachers, or adults in society at large who fail to become mentors and advocates. Jonathan may or may not have been failed by home or neighborhood or society at large.

There are Jonathans in the most impoverished settings. Even a Jonathan from a supportive home, however, needs teachers. It is the teacher who is the keeper of knowledge, a gadfly for persistence, an encourager when the risk seems too great. Twelve-year-old Kathleen understood when she wrote a poem to her teacher:

Push me. See how far I go.
Work me 'til I drop. Then pick me up.
Open a door, and make me run to it before it closes.
Teach me so that I might learn.
But then show me the Tunnel of Experience and let me
   walk through it alone.
And when, near the end, I look back, and I see you in
   the opening with another,
I shall smile.

Points to Ponder for Both Golden and Jonathan

If middle schools are going to be good places for Jonathan and Golden, and if middle school educators are going to move past slogans to action, we must consider several propositions:

There is no time for a linear approach to student needs. We have a pattern in American schools of focusing on high-end learners to the exclusion of troubled learners for a period of time—then turning our rhetoric and practice in the direction of troubled learners, to the exclusion of advanced learners. All the while, we lament that attention to learning needs of those groups robs the "average" student. In middle school, we have been prone to embrace the at-risk learner and to alternate between irritation at, and denial of, the high-end learner. So long as schools take a sort of one-at-a-time approach to its clients, schools will fail many more children than necessary. A given child has only one passage through the middle school years. If it is not Jonathan's "turn" to be attended to and valued, or Golden's, or any other student's, we have a moral obligation to inform his parents that he is not currently "in vogue" and therefore not a priority for talent development.

"The same challenging curriculum" is a myth. The science curriculum that intrigued Greg would have stupefied most other preadolescents. Golden could not have understood *oral* renditions of Poe in seventh grade, let alone *print* versions. It seems virtually impossible that he could have understood the tapestry of symbols in Poe's works that year. Do we make "the same challenging math curriculum" one that Golden can master? One that more typical seventh graders can master? Or do we accept the calculus curriculum that challenged eleven-year-old Theresa and attempt to challenge *all* seventh graders with it? Embracing diversity is our challenge in education, not pretending singularity.

One-size-fits-all instruction is not an acceptable option. Jonathan and Golden differ significantly from each other and from many of their age-mates. If we advocate instructional arrangements in which middle schoolers are treated largely or wholly alike, we will, in the long run, be as unfair to Golden as we were in the days when we overlooked him or when we subscribed to the notion of remediation. We will also continue to assume, by comparison with the norm, that Jonathan is fine and producing high quality work. Middle school students will become discouraged or disenchanted. Middle school teachers will become weary and weighted with the guilt they carry when it is evident that they are losing students. In the end, we will, as we have in the past, revert to separate classes within a very few years.

We need to teach teachers to adjust for student differences, not trick them into doing so. Much of the argument for heterogeneity is that teachers lower expectations for students in homogeneous remedial classes. If teachers receive all students en masse, the logic goes, they automatically raise expectations for struggling learners because of the greater mass of comparatively more advanced learners. There are problems with that theory. First, such a plan will as likely *lower* expectations for students like Jonathan who were in advanced classes as it will raise them for students who were in slower-paced classes. Second, it perpetuates the idea that a single level of expectations will somehow be appropriate for all students. It skirts the more significant reality that in an increasingly diverse classroom, teachers will need to identify individual needs and respond in various ways to those needs. It is also insulting in its implications that (*a*) teachers cannot learn to adjust expectations proactively, and, therefore, (*b*) students must be moved about in ways that cause reactive teacher response.

Differentiated classrooms are a rarity. If we intend to recognize and address individual differences and needs within heterogeneous settings, we have a long way to go. Most teachers are like I was—stymied by the presence of Golden and unaware that Jonathan had any real problems. National studies indicate that little appropriate differentiation of instruction for academically diverse learners currently takes place in classrooms (Tomlinson et al., 1994; Archambault, Westberg, Brown, Hallmark, Zhang, and Emmons 1993; McIntosh, Vaughn, Schumm, Haager, and Lee 1993; Tomlinson In press). The paucity of differentiation has a multitude of causes: our own long histories as students in one-size-fits-all classrooms, our own experiences as practitioners of one-size-fits-all instruction, our general lack of preservice and inservice preparation in teaching academically diverse learners, teach-to-the-test mandates that cause us to drag all learners through the same content, over-dependence on text-driven curricula, discouraging student-teacher ratios,

choppy time blocks that invite dealing with students as a herd, and lack of administrative and policy support for the long-term change process that is required to alter habitual teaching behaviors. There is little guidance in the middle school literature that exhorts us to differentiate instruction or that offers us concrete guidance in how to do so.

Truth or Trap

Golden and Jonathan are real. Most middle school teachers have taught them. Odds are, most of us have taught them less well than they deserve because we taught them as though they were alike. We have to move beyond intoning the belief that both can learn. We know that. It's why we became teachers—why we stayed on. Rather, we need to confront the harder truths: that middle schoolers differ greatly in the ways they learn and in their learning needs; that middle school educators have to be serious students of learner differences and have to respond effectively to those differences; that single-size instruction is going to be a misfit for many middle schoolers; and that we cannot be truly effective so long as we pretend that Golden and Jonathan can flourish in a learning environment that offers them both "the same challenging curriculum."

The inukshuk is out there, stone piled upon stone. Jonathan and Golden need middle school educators who will make it a guidepost rather than a trap.

REFERENCES

Anrig, G. 1992. What we can learn from the Second International Assessment of Educational Progress. Prepared remarks for press conference. Washington, D.C. (5 February).

Archambault, F., K. Westberg, S. Brown, B. Hallmark, W. Zhang, and C. Emmons. 1993. Classroom practices used with gifted third and fourth grade students. *Journal for the Education of the Gifted* 16(2): 103–19.

Denny, S. 1994. How Fairfax fails the "normal" student. *Washington Post* (14 August): C-10.

Freedman, S. 1990. *Small victories: The real world of a teacher, her students and their high school.* New York: Harper and Row.

Kozol, J. 1991. *Savage inequalities: Children in America's schools.* New York: Crown.

McIntosh, R., S. Vaughn, J. Shumm, D. Haager, and O. Lee. 1993. Observations of students with learning disabilities in general education classrooms. *Exceptional Children* 60(3): 249–61.

McLaren, P. 1989. *Life in schools: An introduction to critical pedagogy in the foundations of education.* New York: Longman.

Tomlinson, C. In press. Deciding to differentiate instruction in middle school: One school's journey.

Tomlinson, C., E. Tomchin, C. Callahan, C. Adams, P. Pizzat-Tinnin, C. Cunningham, B. Moore, L. Lutz, C. Roberson, N. Eiss, M. Landrum, S. Hunsaker, and M. Imbeau. 1994. Practices of preservice teachers related to gifted and other academically diverse learners. *Gifted Child Quarterly* 38(3): 106–14.

Multiculturalism:
Practical Considerations
for Curricular Change

TONY R. SANCHEZ

Tony R. Sanchez is an assistant professor of education at Indiana University Northwest, Gary, Indiana.

Many school districts today are jumping on the multicultural bandwagon by adopting, or at least encouraging, a more divisified curriculum. Proponents of multiculturalism call for an interdisciplinary approach that draws from and spans all subject areas, an approach that I believe is the most effective. I offer here a framework designed to be useful to teachers who want to change their personal or curricular perspective from one that is "mainstream" to one that is more "diverse" and are willing to incorporate that new perspective into whatever subject matter they teach.

Unfortunately, misconstruing the purposes or definition of multicultural education, many teachers either back off from it entirely or teach about different groups sequentially, resulting in a fragmented and isolated treatment. We do the latter when we assign specific groups to specific months (Black History Month, Hispanic Heritage Month, Women's History Month). During one of these periods, the attitude is that teachers will deal with that group for thirty days (maximum) and then return to the mainstream curriculum. Multiculturalism, however, belongs within the framework of the existing curriculum.

The Teacher's Role

By exposing our students to other cultures (whether the contributions of various groups or nonmainstream perspectives of an event or concept), we help them learn about other people's lifestyles and values. This awareness in turn may alter negative, stereotypic thinking, reduce intolerance, and promote cooperation (Cohen 1986). It will also expand *your* personal horizons as well as your students'.

As an educator interested in such an outcome, what might your creed be? I suspect something like this: *Within my course I will promote the recognition and understanding of diversity, and teach respect for it. By doing so, I hope not only to provide personal enrichment but also, through my teaching and actions, to help develop positive, productive interactions and attitudes.*

To put this creed into action, you most likely will do the following: teach the perspectives of the mainstream culture (don't assume students already know them); teach the perspectives of other cultures (with the message: they're equally valid to some); and examine similarities and differences between cultures (Hernandez 1989). This last point is certainly the most challenging; *both* similarities and differences should be addressed so that your students move from merely tolerating differences to viewing them as acceptable, desirable, and valuable (Noar 1989).

Implementing a multicultural curriculum requires specific components. These include (1) a teacher willing to critically evaluate his or her personal perspectives, (2) instructional materials that provide diverse but accurate perspectives, and (3) general goals and objectives.

Analyzing Your Attitude

As the teacher, you implement and guide the questioning, reasoning, analysis, and truth-seeking in your classroom. As such, you must consider your personal attitudes toward your subject area—negative and positive—and the fact that they can't be hidden from your students. What exactly is your level of commitment to the value of diverse perspectives?

Coming to grips with your values and attitudes, changing some, and developing sensitivity to diversity will require time—and courage. It will depend on your willingness to work on your new perspective. Without this commitment, you may find yourself saying, "I'm not very comfortable with this diverse curriculum I'm trying out, but I think it's working out." What that really means is, "It's not working because I don't really believe in it." If that becomes the case, back off. Don't deceive yourself and your students. The payoff for this self-examination will be that the ugliness of prejudice, rejection, and exclusion—all results of ignorance and misinformation—will have no place in your classroom. You will be sensitizing your students not only to the mechanics of learning but also to their own worth and value. The rest of the process will be anticlimactic by comparison with this step.

Choosing Instructional Materials

In the next step of the process, you examine and select instructional materials that reflect accurate, quality (i.e., true) information. Choose materials that you're comfortable with, that won't require a radical change in your style (a change that many teachers needlessly fear).

Danger of Relying on Textbooks

Textbooks, as we know, account for most of the teaching/learning process (Sewall 1987). Furthermore, "Teachers tend to not only rely on, but believe in, the textbook as the source of knowledge" (Fitzgerald 1979).

Recent evaluations indicate that a diverse curriculum requires a change in this attitude. Various cultural/ethnic groups have brought attention to bear on the depiction of their respective cultures in textbooks (Garcia and Florez-Tighe 1986). The attitude shared by these groups can be summed up as follows: "The sole false perspective is that which claims to be the only one there is" (Gasset, cited in Smith and Otero 1982). The multicultural movement does *not* require abandonment of the mainstream perspective. This would only lead to isolated enclaves, fragmentation, and polarization. On the contrary, the movement promotes integrating a variety of perspectives, which must include the mainstream (Banks 1991).

Bias in textbooks appears in several forms, including stereotyping, omissions, distortions, overrepresentation in certain contexts, romanticized portrayals, token representations, and biased language. As educators, we need to examine and evaluate these materials in terms of content, language, and illustrations. Though textbook bias has been reduced in some quarters, it still remains, its manifestations sometimes blatant and other times subtle (Garcia and Florez-Tighe 1986).

How do we go about identifying such bias? We will need to explore, compare, contrast, question, and evaluate information from multiple sources (which may include students, peers, and the community). Eventually, we will strengthen our evaluative skills so that we can uncover discrepancies and contradictions. Analyzing and questioning the accuracy of the content we teach may represent a major departure for us, but it may also keep us from becoming "adults who believe everything they read—or read only what they wish to

believe" (Klein 1985, 27). Passing on critical reading skills to our students may ultimately be our greatest legacy to them.

Guidelines for Multicultural Curriculum

Here are some basic guidelines to keep in mind as you purposively change your curricular perspective (Gaines 1992):

Go beyond a trivializing, "tourist" curriculum. A diversity curriculum is more than holidays, special months, food, and costumes. Rather, it means coming to know the values, viewpoints, and meaningful traditions that characterize individuals and groups (and you can still include food and costumes). These interpretations must be regular, built-in components of your subject area.

Go beyond tokenism. Do you enrich your class with African American or Hispanic perspectives simply because you have some black or Mexican students? Or, instead, do you employ multiple, unbiased perspectives because you recognize the value of alternative interpretations and want to promote acceptance and respect for different experiences and viewpoints? The former approach is characteristic of a teacher who doesn't really believe in or is uncomfortable with the notion of diversity in his or her subject area; the teacher's efforts will come off as phony. The latter approach characterizes a teacher who appreciates diversity.

Go beyond stereotyping. Give students continuous opportunities to examine images for accuracy. Too often a student's stereotypic perception goes unchallenged and therefore becomes solidified as truth. In this regard, you must expect to handle incidences of bias and ignorance that arise in the classroom. What should you do on such occasions? Here are four pieces of advice that I have found helpful:

1. *Don't ignore comments or questions that reflect misinformation.* Address the issue while a direct connection to the goals of the curriculum can still be made. Your silence on such matters can only be interpreted as confirmation.

2. *Don't excuse comments or questions that could be interpreted as culturally or racially insulting.* The students who are targets of such remarks (which can very quickly escalate into full-blown classroom incidents) will segregate themselves for protection—something that you didn't provide.

3. *Don't be afraid to step in to handle and clarify a situation.* Doing something on the spot is certainly preferable to doing nothing and allowing things to fester.

4. *Don't forget your commitment.* Your mission in establishing a diverse curriculum is to expand your students' knowledge so that they will develop more positive attitudes and behaviors that will enable them to interact effectively in our diverse society. Your responsibility in the mission is consistency.

Goals and Objectives

What learning outcomes should a multicultural curriculum promote? The following goals are frequently found in a diversified curriculum (Hernandez 1989; Kosmoski 1989):

To help students recognize and understand the values and experiences of one's own ethnic/cultural heritage

To promote sensitivity to diverse ethnicities/cultures through exposure to other cultural perspectives

To develop an awareness and respect for the similarities and differences among diverse groups

To identify, challenge, and dispel ethnic/cultural stereotyping, prejudice, and discrimination in behavior, textbooks, and other instructional materials

Goals are, of course, intended to be guidelines. A multicultural curriculum can only be effective when the teacher is given choices as to how to achieve such goals within his or her subject area or grade level. An inappropriate or too narrowly focused curriculum—a product of haste and pressure to conform—will likely result when teachers are not free to make those decisions. How to integrate a multicultural perspective into the curriculum rather than making it a blatant "add-on" is the main issue they face. Teachers usually approach this task by trial and error. Using a single, all-encompassing model to implement a diverse curriculum is not a good idea because no model can provide what is effective for all students at all times and under all circumstances. Rather, the teacher must systematically incorporate content and strategies in a comfortable balance. The process requires time, with the teacher "testing the waters" on a by-unit or by-lesson basis.

As an initial effort, many teachers employ a "cultural" unit or lesson in their standard monocentric curricula. It is usually additive instead of integral, but it serves the important purpose of "breaking the multicultural ice." Such an initial effort is almost always necessary to allow the educator to comfortably ease into a truly diverse curriculum.

Development and implementation of a multicultural curriculum must eventually be evaluated for effectiveness (California State Department of Education 1979). What must be assessed? Three chief components are (1) achievement; (2) student behavior; and (3) student attitudes (Hernandez 1989). Achievement, the primary focus of American education, can be fairly assessed through various conventional measures. Student behavior can be monitored

and evaluated formally (questionnaires, surveys, discussion groups, reduced number of disruptive incidents) and informally (teacher observations of cooperative interactions, voluntary student participation and assistance, student willingness to explore cultural similarities and differences). Student attitudes are the most difficult to assess for change. The validity of evaluation is dependent on the instrument used and should always be interpreted with caution. Research indicates that attitude change as a goal of multicultural education is indeed feasible. Studies of the use of content and strategies to change cultural/ethnic/racial attitudes and reduce prejudice show positive results, even when complex, multiple variables, such as age, socioeconomic status, and social institutions, are involved (Sanchez 1991). Establishing the foundation for such change—through diverse content and teacher modeling—cannot guarantee positive attitude changes. As educators, however, we must be willing to take the chance that this endeavor will promote understanding, acceptance, and respect.

REFERENCES

Banks, J. A. 1991. *Teaching strategies for ethnic studies.* 5th ed. Needham Heights, Mass.: Allyn and Bacon.

California State Department of Education. 1979. *Guide for multicultural education.* Sacramento, Calif.: California State Department of Education.

Cohen, C. B. 1986. Teaching about ethnic diversity. *ERIC Digest* 32: 1–2.

Fitzgerald, F. 1979. *America revisited.* Boston, Mass.: Atlantic Monthly Press/Little, Brown.

Gaines, L. 1992. What you can do. *Creative Classroom* (Sept.): 115.

Garcia, J., and V. Florez-Tighe. 1986. The portrayal of Blacks, Hispanics, and Native Americans in recent basal reading series. *Equity and Excellence* 22(4-6): 72–76.

Hernandez, H. 1989. *Multicultural education.* Columbus, Ohio: Merrill.

Klein, G. 1985. *Reading into racism.* London: Routledge and Kegan Paul.

Kosmoski, G. J. 1989. *Multicultural education.* Chicago: Third World Press.

Noar, G. 1989. *Sensitizing teachers to ethnic groups.* Needham Heights, Mass.: Allyn and Bacon.

Sanchez, T. R. 1991. *The effects of knowledge acquisition about Blacks on the racial attitudes of White high school sophomores.* Ann Arbor, Mich.: University Microfilms, Inc.

Sewall, G. T. 1987. *American history textbooks: An assessment of quality.* New York: Columbia University, Teachers College, Educational Excellence Network.

Smith, G. R., and G. Otero. 1982. *Teaching about cultural awareness.* Denver, Col.: University of Denver, Center for Teaching International Relations.

Learning and Instruction

Information Processing/Cognitive Learning (Articles 19–21)
Learning (Articles 22–26)
Instructional Strategies (Articles 27–29)

Learning can be broadly defined as a relatively permanent change in behavior or thinking due to experience. Learning is not a result of change due to maturation. Changes in behavior and thinking of students result from complex interactions between their individual characteristics and environmental factors. A continuing challenge in education is understanding these interactions so that learning can be enhanced. This unit focuses on approaches within educational psychology that represent different ways of viewing the learning process and related instructional strategies. Each approach to learning emphasizes a different set of personal and environmental factors that influence certain behaviors. While no one approach can fully explain learning, each is a valuable contribution to our knowledge about the process.

The discussion of each learning approach includes suggestions for specific techniques and methods of teaching to guide teachers in understanding student behavior and in making decisions about how to teach. The articles in this section reflect a recent emphasis on applied research conducted in schools and on constructivist theories. The relatively large number of articles on information processing/cognitive learning and instruction, as opposed to behaviorism, also reflects a change in emphasis. Behaviorism, however, remains important in our understanding of learning and instruction.

Researchers have recently made significant advances in understanding the way our minds work. Information processing refers to the way that the mind receives sensory information, stores it as memory, and recalls it for later use. This procedure is basic to all learning, no matter what teaching approach is taken, and we know that the method used in processing information determines to some extent how much and what we remember. The essays in the first subsection present some of the fundamental principles of information processing, including important new developments in human intelligence.

For years, behaviorism was the best-known approach to learning. Most practicing and prospective teachers are familiar with concepts such as classical conditioning, reinforcement, and punishment, and there is no question

that behaviorism has made significant contributions to understanding learning. But behaviorism has also been subject to much misinterpretation, in part because it seems so simple. In fact, the effective use of behavioristic principles is complex and demanding, as debate presented in the articles in the second subsection point out.

Humanistic/social psychological learning emphasizes the affective, social, moral, and personal development of students. Humanistic learning involves acceptance of the uniqueness of each individual, stressing character, feelings, values, and self-worth. To the humanist, learning is not simply a change in behavior or thinking; learning is also the discovery of the personal meaning of information. Social psychology is the study of the nature of interpersonal relationships in social situations. In education, this approach looks at teacher-pupil relationships and group processes to derive principles of interaction that affect learning.

Instructional strategies are the teacher behaviors and methods of conveying information that affect learning. Teaching methods or techniques can vary greatly, depending on objectives, group size, types of students, and personality of the teacher. For example, discussion classes are generally more effective for enhancing thinking skills than are individualized sessions or lectures. For the final subsection, major instructional strategies to illustrate a variety of approaches have been selected. The first subsection article describes how the classroom climate can be assessed and the findings used for teaching. Strategies to promote learning through the use of cognitive maps and study guides are summarized in the next article, while the article by David Brown examines the growing importance of technology in the classroom.

Looking Ahead: Challenge Questions

Compare and contrast the different approaches to learning. What approach do you think is best, and why? What factors are important to your answer (e.g., objectives, types of students, setting, personality of the teacher)?

What teaching strategies could you use to promote greater student retention of material? What are good ways to attract and keep students' attention? Must a teacher be an "entertainer"? Why or why not?

How can a teacher promote positive self-esteem, values, character, caring, and attitudes? How are they related to cognitive learning? How much emphasis should be put on cultivating character or positive student interactions? How would you create a "caring" classroom? Discuss whether or not this would interfere with achievement of cognitive learning targets.

How can technology be used productively in the classroom? What learning theories should be used as a basis for instruction that utilizes technology?

Making Information Memorable: Enhanced Knowledge Retention and Recall Through the Elaboration Process

DONN RITCHIE and BELINDA DUNNICK KARGE

In recent years there has been a concerted effort to reduce the amount of instructional time teachers spend on facts in lieu of increasing students' ability to comprehend a domain's higher level principles (American Association for the Advancement of Science, 1993; National Council of Teachers of Mathematics, 1991). When we consider the vast amount of information in most subject areas, this strategy seems wise, for the chance of a teacher being able to cover all the basic knowledge in any one subject area is remote. Regardless of the subject area, however, higher order processes (i.e., analysis, synthesis, and evaluation) are based on specific facts, and these facts must be understood before higher level concepts or principles can be grasped. Many students, including those with special needs, may experience difficulty when attempting to learn basic facts, retain new information, or generalize knowledge from one setting to another (e.g., from the learning disabilities resource room to the general classroom). So how can we best help these students acquire, retain, and recall knowledge?

Although teachers cannot alter students' preferred learning method, initial background knowledge, or innate intelligence, they can incorporate instructional techniques that help students to retain and recall information (Denham & Lieberman, 1980; Englert, 1983). One such technique that helps make information more memorable is a process known as elaboration.

Elaboration

Cognitive psychologists generally agree that for information to be retained in the long-term memory, it is imperative that students elaborate on the new material (Anderson, 1990; Gagné, 1985; Roehler & Duffy, 1984). Elaboration occurs when students think about a specific piece of information and construct a memory link between that piece and some related information already held in their long-term memory. However, the related information is more substantive than that used in literal comprehension. To elaborate, students must go through a thoughtful pause during which new memories are created and linked to existing mental structures (i.e., the new information is integrated with prior knowledge). This link could be anything that serves to connect the new information to that stored in long-term memory, such as inferences, continuations, examples, or details (Gagné, 1985).

With the continual expansion of knowledge, many teachers feel obligated to increase the amount of information delivered in their classes. When this occurs, information is often presented without time for students to use self-generated or teacher-generated elaborations. Even students with a strong desire to learn will suffer a reduction in their ability to recall information in these situations. In fact, Anderson (1990) found that students who elaborate on material, even without knowing of a later test, achieve higher test scores than students who are aware of an impending test but do not have time to elaborate.

Many researchers have suggested that strategy deficits relate directly to many of the educational problems that students with special needs encounter (Deshler & Schumaker, 1986; Paris & Jacobs, 1984; Simmons, Kameenui, & Darch, 1988). A strategy is an individual's approach to a task (Deshler & Lenz, 1989). Because the ability to recall information is such an important aspect of school learning, a variety of memory improvement strate-

Donn Ritchie *is an associate professor in the Department of Educational Technology at San Diego State University.* ***Belinda Dunnick Karge*** *is a professor in the Department of Special Education at California State University, Fullerton.*

gies have been identified and researched. These strategies are taught to students either intentionally or intuitively by concerned teachers and parents. They are also offered in formal courses and sold to the public by private firms. Many of the procedures are somewhat general. They prompt students to elaborate on material simply by directing them to paraphrase, summarize, draw inferences, or generate a series of questions and answers. Other methods are more specific and prescribe methods to elaborate individual facts or lessons.

Sometimes the cognitive strategies necessary for efficient and accurate learning are unknown to the low achieving student. A grammatical rule may be learned, yet the student may not be able to generalize the rule and use it when writing a paragraph or an essay (Lucking & Manning, 1996). The students need to be taught specific elaborative methods to assure proper generalization of the knowledge they have attained.

In this article we examine 11 elaborative methods (see Table 1). Rather than provide abstract concepts, each method is illustrated with a specific example. We have taken examples from a geology class, specifically on formations generated by erosion. It is important to note, however, that the elaborative methods we suggest apply to all subject domains.

Microlevel Elaborations

Although there are numerous types, elaborations can be divided into two basic groups: microlevel and macrolevel elaborations. Whereas macrolevel elaborations help students to establish mental models that facilitate comprehension of entire lessons, microlevel elaborations help students remember specific pieces of information in the lesson. To examine microlevel elaborations, it helps to divide them into two subgroups: transformational and situational elaborations (see Table 1).

Transformational elaborations. Students sometimes lack basic knowledge structures in a content domain to which new information can be related. In these cases, elaborations can be made through a transformation of the new material (Levin, 1982, as cited in Pressley, Johnson, & Symons, 1987). This transformation is accomplished by associating the new material with a word which is acoustically similar, by using visual stimuli to identify critical attributes, or by rearranging the pieces of information into a new presentation. In other words, the new material is coded by introducing relationships that are neither naturally nor semantically inherent in it.

There are three distinct types of transformational microlevel elaborations. Probably the most common is the listing of keywords. This elaboration has its strongest practicality when two or more facts need to be tied together, such as in vocabulary definitions. In this process, the student first establishes an association between the new word and an acoustically similar word (keyword) already in the student's vocabulary. Next, the student encodes a meaningful relationship between the keyword and the information to be associated with the new word. An example of this type of elaboration, one common in geology classes, helps students remember where stalactites and stalagmites form in caves. Instead of having students memorize the points of formation by rote, the teacher can explain that stalactites have to hold on tight (tite) because they hang from the ceiling. This association provides the new vocabulary word, *stalactite*, with a link to its meaning. The keyword method is especially useful when forming associations between pieces of information that, for the student, may have no obvious or logical relationship to one another (especially important for students with learning disabilities and young children).

A second type of transformational microlevel elaboration is mathemagenic (Merrill, 1983). This elaboration requires the teacher or student to identify a critical attribute, with the help of a visual stimulus, such as arrows, boldface type, or colors, to draw attention to an important feature. An example would be for a teacher to circle the letter *g* in *stalagmite*, and the letter *c* in *stalactite*. If the visual aid is coupled with the use of a keyword mnemonic that states that *g* stands for *ground* and *c* stands for *ceiling*, students should more easily remember which formation is located on the floor and which is located on the ceiling of a cave. Providing students with a visual model has been found to improve the performance of students with learning disabilities considerably (Rivera & Smith, 1988).

TABLE 1
Elaboration Names and Implementation Procedures

Microlevel	Implementation
Transformational	Alter content to make it memorable.
Keyword	Associate to acoustically similar word.
Mathemagenic	Identify critical attribute with visual stimulus.
Representational	Reconfigure material to personal format.
Situational	Build on meaning found in context.
Precise contextual	Add additional content to strengthen link in context.
Imagery	Have students visualize the content.
Prerequisite	Introduce related material prior to content.

Macrolevel	Implementation
Generality	Compare new content to what students already know.
Advanced organizer, comparative	Compare to existing knowledge in this subject.
Experiential	Compare to students' personal experiences.
Analogy	Compare to knowledge in different subject domain.
General-to-detailed	Present global idea, then relate to specific content.
Epitome	Teach simple, concrete ideas related to lesson content
Advanced organizer, expository	Teach abstract ideas before lesson content.

The final type of transformational microlevel elaboration is representational. In this method, the student constructs a new means of representing the information, by using a chart, graph, drawing, or formula (Merrill, 1983). Representational elaborations allow students to rearrange information and then encode it in a novel or personal way, which makes it easier to recall at a later time. One form of representational elaboration, which is gaining interest in educational research, is known as concept mapping. In concept mapping, students develop "two dimensional diagrams that illustrate relationships between ideas in a content area" (Jonassen, Beissner, & Yacci, 1993, p. 155). In developing concept maps, students draw two or more concepts connected by a linking word that identifies the bridging relationship. As students reformat the concepts and relationships into the new representation, they create links among the pieces of information, thereby increasing and strengthening the relationship. For instance, after reading a text on erosional forces and their resulting deposits, students could be asked to list the three major agents of erosion (water, wind, and glaciers) and then develop a table, or draw a concept map, depicting the relationships between the agent and associated formations. Using graphics in combination with teacher-mediated mnemonic instruction is an excellent way to increase mastery of content material for students with learning disabilities (Mastropieri, Scruggs, McLoone, & Levine, 1985).

Although the simpler of the two main types of microlevel elaborations, transformational elaborations can be an important means to acquiring new knowledge. These mnemonic devices, both verbal and pictorial, are widely used and can even be helpful in teaching quite young children (Foley & Wilder, 1989). The few students who appear not to benefit from instruction in keyword strategies are those who have previously developed and readily employ sophisticated elaborative strategies without external prompts (Pressley et al., 1987).

Situational elaborations. Situational elaborations are the second major type of microlevel elaborations. Instead of trans-

forming material, they build on natural and meaningful associations or inferences found within the context of the lesson. For example, the construction of mental images that depict the meaning of the material, and the establishment of appropriate schema before introducing related ideas.

The first of these methods is called precise contextual elaborations (Stein et al., 1982). These elaborations provide tightly knit links between ideas in the text and the students' existing knowledge structure. They are developed as an additional thought that makes otherwise arbitrary relationships intelligible.

In a study by Stein et al. (1982), students were read incomplete phrases similar to "The extremely strong river deposited the sand . . ." and were then asked to complete the sentence with a phrase of their own to make the sentence more meaningful. Within all ability groups, it was found that students who made precise elaborations (such as adding the phrase "over the entire city," which would require a strong river) had a much better recall level of the statements than those who made imprecise elaborations (such as adding the phrase "one grain at a time," which would not require a strong river). Students who exhibited academic success were more likely to generate precise elaborations by themselves than were less successful students.

A second type of situational elaboration uses mental imagery. This method

requires students to visualize the information or situation that has just been presented to them. The teacher then asks students how they perceive the situation. Accurate student-generated concepts are reinforced, and inaccurate ones are corrected. This method is beneficial because it repeats information gained through prose or lecture format and makes concepts more concrete. For example, in teaching students that geologists classify streams as youthful, mature, and old-age, teachers can reveal a few pertinent facts, then ask students to visualize and state how these streams may appear in nature. Correct assumptions (i.e., a youthful

---

Microlevel elaborations assist students in the retention of individual facts, macrolevel elaborations facilitate retention of entire lessons.

---

stream rushes straight ahead whereas an old-age stream meanders slowly from side to side) are reinforced. Classroom experience has shown that students who exhibit learning problems recall these self-generated imagery characteristics more readily than those stated by a teacher.

The third and final type of situational elaboration is called prerequisite elaboration. This type of elaboration is used to establish or reinforce a concept by bringing associated or related knowledge into the working memory before the introduction or review of a new concept. Ellis, Deshler, Lenz, Schumaker, and Clark (1993) validated the importance of prerequisite elaboration for students with mild disabilities. They found that students often exhibit less confusion and frustration when necessary skills or vocabulary are introduced early in a lesson. Similar to Ausubel's (1968) advanced organizer (a macrolevel elaboration), this method is used to impart knowledge on a specific, single concept. A geological example would be for a teacher to first remind students how the word "terminal" is used in everyday conversation to indicate the end of something. If an explanation of the glacial deposit known as a "terminal moraine" is then introduced, students will be better able to remember that a terminal moraine is found at the front end of a glacier, where advancement ceased and the glacier began to retreat.

Macrolevel Elaborations

Whereas microlevel elaborations assist students in the retention of individual

nizer would act as an "ideational scaffolding for the stable incorporation and retention of more detailed and differentiated material that follows" (p. 148). This scaffolding, or framework, is set up to establish an anchor point for forthcoming facts to attach themselves. Anchor points allow for easier integration and discrimination between new material and established, comparative knowledge. An example would be for a teacher to ask students to recall information on the deposition and composition of sand dunes. After allowing time for students to bring this knowledge to their working memory, the teacher may then describe a wind-blown soil deposit known as loess, comparing it to and contrasting it with the students' knowledge of sand dunes. The use of

on deposits found around hot springs, the information will be more readily assimilated because of their experience with the deposits formed in the beaker.

The third type of generality elaboration exists in the form of an analogy. With analogies, teachers relate new ideas to similar cognitive structures held by the students. For instance, if the concept being taught deals with the relative ages of sedimentary deposits, the teacher can make an analogy to the ages of successive layers of asphalt shingles placed on a building. As long as students understand an analogy's conceptual framework, they should be able to assimilate related concepts (Brown, 1994) and develop a level of comfort and security in connecting new ideas to their existing knowledge (Dagher, 1994).

General-to-detailed elaborations. The final type of macrolevel elaboration, which also assists in the sequencing of instruction, is the general-to-detailed elaboration. Reigeluth's (1983) elaboration theory of instruction is one such example. This elaboration begins with an "epitome" of the material to be learned, which is "a special kind of overview that teaches a few general, simple, and fundamental (but not abstract) ideas. The remainder of the instruction presents progressively more detailed ideas, which elaborate on earlier ones" (p. 338). Englert (1984) found similar evidence in working with students with disabilities. Teaching simple, concrete ideas that are related to the content of the lesson, then adding details, is a highly effective strategy to accentuate learning with this population.

Reigeluth compares his strategy to a zoom lens. When the lesson first begins, students view information through a wide-angle lens, which allows them to see the major parts and relationships between the parts. Students then have the ability to zoom in to look at individual parts in greater detail. This zooming in and out allows students to see how individual parts fit into the large picture, to see how the knowledge is structured, and to build a mental model of the information around the epitome.

If the class is studying erosional deposits, an example of an epitome would be that all erosional agents (wind, water,

---

There is little doubt that both the micro- and macrolevel elaborations increase students' ability to retain and recall information.

---

facts, macrolevel elaborations facilitate retention of entire lessons by first establishing relevant mental models to which students can associate new information. Although there are numerous types of macrolevel elaborations, they can be divided into two main groups: (a) generalities and (b) general-to-detailed. As with all elaborations, each allows for enhanced retention and recall of information by relating incoming material to existing cognitive structures (see Table 1).

Generality elaborations. There are three types of generality elaborations, each presenting a unified description of a similar topic and then relating this description to information that students are about to learn. Ausubel (1968) formally promoted this strategy, which he labeled a "comparative advanced organizer." The orga-

generalization and adaptation of learning strategies for students with disabilities (Ellis, Lenz, & Sabornie, 1987) and the importance of advance organizers for potentially low performing students in the secondary content classroom (Lenz, Alley, & Schumaker, 1987) have been well documented.

Experiential elaborations are a second type that can be included in the subgroup of generality elaborations. This elaboration uses students' personal experiences to make new information more memorable. These experiences can come from everyday life or be generated shortly before instruction by the teacher. For instance, if students set out a heated, saturated saltwater solution to evaporate over night, they will find mineral deposits in the beaker the following day. If the students' next classroom discussion focuses and glaciers) carry material until their speed decreases, at which time the materials are dropped and deposits are formed. At the next level of elaboration, the different types of erosional agents would be examined and an explanation of how these agents carry and deposit material would be presented. As students progress through the lesson, each ensuing level of instruction elaborates back to preceding levels, explaining the content in more detail.

Ausubel (1968) developed a somewhat similar technique that incorporated the general-to-detailed idea in his expository advanced organizer. Instead of presenting a few simple concepts as with an epitome, this elaboration method starts with an abstract idea that is more general and inclusive than the information presented later in the lesson. Once students become familiar with the abstract idea, they are given more detailed information that has an anchor point from which the meaning can be conceptualized. In geology, initial instruction may include the concept that erosion is an unending natural force, and if it is not counterbalanced, the resulting deposits will eventually fill in the world's ocean basins. Later instruction could detail the force that causes erosion as well as counteracting forces that push up the land.

Discussion

Implications for Educators

There is little doubt that both the micro- and macrolevel elaborations increase students' ability to retain and recall information. In addition, critical thinking may be promoted as students compare and contrast their previous knowledge to newly obtained knowledge during the process of elaboration (Stein, 1989). With these potential benefits, it is imperative that educators provide either teacher-generated elaborations or time for students to develop their own. When teachers distribute material or lecture to their classes without regard to the internal learning process of the student, those who are low performers are likely to interpret material in an arbitrary or verbatim fashion and learn through shallow processing methods, such as repetition, memorizing specific texts, or cramming for examinations.

Such methods limit students' assimilation of material or require that they spend additional time studying for comprehension.

Because individuals differ in their ability to elaborate, it is important that teachers encourage students with special needs to develop the skills of elaborating material on their own and to practice the various elaborative processes. Unfortunately, students do not gain a full understanding of the process of elaboration either by being told how to execute elaborative strategies or simply by being exposed to elaborated materials (Pressley et al., 1987). Rather, students need to be taught the techniques systematically and given the chance to implement and practice the processes over time. It is also important for teachers to instruct students in the use of multiple elaborative strategies because some are better assimilated than others, and some are better suited for specific types of problems. Exposure to different types of strategies may help students establish the general tendency to be more elaborative (Pressley et al., 1987), and individual differences in preference and prior knowledge will allow some strategies to be more easily retained and employed than others (Weinstein, Ridley, Dahl, & Weber, 1989). In addition, memory for a specific piece of information has been found to be related to the number of elaborations developed around that information (Anderson, 1990).

Conclusion

If we assume that students will always be required to master a certain amount of specific subject matter, then it is to the teacher's advantage to use strategies that help students remember information more easily. Although the learning strategies employed by a teacher and a student's prior knowledge, aptitude, and interest in subject matter all influence how well a student learns new material, comprehension is also affected by the student's ability to generate useful elaborations. We have presented 11 techniques to help establish the elaborative process for learning individual facts as well as for assimilating entire lessons (see Table 1). These techniques do more than just help students recall information for exams; they help students retain and access per-

tinent knowledge for use later in life. Because of the power of elaborative techniques, the process of teaching and using elaborations should be of paramount importance to teachers, authors, parents, and students both with and without disabilities. As both general and special educators seek best practices related to collaborative teaching environments (Karge, McClure, & Patton, 1995; Wilhite & Cessna, 1996) and inclusive settings (Cessna & Skiba, 1996; Whinnery, King, Evans, & Gable, 1995), administrators and principals seek ways to assist teachers (Lasky, Karge, Robb, & McCabe, 1995), and parents reach out to support the schools (Mostert, 1996), it is critical that all work together to use effective, efficient teaching practices. The trained use of elaborative techniques can enhance the learning potential of students with disabilities by assisting with both basic skill and higher level comprehension and retention.

REFERENCES

American Association for the Advance of Science. (1993). *Benchmarks for science literacy: Project 2061*. New York: Oxford University Press.

Anderson, J. (1990). *Cognitive psychology and its implications*. (3rd ed.). New York: W. H. Freeman.

Ausubel, D. B. (1968). *Educational psychology: A cognitive view*. New York: Holt, Rinehart, and Winston.

Brown, D. E. (1994). Facilitating conceptual change using analogies and explanatory models. *International Journal of Science Education, 16*(2), 201–214.

Cessna, K. K. & Skiba, R. J. (1996). Needs-based services: A responsible approach to inclusion. *Preventing School Failure, 40*, 117–123.

Dagher, Z. R. (1994). Does the use of analogies contribute to conceptual change? *Science Education, 78*, 601–614.

Denham, C. & Lieberman, A. (Eds.). (1980). *Time to learn*. Washington, DC: National Institute of Education.

Deshler, D. D., & Lenz, B. K. (1989). The strategies instructional approach. *International Journal of Disability, Development and Education, 36*, 203–224.

Deshler, D. D., & Schumaker, J. B., (1986). Learning strategies: An instructional alternative for low-achieving adolescents. *Exceptional Children, 52*(6), 583–590.

Ellis, E. S., Deshler, D. D., Lenz, B. K., Schumaker , J. B., & Clark, F. L. (1993). In Meyen, E. L., Vergason, G. A., Whelan, R. J. (Eds.), *Educating students with mild disabilities*. (pp. 151–155), Denver: Love.

Ellis, E. S., Lenz, B. K., & Sabornie, E. J. (1987). Generalization and adaptation of learning strategies to natural environments: Part 1. Critical agents. *Remedial and Special Education, 8*(1), 6–21.

Englert, C. S. (1983). Measuring special education

teacher effectiveness, *Exceptional Children, 50*(1), 247–254.

Englert, C. S. (1984). Effective direct instruction practices in special education settings. *Remedial and Special Education, 5,* 38–47.

Foley, M. A., & Wilder, A. (1989, April). *Developmental comparisons of the effects of type of imaginal elaboration on memory.* Paper presented at the biennial meeting of the Society for Research in Child Development. Kansas City, MO.

Gagné, E. D. (1985). *The cognitive psychology of school learning.* Boston: Little, Brown and Company.

Jonassen, D. H., Beissner, K., & Yacci, M. (1993). *Structural knowledge.* Hillsdale, NJ: Lawrence Erlbaum Associates.

Karge, B. D., McClure, M., & Patton, P. L. (1995). The success of collaboration resource programs for students with disabilities in grades 6 through 8. *Remedial and Special Education, 16*(2), 79–89.

Lasky, B., Karge, B. D., Robb, S. M., & McCabe, M. (1995). How principals can help the beginning special education teacher. *National Association of Secondary School Principals, 79*(568), 1–14.

Lenz, B. K., Alley, G. R., & Schumaker, J. B., (1987). Activating the inactive learner: Advance organizers in the secondary content classroom. *Learning Disability Quarterly, 10*(1), 53–67.

Levin, J. (1982). Pictures as prose-learning devices. In A. Flammer & W. Kintsch (Eds.), *Discourse processing.* (pp. 412–444). Amsterdam: North-Holland.

Lucking, R., & Manning, M. L. (1996). Instruction for low-achieving young adolescents: Addressing the challenge of a generation imperiled. *Preventing School Failure, 40*(2), 82–87.

Mastropieri, M. A., Scruggs, T. E., McLoone, B., & Levine, J. R., (1985). Facilitating the acquisition of science classifications in learning disabled students. *Learning Disability Quarterly, 8,* 299–309.

Merrill, M. D. (1983). Component display theory. In C. M. Reigeluth (Ed.), *Instructional theories and models: An overview of their current status* (pp. 278–333). Hillsdale, NJ: Erlbaum.

Mostert, M. P. (1996). Interprefessional collaboration in schools: Benefits and barriers in practice. *Preventing School Failure, 40*(3), 135–138.

National Council of Teachers of Mathematics. (1991). *Professional standards for teaching mathematics.* Reston, VA: Author.

Paris, S. G., & Jacobs, J. E. (1984). The benefits of informed instruction for children's reading awareness and comprehension skills. *Child Development, 55,* 2083–2093.

Pressley, M., Johnson, C. J., & Symons, S. (1987). Elaborating to learn and learning to elaborate. *Journal of Learning Disabilities, 20*(2), 76-91.

Reigeluth, C. M. (1983). Elaboration theory of instruction. In C. M. Reigeluth (Ed.) *Instructional theories and models: An overview of their current status* (pp. 335–381). Hillsdale, NJ: Erlbaum.

Roehler, L. R., & Duffy, G. G. (1984). Direct explanation of comprehension processes. In G. G. Duffy, L. R. Roehler, & J. Mason (Eds.), *Comprehension instruction: Perspectives and suggestions* (pp. 265–280). New York: Longman.

Rivera, D. & Smith, D. D. (1988). Using a demonstration strategy to teach midschool students with learning disabilities how to compute long division. *Journal of Learning Disabilities, 21*(1), 77–81.

Simmons, D. C., Kameenui, E. J., & Darch, C. (1988). Learning disabled children's metacognition of selected textual features. *Learning Disabilities Quarterly, 11*(1), 380–395.

Stein, B., Bransford, J., Franks, J., Owings, R., Vye, N., & McGraw, W. (1982). Differences in the precision of self-generated elaborations. *Journal of Experimental Psychology, 111,* 399–405.

Stein, V. (1989). Elaboration: Using what you know. (Reading-to-Write Report No. 6, Technical Report No. 25). *Office of Educational Research and Improvement*, Washington, DC (ERIC Document Reproduction Service No. ED 306 596).

Weinstein, C. E., Ridley, D. S., Dahl, T., & Weber, E. S. (1989). Helping students develop strategies for effective learning. *Educational Leadership, 46*(4), 17–19.

Whinnery, K. W., King, M., Evans, W. H. & Gable, P. A. (1995). Perceptions of students with learning disabilities: Inclusion versus pull-out services. *Preventing School Failure, 40*(1), 5–9.

Wilhite, K. & Cessna, K. K. (1996). Safeguarding the education of incarcerated juvenile offenders: The critical role of state departments of education, *Preventing School Failure, 40*(2), 56–59.

The First Seven . . . and the Eighth

A Conversation with Howard Gardner

Human intelligence continues to intrigue psychologists, neurologists, and educators. What is it? Can we measure it? How do we nurture it?

Kathy Checkley

Howard Gardner's theory of multiple intelligences, described in Frames of Mind (1985), *sparked a revolution of sorts in classrooms around the world, a mutiny against the notion that human beings have a single, fixed intelligence. The fervor with which educators embraced his premise that we have multiple intelligences surprised Gardner himself. "It obviously spoke to some sense that people had that kids weren't all the same and that the tests we had only skimmed the surface about the differences among kids," Gardner said.*

Here Gardner brings us up-to-date on his current thinking on intelligence, how children learn, and how they should be taught.

How do you define intelligence?

Intelligence refers to the human ability to solve problems or to make something that is valued in one or more cultures. As long as we can find a culture that values an ability to solve a problem or create a product in a particular way, then I would strongly consider whether that ability should be considered an intelligence.

First, though, that ability must meet other criteria: Is there a particular representation in the brain for the

ability? Are there populations that are especially good or especially impaired in an intelligence? And, can an evolutionary history of the intelligence be seen in animals other than human beings?

I defined seven intelligences (see box) in the early 1980s because those intelligences all fit the criteria. A decade later when I revisited the task, I found at least one more ability that clearly deserved to be called an intelligence.

That would be the naturalist intelligence. What led you to consider adding this to our collection of intelligences?

Somebody asked me to explain the achievements of the great biologists, the ones who had a real mastery of taxonomy, who understood about different species, who could recognize patterns in nature and classify objects. I realized that to explain that kind of ability, I would have to manipulate the other intelligences in ways that weren't appropriate.

So I began to think about whether the capacity to classify nature might be a separate intelligence. The naturalist ability passed with flying colors. Here are a couple of reasons: First, it's an ability we need to survive as human beings. We need, for example, to know which animals to hunt and which to run away from. Second, this ability isn't restricted to human beings. Other animals need to have a naturalist intelligence to survive. Finally, the big selling point is that brain evidence supports the existence of the naturalist intelligence. There are certain parts of the brain particularly dedicated to the recognition and the naming of what are called "natural" things.

How do you describe the naturalist intelligence to those of us who aren't psychologists?

The naturalist intelligence refers to the ability to recognize and classify plants, minerals, and animals, including rocks and grass and all variety of flora and fauna. The ability to recognize cultural artifacts like cars or sneakers may also depend on the naturalist intelligence.

Now, everybody can do this to a certain extent—we can all recognize dogs, cats, trees. But, some people from an early age are extremely good at recognizing and classifying artifacts. For example, we all know kids who, at age 3 or 4, are better at recognizing dinosaurs than most adults.

Darwin is probably the most famous example of a naturalist because he saw so deeply into the nature of living things.

Are there any other abilities you're considering calling intelligences?

Well, there may be an existential intelligence that refers to the human inclination to ask very basic questions about existence. Who are we? Where do we come from? What's it all about? Why do we die? We might say that existential intelligence allows us to know the invisible, outside world. The only reason I haven't given a seal of approval to the existential intelligence is that I don't think we have good brain evidence yet on its existence in the nervous system—one of the criteria for an intelligence.

You have said that the theory of multiple intelligences may be best understood when we know what it critiques. What do you mean?

The standard view of intelligence is that intelligence is something you are born with; you have only a certain amount of it; you cannot do much about how much of that intelligence you have; and tests exist that can tell you how smart you are. The theory of multiple intelligences challenges that view. It asks, instead,

© Susie Fitzhugh

"Given what we know about the brain, evolution, and the differences in cultures, what are the sets of human abilities we all share?"

My analysis suggested that rather than one or two intelligences, all human beings have several (eight) intelligences. What makes life interesting, however, is that we don't have the same strength in each intelligence area, and we don't have the same amalgam of intelligences. Just as we look different from one another and have different kinds of personalities, we also have different kinds of minds.

This premise has very serious educational implications. If we treat everybody as if they are the same, we're catering to one profile of intelligence, the lan-

School matters, but only insofar as it yields something that can be used once students leave school.

guage-logic profile. It's great if you have that profile, but it's not great for the vast majority of human beings who do not have that particular profile of intelligence.

Can you explain more fully how the theory of multiple intelligences challenges what has become known as IQ?

The theory challenges the entire notion of IQ. The IQ test was developed about a century ago as a way to determine who would have trouble in school. The test measures linguistic ability, logical-mathematical ability, and, occasionally, spatial ability.

What the intelligence test does not do is inform us about our other intelligences; it also doesn't look at other virtues like creativity or civic mindedness, or whether a person is moral or ethical.

We don't do much IQ testing anymore, but the shadow of IQ tests is still with us because the SAT—arguably the most potent examination in the world—is basically the same kind of disembodied language-logic instrument.

The truth is, I don't believe there is such a general thing as scholastic aptitude. Even so, I don't think that the SAT will fade until colleges indicate that they'd rather have students who know how to use their minds well—students who may or may not be good test takers, but who are serious, inquisitive, and know how to probe and problem-solve. That is really what college professors want, I believe.

Can we strengthen our intelligences? If so, how?

We can all get better at each of the intelligences, although some people will improve in an intelligence area more readily than others, either because biology gave them a better brain for that intelligence or because their culture gave them a better teacher.

Teachers have to help students use their combination of intelligences to be successful in school, to help them learn whatever it is they want to learn, as well as what the teachers and society believe they have to learn.

Now, I'm not arguing that kids shouldn't learn the literacies. Of course they should learn the literacies. Nor am I arguing that kids shouldn't learn the disciplines. I'm a tremendous champion of the disciplines. What I argue against is the notion that there's only one way to learn how to read, only one way to learn how to compute, only one way to learn about biology. I think that such contentions are nonsense.

It's equally nonsensical to say that everything should be taught seven or eight ways. That's not the point of the MI theory. The point is to realize that any topic of importance, from any discipline, can be taught in more than one way. There are things people need to know, and educators have to be extraordinarily imaginative and persistent in helping students understand things better.

A popular activity among those who are first exploring multiple intelligences is to construct their own intellectual profile. It's thought that when teachers go through the process of creating such a profile, they're more likely to recognize and appreciate the intellectual strengths of their students. What is your view on this kind of activity?

My own studies have shown that people love to do this. Kids like to do it, adults like to do it. And, as an activity, I think it's perfectly harmless.

I get concerned, though, when people think that determining your intellectual profile—or that of someone else—is an end in itself.

You have to use the profile to understand the ways in which you seem to learn easily. And, from there, determine how to use those strengths to help you become more successful in other endeavors. Then, the profile becomes a way for you to understand yourself better, and you can use that understanding to catapult yourself to a better level of understanding or to a higher level of skill.

How has your understanding of the multiple intelligences influenced how you teach?

As long as you can lose one ability while others are spared, you cannot just have a single intelligence.

My own teaching has changed slowly as a result of multiple intelligences because I'm teaching graduate students psychological theory and there are only so many ways I can do that. I am more open to group work and to student projects of various sorts, but even if I wanted to be an "MI professor" of graduate students, I still have a certain moral obligation to prepare them for a world in which they will have to write scholarly articles and prepare theses.

Where I've changed much more, I believe, is at the workplace. I direct research projects and work with all kinds of people. Probably 10 to 15 years ago, I would have tried to find people who were just like me to work with me on these projects.

I've really changed my attitude a lot on that score. Now I think much more in terms of what people are good at and in putting together teams of people whose varying strengths complement one another.

How should thoughtful educators implement the theory of multiple intelligences?

Although there is no single MI route, it's very important that a teacher take individual differences among kinds very seriously. You cannot be a good MI teacher if you don't want to know each child and try to gear how you teach and how you evaluate to that particular child. The bottom line is a deep interest in children and how their minds are different from one another, and in helping them use their minds well.

Now, kids can be great informants for teachers. For example, a teacher might say, "Look, Benjamin, this obviously isn't working. Should we try using a picture?" If Benjamin gets excited about that approach, that's a pretty good clue to the teacher about what could work.

The theory of multiple intelligences, in and of itself, is not going to solve anything in our society, but linking the multiple intelligences with a curriculum focused on understanding is an extremely powerful intellectual undertaking.

When I talk about understanding, I mean that students can take ideas they learn in school, or anywhere for that matter, and apply those appropriately in new situations. We know people truly understand something when they can represent the knowledge in more than one way. We have to put understanding up front in school. Once we have that goal, multiple intelligences can be a terrific handmaiden because understandings involve a mix of mental representations, entailing different intelligences.

People often say that what they remember most about school are those learning experiences that were linked to real life. How does the theory of multiple intelligences help connect learning to the world outside the classroom?

The theory of multiple intelligences wasn't based on school work or on tests. Instead, what I did was look at the world and ask, What are the things that people do in the world? What does it mean to be a surgeon? What does it mean to be a politician? What does it mean to be an artist or a sculptor? What abilities do you need to do those things? My theory, then, came from the things that are valued in the world.

So when a school values multiple intelligences, the relationship to what's valued in the world is patent. If you cannot easily relate this activity to something that's valued in the world, the school has probably

© Susie Fitzhugh

lost the core idea of multiple intelligences, which is that these intelligences evolved to help people do things that matter in the real world.

School matters, but only insofar as it yields something that can be used once students leave school.

The Intelligences, in Gardner's Words

■ Linguistic intelligence is the capacity to use language, your native language, and perhaps other languages, to express what's on your mind and to understand other people. Poets really specialize in linguistic intelligence, but any kind of writer, orator, speaker, lawyer, or a person for whom language is an important stock in trade highlights linguistic intelligence.

■ People with a highly developed logical-mathematical intelligence understand the underlying principles of some kind of a causal system, the way a scientist or a logician does; or can manipulate numbers, quantities, and operations, the way a mathematician does.

■ Spatial intelligence refers to the ability to represent the spatial world internally in your mind—the way a sailor or airplane pilot navigates the large spatial world, or the way a chess player or sculptor represents a more circumscribed spatial world. Spatial intelligence can be used in the arts or in the sciences. If you are spatially intelligent and oriented toward the arts, you are more likely to become a painter or a sculptor or an architect than, say, a musician or a writer. Similarly, certain sciences like anatomy or topology emphasize spatial intelligence.

■ Bodily kinesthetic intelligence is the capacity to use your whole body or parts of your body—your hand, your fingers, your arms—to solve a problem, make something, or put on some kind of a production. The most evident examples are people in athletics or the performing arts, particularly dance or acting.

■ Musical intelligence is the capacity to think in music, to be able to hear patterns, recognize them, remember them, and perhaps manipulate them. People who have a strong musical intelligence don't just remember music eas-

ily—they can't get it out of their minds, it's so omnipresent. Now, some people will say, "Yes, music is important, but it's a talent, not an intelligence." And I say, "Fine, let's call it a talent." But, then we have to leave the word *intelligent* out of *all* discussions of human abilities. You know, Mozart was damned smart!

■ Interpersonal intelligence is understanding other people. It's an ability we all need, but is at a premium if you are a teacher, clinician, salesperson, or politician. Anybody who deals with other people has to be skilled in the interpersonal sphere.

■ Intrapersonal intelligence refers to having an understanding of yourself, of knowing who you are, what you can do, what you want to do, how you react to things, which things to avoid, and which things to gravitate toward. We are drawn to people who have a good understanding of themselves because those people tend not to screw up. They tend to know what they can do. They tend to know what they can't do. And they tend to know where to go if they need help.

■ Naturalist intelligence designates the human ability to discriminate among living things (plants, animals) as well as sensitivity to other features of the natural world (clouds, rock configurations). This ability was clearly of value in our evolutionary past as hunters, gatherers, and farmers; it continues to be central in such roles as botanist or chef. I also speculate that much of our consumer society exploits the naturalist intelligences, which can be mobilized in the discrimination among cars, sneakers, kinds of makeup, and the like. The kind of pattern recognition valued in certain of the sciences may also draw upon naturalist intelligence.

How can teachers be guided by multiple intelligences when creating assessment tools?

We need to develop assessments that are much more representative of what human beings are going to have to do to survive in this society. For example, I value literacy, but my measure of literacy should not be whether you can answer a multiple-choice question that asks you to select the best meaning of a paragraph. Instead, I'd rather have you read the paragraph and list four questions you have about the paragraph and figure out how you would answer those questions. Or, if I want to know how you can write, let me give you a stem and see whether you can write about that topic, or let me ask you to write an editorial in response to something you read in the newspaper or observed on the street.

The current emphasis on performance assessment is well supported by the theory of multiple intelligences. Indeed, you could not really be an advocate of multiple intelligences if you didn't have some dissatisfaction with the current testing because it's so focused on short-answer, linguistic, or logical kinds of items.

MI theory is very congenial to an approach that says: one, let's not look at things through the filter of a short-answer test. Let's look directly at the performance that we value, whether it's a linguistic, logical, aesthetic, or social performance; and, two, let's never pin our assessment of understanding on just one particular measure, but let's always allow students to show their understanding in a variety of ways.

You have identified several myths about the theory of multiple intelligences. Can you describe some of those myths?

One myth that I personally find irritating is that an intelligence is the same as a learning style. Learning styles are claims about ways in which individuals purportedly approach everything they do. If you are planful, you are supposed to be planful about everything. If you are logical-sequential, you are supposed to be logical-sequential about everything. My own research and observations suggest that that's a dubious assumption. But whether or not that's true, learning styles are very different from multiple intelligences.

Multiple intelligences claims that we respond, individually, in different ways to different kinds of content, such as language or music or other people. This is very different from the notion of learning style.

You can say that a child is a visual learner, but that's not a multiple intelligences way of talking about things. What I would say is, "Here is a child who very easily represents things spatially, and we can draw upon that strength if need be when we want to teach the child something new."

Another widely believed myth is that, because we have seven or eight intelligences, we should create seven or eight tests to measure students' strengths in each of those areas. That is a perversion of the theory. It's re-creating the sin of the single intelligence quotient and just multiplying it by a larger number. I'm personally against assessment of intelligences unless such a measurement is used for a very specific learning purpose—we want to help a child understand her history or his mathematics better and, therefore, want to see what might be good entry points for that particular child.

What experiences led you to the study of human intelligence?

It's hard for me to pick out a single moment, but I can see a couple of snapshots. When I was in high

© Susie Fitzhugh

school, my uncle gave me a textbook in psychology. I'd never actually heard of psychology before. This textbook helped me understand color blindness. I'm color blind, and I became fascinated by the existence of plates that illustrated what color blindness was. I could actually explain why I couldn't see colors.

Another time when I was studying the Reformation, I read a book by Erik Erikson called *Young Man Luther* (1958).[1] I was fascinated by the psychological motivation of Luther to attack the Catholic Church. That fascination influenced my decision to go into psychology.

The most important influence was actually learning about brain damage and what could happen to people when they had strokes. When a person has a stroke, a certain part of the brain gets injured, and that injury can tell you what that part of the brain does. Individuals who lose their musical abilities can still talk. People who lose their linguistic ability still might be able to sing. That understanding not only

brought me into the whole world of brain study, but it was really the seed that led ultimately to the theory of multiple intelligences. As long as you can lose one ability while others are spared, you cannot just have a single intelligence. You have to have several intelligences.

1. See Erik Erikson, *Young Man Luther* (New York: W. W. Norton, 1958).

Howard Gardner is Professor of Education at Harvard Graduate School of Education and author of, among other books, *The Unschooled Mind: How Children Think and How Schools Should Teach* (1991). He can be reached at Roy B. Larsen Hall, 2nd Floor, Appian Way, Harvard Graduate School of Education, Cambridge, MA 02138. **Kathy Checkley** is a staff writer for *Update* and has assisted in the development of ASCD's new CD-ROM, *Exploring Our Multiple Intelligences*, and pilot online project on multiple intelligences.

Styles of Thinking, Abilities, and Academic Performance

ELENA L. GRIGORENKO

ROBERT J. STERNBERG
Yale University

ABSTRACT: *This study was designed to investigate the role of thinking styles in academic performance. Participants were 199 gifted students enrolled in the Yale Summer School Program. Their abilities were evaluated by the Sternberg Triarchic Abilities Test; their academic performance was judged by independent raters blind to the conditions of the study; and their thinking styles were measured by two converging self-report questionnaires. The results of the study show that, after controlling for levels of abilities, styles of thinking significantly contribute to prediction of academic performance. Moreover, equally able thinkers of different styles tend to do better in different assessment settings.*

A cornerstone of modern educational psychology is that a student's level of abilities is one of the major predictors of school success. Though psychologists or educators may differ significantly on the details and on theory, there is established evidence that abilities matter (e.g., Carroll, 1993; Gardner, H., 1983; Guilford, 1967; Horn, 1994; Spearman, 1927; Sternberg, 1985, 1986, 1988b; Thurstone, 1938).

Yet abilities do not predict school performance completely. In the search for other variables that contribute to school achievement, researchers have devoted considerable attention to the so-called *stylistic aspects* of cognition. The idea of a style reflecting a person's typical or habitual mode of problem-solving, thinking, perceiving, and remembering was initially introduced by Allport (1937). Since then, researchers have developed various theories in attempts to understand the reality of styles (see Curry, 1983; Grigorenko

& Sternberg, 1995; Kagan & Kogan, 1970; Kogan, 1983; Riding & Cheema, 1991; Sternberg, 1988a; Vernon, 1973). In an examination of the literature on styles, Grigorenko and Sternberg (1995) found three general approaches to stylistic aspects of learning.

The first approach is cognition-centered, dealing with cognitive styles. Theorists and researchers in this area have sought to investigate "the characteristic, self-consistent modes of functioning which individuals show in their perceptual and intellectual activities" (Witkin, Oltman, Raskin, & Karp, 1971, p. 3). Some of the main styles studied in this literature have been leveling-sharpening (i.e., a tendency to be hypersensitive to small differences versus a tendency to maximize assimilation; Klein, 1954), equivalence range (i.e., a spontaneous differentiation of heterogeneous items into a complex of related groups; Gardner, R., 1953), field dependence-independence (i.e.,

From *Exceptional Children*, Spring 1997, pp. 295-312. © 1997 by The Council for Exceptional Children. Reprinted by permission.

an ability to differentiate an object from the context; Witkin, 1973), and impulsivity-reflectivity (i.e., a tendency to reflect/disregard alternative solutions; Kagan, 1958). There also have been attempts to integrate specific cognitive styles into a larger framework of cognitive functioning. Kagan and Kogan (1970) have matched particular cognitive styles with stages of problem-solving. Fowler (1977, 1980) and Santostefano (1986) have incorporated the notion of styles into a developmental framework, and Royce and Powell (1983) have conceptualized styles as higher-order strategies that control the deployment of lower-order abilities.

A second approach to studying styles is personality-centered. The theory of Myers and Myers (1980), based on the work of Jung (1923), follows this approach. Myers and Myers have distinguished among two attitudes, extroversion and introversion; two perceptual functions, intuition and sensing; two judgmental functions, thinking and feeling; and two ways of dealing with the outer world, judgment and perception. Gregorc (1984) has distinguished between two ways of handling each of space and time. Thus, people can be classified as abstract or concrete with respect to space, and as sequential or random with respect to time. Miller (1987, 1991) has proposed a somewhat different taxonomy, distinguishing among analytic versus holistic, objective versus subjective, and emotionally stable versus emotionally unstable individuals.

The third approach is activity-centered and tends to focus on styles of learning and teaching. These theories have probably had the most direct application in the classroom. For example, Kolb (1974) has identified four styles of learning: convergent versus divergent and assimilational versus accommodational. Dunn and Dunn (1978) have categorized styles in terms of preferred elements in a learning situation, such as various aspects of the environment (e.g., sound and light) and various aspects of interaction with the self and others (e.g., peers and adults). Renzulli and Smith (1978) have distinguished preferred styles of work in the classroom, such as projects, drill and recitation, and peer teaching. A theory of the same kind but more oriented toward the world of work is that of Holland (1973), who has distinguished among realistic, investigative, artistic, social, and enterprising styles on the job.

These three approaches differ not only in the focus of their interest, but also in the ways they address the functional aspects of styles, mentioned previously. The cognition- and the personality-centered approaches typically imply that styles are either-or constructs (a person could be either field-independent, or field-dependent, but not both). In these approaches, styles are consistent across various tasks and situations, and can be modified very little, if at all, by training during the life span. Cognitive and personality styles are most often viewed as structures, where the focus is placed on stability over time; as such, styles are "givens" in a training or educational setting (Riding & Cheema, 1991). Cognition- and personality-centered theories also usually have built-in evaluating attitudes, assuming that certain styles are better than others: It is often more beneficial in modern society to be reflective rather than impulsive, or sequential rather than random. These styles are measured primarily by specially designed laboratory tasks. In contrast, styles defined in the third, activity-centered approach are measured by methods more easily usable in educational environments. Most authors working in the activity-centered framework view styles as processes, which can be built on and used to compensate for or to remediate weaknesses. In this interpretation, styles are seen as dynamic, not as "frozen forever." There are also no "bad or good" styles—the aim is to find or develop "optimal" styles for particular situations.

THEORY OF MENTAL SELF-GOVERNMENT

Our goal was to build on this work using the theory of mental self-government (Sternberg, 1988a, 1990, 1994). The objective of the theory is to integrate various approaches to style and to provide new directions for theory applied to educational practice.

The basic idea of the theory of mental self-government (Sternberg, 1988a, 1994) is that people, like societies, have to organize or govern themselves. Thus, the theory addresses the question of how people govern and manage their everyday cognitive activities, within the school and without. In the theory of mental self-government, a style of thinking is defined as a preferred way of thinking. It is not an ability, but rather a *favored way of expressing or using one or more abilities.* Two or more people with the same levels or patterns of abilities might nevertheless have very different styles of thinking. Also, two people with similar personality characteristics might differ in their thinking styles. Thus, styles of thinking do not reside in the domain of abilities or in the domain of personality, but at the interface between the two (Sternberg, 1988a, 1988b, 1994).

The theory is organized into five major parts: functions, forms, levels, scope, and leanings of mental self-government (see Table 1). Because scope was not used in our studies, we do not describe it further. The basic idea, then, is that people can be characterized and assessed with regard to habitual functions, forms, levels, and leanings in their cognitive activities.

The theory of mental self-government is rooted in previous work on styles, and so it shares some characteristics with earlier theories. The theory of thinking styles addresses all three domains—the domain of cognition, the domain of personality, and the domain of activity: We view thinking styles as buffers between such internal characteristics as ability and personality, on the one hand, and the external situation, on the other. The theory of mental self-government provides an insight into individually preferred ways of thinking in various activities. Similar to the cognition- and the personality-centered approaches, some thinking styles imply distinct poles: A person can be either local or global, liberal or conservative, but not both (see Table 1 for definitions of these styles). On the contrary, other thinking styles (e.g., legislative, judicial, and executive), like activity-based styles, are not polarizable, because they represent distinct categories that do not lie on a continuum.

The space of thinking styles is multidimensional; the different styles are not orthogonal to each other and tend to correlate and to form profiles. Thus, for example, the executive style often correlates with the conservative style, whereas the legislative style tends to be associated with the liberal one (Martin, 1989). Moreover, although people have a general profile of the ways they choose to think, thinking styles can vary across tasks and situations. A student's preferred style in mathematics, for example, may not necessarily be his or her preferred style in a cooking class. Thus, similarly to the activity-based approach, we view styles as dynamic and adaptive, subject to change and optimization. Unlike the cognition- or the personality-based approaches to styles, we believe that the thinking styles are not fixed, but rather can vary across the life span. The styles that may lead to adaptive performance (either in learning or teaching) at the elementary-school level are not necessarily those that will work best in advanced graduate school training or at work. For example, teachers at the primary level of education tend to favor students with creative thinking styles more than do teachers at the secondary level (Sternberg & Grigorenko, 1995).

Styles are, at least in part, socialized (Sternberg, 1988a; Sternberg & Grigorenko, 1995), and

may undergo developmental changes. No thinking style is, in any absolute sense, "good" or "bad." Rather, it can be more or less adaptive for a given task or situation, and what is adaptive in one setting may not be in another.

Finally, thinking styles manifest themselves in any activity, and therefore can be measured in an ecologically valid situation, as well as in a laboratory setting. In other words, thinking styles are reflected in styles of learning and teaching, styles of working and playing, and so on.

In our previous studies (Grigorenko & Sternberg, in press; Sternberg & Grigorenko, 1993, 1995), we operationalized the theory of thinking styles and applied it to various educational activities—in particular, learning and teaching. Our most relevant findings were that there was a significant variation of styles among teachers and students, and that students' thinking styles were predictive of their school success. In the present study, we have attempted to extend our research on thinking styles into the area of gifted education.

METHOD

This study was a part of a large-scale effort to validate Sternberg's *triarchic model of intelligence* (Sternberg, 1985, 1986, 1988b). The triarchic theory distinguishes among three kinds of intellectual giftedness: analytic, creative, and practical. In brief, the theory suggests that individuals gifted in these different ways excel in different activities: The analytically gifted are strong in analyzing, evaluating, and critiquing; the creatively gifted are good at discovering, creating, and inventing; and the practically gifted are strong in implementing, utilizing, and applying. A complete account of the larger study has been presented elsewhere (Sternberg & Clinkenbeard, 1995; Sternberg, Ferrari, Clinkenbeard, & Grigorenko, in press). In this article, we present only the components of the study relevant to thinking styles.

Study Questions

The general purpose of this study was to investigate relations between different types of abilities (as defined by the triarchic theory) and different thinking styles (as defined by the theory of mental self-government). We addressed four research questions, as follows:

1. *Is there a relationship between thinking styles and abilities?* In other words, did stylistic preferences differ for gifted and nongifted students? More specifically, did stylistic preferences differ

among gifted students of different abilities? For example, did creative students tend to be more legislative, and analytical students tend to be more judicial?

2. *After controlling for level of students' abilities, to what degree do thinking styles predict perfor-*

mance? In other words, when the level of abilities was accounted for, did styles contribute anything to understanding variability in academic performance?

3. *Given that four different instructional types (analytical, creative, practical, and traditional) were*

TABLE 1
Styles of Mental Self-Government

Styles	Characterization	Example Relevant to School Settings
Functions		
Legislative	is concerned with creating, formulating, imagining, and planning; likes to formulate his or her own activities	students who like to approach assignments in their own ways, who like to wander off from their textbooks, who like to explore, to do science projects, to write poetry and stories, to compose music, and to create original artworks
Executive	is concerned with implementing and doing; likes to pursue activities structured by others	students who are always ready for the class, who know the assigned material very well, who prefer solving problems over formulating them and like developing someone else's idea more than suggesting their own
Judicial	is concerned with judging, evaluating, and comparing; likes to judge the products of others' activities, or to judge the others themselves	students who like to comment and to critique, who enjoy writing critical essays and commentaries, who prefer evaluating others' ideas over formulating or implementing them
Forms		
Monarchic	tends to focus single-mindedly on one goal or need at a time; a single goal or way of doing things predominates	students who like to engage in single projects, whether in art, science, history, or business
Hierarchic	tends to allow for multiple goals, each of which may have a different priority; knows how to perform multiple tasks within the same time frame, setting priorities for getting them done	students who know how to divide homework so that more time and energy are devoted to more important and more difficult assignments
Oligarchic	tends to allow for multiple goals, all of which are equally important; likes to do multiple tasks within the same time frame but has difficulty setting priorities for getting them done	students who start many projects simultaneously, but have trouble finishing them because there is not enough time and because priorities of the projects have not been set
Anarchic	tends to eschew rules, procedures, and formal systems; often has difficulty adjusting to the school as a system	students who do not do much planning and tend to choose projects they work on in a random way; do not like to follow the established curriculum and have difficulties meeting deadlines

TABLE 1
(Continued)

Styles	Characterization	Example Relevant to School Settings
Levels		
Global	prefers to deal with the large picture and abstractions	students who like writing on the global message and meaning of a work of art, or on the significance of a particular discovery for mankind
Local	prefers dealing with details and concrete issues	students who like writing on the components of a work of art, or on the details of an experiment
Leaning		
Liberal	likes to do things in new ways, to have change in his or her life, and to defy conventions	students who like figuring out how to operate new equipment and like non-traditional challenging tasks
Conserva-tive	likes traditions and stability; prefers doing things in tried and true ways	students who like to be shown all the steps of operating equipment and like to be given precise instructions for performing a task

used, do students with certain thinking styles who are placed in a particular instructional group that is matched or mismatched with their ability, perform any better than students with other thinking styles? For example, did creative students, scoring high on the judicial thinking style and placed in the group with analytical instruction, perform better than creative students in the same group, but with lower scores on the judicial thinking style?

4. *Given that various tools of performance evaluation (homework, written examinations, and a project) were used in this study, did students with particular thinking styles do better in one form of evaluation than another? In other words, did specific forms of evaluation benefit students with particular thinking styles?*

Participants

Participants were high school students, ranging in age from 13 to 16 years, who attended the 1993 Yale Summer Psychology Program (YSPP). The program was advertised through brochures and newsletters distributed to schools in the United States and other countries. Schools were asked to submit nominations of gifted students to the Program Committee of the YSPP. A selection procedure was based on the students' performance on the Sternberg Triarchic Abilities Test (STAT), Level H, designed for advanced high school and college students (Sternberg, 1993). The STAT was sent to schools that placed nominations. The test was administered to the nominated students in their own schools.

A total of 199 students (146 females and 53 males) were selected for participation in the summer program of 1993. (Altogether the YSPP enrolled 225 students, of whom 25 were admitted for pay, to provide tuition for eligible students. These 25 students were excluded from further analyses. Moreover, one student was expelled for discipline problems.)

Of these students, 3 (1.5%) were entering grade 9, 25 (12.6%) were entering Grade 10, 77 (38.7%) were entering Grade 11, and 94 (47.2%) were entering Grade 12. The program participants were fairly widely distributed ethnically (based on students' own reports): 60% European American, 11% African American, 6% Hispanic American, and 17% American from another ethnic minority. Further, 4% of the students were from South Africa, and 2% "other."

Materials and Procedures

Different instruments were used for identification, performance assessment, and styles evaluation. All instruments were developed prior to the study, and complete accounts of their psychometric properties can be found elsewhere. Thus, only brief technical descriptions will be provided here.

Identification. Identification and classification of students into ability groups were done using the results of the STAT multiple-choice and essay subtests. There are nine multiple-choice subtests, each including 2 sample items and 4 test items, for a total of 36 items (for details, see Sternberg et al., in press). The item types on the nine multiple-choice subtests are: (1) analytic-verbal—inferring the meanings of neologisms from natural contexts; (2) analytic-quantitative—inferring subsequent numbers on the basis of series of numbers; (3) analytic-figural—inferring the missing part of each matrix based on the matrix's overall structure; (4) practical-verbal—performing everyday reasoning; (5) practical-quantitative—performing everyday math; (6) practical-figural—performing route planning; (7) creative-verbal—solving verbal analogies preceded by counterfactual premises; (8) creative-quantitative—learning and applying novel number operations; (9) creative-figural—extracting and applying rules for figure transformations. The three essay subtests involved analytical thinking (requiring students to analyze the advantages and disadvantages of having police or security guards in a school building), creative thinking (requiring students to describe how they would reform their school system to produce an ideal one), and practical thinking (requiring students to specify a problem in their life, and to state three practical solutions for solving it). Multiple-choice subtests and essays were standardized, and then three primary STAT scores (analytical, creative, and practical) were obtained. The details of the validation of the STAT have been described in detail elsewhere (Sternberg & Clinkenbeard, 1995; Sternberg et al., in press). In brief, a varimax-rotated principal components analysis of the multiple-choice subtests of the STAT resulted in 9 specific factors (factor loadings varied from .92 to .98) with approximately equal eigenvalues, which ranged from 1.01 to 0.98. The factor structure shows that each subtest represents a unique process (analytic, creative, practical)—content (verbal, quantitative, figural) combination, suggesting that the STAT does tap into different abilities, instead of simply measuring Spearman's general ability (*g*, Spearman, 1927). The Kuder-Richardson-20 (KR-20) reliability coefficients for multiple-choice items ranged from .49 to .64. The interrater agreement on the essays ranged from .58 to .69. The multiple-choice subtests scores correlated with essay questions at $p < .01$. The correlations with the Watson-Glaser Critical Thinking Appraisal and the Concept Mastery tests used for external validation were significant, but of moderate magnitude.

Based on their STAT performance, all students enrolled in the program were classified into five different groups. The STAT subtest scores were standardized, so they could be compared across different subtests. Students were identified as "high" in an aspect of ability based on their strongest test attainment and their score in respect to the group average. Thus, we first constructed three groups: (a) a group in which students demonstrated a high level of analytical ability ($N = 39$, 19.6%); (b) a group in which students were high in creative ability ($N = 38$, 19.1%); and (c) a group in which students were high in practical ability ($N = 35$, 17.6%). For students to be classified as "high" in analytic, creative, or practical ability, their total score for a given ability was required to be at least a half-standard deviation above the group average and at least a half-standard deviation above their own scores for the other two abilities measured by the STAT (e.g., analytic higher than creative and practical). Although the half-standard deviation criterion might sound weak, recall that all students entering the program were first nominated as gifted by their schools.

For the fourth group, we defined a "balanced" gifted group ($N = 40$, 20.1%). For students to be classified as balanced, they had to score above the group average for all three abilities. Finally, the fifth group was composed of students who scored at or below the group average for all three abilities ($N = 47$, 23.6%). These students were classified as not identified as gifted.

Instruction. Students were given an intensive, 4-week, college-level psychology course. The course consisted of three main components: the *text* (Sternberg, 1995), the *lecture series*, and the *afternoon sections*. The first two components were common to all groups, whereas the last constituted the treatment and diverged across groups. There were four types of afternoon sections, in which section leaders emphasized different skills: memory (traditional educational paradigm), analytical thinking, creative thinking, or practical thinking. The students were divided among instructional groups in such a way that all groups had close to equal numbers of students of each of the five types of ability patterns. Thus, some students were placed in groups in which the type of afternoon section matched their abilities ($N = 83$, e.g., 10 of 38 creative students were placed in groups in which the section leaders taught for creative thinking), while the remaining students were mismatched ($N = 113$, e.g., 9 creative students were place in groups with the section leaders teaching for practical thinking).

Performance Assessment. In our previous studies on thinking styles, we found that thinking styles predict school success: Students were viewed by their teachers as achieving at higher levels when the students' profiles of styles matched those of their teachers (Sternberg & Grigorenko, 1995). In other words, teachers appear to value more highly students who are stylistically similar to themselves. However, the evaluation of academic performance was done through students' class grades: that is, it could have been confounded with teachers' subjective perception of a given student. Thus, we were able to show that thinking styles were relevant to school performance, but our measures of school performance were, most likely, confounded with the teacher's view of a given student. In the present study, we had a chance to eliminate the possible bias that may have resulted from the use of class grades as indicators of academic performance. In this study, students' performance was rated by independent raters, who had never met the students and thus made their judgments based only on the quality of students' writing.

All students received identical kinds of assessments: two major homework assignments, a final project, and two exams. Each of the assessments involved various tasks testing for analytical, creative, and practical skills. Some examples of assessments are (a) compare Freud's theory of dreaming to Jung's [analytical]; (b) design an experiment to test a theory of dreaming [creative]; and (c) discuss the implications of Jung's theory of dreaming for your life [practical].

Four raters scored all performance assessments, rating each task for a corresponding ability (e.g., analytic ratings for the analytic performances). All ratings were on a scale of 1 (low) to 9 (high). The effective reliabilities of quality ratings for four raters varied from .73 to .96. Principal-components analyses were used to extract the common variance in the ratings of the four judges for each of the analytic, creative, and practical ratings for the three types of assessments. The first principal-component score of these analyses was then used to assess achievement in the following analyses. Thus, there were six resulting factor scores: three abilities (analytic, creative, and practical), evaluated in three different assessment settings (two homework assignments, a final project, and two exams).

Using these scores, we created six summary measures. Three measures reflected students' performance on all homework assignments, all exams, and the final project. Three other measures reflected students' performance on analyti-

cal, creative, and practical tasks in different assessment settings. These six measures were used in the further analyses.

Evaluation of Styles. In the present study, students' thinking styles were evaluated in two different ways: (a) a self-report questionnaire and (b) a set of thinking-styles tasks. Detailed descriptions of the thinking-styles instruments can be found elsewhere (Grigorenko & Sternberg, in press; Sternberg & Grigorenko, 1995). The purpose of having different measures was to have converging operations (Garner, Hake, & Eriksen, 1956) that measured the same constructs. In this way, sources of bias and error associated with individual measures would be reduced (Campbell & Fiske, 1959). The thinking styles measures are as follows:

- *Thinking Styles Questionnaire (TSQ).* This questionnaire consisted of 104 items, 8 for each of 13 scales: legislative, executive, judicial, monarchic, hierarchic, oligarchic, anarchic, global, local, liberal, conservative, internal, and external. Items were in the form of a Likert scale with ratings ranging from 1 (low) to 7 (high). In the further analyses, we used only 11 scales: Internal and external styles were excluded, because the other thinking styles measure (see the following description) did not include the tasks measuring these styles. The scales' internal consistency coefficients, obtained from an independent sample of school students prior to the study, ranged from .55 to .83 (see Table 2), suggesting adequate reliability of the instrument.

- *Set of Thinking Styles Tasks for Students (STS).* The STS was a set of 16 different tasks and preference items for students. The tasks and preference items were assumed to map directly onto 11 thinking styles: legislative, executive, judicial, monarchic, hierarchic, oligarchic, anarchic, global, local, liberal, and conservative. Students had to solve problems and make choices, and every response was coded via a scoring map of correspondence between responses and styles. For each scale, the sum of the scores across tasks and preference items was considered to be a measure of the thinking style. When preferences and choices were reordered into dichotomous form, the KR-20 reliability coefficients ranged from .59 to .74 (Sternberg & Grigorenko, 1995).

Examples of items from the TSQ and STS, as well as internal-consistency alpha reliabilities of subscales (calculated on independent but comparable samples of students not involved in these studies), are shown in Table 2. The correlations between corresponding scales of the TSQ and STS varied between $r = .45$ ($N = 277$, $p < .0001$) for the conservative style and $r = .20$ ($N = 277$, $p < .001$) for the global style.

Principal-components analyses were used to extract the common variance in the scale scores obtained from the TSQ and STS. The first principal-component scores were then used as measures of the styles in the data analyses. The variance explained by the first principal component of each style was 64% for legislative; 69% for executive; 61% for judicial; 58% for monarchic; 50% for hierarchic; 52% for oligarchic; 50% for anarchic; 60% for global; 63% for local; 72% for liberal; and 72% for conservative. This procedure allowed us to separate out questionnaire-specific measurement error, at least to some extent, and to pre-

TABLE 2

Examples of Some of the Items and Reliability Coefficients of the Scales of the Thinking Styles Questionnaire (TSQ) and the Set of Thinking Styles Tasks for Students (STS)

Style	Sample Item	Reliability (α)
Thinking Styles Questionnaire (TSQ)		$N = 277$
Legislative	When faced with a problem, I use my own ideas and strategies to solve it.	.81
Executive	Before starting a task or project, I check to see what method or procedure should be used.	.83
Judicial	I enjoy work that involves analyzing, grading, or comparing things.	.73
Monarchic	I like to concentrate on one task at a time.	.84
Hierarchic	In talking or writing down ideas, I like to have the issues organized in order of importance.	.81
Oligarchic	I prefer to work on a project or task that is acceptable and approved by my peers.	.54
Anarchic	When there are many important things to do, I try to do as many as I can in whatever time I have.	.55
Global	I care more about the general effect than about details of a task I have to do.	.83
Local	I like to collect detailed or specific information for projects I work on.	.66
Liberal	I like to change routines in order to improve the way tasks are done.	.88
Conservative	I like situations where I can follow a set routine.	.83

Set of Thinking Styles Tasks for Students (STS)

Item Examples:

When I am studying literature, I prefer: (a) to make up my own story with my own characters and my own plot *(legislative)*; (b) to evaluate the author's style, to criticize the author's ideas, and to evaluate characters' actions *(judicial)*; (c) to follow the teacher's advice and interpretations of author's positions, and to use the teacher's way of analyzing literature *(executive)*; (d) to do something else (please describe your preferences in the space below).

An example of a task to distinguish among oligarchic, hierarchical, monarchic, and anarchic thinking styles is: You are the mayor of a large northeastern city. You have a city budget this year of $100 million. Below is a list of prob-

TABLE 2
(Continued)

lems currently facing your city. Your job is to decide how you will spend the $100 million available to improve your city. Next to each problem is the projected cost to eliminate a problem entirely. In the space on the next page, list each problem on which you will spend city money and how much money you will budget for that problem. Whether you spend money on one, some, or all problems is up to you, but be sure your plan will not exceed the $100 million available. Whether you spend all the money to solve one or a few problems or divide the money partially to solve many problems is up to you. You have one additional problem—you are up for reelection next year, so consider public opinion when making your decisions.

Problems facing your city:
(1) Drug problem ($100,000,000); (2) The roads (they are old, full of potholes, and need to be repaired) ($25,000,000); (3) You have no new land for landfill and you need to build a recycling center ($25,000,000); (4) You need shelters for the homeless ($50,000,000); (5) You must replace subway cars and city buses; you need to buy new ones for the public transportation system ($50,000,000); (6) The public school teachers are demanding a salary increase and they are going to go on strike ($30,000,000); (7) Sanitation workers are demanding a salary increase and they are going to go on strike ($30,000,000); (8) An increase in unemployment has increased the number of welfare recipients ($80,000,000); (9) The AIDS epidemic has created the need for public education on AIDS prevention and you need to build an AIDS hospital ($100,000,000); and (10) You need to build a new convention center to attract out-of-state tourists. This could generate additional revenue for the next fiscal year ($70,000,000).

---

serve for further analyses the styles scores reflecting only variance shared by the two instruments.

Some styles were highly correlated (e.g., local and global, $r = -.67$, $p < .001$). To reduce the factor space of styles (i.e., to decrease the number of dependent variables), we performed factor analyses with varimax rotation, using the factor scores described previously. The outcome of this analysis was a nine-factor structure, which explained 98% of the total variance. Four of the styles created two factors with different directions of factor loadings (FL). Thus, liberal and conservative styles loaded on one factor; FLs were .90 and -.89, respectively. Global and local styles also created a two-pole factor, with FLs of .93 and -.90, respectively. All other styles formed independent factors. The FLs were as follows: judicial, .99; executive, .81; legislative, .82; monarchic, .98; hierarchic, .97; oligarchic, .99; and anarchic, .99. The factor scores of these 9 factors (local-global, liberal-conservative, judicial, executive, legislative, hierarchic, oligarchic, monarchic, and anarchic) were used in the further analyses.

RESULTS

Based on the results of our previous work (Grigorenko & Sternberg, in press; Sternberg & Grigorenko, 1993, 1995) and in correspondence with the research questions of this study, we formed a set of working hypotheses:

1. *We expected to find no association of styles with abilities.* That is, we did not expect to find that students with different ability patterns would demonstrate consistent stylistic preferences.

2. *We expected that at least some thinking styles would contribute to predictions of overall academic performance,* although we did not specify which ones.

3. *We did not expect to find any difference in academic performance of matched versus mismatched students of different styles.* That is, we did not expect to find any interaction effects between types of instruction (being matched/mismatched) and thinking styles. For example, we did not expect judicial creative students to perform better in the analytical instruction group than did legislative creative students in this group.

4. *We expected that students with certain thinking styles would perform better in some forms of evaluation than in others.*

We present the results of our study with respect to the formulated research questions.

Styles, Abilities, Gender, and Grade

In the first set of analyses, we tested whether there were any group differences between styles for male versus female students, for students of differing ability patterns, and for students in different school grades. Multivariate analysis of variance was used. None of the main effects or interaction effects was significant. Thus, students' thinking styles did not differ across sex, grade, or ability patterns.

When Abilities Are Taken Into Account, Do Styles Still Predict Academic Performance?

We explored the question of whether thinking styles add anything to the explanatory power of ability measures for predicting academic performance. First, we computed correlations between academic performance measures, STAT scores, and the measures of the thinking styles (Table 3). All three STAT components correlated significantly with the assessments of performance across different abilities (the correlations ranged from $r = .34$, $p < .0001$ to $r = .15$, $p < .05$). Seven out of nine correlations between the STAT components and types of assessments were also significant, but practical and creative components of the STAT did not correlate significantly with performance on the homework assignments. It is important to note the fairly high correlations between all academic performance measures and scores on the analytical subtest of the STAT. These correlations were stronger than the diagonal correlations between subtests of the STAT and corresponding performance measures. We explain the presence of these correlations as a reflection of the fact that students' performance on all of the assignments, exams, and the final project were inevitably confounded with the general ability of each student to understand and analyze the theory with which he or she was working. This occurred despite our efforts to formulate the tasks in the manner most suitable for each of the studied abilities. The magnitude of these off-diagonal correlations, however, does not differ significantly from the magnitude of the diagonal correlations. For example, even the largest discrepancy, $r = .34$ versus $r = .17$, did not represent a significant difference: $z = 1.82$, $p > .05$. In other words, the presence of these off-diagonal correlations statistically does not undermine the discriminant validity of the STAT.

Only five styles correlated significantly with measures of performance. Indicators of the judicial style correlated significantly with performance on all tasks and in all assessment settings. In addition, students with the legislative style tended to perform better on both the final projects and the exams and on both the analytical and creative measures. On the contrary, the performance of executive students was worse on the final project and on both the creative and analytical tasks. Liberal students tended to do better on the final project, and hierarchical students did better on the creative assignments. Thus, the correlational pattern suggests that the judicial, legislative, and ex

ecutive styles showed significant associations with academic performance. In particular, students with higher scores on the legislative and judicial thinking styles tended to do better, whereas students who scored high on the executive style tended to do worse, on average.

Among the correlations between the thinking styles measures and the STAT components, only the association between the STAT creative component and the liberal-conservative styles factor was significant ($r = .22$, $p < .005$), with liberal students being more creative. This general lack of associations between the styles and the ability measures largely supports our predictions of no differences on thinking styles in groups of students with different ability patterns. Of course, we cannot prove the null hypothesis.

Thus, the simple correlational analyses suggested that students' performance was associated not only with their levels and patterns of abilities, but also with their thinking styles. Moreover, the amount of variance explained by the STAT subtests in the measures of performance was of the same magnitude as the amount of variance explained by some of the styles (e.g., judicial). In addition, the fact that there was only one significant correlation between the STAT measures and the thinking styles suggests that associations of thinking styles with academic performance are independent of the correlations between academic performance and abilities.

To test further the predictive power of styles, we performed a series of multiple-regression analyses in which the predicted variables were the measures of achieved performance on tasks requiring use of various abilities and performance on various tasks in different assessment settings, and the predictors were the measures on the corresponding STAT component and the five thinking styles that were found to be correlated with the measures of academic performance. Thus the multiple-regression equations were both theoretically based and used the information obtained in the correlation analyses.

The independent variables predicted 16% of the variance in the summary measure of performance on the analytic tasks ($F = 5.3$, $p < .0001$). The variables that contributed significantly were the STAT analytic component ($F = 13.2$, $p < .0005$, $B = .18$), judicial style ($F = 3.6$, $p < .05$, $B = .09$), legislative style ($F = 5.0$, $p < .05$, $B = .11$), and executive style ($F = 3.4$, $p < .05$, $B = -.10$). For performance on the creative tasks, the predictors explained 15% of the variance ($F = 5.0$, $p < .0001$). Significant contributions to the explained variance were from the STAT creative component ($F = 7.3$, $p < .05$, $B = .14$), judicial style ($F = 6.8$,

TABLE 3
Correlations of Abilities, Academic Performance, and Styles

Item	Performance					
	Analytic	*Creative*	*Practical*	*Homework*	*Exams*	*Project*
Abilities						
STAT-Analytical	.25*	.34*	.34*	.26*	.27*	.31*
STAT-Creative	.15*	.21*	.20*	.13	.16*	.20*
STAT-Practical	.15*	.17*	.17*	.12	.18*	.15*
Thinking styles (factor scores)						
Legislative	.17*	.16*	.14	.12	.14*	.17*
Judicial	.15*	.20*	.23*	.21*	.18*	.15*
Executive	-.15*	-.16*	-.10	-.12	-.07	-.18*
Monarchic	-.06	-.06	-.08	-.05	-.04	-.10
Hierarchic	.06	.16*	.11	.13	.07	.08
Oligarchic	-.06	-.11	-.11	-.12	-.11	.03
Anarchic	-.08	-.13	-.12	-.10	-.08	-.12
Local-Global	.07	.04	.09	.05	.01	.12
Liberal-Conservative	.14	.10	.08	.03	.09	.16

Note: STAT = Sternberg Triarchic Abilities Test, Level H.

* $p < .05$.

$p < .01$, $B = .13$), and executive style ($F = 4.3$, $p < .05$, $B = -.11$). Finally, the independent variables predicted 13% of the variance in performance on the practical tasks ($F = 4.1$, $p < .001$, $B = .18$). Only two variables contributed significantly: the practical component of the STAT ($F = 6.7$, $p < .01$, $B = .14$) and judicial style ($F = 10.6$, $p < .001$, $B = .17$). Thus, performance on the analytic, creative, and practical tasks is dependent not only on the level of the corresponding ability, but also on stylistic preferences. In general, the more judicial or legislative a student was, the better his or her performance was, whereas the more executive a student was, the worse was his or her performance.

The results of the multiple-regression analyses predicting performance on various tasks in different assessment settings were homogeneous. For all three overall dependent measures

(exam, homework, and final project evaluations), the analytical component of the STAT was the best predictor ($p < .0001$ in all three models, B ranging from .24 to .27). The judicial style made a statistically significant contribution in explaining variation in performance on the exams ($F = 6.3$, $p < .01$, $B = .15$), on homework ($F = 8.0$, $p < .005$, $B = .15$), and on the final project ($F = 3.3$, $p < .05$, $B = .10$). Moreover, three other styles contributed significantly to prediction of final project performance: the legislative style ($F = 5.1$, $p < .05$, $B = .13$), the liberal style ($F = 3.8$, $p < .05$, $B = .12$), and the executive style ($F = 4.4$, $p < .05$, $B = -.13$).

Styles and Different Types of Instruction

In the previous analyses, we investigated the predictive power of styles for academic performance over and above abilities across all groups, regardless of the type of instruction. The question for the following set of analyses was whether styles make a difference in academic performance of matched versus mismatched students, that is, whether there is an interaction effect between type of instruction (matched/mismatched) and thinking styles. For example, do judicial creative students perform better in the analytical instruction group than do legislative creative students?

At the first stage of these analyses, we conducted analysis of variance to ensure that there were no accidental clusterings of thinking styles within different instructional groups or within groups of matched and mismatched students. There were not. At the second stage, we performed two series of multiple-regression analyses of academic performance, testing for (a) possible interaction effects between thinking styles and type of instruction, and (b) possible interaction effects between thinking styles and matched/mismatched placement. No main or interaction effects with type of instruction were found. There was an effect of match for the summary score on analytic tasks and homework assignments, with matched students doing better than mismatched students, but no interaction effects with thinking styles were found.

Styles and Different Types of Evaluation

Finally, a last set of analyses was based on the hypothesis that various assessment methods might favor different thinking styles (Sternberg, 1994). Specifically, we suggested that while types of assessments do not differentially benefit students of different ability patterns (e.g., creative students would do as well on the homework assignments as on the exams), various types of evaluation could be differentially beneficial for students of different styles (e.g., a judicial student would do better on the exams than on the final project).

To perform these analyses, we recoded the thinking-styles scores. We analyzed the distribution of thinking styles scores in the sample and adapted a cut-point of 1.5 standard deviations to detect the 10%-15% of the students who scored the highest on each of the 11 styles (we used raw scores on thinking styles in these analyses). (Due to the limited size of our sample, we could not adapt a traditional conservative cut-off score of 2 standard deviations above the mean.)

These students were considered to be "high" on a given style. Then we carried out analyses of variance to test whether members of the high groups performed better in particular assessment settings than in others. Table 4 shows the results of these analyses. The table shows that there is a significant difference in performance of

highly judicial, highly liberal, and highly oligarchic thinkers versus all other students on exams, judicial thinkers versus other students on homework, and executive and anarchic thinkers versus other students on the final project. Moreover, certain combinations of styles (e.g., judicial and global) tend to enhance the performance in different assessment situations.

The patterns of the means suggest that the exam format was most favorable for judicial thinkers (μ= .39 in the group of highly judicial students versus μ = -.03 in the group of other students) and for thinkers of other styles who were also high on the judicial style. This format of assessment was least beneficial for legislative/global thinkers (μ = -2.11 in the group of legislative-global thinkers versus μ = -.04 or higher in other groups), and was disadvantageous as well for oligarchic students (μ = -.44 in the group of oligarchic thinkers versus μ = .02 in the group of other students).

The format of the independent final project was the least beneficial for executive students (μ = -.44 among executive thinkers versus μ = .07 in the group of all other students) and, moreover, for students with virtually all combinations of other styles with the executive style. In addition, anarchic students tended to do worse than did all other students combined (μ = -.37 versus μ = .08, respectively). The independent project was the most favorable for legislative/local (μ = 2.30 versus μ = .29 or lower in other groups), legislative/anarchic (μ = .51 versus μ = .05 or lower in other groups), and legislative/liberal (μ = 2.28 versus μ = .29 or lower in other groups) thinkers.

Homework assignments were quite variable, and, in addition, there were few constraints on how they had to be done; for example, a student could request a consultation with a teaching fellow, or a group of students could complete the assignments together. Thus, this particular type of assessment did not appear to be consistently beneficial for students with any particular stylistic preferences, except for judicial thinkers (μ = .40 versus μ = -.04 in the group of all other students).

DISCUSSION

This study attempted to investigate patterns of thinking styles in a group of gifted children. We obtained the following results, in summary:

- There are no differences in thinking styles between groups of students with different ability patterns.

- Certain thinking styles contribute significantly to prediction of academic performance.
- The degree of this contribution is not affected by the type of instruction students are given.
- Students with particular thinking styles do better in some forms of evaluation than in others.

A few interesting conclusions can be drawn from the results. First, we saw no distinct patterns of particular thinking styles among the students by abilities, gender, or grade. These results are similar to those of our previous findings in a sample of unselected (nongifted) students in four different schools (Sternberg & Grigorenko, 1995). Thus, in two independent groups of students, we found no direct links between styles and abilities. A variety of styles can be associated with high levels of ability. Moreover, various types of abilities can be associated with a given style.

The finding of no difference in profiles of styles in males versus females is also not a surprising one: Previously we also found no association between students' gender and their styles (Sternberg & Grigorenko, 1995). A lack of grade differences in styles might be explained by the fact that in both studies we worked primarily with high-school students, limiting the age range of participants to 12-17 years of age. We intentionally limited our samples to this age range due to the fact that we used self-report questionnaires requiring a certain level of metacognitive capacities to reflect stable patterns of preferences and behaviors (Schwab-Stone, Fallon, Briggs, & Crowther, 1994). However, the theory of mental self-government assumes the presence of developmental changes in stylistic preferences; future studies, implementing measures other than self-report ones, might show significant age/grade effects.

In our larger-scale study (Sternberg & Clinkenbeard, 1995; Sternberg et al., in press), we found a significant instruction-by-ability interaction and showed that performance of students with a certain ability pattern was higher on the tasks corresponding to their abilities if these students were placed in a matching instructional

TABLE 4
Styles and Types of Assessment

Styles	Exams	Homework Assignments	Final Paper
Judicial	$F(1, 186) = 3.3, p < .05$	$F(1, 186) = 5.8, p < .05$	
Executive			$F(1,186) = 4.1, p < .05$
Liberal	$F(1,186) = 3.3, p < .05$		
Oligarchic	$F(1,186) = 4.3, p < .05$		
Anarchic			$F(1, 186) = 4.4, p < .05$
Legislative*Global	$F(3,186) = 3.6, p < .01$		
Legislative*Local			$F(3,186) = 3.6, p < .05$
Legislative*Liberal			$F(3,186) = 3.6, p < .05$
Legislative*Anarchic			$F(3,186) = 2.8, p < .05$
Judicial*Global	$F(3,184) = 2.3, p < .05$		
Judicial*Hierarchic	$F(3,186) = 4.5, p < .005$	$F(3,186) = 2.5, p < .05$	
Executive*Global			$F(3,186) = 4.9, p < .005$
Executive* Conservative			$F(3,186) = 4.1, p < .01$
Executive*Anarchic			$F(3,186) = 2.9, p < .05$

Note: The table shows only the styles and the combination of the styles that yielded statistically significant results. The significance values are corrected for multiple comparisons by adjusting *p* values.

group (e.g., analytical students placed in the groups with analytical instructions did better on the analytical tasks than did other students). In this study, due to the study design, we had a chance to investigate how, if at all, thinking styles modify the relationships between ability type and the mode of instruction. We discovered no significant buffering effects that could have been attributed to styles. For example, creative students, placed in instructional groups that did not match their ability, did not differ in their performance when their styles were taken into account. These findings, however, should be interpreted with caution: The whole program took only 4 weeks; and it is possible that there simply was not enough time for stylistic differences to manifest themselves.

Further, in the present study, we had a unique opportunity to evaluate the contribution various thinking styles made to students' performance in a given situation, when these evaluations were conducted by psychologists who did not meet the students in person, but judged their performance on the basis of their writing. Of course, a valid argument could be made that such a type of evaluation is biased in favor of students with a high level of writing skills. Yet, taking into account this drawback of our evaluation system, we think that these assessments were less subjective than traditional school teachers' grades, and therefore provided us with an opportunity to test whether thinking styles predict students' performance, over and above the students' abilities. This particular aspect of the design was especially interesting, due to the fact that in our previous research we showed that teachers tend to overestimate the extent to which their students share their own styles, and that students in fact receive higher grades and more favorable evaluations when their styles more closely match those of their teachers (Sternberg & Grigorenko, 1995). Thus, the opportunity to separate teacher-dependent variance in performance assessment and to study the "purer" contributions of ability and styles was explored.

We found that students' performance was associated not only with their levels and types of abilities, but also with at least three thinking styles (judicial, executive, and legislative). The highest predictive power was demonstrated by the judicial style. But, in interpreting these results, we should say that a significant portion of the YSPP academic activities was based on analytical work, which involved comparing, contrasting, and evaluating. Even though special "create-and-implement" tasks were designed to benefit creative and practical students, these tasks were based on ma-

terial that needed to be critically evaluated by a student. Thus, even the creative and practical tasks in our program involved a significant amount of analytical effort. We might have found a different "most favorable style" were the same study carried out in an art school or a boy/girl-scout program. However, the most general conclusion remains the same: Styles add to our understanding of students' performance, and therefore should be taken into consideration in school settings.

Yet one more illustration of the importance of the styles came from the last, and probably the most interesting part of the study, where we compared the performance of students in "high" and "other" groups in a particular style. In these analyses, we detected a number of interaction effects between various styles and different assessment procedures. We found that the examination format was most beneficial for judicial students, whereas the final projects favored legislative students and disadvantaged executive students. Although our sample was not large enough to study interactions between various styles in more detail, the results clearly suggest that different types of assessment benefit different types of thinkers (see also Sternberg, 1994). The take-home message of these analyses is that styles do matter, and teachers should systematically vary their assessment to meet the needs of a larger number of students.

These latter analyses are of practical value. A teacher of gifted students should try to assess the students' performance by using an array of different assessment procedures. Independent of their patterns of abilities, gifted students of different thinking styles tend to perform better when the method of assessment matches their thinking styles. Our results, obtained in this and other studies, suggest that short-answer/multiple-choice items appear to be most beneficial for executive, local, judicial, and hierarchic thinkers. Macroanalytic essays are advantageous for judicial-global students, whereas microanalytic essays will be advantageous for judicial-local thinkers. Timed assignments may be beneficial for hierarchic students and detrimental for anarchic ones. Monarchic students tend to shine when the assignment requires high commitment, whereas oligarchic students are able to divide their resources equally between a number of tasks. Open-ended assignments, projects, and portfolios will benefit legislative thinkers and may frustrate executive ones.

In summary, the diversity of styles among students implies that students need a variety of means of assessment to maximize and show to an optimal extent their talents and achievements.

REFERENCES

Allport, G. (1937). *Personality: A psychological interpretation.* New York: Holt.

Campbell, D. T., & Fiske, D. W. (1959). Convergent and discriminant validation by the multitrait multimethod matrix. *Psychological Bulletin, 56,* 81-105.

Carroll, J. B. (1993). *Human cognitive abilities: A survey of factor-analytic studies.* New York, NY: Cambridge University Press.

Curry, L. (1983). An organization of learning styles theory and constructs. *ERIC Document.* 235 185.

Dunn, R., & Dunn, K. (1978). *Teaching students through their individual learning styles.* Reston, VA: Reston Publishing.

Fowler, W. (1977). Sequence and styles in cognitive development. In F. Weizmann & I. Uzgiris (Eds.), *The structuring of experience* (pp. 265-295). New York: Plenum Press.

Fowler, W. (1980). Cognitive differentiation and developmental learning. In H. Rees & L. Lipsitt (Eds.), *Advances in child development and behavior, Vol. 15* (pp. 163-206). New York: Academic Press.

Gardner, H. (1983). *Frames of mind: The theory of multiple intelligences.* New York: Basic Books.

Gardner, R. (1953). Cognitive style in categorizing behavior. *Perceptual and Motor Skills, 22,* 214-233.

Garner, W. R., Hake, H. W., & Eriksen, C. W. (1956). Operationism and the concept of perception. *Psychological Review, 63,* 149-159.

Gregorc, A. F. (1984). Style as a symptom: A phenomenological perspective. *Theory Into Practice, 23,* 51-55.

Grigorenko, E. L., & Sternberg, R. J. (1995). Thinking styles. In D. H. Saklofske & M. Zeidner (Eds.) *International handbook of personality and intelligence* (pp. 205-229). New York: Plenum Press.

Grigorenko, E. L., & Sternberg, R. J. (in press). Styles of thinking in school settings. *Vestnik Moskovskogo Universiteta. Seria 14. Psikhologia.*

Guilford, J. P. (1967). *The nature of human intelligence.* New York: McGraw-Hill.

Holland, J. L. (1973). *Making vocational choices: A theory of careers.* Englewood Cliffs, NJ: Prentice-Hall.

Horn, J. L. (1994). Theory of fluid and crystallized intelligence. In R. J. Sternberg (Ed.), *The encyclopedia of human intelligence. Vol. 1* (pp. 443-451). New York: Macmillan.

Jung, C. (1923). *Psychological types.* New York: Harcourt Brace.

Kagan, J. (1958). The concept of identification. *Psychological Review, 65,* 296-305.

Kagan, J., & Kogan, N. (1970). Individual variation in cognitive processes. In P. A. Mussen (Ed.), *Carmichael's manual of child psychology. Vol. 1* (pp. 1273-1365). New York: Wiley.

Klein, G. S. (1954). Need and regulation. In M. R. Jones (Ed.), *Nebraska symposium on motivation* (pp. 474-505). Lincoln: University of Nebraska Press.

Kogan, N. (1983). Stylistic variation in childhood and adolescence: Creativity, metaphor, and cognitive style. In P. H. Mussen (Ed.), *Handbook of child psychology, Vol. 3* (pp. 630-706). New York: Wiley.

Kolb, D. A. (1974). On management and the learning process. In D. A. Kolb, I. M. Rubin, & J. M. McIntyre (Eds.), *Organizational psychology* (pp. 239-252). Englewood Cliffs, NJ: Prentice-Hall.

Martin, M. (1989). *Mind as mental self-government: Construct validation of a theory of intellectual styles.* Unpublished manuscript, Yale University, New Haven, Connecticut.

Miller, A. (1987). Cognitive styles: An integrated model. *Educational Psychology, 7,* 251-268.

Miller, A. (1991). Personality types, learning styles and educational goals. *Educational Psychology, 11,* 217-238.

Myers, I. B., & Myers, P. B. (1980). *Gifts differing.* Palo Alto, CA: Consulting Psychologists Press.

Renzulli, J. S., & Smith, L. H. (1978). *Learning styles inventory.* Mansfield Center, CT: Creative Learning Press.

Riding, R., & Cheema, I. (1991). Cognitive styles: An overview and integration. *Educational Psychology, 11,* 193-215.

Royce, J., & Powell, A. (1983). *Theory of personality and individual differences: Factors, systems and process.* Englewood Cliffs, NJ: Prentice-Hall.

Santostefano, S. (1986). Cognitive controls, metaphors and contexts: An approach to cognition and emotion. In D. Bearison & H. Zimiles (Eds.), *Thought and emotion: Developmental perspectives* (pp. 217-238). Hillsdale, NJ: Lawrence Erlbaum.

Schwab-Stone, M., Fallon, T., Briggs, M., & Crowther, B. (1994). Reliability of diagnostic reporting for children 6-11 years: A test-retest study of the Revised Diagnostic Schedule for Children. *The American Journal of Psychiatry, 157,* 1048-1054.

Spearman, C. (1927). *The abilities of man.* New York: Macmillan.

Sternberg, R. J. (1985). *Beyond IQ: A triarchic theory of human intelligence.* New York: Cambridge University Press.

Sternberg, R. J. (1986). *Intelligence applied: Understanding and increasing your intellectual skills.* San Diego: Harcourt Brace.

Sternberg, R. J. (1988a). Mental self-government: A theory of intellectual styles and their development. *Human Development, 31,* 197-224.

Sternberg, R. J. (1988b). *The triarchic mind: A new theory of human intelligence.* New York: Viking.

Sternberg, R. J. (1990). Thinking styles: Keys to understanding student performance. *Phi Delta Kappan, 71,* 366-371.

Sternberg, R. J. (1993). *Sternberg Triarchic Abilities Test.* Unpublished test.

Sternberg, R. J. (1994). Allowing for thinking styles. *Educational Leadership, 52*(3), 36-39.

Sternberg, R. J. (1995). *In search of the human mind.* Orlando, FL: Harcourt Brace.

Sternberg, R. J., & Clinkenbeard, P. (1995). A triarchic view of identifying, teaching, and assessing gifted children. *Roeper Review, 17,* 225-260.

Sternberg, R. J., Ferrari, M., Clinkenbeard, P., & Grigorenko, E. L. (in press). Identification, instruction, and assessment of gifted children: A construct validation of a triarchic model. *Gifted Child Quarterly.*

Sternberg, R. J., & Grigorenko, E. L. (1993). Thinking styles and the gifted. *Roeper Review, 16,* 122-130.

Sternberg, R. J., & Grigorenko, E. L. (1995). Styles of thinking in the school. *European Journal of High Ability, 6*(2), 1-19.

Thurstone, L. L. (1938). *Primary mental abilities.* Chicago: University of Chicago Press.

Vernon, P. (1973). Multivariate approaches to the study of cognitive styles. In J. R. Royce (Ed.), *Contributions of multivariate analysis to psychological theory* (pp. 139-157). London: Academic Press.

Witkin, H. A. (1973). *The role of cognitive style in academic performance and in teacher-student relations.* Unpublished report, Educational Testing Service. Princeton, New Jersey.

Witkin, H. A., Oltman, P. K., Raskin, E., & Karp, S. A. (1971). *Embedded Figures Test, Children's Embedded Figures Test, Group Embedded Figures Test.* Manual. Palo Alto: Consulting Psychologist Press.

ABOUT THE AUTHORS

ELENA L. GRIGORENKO, Associate Research Scientist, Department of Psychology and Child Study Center; and **ROBERT J. STERNBERG,** IBM Professor of Psychology and Education, Department of Psychology, Yale University, New Haven, Connecticut.

This research was supported under the Javits Act Program (Grant #R206R50001) as administered by the Office of Educational Research and Improvement of the U.S. Department of Education. Grantees undertaking such projects are encouraged to express their professional judgments freely. This article, therefore, does not necessarily represent positions or policies of the government, and no official endorsement should be inferred.

We are grateful to Pamela Clinkenbeard and Michel Ferrari for their assistance in data collection.

Copies of the instruments may be obtained at cost from the authors. Address requests for reprints to Robert J. Sternberg, Department of Psychology, Yale University, Box 208205, New Haven, CT 06520-8205 (E-mail: sterobj@yalevm.cis.yale.edu).

Manuscript received January 1996; revision accepted April 1996.

The Rewards of Learning

To teach without using extrinsic rewards is analogous to asking our students to learn to draw with their eyes closed, Mr. Chance maintains. Before we do that, we should open our own eyes.

Paul Chance

Paul Chance (Eastern Shore Maryland Chapter) is a psychologist, writer, and teacher. He is the author of Thinking in the Classroom *(Teachers College Press, 1986) and teaches at James H. Groves Adult High School in Georgetown, Del.*

A man is seated at a desk. Before him lie a pencil and a large stack of blank paper. He picks up the pencil, closes his eyes, and attempts to draw a four-inch line. He makes a second attempt, a third, a fourth, and so on, until he has made well over a hundred attempts at drawing a four-inch line, all without ever opening his eyes. He repeats the exercise for several days, until he has drawn some 3,000 lines, all with his eyes closed. On the last day, he examines his work. The question is, How much improvement has there been in his ability to draw a four-inch line? How much has he learned from his effort?

E. L. Thorndike, the founder of educational psychology and a major figure in the scientific analysis of learning, performed this experiment years ago, using himself as subject.[1] He found no evidence of learning. His ability to draw a four-inch line was no better on the last day than it had been on the first.

The outcome of this experiment may seem obvious to us today, but it was an effective way of challenging a belief widely held earlier in this century, a belief that formed the very foundation of education at the time: the idea that "practice makes perfect."

It was this blind faith in practice that justified countless hours of rote drill as a standard teaching technique. Thorndike's experiment demonstrated that practice in and of itself is not sufficient for learning. Based on this and other, more formal studies, Thorndike concluded that prac-

tice is important only insofar as it provides the opportunity for reinforcement.

To reinforce means to strengthen, and among learning researchers *reinforcement* refers to a procedure for strengthening behavior (that is, making it likely to be repeated) by providing certain kinds of consequences.[2] These consequences, called *reinforcers,* are usually events or things a person willingly seeks out. For instance, we might teach a person to draw a four-inch line with his eyes closed merely by saying "good" each time the effort is within half an inch of the goal. Most people like to succeed, so this positive feedback should be an effective way of reinforcing the appropriate behavior.

Hundreds of experimental studies have demonstrated that systematic use of reinforcement can improve both classroom conduct and the rate of learning. Yet the systematic use of reinforcement has never been widespread in American schools. In *A Place Called School*, John Goodlad reports that, in the elementary grades, an average of only 2% of class time is devoted to reinforcement; in the high schools, the figure falls to 1%.[3]

THE COSTS OF REWARD

There are probably many reasons for our failure to make the most of reinforcement. For one thing, few schools of education provide more than cursory instruction in its use. Given Thorndike's finding about the role of practice in learning, it is ironic that many teachers actually use the term *reinforcement* as a synonym for *practice.* ("We assign workbook exercises for reinforcement.") If schools of education do not teach future teachers the nature of reinforcement and how to use it effectively, teachers can hardly be blamed for not using it.

The unwanted effects of misused reinforcement have led some teachers to shy away from it. The teacher who sometimes lets a noisy class go to recess early will find the class getting noisier before recess. If high praise is reserved for long-winded essays, students will develop wordy and redundant writing styles. And it should surprise no one if students are seldom original in classrooms where only conventional work is admired or if they are uncooperative in classrooms where one can earn recognition only through competition. Reinforcement is powerful stuff, and its misuse can cause problems.

Another difficulty is that the optimal use of reinforcement would mean teaching in a new way. Some studies suggest that maximum learning in elementary and middle schools might require very high rates of reinforcement, perhaps with teachers praising someone in the class an average of once every 15 seconds.[4] Such a requirement is clearly incompatible with traditional teaching practices.

Systematic reinforcement can also mean more work for the teacher. Reinforcing behavior once every 15 seconds means 200 reinforcements in a 50-minute period — 1,000 reinforcements in a typical school day. It also implies that, in order to spot behavior to reinforce, the teacher must be moving about the room, not sitting at a desk marking papers. That may be too much to ask. Some studies have found that teachers who have been taught how to make good use of reinforcement often revert to their old style of teaching. This is so even though the teachers acknowledge that increased use of reinforcement means fewer discipline problems and a much faster rate of learning.[5]

Reinforcement also runs counter to our Puritan traditions. Most Americans have

From *Phi Delta Kappan*, November 1992, pp. 200-207. © 1992 by Paul Chance. Reprinted by permission.

always assumed — occasional protestations to the contrary notwithstanding — that learning should be hard work and at least slightly unpleasant. Often the object of education seems to be not so much to teach academic and social skills as to "build character" through exposure to adversity. When teachers reinforce students at a high rate, the students experience a minimum of adversity and actually enjoy learning. Thus some people think that reinforcement is bad for character development.

All of these arguments against reinforcement can be countered effectively. Schools of education do not provide much instruction in the practical use of reinforcement, but there is no reason why they cannot do so. Reinforcement can be used incorrectly and with disastrous results, but the same might be said of other powerful tools. Systematic use of reinforcement means teaching in a new way, but teachers can learn to do so.[6] A great deal of reinforcement is needed for optimum learning, but not all of the reinforcement needs to come from the teacher. (Reinforcement can be provided by computers and other teaching devices, by teacher aides, by parents, and by students during peer teaching and cooperative learning.) No doubt people do sometimes benefit from adversity, but the case for the character-building properties of adversity is very weak.[7]

However, there is one argument against reinforcement that cannot be dismissed so readily. For some 20 years, the claim has been made that systematic reinforcement actually undermines student learning. Those few teachers who make extensive use of reinforcement, it is claimed, do their students a disservice because reinforcement reduces interest in the reinforced activity.

Not all forms of reinforcement are considered detrimental. A distinction is made between reinforcement involving intrinsic reinforcers — or rewards, as they are often called — and reinforcement involving extrinsic rewards.[8] Only extrinsic rewards are said to be harmful. An *intrinsic reward* is ordinarily the natural consequence of behavior, hence the name. We learn to throw darts by seeing how close the dart is to the target; learn to type by seeing the right letters appear on the computer screen; learn to cook from the pleasant sights, fragrances, and flavors that result from our culinary efforts; learn to read from the understanding we get from the printed word; and

learn to solve puzzles by finding solutions. The Japanese say, "The bow teaches the archer." They are talking about intrinsic rewards, and they are right.

Extrinsic rewards come from an outside source, such as a teacher. Probably the most ubiquitous extrinsic reward (and one of the most effective) is praise. The teacher reinforces behavior by saying "good," "right," "correct," or "excellent" when the desired behavior occurs. Other extrinsic rewards involve nonverbal behavior such as smiles, winks, thumbs-up signs, hugs, congratulatory handshakes, pats on the back, or applause. Gold stars, certificates, candy, prizes, and even money have been used as rewards, but they are usually less important in teaching — and even in the maintenance of good discipline — than those mentioned earlier.

The distinction between intrinsic and extrinsic rewards is somewhat artificial. Consider the following example. You put money into a vending machine and retrieve a candy bar. The behavior of inserting money into a vending machine has been reinforced, as has the more general behavior of interacting with machines. But is the food you receive an intrinsic or an extrinsic reward? On the one hand, the food is the automatic consequence of inserting money and pressing buttons, so it would appear to be an intrinsic reward. On the other hand, the food is a consequence that was arranged by the designer of the machine, so it would seem to be an extrinsic reward.[9]

Though somewhat contrived, the distinction between intrinsic and extrinsic rewards has been maintained partly because extrinsic rewards are said to be damaging.[10] Are they? First, let us be clear about the charge. The idea is that — if teachers smile, praise, congratulate, say "thank you" or "right," shake hands, hug, give a pat on the back, applaud, provide a certificate of achievement or attendance, *or in any way provide a positive consequence (a reward) for student behavior* — the student will be less inclined to engage in that behavior when the reward is no longer available.

For example, teachers who offer prizes to students for reading books will, it is said, make the children less likely to read when prizes are no longer available. The teacher who reads a student's story aloud to the class as an example of excellent story writing actually makes the student less likely to write stories in the future, when such public approval is not forth-

coming. When teachers (and students) applaud a youngster who has given an excellent talk, they make that student disinclined to give talks in the future. The teacher who comments favorably on the originality of a painting steers the young artist away from painting. And so on. This is the charge against extrinsic rewards.

No one disputes the effectiveness of extrinsic rewards in teaching or in maintaining good discipline. Some might therefore argue that extrinsic rewards should be used, even if they reduce interest in learning. Better to have students who read only when required to do so, some might say, than to have students who cannot read at all.

But if rewards do reduce interest, that fact is of tremendous importance. "The teacher may count himself successful," wrote B. F. Skinner, "when his students become engrossed in his field, study conscientiously, and do more than is required of them, but *the important thing is what they do when they are no longer being taught*" (emphasis added).[11] It is not enough for students to learn the three R's and a little science and geography; they must be prepared for a lifetime of learning. To reduce their interest in learning would be a terrible thing — even if it were done in the interest of teaching them effectively.

The question of whether rewards adversely affect motivation is not, then, of merely academic or theoretical importance. It is of great practical importance to the classroom teacher.

Extrinsic rewards are said to be damaging. Are they? First, let us be clear about the charge.

More than 100 studies have examined this question.[12] In a typical experiment, Mark Lepper and his colleagues observed 3- to 5-year-old nursery school children playing with various kinds of toys.[13] The toys available included felt tip pens of various colors and paper to draw on. The researchers noted the children's inclination to draw during this period. Next the researchers took the children aside and asked them to draw with the felt tip pens. The researchers promised some children a "Good Player Award" for drawing. Other children drew pictures without receiving an award.

Two weeks later, the researchers returned to the school, provided felt tip pens and paper, and observed the children's inclination to draw. They found that children who had been promised an award spent only half as much time drawing as they had originally. Those students who had received no award showed no such decline in interest.

Most studies in this area follow the same general outline: 1) students are given the opportunity to participate in an activity without rewards; 2) they are given extrinsic rewards for participating in the activity; and 3) they are again given the opportunity to participate in the activity without rewards.

The outcomes of the studies are also fairly consistent. Not surprisingly, there is usually a substantial increase in the activity during the second stage, when extrinsic rewards are available. And, as expected, participation in the activity declines sharply when rewards are no longer available. However, interest sometimes falls below the initial level, so that students are less interested in the activity than they had been before receiving rewards. It is this net loss of motivation that is of concern.

Researchers have studied this decline in motivation and found that it occurs only under certain circumstances. For example, the effect is most likely to occur when the initial interest in the activity is very high, when the rewards used are *not* reinforcers, and when the rewards are held out in advance as incentives.[14]

But perhaps the best predictor of negative effects is the nature of the "reward contingency" involved. (The term *reward contingency* has to do with the nature of the relationship between behavior and its reward.) Alyce Dickinson reviewed the research literature in this area and identified three kinds of reward contingency:[15]

Task-contingent rewards are available for merely participating in an activity, without regard to any standard of performance. Most studies that find a decline in interest in a rewarded activity involve task-contingent rewards. In the Lepper study described above, for instance, children received an award for drawing *regardless of how they drew*. The reward was task-contingent.

Performance-contingent rewards are available only when the student achieves a certain standard. Performance-contingent rewards sometimes produce negative results. For instance, Edward Deci offered college students money for solving puzzles, $1 for each puzzle solved. The rewarded students were later less inclined to work on the puzzles than were students who had not been paid. Unfortunately, these results are difficult to interpret because the students sometimes failed to meet the reward standard, and failure itself is known to reduce interest in an activity.[16]

Success-contingent rewards are given for good performance and might reflect either success or progress toward a goal. Success-contingent rewards do not have negative effects; in fact, they typically *increase* interest in the rewarded activity. For example, Ross Vasta and Louise Stirpe awarded gold stars to third- and fourth-graders each time they completed a kind of math exercise they enjoyed. After seven days of awards, the gold stars stopped. Not only was there no evidence of a loss in interest, but time spent on the math activity actually increased. Nor was there any decline in the quality of the work produced.[17]

Dickinson concludes that the danger of undermining student motivation stems not from extrinsic rewards, but from the use of inappropriate reward contingencies. Rewards reduce motivation when they are given without regard to performance or when the performance standard is so high that students frequently fail. When students have a high rate of success and when those successes are rewarded, the rewards *do not have negative effects*. Indeed, success-contingent rewards tend to increase interest in the activity. This finding, writes Dickinson, "is robust and consistent." She adds that "even strong opponents of contingent rewards recognize that success-based rewards do not have harmful effects."[18]

The evidence, then, shows that extrinsic rewards can either enhance or reduce interest in an activity, depending on how they are used. Still, it might be argued that, because extrinsic rewards *sometimes* cause problems, we might be wise to avoid their use altogether. The decision not to use extrinsic rewards amounts to a decision to rely on alternatives. What are those alternatives? And are they better than extrinsic rewards?

ALTERNATIVES TO REWARDS

Punishment and the threat of punishment are — and probably always have been — the most popular alternatives to extrinsic rewards. Not so long ago, lessons were "taught to the tune of a hickory stick," but the tune was not merely tapped on a desk. Students who did not learn their lessons were not only beaten; they were also humiliated: they sat on a stool (up high, so everyone could see) and wore a silly hat.

Gradually, more subtle forms of punishment were used. "The child at his desk," wrote Skinner, "filling in his workbook, is behaving primarily to escape from the threat of a series of minor aversive events — the teacher's displeasure, the criticism or ridicule of his classmates, an ignominious showing in a competition, low marks, a trip to the office 'to be talked to' by the principal, or a word to the parent who may still resort to the birch rod."[19] Skinner spent a lifetime inveighing against the use of such "aversives," but his efforts were largely ineffective. While extrinsic rewards have been condemned, punishment and the threat of punishment are widely sanctioned.

Punishment is popular because, in the short run at least, it gets results. This is illustrated by an experiment in which Deci and Wayne Cascio told students that, if they did not solve problems correctly within a time limit, they would be exposed to a loud, unpleasant sound. The threat worked: all the students solved all the problems within the time limit, so the threat never had to be fulfilled. Students who were merely rewarded for correct solutions did not do nearly as well.[20]

But there are serious drawbacks to the use of punishment. For one thing, although punishment motivates students to learn, it does not teach them. Or, rather, it teaches them only what *not* to do, not what *to* do. "We do not teach [a student] to learn quickly," Skinner observed, "by punishing him when he learns slowly, or to recall what he has learned by punishing him when he forgets, or to think logically by punishing him when he is illogical."[21]

Punishment also has certain undesirable side effects.[22] To the extent that punishment works, it works by making students anxious. Students get nervous before a test because they fear a poor grade, and they are relieved or anxious when they receive their report card depending on whether or not the grades received will result in punishment from their parents.[23] Students can and do avoid the anxiety caused by such punishment by cutting classes and dropping out of school. We do the same thing when we cancel or "forget" a dental appointment.

Another response to punishment is aggression. Students who do not learn easily — and who therefore cannot readily avoid punishment — are especially apt to become aggressive. Their aggression often takes the form of lying, cheating, stealing, and refusing to cooperate. Students also act out by cursing, by being rude and insulting, by destroying property, and by hitting people. Increasingly, teachers are the objects of these aggressive acts.

Finally, it should be noted that punishment has the same negative impact on intrinsic motivation as extrinsic rewards are alleged to have. In the Deci and Cascio study just described, for example, when students were given the chance to work on puzzles with the threat of punishment removed, they were less likely to do so than were students who had never worked under the threat of punishment.[24] Punishment in the form of criticism of performance also reduces interest in an activity.[25]

Punishment is not the only alternative to the use of extrinsic rewards. Teachers can also encourage students. Encouragement consists of various forms of behavior intended to induce students to perform. We encourage students when we urge them to try, express confidence in their ability to do assignments, and recite such platitudes as "A winner never quits and a quitter never wins."[26]

In encouraging students, we are not merely urging them to perform, however; we are implicitly suggesting a relationship between continued performance and certain consequences. "Come on, Billy — you can do it" means, "If you persist at this task, you will be rewarded with success." The power of encouragement is ultimately dependent on the occurrence of the implied consequences. If the teacher tells Billy he can do it and if he tries

and fails, future urging by the teacher will be less effective.

Another problem with encouragement is that, like punishment, it motivates but does not teach. The student who is urged to perform a task is not thereby taught how to perform it. Encouragement is a safer procedure than punishment, since it is less likely to provoke anxiety or aggression. Students who are repeatedly urged to do things at which they ultimately fail do, however, come to distrust the judgment of the teacher. They also come to believe that they cannot live up to the expectations of teachers — and therefore must be hopelessly stupid.

Intrinsic rewards present the most promising alternative to extrinsic rewards. Experts on reinforcement, including defenders of extrinsic rewards, universally sing the praises of intrinsic rewards. Unlike punishment and encouragement, intrinsic rewards actually teach. Students who can see that they have solved a problem correctly know how to solve other problems of that sort. And, unlike extrinsic rewards, intrinsic rewards do not depend on the teacher or some other person.

But there are problems with intrinsic rewards, just as there are with extrinsic ones. Sometimes students lack the necessary skills to obtain intrinsic rewards. Knowledge, understanding, and the aesthetic pleasures of language are all intrinsic rewards for reading, but they are not available to those for whom reading is a difficult and painful activity.

Often, intrinsic rewards are too remote to be effective. If a student is asked to add 3 + 7, what is the intrinsic reward for answering correctly? The student who learns to add will one day experience the satisfaction of checking the accuracy of a restaurant bill, but this future reward is of no value to the youngster just learning to add. Though important in maintaining what has been learned, intrinsic rewards are often too remote to be effective reinforcers in the early stages of learning.

One problem that often goes unnoticed is that the intrinsic rewards for academic work are often weaker than the rewards available for other behavior. Students are rewarded for looking out the window, daydreaming, reading comic books, taking things from other students, passing notes, telling and listening to jokes, moving about the room, fighting, talking back to the teacher, and for all sorts of activities that are incompatible

with academic learning. Getting the right answer to a grammar question might be intrinsically rewarding, but for many students it is considerably less rewarding than the laughter of one's peers in response to a witty remark.

While intrinsic rewards are important, then, they are insufficient for efficient learning.[27] Nor will encouragement and punishment fill the gap. The teacher must supplement intrinsic rewards with extrinsic rewards. This means not only telling the student when he or she has succeeded, but also praising, complimenting, applauding, and providing other forms of recognition for good work. Some students may need even stronger reinforcers, such as special privileges, certificates, and prizes.

REWARD GUIDELINES

Yet we cannot ignore the fact that extrinsic rewards can have adverse effects on student motivation. While there seems to be little chance of serious harm, it behooves us to use care. Various experts have suggested guidelines to follow in using extrinsic rewards.[28] Here is a digest of their recommendations:

1. Use the weakest reward required to strengthen a behavior. Don't use money if a piece of candy will do; don't use candy if praise will do. The good effects of reinforcement come not so much from the reward itself as from the reward contingency: the relationship between the reward and the behavior.

2. When possible, avoid using rewards as incentives. For example, don't say, "If you do X, I'll give you Y." Instead, ask the student to perform a task and then provide a reward for having completed it. In most cases, rewards work best if they are pleasant surprises.

3. Reward at a high rate in the early stages of learning, and reduce the frequency of rewards as learning progresses. Once students have the alphabet down pat, there is no need to compliment them each time they print a letter correctly. Nor is there much need to reward behavior that is already occurring at a high rate.

4. Reward only the behavior you want repeated. If students who whine and complain get their way, expect to see a lot of whining and complaining. Similarly, if you provide gold stars only for the three best papers in the class, you are rewarding competition and should not be surprised if students do not cooperate

with one another. And if "spelling doesn't count," don't expect to see excellent spelling.

5. Remember that what is an effective reward for one student may not work well with another. Some students respond rapidly to teacher attention; others do not. Some work well for gold stars; others don't. Effective rewards are ordinarily things that students seek — positive feedback, praise, approval, recognition, toys — but ultimately a reward's value is to be judged by its effect on behavior.

6. Reward success, and set standards so that success is within the student's grasp. In today's heterogeneous classrooms, that means setting standards for each student. A good way to do this is to reward improvement or progress toward a goal. Avoid rewarding students merely for participating in an activity, without regard for the quality of their performance.

7. Bring attention to the rewards (both intrinsic and extrinsic) that are available for behavior from sources *other than the teacher*. Point out, for example, the fun to be had from the word play in poetry or from sharing a poem with another person. Show students who are learning computer programming the pleasure in "making the computer do things." Let students know that it's okay to applaud those who make good presentations so that they can enjoy the approval of their peers for a job well done. Ask parents to talk with their children about school and to praise them for learning. The goal is to shift the emphasis from rewards provided by the teacher to those that will occur even when the teacher is not present.[29]

Following these rules is harder in practice than it might seem, and most teachers will need training in their implementation. But reinforcement is probably the most powerful tool available to teachers, and extrinsic rewards are powerful reinforcers. To teach without using extrinsic rewards is analogous to asking our students to learn to draw with their eyes closed. Before we do that, we should open our own eyes.

1. The study is described in E. L. Thorndike, *Human Learning* (1931; reprint ed., Cambridge, Mass.: MIT Press, 1966).

2. There are various theories (cognitive, neurological, and psychosocial) about why certain consequences reinforce or strengthen behavior. The important thing for our purposes is that they do.

3. John I. Goodlad, *A Place Called School: Prospects for the Future* (New York: McGraw-Hill, 1984). Goodlad complains about the "paucity of praise" in schools. In doing so, he echoes B. F. Skinner, who wrote that "perhaps the most serious criticism of the current classroom is the relative infrequency of reinforcement." See B. F. Skinner, *The Technology of Teaching* (Englewood Cliffs, N.J.: Prentice-Hall, 1968), p. 17.

4. Bill L. Hopkins and R. J. Conard, "Putting It All Together: Superschool," in Norris G. Haring and Richard L. Schiefelbusch, eds., *Teaching Special Children* (New York: McGraw-Hill, 1975), pp. 342-85. Skinner suggests that mastering the first four years of arithmetic instruction efficiently would require something on the order of 25,000 reinforcements. See Skinner, op. cit.

5. See, for example, Bill L. Hopkins, "Comments on the Future of Applied Behavior Analysis," *Journal of Applied Behavior Analysis*, vol. 20, 1987, pp. 339-46. In some studies, students learned at double the normal rate, yet most teachers did not continue reinforcing behavior at high rates after the study ended.

6. See, for example, Hopkins and Conard, op. cit.

7. For example, Mihaly Csikszentmihalyi found that adults who are successful and happy tend to have had happy childhoods. See Tina Adler, "Support and Challenge: Both Key for Smart Kids," *APA Monitor*, September 1991, pp. 10-11.

8. The terms *reinforcer* and *reward* are often used interchangeably, but they are not really synonyms. A reinforcer is defined by its effects: an event that strengthens the behavior it follows is a reinforcer, regardless of what it was intended to do. A reward is defined by social convention as something desirable; it may or may not strengthen the behavior it follows. The distinction is important since some studies that show negative effects from extrinsic rewards use rewards that are *not* reinforcers. See Alyce M. Dickinson, "The Detrimental Effects of Extrinsic Reinforcement on 'Intrinsic Motivation,' " *The Behavior Analyst*, vol. 12, 1989, pp. 1-15.

9. John Dewey distrusted the distinction between extrinsic and intrinsic rewards. He wrote that "what others do to us when we act is as natural a consequence of our action as what the fire does to us when we plunge our hands in it." Quoted in Samuel M. Deitz, "What Is Unnatural About 'Extrinsic Reinforcement'?," *The Behavior Analyst*, vol. 12, 1989, p. 255.

10. Dickinson writes that "several individuals have demanded that schools abandon reinforcement procedures for fear that they may permanently destroy a child's 'love of learning.' " See Alyce M. Dickinson, "Exploring New Vistas," *Performance Management Magazine*, vol. 9, 1991, p. 28. It is interesting to note that no one worries that earning a school letter will destroy a student's interest in sports. Nor does there seem to be much fear that people who win teaching awards will suddenly become poor teachers. For the most part, only the academic work of students is said to be put at risk by extrinsic rewards.

11. Skinner, p. 162.

12. For reviews of this literature, see Edward L. Deci and Richard M. Ryan, *Intrinsic Motivation and Self-Determination in Human Behavior* (New York: Plenum, 1985); Dickinson, "The Detrimental Effects"; and Mark R. Lepper and David Greene, eds., *The Hidden Costs of Reward: New Perspectives on the Psychology of Human Motivation* (Hillsdale, N.J.: Erlbaum, 1978).

13. Mark R. Lepper, David Greene, and Richard E. Nisbett, "Undermining Children's Intrinsic Interest with Extrinsic Rewards," *Journal of Personality and Social Psychology*, vol. 28, 1973, pp. 129-37.

14. See, for example, Dickinson, "The Detrimental Effects"; and Mark Morgan, "Reward-Induced Decrements and Increments in Intrinsic Motivation," *Review of Educational Research*, vol. 54, 1984, pp. 5-30. Dickinson notes that studies producing negative effects are often hard to interpret since other variables (failure, deadlines, competition, and so on) could account for the findings. By way of example, she cites a study in which researchers offered a $5 reward to top performers. The study was thus contaminated by the effects of competition, yet the negative results were attributed to extrinsic rewards.

15. Dickinson, "The Detrimental Effects."

16. Edward L. Deci, "Effects of Externally Mediated Rewards on Intrinsic Motivation," *Journal of Personality and Social Psychology*, vol. 18, 1971, pp. 105-15.

17. Ross Vasta and Louise A. Stirpe, "Reinforcement Effects on Three Measures of Children's Interest in Math," *Behavior Modification*, vol. 3, 1979, pp. 223-44.

18. Dickinson, "The Detrimental Effects," p. 9. See also Morgan, op. cit.

19. Skinner, p. 15.

20. Edward L. Deci and Wayne F. Cascio, "Changes in Intrinsic Motivation as a Function of Negative Feedback and Threats," paper presented at the annual meeting of the Eastern Psychological Association, Boston, May 1972. This paper is summarized in Edward L. Deci and Joseph Porac, "Cognitive Evaluation Theory and the Study of Human Motivation," in Lepper and Greene, pp. 149-76.

21. Skinner, p. 149.

22. For more on the problems associated with punishment, see Murray Sidman, *Coercion and Its Fallout* (Boston: Authors Cooperative, Inc., 1989).

23. Grades are often referred to as rewards, but they are more often punishments. Students study not so much to receive high grades as to avoid receiving low ones.

24. Deci and Cascio, op. cit.

25. See, for example, Edward L. Deci, Wayne F. Cascio, and Judy Krusell, "Sex Differences, Positive Feedback, and Intrinsic Motivation," paper presented at the annual meeting of the Eastern Psychological Association, Washington, D.C., May 1973. This paper is summarized in Deci and Porac, op. cit.

26. It should be noted that encouragement often closely resembles reinforcement in form. One teacher may say, "I know you can do it, Mary," as Mary struggles to answer a question; another teacher may say, "I knew you could do it, Mary!" when Mary answers the question correctly. The first teacher is encouraging; the second is reinforcing. The difference is subtle but important.

27. Intrinsic rewards are more important to the maintenance of skills once learned. An adult's skill at addition and subtraction is not ordinarily maintained by the approval of peers but by the satisfaction that comes from balancing a checkbook.

28. See, for example, Jere Brophy, "Teacher Praise: A Functional Analysis," *Review of Educational Research*, vol. 51, 1981, pp. 5-32; Hopkins and Conard, op. cit.; and Dickinson, "The Detrimental Effects."

29. "Instructional contingencies," writes Skinner, "are usually contrived and should always be temporary. If instruction is to have any point, the behavior it generates will be taken over and maintained by contingencies in the world at large." See Skinner, p. 144.

Rewards Versus Learning: A Response to Paul Chance

Mr. Kohn raises some questions about Paul Chance's article in the November 1992 Kappan* and suggests that an engaging curriculum — not manipulating children with artificial incentives — offers a genuine alternative to boredom in school and to diminished motivation when school lets out.

....

ALFIE KOHN

ALFIE KOHN is an independent scholar living in Cambridge, Mass., who writes and lectures widely on human behavior and education. His newest book is Punished by Rewards: The Trouble with Gold Stars, Incentive Plans, A's, Praise, and Other Bribes *(Houghton Mifflin, October 1993). ©1993, Alfie Kohn.*

I N THE COURSE of offering some suggestions for how educators can help children become more generous and empathic ("Caring Kids: The Role of the Schools," March 1991), I argued that manipulating student behavior with either punishments or rewards is not only unnecessary but counterproductive. Paul Chance, taking exception to this passage, wrote to defend the use of rewards (Backtalk, June 1991). Now, following the publication of his longer brief for behaviorism ("The Rewards of Learning," November 1992), it is my turn to raise some questions — and to continue what I hope is a constructive

[*See Annual Editions Article 22. Ed.]

dialogue between us (not to mention a long overdue examination of classroom practices too often taken for granted).

To begin, I should mention two points where our perspectives converge. Neither of us favors the use of punishment, and both of us think that rewards, like other strategies, must be judged by their long-term effects, including what they do for (or to) children's motivation. Chance and I disagree, however, on the nature of those effects.

Rewards, like punishments, can usually get people to do what we want for a while. In that sense, they "work." But my reading of the research, corroborated by real-world observation, is that rewards can never buy us anything more than short-term compliance. Moreover, we — or, more accurately, the people we are rewarding — pay a steep price over time for our reliance on extrinsic motivators.

REWARDS ARE INHERENTLY CONTROLLING

Applied behaviorism, which amounts to saying, "Do this and you'll get that," is essentially a technique for controlling people. In the classroom, it is a way of doing things *to* children rather than working *with* them. Chance focuses on the empirical effects of rewards, but I feel obliged to pause at least long enough to stress that moral issues are involved here regardless of whether we ultimately endorse or oppose the use of rewards.

By now it is not news that reinforcement strategies were developed and refined through experiments on laboratory animals. Many readers also realize that underlying the practice of reinforcement is a theory — specifically, the assumption that humans, like all organisms, are

basically inert beings whose behavior must be elicited by external motivation in the form of carrots or sticks. For example, Alyce Dickinson, the author Chance cites six times and from whom he borrows the gist of his defense of rewards, plainly acknowledges the central premise of the perspective she and Chance share, which is that "all behavior is ultimately initiated by the external environment."[1] Anyone who recoils from this theoretical foundation ought to take a fresh look at the real-world practices that rest on it.

I am troubled by a model of human relationship or learning that is defined by control rather than, say, persuasion or mutual problem solving. Because the reinforcements themselves are desired by their recipients, it is easy to miss the fact that using them is simply a matter of "control[ling] through seduction rather than force."[2] Rewards and punishments (bribes and threats, positive reinforcements and "consequences" — call them what you will) are not really opposites at all. They are two sides of the same coin. The good news is that our options are not limited to variations on the theme of behavioral manipulation.[3]

REWARDS ARE INEFFECTIVE

The question of how well rewards *work*, apart from what they do to children's long-term motivation, is dispatched by Chance in a single sentence: "No one disputes the effectiveness of extrinsic rewards in teaching or in maintaining good discipline" (p. 203). I found myself rereading the paragraph in which this extraordinary claim appears, searching for signs that Chance was being ironic.

In point of fact, the evidence overwhelmingly demonstrates that extrinsic rewards are ineffective at producing lasting change in attitudes or even behaviors. Moreover, they typically do not enhance – and often actually impede – performance on tasks that are any more complex than pressing a bar. This evidence, which I have been sorting through recently for a book-length treatment of these issues (*Punished by Rewards*, scheduled for publication this fall), is piled so high on my desk that I fear it will topple over. I cannot review all of it here; a few samples will have to do.

Consider first the matter of behavior change. Even behaviorists have had to concede that the token economy, a form of behavior modification once (but, mercifully, no longer) popular for controlling people in institutions, doesn't work. When the goodies stop, people go right back to acting the way they did before the program began.[4] Studies have found that rewarding people for losing weight,[5] quitting smoking,[6] or using seat belts[7] is typically less effective than using other strategies – and often proves worse than doing nothing at all.

Children whose parents make frequent use of rewards or praise are likely to be less generous than their peers.[8] On reflection, this makes perfect sense: a child promised a treat for acting responsibly has been given no reason to keep behaving that way when there is no longer a reward to be gained for doing so. The implications for behavioristic classroom management programs such as Assertive Discipline, in which children are essentially bribed or threatened to conform to rules that the teacher alone devises, are painfully clear.

Rewards (like punishments) can get people to do what we want in the short term: buckle up, share a toy, read a book. In that sense, Chance is right that their effectiveness is indisputable. But they rarely produce effects that survive the rewards themselves, which is why behaviorists are placed in the position of having to argue that we need to keep the goodies coming or replace one kind of reward with another (e.g., candy bars with grades). The fact is that extrinsic motivators do not alter the attitudes that underlie our behaviors. They do not create an enduring *commitment* to a set of values or to learning; they merely, and temporarily, change what we do. If, like Skinner, you think there is nothing to humans other than what we do, then this criticism will not trouble you. If, on the

---

*T*he good news is that our options are not limited to variations on the theme of behavioral manipulation.

---

other hand, you think that our actions reflect and emerge from who we *are* (what we think and feel, expect and will), then you have no reason to expect interventions that merely control actions to work in the long run.

As for the effect on performance, I know of at least two dozen studies showing that people expecting to receive a reward for completing a task (or for doing it successfully) don't perform as well as those who expect nothing. The effect is robust for young children, older children, and adults; for males and females; for rewards of all kinds (including money, grades, toys, food, and special privileges). The tasks in these studies range from memorizing facts to engaging in creative problem solving, from discriminating between similar drawings to designing collages. In general, the more cognitive sophistication and open-ended thinking required, the worse people do when they are working for a reward.[9]

At first researchers didn't know what to make of these findings. (A good sign that one has stumbled onto something important is the phrase "contrary to hypothesis" in a research report.) "The clear inferiority of the reward groups was an unexpected result, unaccountable for by theory or previous empirical evidence," a pair of experimenters confessed in 1961.[10] Rewards "have effects that interfere with performance in ways that we are only beginning to understand," said Janet Spence (later president of the American Psychological Association) in 1971.[11] Since then, most researchers – with the exception of a small cadre of un-

reconstructed behaviorists – have gotten the message that, on most tasks, a Skinnerian strategy is worse than useless: it is counterproductive.

REWARDS MAKE LEARNING LESS APPEALING

Even more research indicates that rewards also undermine *interest* – a finding with obvious and disturbing implications for the use of grades, stickers, and even praise. Here Chance concedes there may be a problem but, borrowing Dickinson's analysis, assures us that the damage is limited. Dickinson grants that motivation tends to decline when people are rewarded just for engaging in a task and also when they receive performance-contingent rewards – those "based on performance standards" (Dickinson) or "available only when the student achieves a certain standard" (Chance).

But Dickinson then proceeds to invent a new category, "success-contingent" rewards, and calls these innocuous. The term means that, when rewards are given out, "subjects are told they have received the rewards because of good performance." For Chance, though, a "success-contingent" reward is "given for good performance and might reflect either success or progress toward a goal" – a definition that appears to diverge from Dickinson's and that sounds quite similar to what is meant by "performance-contingent." As near as I can figure, the claim both Dickinson and Chance are making is that, when people come away thinking that they have done well, a reward for what they have achieved doesn't hurt. On this single claim rests the entire defense against the devastating charge that by rewarding students for their achievement we are leading them to see learning as a chore. But what does the research really say?

Someone who simply glances at the list of studies Dickinson offers to support her assertion might come away impressed. Someone who takes the time to read those studies will come away with a renewed sense of the importance of going straight to the primary source. It turns out that two of the studies don't even deal with rewards for successful performance.[12] Another one actually *disproves* the contention that success-contingent rewards are harmless: it finds that this kind of reward not only undermines intrinsic motivation but is more destructive than rewards given just for engaging in the task![13]

The rest of the studies cited by Dickinson indicate that some subjects in laboratory experiments who receive success-contingent rewards are neither more nor less interested in the task than those who get nothing at all. But Dickinson curiously omits a number of *other* studies that are also set up so that some subjects succeed (or think they succeed) at a task and are presented with a reward. These studies have found that such rewards *do* reduce interest.[14]

Such a result really shouldn't be surprising. As Edward Deci and his colleagues have been pointing out for years, adults and children alike chafe at being deprived of a sense of self-determination. Rewards usually feel controlling, and rewards contingent on performance ("If you do a good job, here's what I'll give you") are the most controlling of all. Even the good feeling produced by doing well often isn't enough to overcome that fact. To the extent that information about how well we have done *is* interest-enhancing, this is not an argument for Skinnerian tactics. In fact, when researchers have specifically compared the effects of straightforward performance feedback ("Here's how you did") and performance-contingent rewards ("Here's a goody for doing well"), the latter undermined intrinsic motivation more than the former.[15]

Finally, even if all the research really did show what Dickinson and Chance claim it does, remember that outside of the laboratory people often fail. That result is more likely to be de-motivating when it means losing out on a reward, such as an A or a bonus. This Chance implicitly concedes, although the force of the point gets lost: students do not turn off from failing per se but from failing when a reward is at stake. In learning contexts free of extrinsic motivators, students are more likely to persist at a task and to remain interested in it even when they don't do it well.

All of this means that getting children to think about learning as a way to receive a sticker, a gold star, or a grade — or, even worse, to get money or a toy *for* a grade, which amounts to an extrinsic motivator for an extrinsic motivator — is likely to turn learning from an end into a means. Learning becomes something that must be gotten through in order to receive the reward. Take the depressingly pervasive program by which children receive certificates for free pizza when they

have read a certain number of books. John Nicholls of the University of Illinois comments, only half in jest, that the likely consequence of this program is "a lot of fat kids who don't like to read."

Educational psychologists such as Nicholls, Carol Dweck, and Carole Ames keep finding that when children are led to concentrate on their performance, on how well they are doing — an inevitable consequence of the use of rewards or punishments — they become less interested in *what* they are doing. ("Do we have to know this? Will it be on the test?") I am convinced that one of the primary obligations of educators and parents who want to promote a lasting commitment to learning is to do everything in their power to help students forget that grades exist.

REWARDS IGNORE CURRICULAR QUESTIONS

One last point. Chance's defense of the Skinnerian status quo might more properly have been titled "The Rewards *for* Learning." My interest is in the rewards *of* learning, a concern that requires us to ask whether we are teaching something *worth* learning. This is a question that behaviorists do not need to ask; it is enough to devise an efficient technique to reinforce the acquisition of whatever happens to be in someone's lesson plan.

Chance addresses the matter of intrinsic motivation just long enough to dismiss it as "too remote to be effective." He sets up a false dichotomy, with an abstract math problem on one side (Why would a child be motivated to learn that 7 + 3 = 10? he wants to know) and reinforcements (the solution to this problem) on the other. Indeed, if children are required to fill in an endless series of blanks on worksheets or to memorize meaningless, disconnected facts, they may *have* to be bribed to do so. But Chance seems oblivious to exciting developments in the field of education: the whole-language movement, the emphasis on "learner-centered" learning, and the entire constructivist tradition (in which teaching takes its cue from the way each child actively constructs meaning and makes sense of the world rather than treating students as passive responders to environmental stimuli).

I invite Chance to join the campaign for an engaging curriculum that is connected to children's lives and interests, for an approach to pedagogy in which students

are given real choices about their studies, and for classrooms in which they are allowed and helped to work with one another. Pursuing these approaches, not manipulating children with artificial incentives, offers a *real* alternative to boredom in school and to diminished motivation when school lets out.

---

1. Alyce M. Dickinson, "The Detrimental Effects of Extrinsic Reinforcement on 'Intrinsic Motivation,' " *The Behavior Analyst*, vol. 12, 1989, p. 12. Notice the quotation marks around "intrinsic motivation," as if to question the very existence of the phenomenon — a telltale sign of Skinnerian orthodoxy.

2. Edward L. Deci and Richard M. Ryan, *Intrinsic Motivation and Self-Determination in Human Behavior* (New York: Plenum, 1985), p. 70.

3. Behaviorists are apt to rejoin that control is an unavoidable feature of all relationships. In response I would point out that there is an enormous difference between saying that even subtle reinforcements can be controlling and asserting that all human interaction is best described as an exercise in control. The latter takes on faith that selfhood and choice are illusions and that we do only what we have been reinforced for doing. A far more defensible position, it seems to me, is that some forms of human interaction are controlling and some are not. The line might not be easy to draw in practice, but the distinction is still meaningful and important.

4. "Generally, removal of token reinforcement results in decrements in desirable responses and a return to baseline or near-baseline levels of performance," as the first major review of token economies concluded. In fact, not only does the behavior fail "to generalize to conditions in which [reinforcements] are not in effect" — such as the world outside the hospital — but reinforcement programs used each morning generally don't even have much effect on patients' behavior during the afternoon! See Alan E. Kazdin and Richard R. Bootzin, "The Token Economy: An Evaluative Review," *Journal of Applied Behavior Analysis*, vol. 5, 1972, pp. 359-60. Ten years later, one of these authors — an enthusiastic proponent of behavior modification, incidentally — checked back to see if anything had changed. "As a general rule," he wrote, with an almost audible sigh, "it is still prudent to assume that behavioral gains are likely to be lost in varying degrees once the client leaves the program." See Alan E. Kazdin, "The Token Economy: A Decade Later," *Journal of Applied Behavior Analysis*, vol. 15, 1982, pp. 435-37. Others reviewing the research on token economies have come to more or less the same conclusion.

5. The only two studies I am aware of that looked at weight loss programs to see what happened when people were paid for getting slimmer found that the incentives either had no effect or were actually counterproductive. See Richard A. Dienstbier and Gary K. Leak, "Overjustification and Weight Loss: The Effects of Monetary Reward," paper presented at the annual meeting of the American Psychological Association, Washington, D.C., September 1976; and F. Matthew Kramer et al., "Maintenance of Successful Weight Loss Over 1 Year: Effects of Financial Contracts for Weight Maintenance or Participation in Skills Training," *Behavior Therapy*, vol. 17, 1986, pp. 295-301.

6. A very large study, published in 1991, recruited subjects for a self-help program designed to help people quit smoking. Three months later, those who had been offered a prize for turning in weekly prog-

ress reports were lighting up again more often than were those who had received a no-reward treatment — and even more than those who didn't take part in any program at all. In fact, for people who received both treatments, "the financial incentive somehow diminished the positive impact of the personalized feedback." See Susan J. Curry et al., "Evaluation of Intrinsic and Extrinsic Motivation Interventions with a Self-Help Smoking Cessation Program," *Journal of Consulting and Clinical Psychology*, vol. 59, 1991, p. 323.

7. A committed behaviorist and his colleagues reviewed the effects of 28 programs used by nine different companies to get their employees to use seat belts. Nearly half a million vehicle observations were made over six years in the course of this research. The result: programs that rewarded people for wearing their seat belts were the least effective over the long haul. The author had to confess that "the greater impact of the no-reward strategies from both an immediate and [a] long-term perspective . . . [was] not predicted and [is] inconsistent with basic reinforcement theory." See E. Scott Geller et al., "Employer-Based Programs to Motivate Safety Belt Use: A Review of Short-Term and Long-Term Effects," *Journal of Safety Research*, vol. 18, 1987, pp. 1-17.

8. Richard A. Fabes et al., "Effects of Rewards on Children's Prosocial Motivation: A Socialization Study," *Developmental Psychology*, vol. 25, 1989, pp. 509-15. Praise appears to have a similar detrimental effect; see Joan E. Grusec, "Socializing Concern for Others in the Home," *Developmental Psychology*, vol. 27, l991, pp. 338-42. See also the studies reviewed in Alfie Kohn, *The Brighter Side of Human Nature: Altruism and Empathy in Everyday Life* (New York: Basic Books, 1990), pp. 201-4.

9. A complete bibliography will be available in my forthcoming book, *Punished by Rewards*. Readers unwilling to wait might wish to begin by reading Mark R. Lepper and David Greene, eds., *The Hidden Costs of Rewards* (Hillsdale, N.J.: Erlbaum, 1978), and some of Teresa Amabile's work from the 1980s documenting how rewards kill creativity.

10. Louise Brightwell Miller and Betsy Worth Estes, "Monetary Reward and Motivation in Discrimination Learning," *Journal of Experimental Psychology*, vol. 61, 1961, p. 503.

11. Janet Taylor Spence, "Do Material Rewards Enhance the Performance of Lower-Class Children?," *Child Development*, vol. 42, 1971, p. 1469.

12. In one of the studies, either money or an award was given to children just for taking part in the experiment — and both caused interest in the task to decline. See Rosemarie Anderson et al., "The Undermining and Enhancing of Intrinsic Motivation in Preschool Children," *Journal of Personality and Social Psychology*, vol. 34, 1976, pp. 915-22. In the other, a total of three children were simply praised ("good," "nice going") whenever they engaged in a task; no mention was made of how well they were performing. See Jerry A. Martin, "Effects of Positive and Negative Adult-Child Interactions on Children's Task Performance and Task Preferences," *Journal of Experimental Child Psychology*, vol. 23, 1977, pp. 493-502.

13. Michael Jay Weiner and Anthony M. Mander, "The Effects of Reward and Perception of Competency upon Intrinsic Motivation," *Motivation and Emotion*, vol. 2, 1978, pp. 67-73.

14. Chance doesn't like Deci's 1971 study, but there are plenty of others. In David Greene and Mark R. Lepper, "Effects of Extrinsic Rewards on Children's Subsequent Intrinsic Interest," *Child Development*,

vol. 45, 1974, pp. 1141-45, children who were promised a reward if they drew very good pictures — and then did receive the reward, along with a reminder of the accomplishment it represented — were less interested in drawing later than were children who got nothing. See also James Garbarino, "The Impact of Anticipated Reward upon Cross-Age Tutoring," *Journal of Personality and Social Psychology*, vol. 32, 1975, pp. 421-28; Terry D. Orlick and Richard Mosher, "Extrinsic Awards and Participant Motivation in a Sport Related Task," *International Journal of Sport Psychology*, vol. 9, 1978, pp. 27-39; Judith M. Harackiewicz, "The Effects of Reward Contingency and Performance Feedback on Intrinsic Motivation," *Journal of Personality and Social Psychology*, vol. 37, 1979, pp. 1352-63; and Richard A. Fabes, "Effects of Reward Contexts on Young Children's Task Interest," *Journal of Psychology*, vol. 121, 1987, pp. 5-19. See too the studies cited in, and conclusions offered by, Kenneth O. McGraw, "The Detrimental Effects of Reward on Performance: A Literature Review and a Prediction Model," in Lepper and Greene, eds., p. 40; Mark R. Lepper, "Extrinsic Reward and Intrinsic Motivation," in John M. Levine and Margaret C. Wang, eds., *Teacher and Student Perceptions: Implications for Learning* (Hillsdale, N.J.: Erlbaum, 1983), pp. 304-5; and Deci and Ryan, p. 78.

15. Richard M. Ryan et al., "Relation of Reward Contingency and Interpersonal Context to Intrinsic Motivation: A Review and Test Using Cognitive Evaluation Theory," *Journal of Personality and Social Psychology*, vol. 45, 1983, pp. 736-50. "Rewards in general appear to have a controlling significance to some extent and thus in general run the risk of undermining intrinsic motivation," the authors wrote (p. 748).

Sticking Up for Rewards

It is ironic that honest feedback or a straightforward contingency between work and rewards should be called manipulative, while "persuasion" and "mutual problem solving" should not, Mr. Chance retorts.

....

PAUL CHANCE

PAUL CHANCE (Eastern Shore Maryland Chapter) is a psychologist, writer, and former teacher. He is the author of Thinking in the Classroom *(Teachers College Press, 1986).*

IT IS DIFFICULT to know how to respond to Alfie Kohn's critique.* It is so disjointed and so full of misrepresentations of fact and theory that it is like a greased pig: one can scarcely get a grip on it, let alone wrestle it to the ground. I will illustrate what I mean with a few examples and then reply to what I believe to be Kohn's major objections.

Item: To reward, Kohn says, is to say to a student, "Do this and you'll get that." But this is only one kind of reward – and one that I specifically advised readers to avoid when possible. It is these "contractual rewards" (or incentives) that are apt to be problematic.[1] My article focused on rewards that provide feedback about performance. Such "informational rewards" reflect effort or the quality of performance (e.g., "Good try, Janet"; "Great job, Billy"). As we shall see, even researchers who criticize contractual rewards do not normally object to informational rewards.

[*See Annual Editions Article 23. Ed.]

Item: Kohn says that I ask, Why would a child be motivated to learn that 7 + 3 = 10? But my question was, *How* can a child learn that 7 + 3 = 10 without some sort of response from the environment? A teacher, a peer tutor, or a computer program may provide the necessary feedback, but the natural environment rarely does. This was the point of E. L. Thorndike's line experiment, described in my article.

Item: Kohn suggests that the use of rewards is manipulative and controlling. It is ironic that honest feedback or a straightforward contingency between work and rewards should be called manipulative, while "persuasion" and "mutual problem solving" should not. Students, I suspect, know the truth of the matter. As for control: a parent rewards a baby's crying when he or she offers a bottle, and the baby rewards the parent's action by ceasing to cry. Each controls the other. Students and teachers exert the same sort of reciprocal control in the classroom.[2]

Item: Nowhere do I suggest that students must "fill in an endless series of blanks on worksheets or memorize meaningless, disconnected facts," nor is there any reason to assume that the use of rewards implies such practices. The truth is that rewards are useful whether the student is memorizing dates, mastering algebra word problems, or learning to think.[3] Some sort of extrinsic reinforcement (informational reward) is usually necessary, in the early stages at least, for learning to occur efficiently.

Item: Kohn refers to "practices too often taken for granted." Evidently he believes the mythology that rewards are widely used in our schools. Yet I noted in my article that John Goodlad found that only 2% of class time is devoted to reinforcement in elementary school – and only 1% in high school.[4] Other research consistently shows that reinforcement is notable by its absence. Harold

Stevenson, for example, compared elementary classrooms in America and Asia. He found pronounced differences in the activities of teachers when students were engaged in seatwork. In half of the classes observed in the Chicago area, the teachers provided no feedback about student performance; this seldom happened in Taiwan and almost never happened in Japan.[5]

Item: I do not assume, as suggested, that "humans, like all organisms, are basically inert beings." Nor do I know any psychologist who would embrace this view. Behavioral psychologists in particular emphasize that we learn by *acting on* our environment. As B. F. Skinner put it: "[People] act on the world, and change it, and are changed in turn by the consequences of their actions."[6] Skinner, unlike Kohn, understood that people learn best in a responsive environment. Teachers who praise or otherwise reward student performance provide such an environment.

Item: Kohn implies that I consider grades a reward. In fact, I noted (as Skinner and others had before me) that grades are more often a form of punishment. Incidentally, F. S. Keller, a behaviorist, proposed a system of education that could eliminate grades. In the Keller plan, students are required to demonstrate mastery of each skill before moving to the next. Mastery of each unit in the curriculum is recorded, so grades become superfluous.[7]

Item: Kohn says that "moral issues are involved." The implication is that I and other teachers who use rewards are immoral. If it is immoral to let students know they have answered questions correctly, to pat a student on the back for a good effort, to show joy at a student's understanding of a concept, or to recognize the achievement of a goal by providing a gold star or a certificate – if this is immoral, then count me a sinner.

The above points illustrate, I think, the slippery nature of Kohn's critique and may lead the reader to question his scholarship and his motives for writing. I now turn to what seem to be his major criticisms of rewards.

✐ Kohn insists that rewards undermine interest in rewarded activities.[8] Notice that Kohn does not argue that *some* rewards – or *some uses of* rewards – undermine interest. There is, in his view, no such thing as a good reward. Simple feedback, praise, smiles, hugs, pats on the back, gold stars, applause, certificates of completion, public and private commendations, prizes, special privileges, money, informational rewards, and contractual rewards – they are all one to Kohn, and they are all bad.

The best-known researchers who have found rewards sometimes troublesome are Edward Deci, Richard Ryan, Mark Lepper, and David Greene. Kohn cites all four in making his case. What he does not tell us (though he must surely know it) is that all of these researchers reject his view.[9]

Deci and Ryan believe that rewards can undermine motivation if used in a controlling way. But they add, "When used to convey to people a sense of appreciation for work well done, [rewards] will tend to be experienced informationally and will *maintain or enhance intrinsic motivation*" (emphasis added).[10]

Lepper and Greene take a similar stand. They note, "If rewards provide [a student] with new information about his ability at a particular task, this may *bolster his feelings of competence and his desire to engage in that task for its own sake*" (emphasis added).[11] They add, "If a child does not possess the basic skills to discover the intrinsic satisfaction of complex activities such as reading, the use of extrinsic rewards may be required to equip him with these skills."[12]

The position taken by Deci, Ryan, Lepper, and Greene reflects the consensus among researchers who are concerned about the possible negative effects of rewards. Mark Morgan, for example, reviewed the research and wrote that "the central finding emerging from the present review is that rewards can have either undermining or enhancing effects depending on circumstances."[13] He concludes that "the evidence seems to support strongly the hypothesis that rewards that emphasize success or competence on a task enhance intrinsic motivation."[14]

✐ Kohn claims that rewards do not work. It is true that not all rewards are

> Certain rewards (e.g., attention, positive feedback, praise) are almost always effective reinforcers when used properly.

reinforcing. Teachers must not assume that a reward will strengthen behavior merely because that is the teacher's intention. What is reinforcing for one student may not be for another. But there is overwhelming evidence that certain rewards (e.g., attention, positive feedback, praise) are almost always effective reinforcers when used properly.

In a study by Bill Hopkins and R. J. Conard, cited in my article, teachers who provided frequent feedback, praise, and other rewards saw much faster learning.[15] Students in these classes advanced at the normal rate in spelling, at nearly twice the normal rate in mathematics, and at more than double the usual rate in reading.[16] Studies showing similar gains, due at least partly to frequent use of rewards (especially feedback and praise), are easily found by those who seek them.[17]

Even contractual rewards may be useful in some circumstances. In one program, high-risk, low-income adolescents and young adults in Lafayette Parish, Louisiana, were paid $3.40 an hour to participate in a summer program of academic instruction and job training. Students gained an average of 1.2 grade levels in reading and 1.5 grade levels in math in just eight weeks.[18]

It may be the case that the Lafayette Parish students stopped reading when money was no longer available. It probably cannot be said, however, that they read less than they did before participating in the program. If students show little or no interest in an activity, it is silly to refuse to provide rewards for fear of undermining their interest in the activity – a point made by Greene and Lepper.[19]

Kohn ignores such evidence and instead cites studies on the use of contractual rewards in weight control, smoking, and seat belt programs.[20] I am (understandably, I think) reluctant to take Kohn's assessment of these programs at face value.[21] But let us assume for the sake of argument that he is right. Note that none of these programs has anything to do with the value of rewards in classroom learning. Kohn's logic is, "If rewards do not help people stop smoking, they cannot help students learn to write." By the same logic, we would have to conclude that since aspirin is of no use in treating cancer, it must not be effective in treating headache. It is a bizarre logic.

✐ The benefits of rewards, says Kohn, are only temporary. Obviously this is not true if we are speaking of academic learning: the child who learns the Pythagorean theorem at the hands of a teacher who provides frequent feedback and praise does not suddenly forget Pythagoras because his next teacher no longer pays attention to his efforts. Nor is there any reason to think that students who are paid to read become illiterate when the money runs out.

But perhaps Kohn has other kinds of learning in mind. Teachers who praise and attend to students when they are on-task will find those students spending less time staring out the window or doodling in their notebooks.[22] If the teacher abruptly stops rewarding on-task behavior, the rate of window staring and doodling will return to its previous level.[23] To conclude from this that teachers should not reward behavior is ridiculous. It is like saying that regular exercise is pointless because your muscles get flabby again when you stop exercising. The point is not to stop.

It should be noted, moreover, that one of the things we can strengthen with rewards is persistence. Once our students are on-task for short periods, we can then begin rewarding longer periods of on-task behavior. We must be careful not to raise the standard too quickly, but we can *gradually* require more from our students. Persistence at other kinds of activities can also be built up by systematically providing rewards (especially praise) for meeting successively higher standards. Many teachers do this over the course of a school year, often without realizing it.

When behavior is rewarded intermittently in this way, it tends to become stronger. That is, it becomes *less* likely to fall off when rewards are no longer available. This is a well-established phenomenon called the partial reinforcement effect (PRE). The PRE reflects the fact that, in an uncertain world, persistence often pays off.

ONE FINAL comment: I realize that this reply to Kohn's remarks will have little impact on most readers. Kohn is selling what educators want to buy — and what many of them have been buying for several decades. It is the philosophy of education that says that students must teach themselves, that the teacher's job is to let students explore and discover on their own, and that teachers can, at most, "facilitate learning."[24]

This philosophy renders the teacher essentially impotent and leads ultimately to the conclusion that, when students fail, it is their own fault.[25] If students do not learn, it is because of some deficiency in them: lack of ability, lack of motivation, hyperactivity, attention deficit disorder — we have lots of choices. The failure is never due to inadequate teaching. Learning depends, after all, on things inside the student, well out of the teacher's reach.

I reject this view. I believe that a fair reading of the research on classroom learning points to a better way. That better way includes a teacher who is actively engaged in the educational process. Such a teacher recognizes the importance of, among other things, providing students with opportunities to perform and providing consequences for that performance. Those consequences include feedback, praise, smiles, and other forms of informational reward. In certain circumstances, they may include contractual rewards. This view of education places responsibility for learning squarely on the teacher's shoulders. Perhaps that is why there is so much opposition to it.

1. B. F. Skinner was not fond of contractual rewards himself, but he agreed that they may sometimes be necessary. See B. F. Skinner, "The Contrived Reinforcer," *The Behavior Analyst*, Spring 1982, pp. 3-8.

2. In an *Industry Week* survey, about one in three employees complained about a lack of praise for their work, a fact reported in Randall Poe and Carol L. Courter, "Fast Forward," *Across the Board*, September 1991, p. 5. Would workers want more praise if they considered it manipulative and controlling?

3. For instance. students can learn to find logical errors in a text by reading texts containing such errors and receiving feedback and praise for their efforts. See Kent R. Johnson and T. V. Joe Layng, "Breaking the Structuralist Barrier: Literacy and Numeracy with Fluency," *American Psychologist*, vol. 47, 1992, pp. 1475-90. For more on the use of rewards to teach thinking, see Paul Chance, *Thinking in the Classroom* (New York: Teachers College Press, 1986), Ch. 9.

4. John I. Goodlad, *A Place Called School: Prospects for the Future* (New York: McGraw-Hill, 1984), p. 112. Goodlad argues that teachers should be taught the skills of "providing students with knowledge of their performance, and giving praise for good work" (p. 127). For the most part they are not taught these skills. Ernest Vargas notes that, "with the exception of a stray course here or there," the 1,200 colleges of education in this country offer little instruction in reinforcement and related techniques. See Ernest A. Vargas, "Teachers in the Classroom: Behaviorological Science and an Effective Instructional Technology," *Youth Policy*, July/August 1988, p. 35.

5. Harold W. Stevenson, "Learning from Asian Schools," *Scientific American*, December 1992, pp. 70-76. Stevenson suggests that the American preference for seatwork and the failure to provide feedback may be due partly to the fact that Americans teach longer hours than their Asian counterparts.

6. Quoted in James G. Holland, "B. F. Skinner (1904-1990)," *American Psychologist*, vol. 47, 1992, p. 667.

7. F. S. Keller, "Goodbye, Teacher . . . ," *Journal of Applied Behavior Analysis*, Spring 1968, pp. 79-89. See also Paul Chance, "The Revolutionary Gentleman," *Psychology Today*, September 1984, pp. 42-48.

8. Studies reporting a loss of interest following rewards typically involve 1) contractual rewards and 2) behavior that is already occurring at a high rate. This is, of course, a misuse of contractual rewards, since the purpose of such rewards is to boost the rate of behavior that occurs *infrequently*.

9. In my article, I provided guidelines for the effective use of rewards. These guidelines were drawn, in part, from the recommendations of Deci, Ryan, Lepper, and Greene.

10. Edward L. Deci and Richard M. Ryan, *Intrinsic Motivation and Self-Determination in Human Behavior* (New York: Plenum, 1985), p. 300.

11. David Greene and Mark R. Lepper, "Intrinsic Motivation: How to Turn Play into Work," *Psychology Today*, September 1974, p. 54. Elsewhere they write that "the effects of rewards depend upon the manner and context in which they are delivered." See Mark R. Lepper and David Greene, "Divergent Approaches," in idem, eds., *The Hidden Costs of Reward* (New York: Erlbaum, 1978), p. 208.

12. Greene and Lepper, p. 54.

13. Mark Morgan, "Reward-Induced Decrements and Increments in Intrinsic Motivation," *Review of Educational Research*, Spring 1984, p. 13.

14. Ibid., p. 9. Another of Kohn's sources, Teresa Amabile, also specifically defends the use of informational rewards. See Teresa Amabile, "Cashing in on Good Grades," *Psychology Today*, October 1989, p. 80. See also idem, *The Social Psychology of Creativity* (New York: Springer-Verlag, 1983).

15. Bill L. Hopkins and R. J. Conard, "Putting It

All Together: Superschool," in Norris G. Haring and Richard L. Schiefelbusch, eds., *Teaching Special Children* (New York: McGraw-Hill, 1975), pp. 342-85.

16. The students also enjoyed school more and were better behaved.

17. See, for example, Charles R. Greenwood et al., "Out of the Laboratory and into the Community," *American Psychologist*, vol. 47, 1992, pp. 1464-74; R. Douglas Greer, "L'Enfant Terrible Meets the Educational Crisis," *Journal of Applied Behavior Analysis*, Spring 1992, pp. 65-69; and Johnson and Layng, op. cit.

18. Steven Hotard and Marion J. Cortez, "Evaluation of Lafayette Parish Job Training Summer Remedial Program: Report Presented to the Lafayette Parish School Board and Lafayette Parish Job Training Department of Lafayette Parish Government," August 1987. Note that this research may not represent the best use of contractual rewards, since payment was only loosely contingent on performance.

19. "Clearly," they write, "if a child begins with no intrinsic interest in an activity, there will be no intrinsic motivation to lose." See Greene and Lepper, p. 54.

20. Note that Kohn cites no evidence that his own preferred techniques — persuasion and mutual problem solving — are effective in helping people lose weight, quit smoking, or use seat belts. Indeed, reward programs have been used to treat these problems precisely because persuasion and education have proved ineffective.

21. For instance, in the study on smoking that Kohn cites, the researchers note that "the incentive was not linked directly to smoking cessation." See Susan J. Curry et al., "Evaluation of Intrinsic and Extrinsic Motivation Interventions with a Self-Help Smoking Cessation Program," *Journal of Consulting and Clinical Psychology*, vol. 59, 1991, p. 309. The researchers rewarded participants for completing progress reports, *not* for refraining from smoking.

22. Teacher attention can be an effective reward for on-task behavior. See R. Vance Hall, Diane Lund, and Deloris Jackson, "Effects of Teacher Attention on Study Behavior," *Journal of Applied Behavior Analysis*, Spring 1968, pp. 1-12.

23. Some might argue that we should merely provide students with more interesting (i.e., intrinsically rewarding) material. While interesting learning materials are certainly desirable, it is probably unrealistic to expect that students will always have interesting material with which to work. It may therefore be desirable for them to learn to concentrate on work even when it is not particularly agreeable.

24. The roots of today's constructivist "revolution" are described in Lawrence A. Cremin, "The Free School Movement," *Today's Education*, September/October 1974, pp. 71-74; and in B. F. Skinner, "The Free and Happy Student," *New York University Education Quarterly*, Winter 1973, pp. 2-6.

25. This is apparently the prevailing view. Galen Alessi has found that school psychologists, for instance, rarely consider poor instruction the source of a student's difficulties. Instead, the student and, in a few cases, the student's parents are said to be at fault. Galen Alessi, "Diagnosis Diagnosed: A Systematic Reaction," *Professional School Psychology*, vol. 3, 1988, pp. 145-51.

The Tyranny of Self-Oriented Self-Esteem

Many modern self-esteem programs emphasize a self-focus, although a focus directed on external-to-self goals may be more productive.

James H. McMillan, Judy Singh, and Leo G. Simonetta

JAMES H. McMILLAN, Ph.D., is a professor of educational studies at Virginia Commonwealth University in Richmond, Virginia. JUDY SINGH is a doctoral student in education at Virginia Commonwealth University. LEO G. SIMONETTA is an assistant professor and social psychologist at the Center for Urban Policy Research at Georgia State University in Atlanta.

In Ryann's second-grade classroom there was a poster on one wall to celebrate each individual student. For one week during the year each student was the "special child" of the class, and the space on the poster indicated unique and valued things about the child, such as a favorite color, hobbies, or family. Students put up pictures and other items to announce publicly what they thought was good about themselves. (Ryann, daughter of one of the authors, liked being a "special child" for a week, but the parent was not as enthusiastic.)

Activities of this type are common in elementary schools, all seeking to boost the self-esteem of the students. They assume that self-esteem is the key to achievement, and in fact much evidence, both anecdotal and research-based, shows that students achieve more with self-esteem. Teachers also seem to accept self-esteem as critical for intellectual development and necessary for students to excel or even achieve needed competence in academic tasks. According to Barbara Lerner, "Teachers generally seem to accept the modern dogma that self-esteem is the critical variable for intellectual development—the master key to learning. Children . . . cannot achieve excellence, or even competence, until their self-esteem is raised."[1]

Linking self-esteem to success and overall well-being is so well accepted that there are many institutes, foundations, task forces, and centers dedicated to promoting self-esteem programs. For example, there is the California Task Force to Promote Self-Esteem and Personal and Social Responsibility, the Center for Self-Esteem, the National Council for Self-Esteem, and the Foundation for Self-Esteem.[2] In addition, an increasing number of books, monographs, audio- and videocassettes stress developing self-esteem, as well as "how to" programs for teachers at all levels. The fundamental idea is that once educators focus on improving students' self-esteem, not only will behavior and achievement improve, but students also will be more satisfied, better adjusted, and happier. The assumption is that concentrating on enhancing self-esteem will produce these positive outcomes.

But is it possible, with the best of intentions, to overemphasize self-esteem with self-oriented activities? What are we teaching our children by encouraging and reinforcing a self-focus, and what are its long-term consequences? Since the mid-'60s, psychology has transformed our way of thinking about explanations for people's behaviors, shifting from out-

What are we teaching our children by encouraging and reinforcing a self-focus, and what are its long-term consequences?

side the self (behaviorism) to within the self. The psychologist Martin Seligman terms our current culture one of "maximal selfs," in which the individual should be gratified, fulfilled, self-actualized, and in control.[3] Seligman argues that this revolutionary change has caused increased depression, hopelessness, and other personal difficulties because of the dual burden of high expectations and self-control. Since the focus is on ourselves as being responsible, and on an expectation that we will be most content and happy if we concentrate on what is best for us, coping with failure to reach our expectations becomes difficult. If Seligman is correct, many facets of current self-esteem programs may be based on fundamentally flawed and misdirected theory. In this article the theory of self-oriented self-esteem programs will be reviewed, with illustrations of suggested practices based on this theory and the results that can be expected from this approach. An alternative theory will be recommended, with suggested practices.

Self-oriented Self-esteem

Many self-esteem programs fundamentally encourage students to think more about themselves, to be more introspective and self-oriented. The idea is that the self can be enhanced by focusing on it positively. Barbara Lerner refers to this as "feel-good-now self-esteem."[4] Jack Canfield, a well-known advocate of self-esteem

enhancement, has suggested several strategies for the classroom that emphasize introspection: 1) assume an attitude of 100 percent responsibility by getting students to think about what they are saying to themselves; 2) focus on the positive—"I spend a lot of my time having students recall, write about, draw, and share their past experiences"; 3) learn to monitor your self-talk by replacing negative thoughts with positive—"I can learn to do anything I want, I am smart, I love and accept myself the way I am"; and 4) identify your strengths and weaknesses.[5]

A popular self-esteem book for educators suggests enhancing self-esteem with one or more of the following: improving self-evaluation skills; developing a sense of personal worth; reflecting on self-esteem; thinking of oneself in positive terms; discovering reasons the individual is unhappy; or examining sources of and influences on self-esteem. Their emphasis is on enhancing students' positive self-perceptions.[6] Such ideas are often implemented in classroom activities that teach students introspective thinking: for example, keeping a journal about themselves and indicating "what I like best about myself";[7] teaching a unit entitled "I Am Great" that emphasizes their individuality through self-portraits, silhouettes of themselves, "who am I," and "coat of arms" exercises;[8] and programs such as Developing Understanding of Self and Others (DUSO), Toward Affective Development, and Dimensions of Personality. Some less-complex programs simply encourage student self-talk with phrases such as "I'm terrific" or "I'm great." All these activities or programs are designed to promote self-acceptance and self-awareness, to help students become aware of their unique characteristics, and to "put children in touch with themselves."[9]

Although these are well-intentioned programs, their encouragement of self-introspection may distort a normal, healthy perspective about oneself into self importance, self gratification, and ultimately selfishness. If

the message is that "me" is most important, will selfishness be viewed as normal and expected? Are we making a virtue of self-preoccupation? If so, such "selfism" may have negative consequences. As William Damon points out, "A young mind might too readily interpret a blanket incantation toward self-esteem as a lure toward self-centeredness."[10] Damon believes that placing the child at the center of the universe is psychologically dangerous because "…it draws the child's attention away from the social realities to which the child must adapt for proper character development."[11] Children taught to place themselves first care most for their own personal experiences, and in doing so they do not learn how to develop respect for others. According to Lerner, the feel-good-now variety of self-esteem eventually leads to unhappiness, restlessness, and dissatisfaction.[12] Finally, Seligman argues that our obsession with self is responsible for an alarming increase in depression and other mental difficulties,[13] and it is well-documented that such problems result from rumination and obsessive thinking about oneself.[14]

There are other negative consequences of overemphasizing self-oriented self-esteem. For most students, and surely young children, the idea of self-esteem is abstract and hard to understand. Generalized statements such as "you're valued," or "you're great," or "you're special" have no objective reality. They are simply holistic messages that, untied to something tangible and real, have little meaning.[15] Teachers making such statements will lose credibility because children are adept at discerning valid feedback from such vague generalizations. Students may develop a skepticism toward and distrust of adults, or even worse may learn to tune them out entirely, as the teacher "shades the truth … [with] … empty rhetoric, transparent flattery, bland distortions of reality."[16] By trying to bolster self-esteem with messages that are not "entirely" true, teachers inadvertently undermine the trust of the child. For students who already have a low self-esteem, such statements reinforce a noncaring attitude from adults. From the perspective of children, caring adults "tell it like it is" and don't hide the truth—they don't cover up or make things up that aren't true.

In contrast, there is ample evidence that our mental health improves as we forget ourselves and focus on activities that are not self-oriented. Often we are most happy when we are so involved in outside pursuits that we don't think about ourselves. This leads us to an alternative theoretical foundation for self-esteem: the notion that healthy self-esteem results not from self-preoccupation and analysis but just the opposite—from **not** being self-oriented but being occupied by interests and pursuits external to self. Indeed, many self-esteem enhancement programs appear to be based on this idea.

Accomplishment and External-to-Self-oriented Self-esteem

As an alternative to the self-orientation approach, we suggest that a healthy esteem results not from self-preoccupation and analysis but from activities that result in meaningful accomplishment or have an external-to-self orientation. Accomplishment means that self-esteem is enhanced as children work hard to meet externally set, reasonable standards of achievement. Lerner calls this "earned" self-esteem: "Earned self-esteem is based on success in meeting the tests of reality—measuring up to standards—at home and in school. It is necessarily hard-won, and develops slowly, but is stable and long-lasting, and provides a secure foundation for further growth and development. It is not a precondition for learning but a product of it."[17]

Achieving meaningful success in schoolwork enhances self-esteem after many years of meeting standards and demands. A foundation for self-esteem based on tangible evidence is internalized by students because it makes sense to them in their social environment. Internally meaningful

> *Accomplishment means that self-esteem is enhanced as children work hard to meet externally set, reasonable standards of achievement.*

performance and accomplishment can be attributed to ability and effort. Such internal attributions underlie a sense of self-efficacy so that the child becomes confident in being a capable learner. Striving for achievement also directs children's thinking off themselves and on something external to themselves. This change in thinking orientation determines self-esteem programs that theoretically are diametrically opposed to self-oriented programs.

Recently there have been signs that psychologists may be changing their views about the emphasis on selfism to enhance self-esteem. Seligman maintains that many have lost a sense of commitment to larger entities outside themselves—country, church, community, family, God, or a purpose that transcends themselves.[18] Without these connections people are left to find meaning and fulfillment in themselves. The negative consequences of de-emphasizing other people, groups, community, and the larger society include vandalism, violence, racial tensions, high divorce rates, and drug abuse. Some psychologists attribute the growth of the "me" generation and selfish behavior to the emphasis on individuality and related themes.[19] Others argue that schools should promote selflessness by emphasizing group welfare over individuals, involvement rather than iso-

lation, and self-denial rather than self-centeredness.

These authors suggest that student well-being is best enhanced by pursuits that take attention away from self, in which one gets "lost." Such pursuits could include a hobby; a concern for helping others; having a purpose or cause bigger than oneself; submitting to duty or to a role in community; or academic success following meaningful effort. The hypothesis is that self-esteem is a by-product of successful external-to-self experiences. The more success a student has in such activities, the stronger his or her own self-esteem will be.

From a social-psychological perspective, participating constructively with others is necessary for positive self-esteem. As stated by Damon:

> Growing up in large part means learning to participate constructively in the social world. This in turn means developing real skills, getting along with others, acquiring respect for social rules and legitimate authority, caring about those in need, and assuming social responsibility in a host of ways. All of these efforts necessarily bring children out of themselves. They require children to orient themselves toward other people and other people's standards.[21]

By focusing outside themselves children learn respect for others and an objective reference for acquiring a stable and meaningful sense of themselves. It is the outward focus that forms the foundation for self-esteem.

Some examples of self-esteem programs appear to be based on this external-to-self hypothesis. One is a successful program in which students are involved in an art project structured to enhance a feeling of belonging and accomplishment. Self-esteem is improved by involving students in meaningful group activity, not by self-introspection.[22] Another program reports that children acquire self-esteem from successful experiences and appropriate feedback in motor skill development.[23] Several other programs also stress successful achievement in affecting self-esteem.[24] In each case the program involves students in some meaningful activity, rather than focusing on themselves.

Conclusion

Clearly, educators need to concentrate their efforts on improving students' self-esteem. The important question is: How should this be done? We have suggested that approaches emphasizing meaningful achievement and external-to-self pursuits will result in more healthy self-esteem than programs that are self-oriented. Teachers and administrators need to design programs directing student attention away from the self, not toward it. Paradoxically, positive self-esteem develops as students forget about self-esteem, focus on external pursuits, and obtain positive feedback following meaningful involvement and effort

Teachers and administrators need to design programs directing student attention away from the self, not toward it.

1. Barbara Lerner, "Self-esteem and Excellence: The Choice and the Paradox," *American Educator* 9 (1985): 10-16.

2. Jack Canfield, "Improving Students' Self-esteem," *Educational Leadership* 48 (1990): 48-50.

3. Martin E. P. Seligman, "Boomer Blues: With Too Great Expectations, the Baby-Boomers Are Sliding into Individualistic Melancholy," *Psychology Today* 22 (1988): 50-55.

4. Lerner, "Self-esteem and Excellence."

5. Canfield, "Improving Students' Self-esteem."

6. James A. Beane and Richard P. Lipka, *Self-concept, Self-esteem, and the Curriculum* (Boston: Allyn and Bacon, 1984).

7. Anne E. Gottsdanker-Willenkens and Patricia Y. Leonard, "All about Me: Language Arts Strategies to Enhance Self-Concept," *Reading Teacher* 37 (1984): 801-802.

8. Richard L. Papenfuss, John D. Curtis, Barbara J. Beier, and Joseph D. Menze, "Teaching Positive Self-concepts in the Classroom," *Journal of School Health* 53 (1983): 618-620.

9. Frederic J. Medway and Robert C. Smith, Jr., "An Examination of Contemporary Elementary School Affective Education Programs," *Psychology in the Schools* 15 (1978): 266.

10. William Damon, "Putting Substance into Self-Esteem: A Focus on Academic and Moral Values," *educational HORIZONS* (fall 1991):13.

11. Ibid., 17.

12. Lerner, "Self-esteem and Excellence."

13. Seligman, "Boomer Blues."

14. Thomas J. Lasley and John Bregenzer, "Toward Selflessness," *Journal of Human Behavior and Learning* 3 (1986): 20-27.

15. Damon, "Putting Substance into Self-esteem."

16. Ibid., 15.

17. Lerner, "Self-esteem and Excellence," 13.

18. Martin E. P. Seligman, *Learned Optimism: The Skill to Conquer Life's Obstacles, Large & Small* (New York: Random House, 1990).

19. Sami I. Boulos, "The Anatomy of the 'Me' Generation," *Education* 102 (1982): 238-242.

20. Lasley and Bregenzer, "Toward Selflessness."

21. William Damon, "Putting Substance into Self-esteem," 16-17.

22. Marilee M. Cowan and Faith M. Clover, "Enhancement of Self-concept through Disciplined-based Art Education," *Art Education* 44 (1991): 38-45.

23. Linda K. Bunker, "The Role of Play and Motor Skill Development in Building Children's Self-confidence and Self-esteem," *Elementary School Journal* 91 (1991): 467-471.

24. David L. Silvernail, *Developing Positive Student Self-concept* (Washington, D.C.: National Education Association, 1987).

The Caring Classroom's Academic Edge

Catherine C. Lewis, Eric Schaps, and Marilyn S. Watson

The Child Development Project has shown that when kids care about one another—and are motivated by important, challenging work—they're more apt to care about learning.

At Hazelwood School in Louisville, Kentucky, pairs of students are scattered around a 2nd–3rd grade classroom. Heads bent together, students brainstorm with their partners why Widower Muldie, of the book *Wagon Wheels*, left his three sons behind when he set off across the wilderness in search of a home site. Although this story of an African-American pioneer family is set in the rural America of more than 100 years ago, these inner-city students have little trouble diving into the assignment: Write a dialogue between Johnnie and Willie Muldie, ages 11 and 8, who are left in charge of their 3-year-old brother.

Teacher Laura Ecken sets the stage:

Let's imagine that we're Johnny and Willie. It's the first night all alone without daddy. We've put little brother to bed, and we're just sitting up talking to each other.

A Salinas, California, student looks to her older "buddy" for help.

Before students launch into their work, Ecken asks the class to discuss "ways we can help our partners." The children demonstrate remarkable forethought about how to work together: "Disagree without being mean." "If your partner says something that don't fit, then work it into another part." "Let your partner say all they want to say."

Over the next hour, students become intensely interested in figuring out what the Muldie boys might have said to each other. The teacher offers no grade or behavioral reward for this task, nor is any needed. Students are friendly, helpful, and tactful, but also determined to write the best dialogue they know how. In one partnership, John says, "We could talk about how much we miss daddy." Cynthia counters: "But daddy's only been gone for a day." After a few exchanges on this point, John and Cynthia agree to talk about "how much we're *going* to miss daddy." In another partnership, Barry makes use of a strategy suggested by a classmate in the preceding discussion: "How about if we use your idea to 'help me hunt for food' later, because right now we're talking about how the boys feel." Students seem remarkably comfortable questioning and expressing disagreement; the easy camaraderie extends to the many partnerships that cross racial and gender lines.

Fruits of Community

That children at Hazelwood School care about learning and about one another seems perfectly natural. But it didn't just happen. The school's staff has worked very hard over the past five years to create what they call "a caring community of learners"—a community whose members feel valued, personally connected to one another, and committed to everyone's growth and learning. Hazelwood's staff—and educators at other

Do students view their classmates primarily as collaborators in learning, or as competitors in the quest for grades and recognition?

From *Educational Leadership,* September 1996, pp, 16-21. © 1996 by Catherine C. Lewis, Eric Schaps, and Marilyn S. Watson. Reprinted by permission.

Five Principles to Practice

How exactly do Child Development Project schools become "caring communities of learners"? They adhere to five interdependent principles, striving for the following.

1. Warm, supportive, stable relationships. Do all members of a school community—students, teachers, staff, parents—know one another as people? Do students view their classmates primarily as collaborators in learning, or as competitors in the quest for grades and recognition? Teachers at our CDP schools carefully examine their approaches, asking, "What kind of human relationships are we fostering?" They recast many old activities.

For example, at one California elementary school, the competitive science fair has become a hands-on family science night that draws hundreds of parents. With awards eliminated, parents are free to focus on the pleasures of learning science with their children. A Dade County, Florida, elementary school removed the competitive costume contest from its Halloween celebration, so that children could enjoy the event without worrying about winners and losers. Other schools took the competition out of PTA membership drives, refocusing them to emphasize participation and celebration of the school's progress.

Teachers also added or redesigned many academic and nonacademic activities so that students could get to know one another and develop a feeling of unity and shared purpose as a class and school. "A big change for me is that on the first morning of school, the classroom walls are blank— no decorations, no rules," explains a teacher from California. Like many of her Child Development Project colleagues, she involves students in interviewing classmates and creating wall displays about "our class" that bring children closer together.

In the first class meetings of the year, students discuss "how we want to be treated by others," and "what kind of class we want to be." From these discussions emerge a few simple principles—"be kind," "show respect," "do

Child Development Project (CDP) schools across the country—believe that creating such a community is crucial to children's learning and citizenship. A growing body of research suggests they are right.

At schools high in "community"— measured by the degree of students' agreement with statements such as "My school is like a family" and "Students really care about each other"—students show a host of positive outcomes. These include higher educational expectations and academic performance, stronger motivation to learn, greater liking for school, less absenteeism, greater social competence, fewer conduct problems, reduced drug use and delinquency, and greater commitment to democratic values (Battistich et al., in press; Bryk and Driscoll 1988; Hom and Battistich 1995).

Our approach in the Child Development Project is to take research findings about how children learn and develop—ethically, socially, and intellectually—and translate them into a comprehensive, practical program with three facets: (1) a classroom program that concentrates on literature-based reading instruction, cooperative learning, and a problem-solving approach to discipline; (2) a school-

wide program of community building and service activities; and (3) a family involvement program.

We originally developed these approaches in collaboration with teachers in California's San Ramon and Hayward school districts. We then extended them, beginning in 1991, to six additional districts nationwide (Cupertino, San Francisco, and Salinas in California; Dade County, Florida.; Jefferson County, Kentucky; and White Plains, New York). In both the original and extension sites, students in CDP schools were studied and compared with students in matched non-project schools (Solomon et al. 1992).

Everything about schooling— curriculum, teaching method, discipline, interpersonal relationships—teaches children about the human qualities that we value.

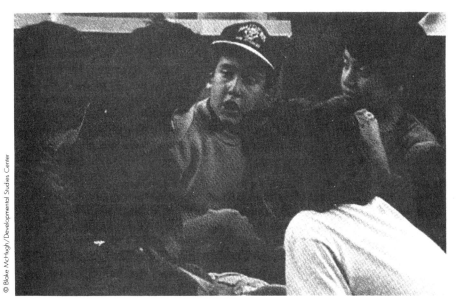

© Blake McHugh/Developmental Studies Center

Students work harder, achieve more, and attribute more importance to schoolwork in classes in which they feel liked, accepted, and respected by the teacher and fellow students.

our best"—that are remarkably similar across diverse schools.

Says one teacher,

> When you invest time up front in having the kids get to know one another, the picked-on child never has a chance to emerge. Kids find out that they share the same favorite food, hobby, or whatever; they see one another as human beings. The child who might have been the nerd in previous years never gets seen

that way because classmates remember that that child's favorite food is McDonald's hamburgers, too.

2. Constructive learning. Children naturally try to make sense of the world—to figure out how magnets work or why friends help. Good teaching fosters these efforts to understand, but also hones them, helping children become ever more skillful, reflective, and self-critical in their pursuit of knowledge. How can teachers support and extend children's natural efforts to learn?

First, educators can provide a coherent curriculum, organized around important concepts, rather than a

potpourri of isolated facts. Second, educators can connect the curriculum with children's own natural efforts to make sense of the world. Children should see mathematics, for example, as a powerful means for understanding the world, not as arbitrary principles that apply only within classroom walls. When children see how the ideas and skills of school help them understand and act upon the world—how they are genuinely useful—they begin to practice these academic skills throughout their home and school lives.

Third, lessons can be set up so that children must weigh new information against what they already know, work through discrepancies, and construct a new understanding. When children make discoveries, struggle to find explanations, and grapple with evidence and views that differ from their own, they are likely to reach more profound levels of understanding than they can achieve through simple rote learning. The students at Hazelwood School who wrote a dialogue between the Muldie boys were constructive learners in all these senses.

Like other books in our project's literature-based program, *Wagon Wheels* pursues important issues: What experiences have shaped the lives of diverse Americans? How have acts of principle, courage, and responsibility shaped history, and how do they shape our own daily lives? These issues are explored not just in literature and social studies, but in class meetings, problem solving, and in many other ways.

In addition, to make sense of an experience that happened long ago, Ecken's students needed to draw on both school learning and their own experiences. Would being left without parents and in charge of a younger brother feel any different in 1878 than in 1994? Finally, the task of writing a dialogue challenged students to take the perspective of the boys in the story and to reconcile their thinking with their partner's perspective.

3. An important, challenging curriculum. In an era of rapid techno-logical change, certain skills and habits are likely to remain important—thoughtful reading, self-critical reflec-tion, clear communication, asking productive questions. But the de facto curriculum defined by commercial text-books and standardized tests often emphasizes something much less enduring—isolated subskills and piece-meal knowledge. Like Jere Brophy and Janet Alleman (1991), we believe that curriculum development must "be driven by major long-term goals, not just short-term coverage concerns." These goals should be broadly conceived to include children's devel-opment as principled, humane citizens.

Numerous critiques of the curriculum in this country argue that it sells chil-dren short by presenting material that is too simple and too easily mastered—for example, basal readers whose barren language and shallow ideas offer little reason to read. That a more challenging curriculum is more compelling to children, even so-called slow learners, is a tenet underlying some recent interventions (Hopfenberg 1993).

4. Intrinsic motivation. What kind of schooling produces eager, lifelong learners? Certainly not schooling that relies on the power of extrinsic rewards—prizes, honors, grades, and so forth. In fact, studies show that these can actually undermine children's interest in learning (Lepper and Greene 1978). Awarding prizes for creating science projects, reading books, running laps, or a host of other worthwhile ends can diminish interest in the activity itself by focusing children's

Faced with a competitive, skill-and-drill curriculum, educationally less-prepared children may preserve their self-esteem by reducing their efforts.

attention on the reward, and by implying that the task is not inherently worthwhile (Kohn 1993). As one sage commentator quipped, "If we want children to read books, we should offer them books as a reward for eating pizzas, not pizzas for reading books."

To minimize extrinsic rewards, educators need a curriculum that is worth learning and a pedagogy that helps students see why it is worth learning. The students writing a dialogue between the Muldie boys were motivated by the task itself. *Wagon Wheels* raised issues of timeless importance, and the teacher took care to introduce the book in a way that piqued students' curiosity and helped them make personal connections to the book.

5. Attention to social and ethical dimensions of learning. Everything about schooling—curriculum, teaching method, discipline, interpersonal relationships—teaches children about the human qualities that we value. As students discuss the experiences of African-American families like the Muldies, they grow ethically and socially. This growth stems from the

content they encounter, the experience of working with classmates, and the reflection following partner work on their difficulties and successes working with others.

Child Development Project teachers scrutinize disciplinary approaches not just for whether they help children behave in the short run, under an adult's surveillance, but whether they

promote children's responsible behavior in the long run. Teachers engage children in shaping the norms of their class and school, so that they see that these norms are not arbitrary standards set by powerful adults, but necessary standards for the well-being of everyone. Teachers also help children develop collaborative approaches to resolving conflicts, guiding them to think about the values needed for humane life in a group. Playground disputes become opportunities for students to learn about the needs and perspectives of other students, and to practice skills of nonviolent problem solving.

Finally, teachers look at the many programs, special events, parent-supported activities, and policies of the school through the lens of social and ethical development. Do these activities help children understand the values that sustain democratic society? Do they give students many opportunities to develop and practice qualities that we want them to have as adults—responsibility, collaboration, tolerance, commitment to the common good, courage to stand up for their beliefs, and so on?

Synergy of Academic and Social Goals

It is common to think of the academic and social goals of schooling as a hydraulic—to imagine that fostering one undermines the other. But when schools attend to all five elements described above, they create environments where children care about one another and about learning.

For example, students work harder, achieve more, and attribute more importance to schoolwork in classes in which they feel liked, accepted, and respected by the teacher and fellow students. Warm, supportive relationships also enable students to risk the

To minimize extrinsic rewards, educators need a curriculum that is worth learning and a pedagogy that helps students see why it is worth learning.

new ideas and mistakes so critical to intellectual growth. It is no coincidence that, to create an environment in which students can discuss classmates' incorrect solutions to math problems, Japanese teachers spend a great deal of time building friendships among children and a feeling of classroom unity.

Schools that provide an important, challenging curriculum, and help children connect it to their own efforts to understand the world, become allies in children's quest for competence—and teachers in those schools have a head start in being seen as supportive, valued adults.

A shift away from competition, rewards, and punishments helps all students—not just the high-achievers—feel like valued members of the classroom community. Faced with a competitive, skill-and-drill curriculum, educationally less-prepared children may preserve their self-esteem by reducing their efforts. They may psychologically withdraw from the classroom or school community, leaving it powerless to influence their social, ethical, or intellectual development (Nicholls 1989).

The caring classroom is not one that avoids criticism, challenge, or mistakes. Parker J. Palmer (1983) has written:

> A learning space needs to be hospitable not to make learning painless but to make the painful things possible... things like exposing ignorance, testing tentative hypotheses, challenging false or partial information, and mutual criticism of thought. [None of these] can happen in an atmosphere where people feel threatened and judged.

Like a family, the caring classroom provides a sense of belonging that allows lively, critical discussions and risk-taking.

Countering Conventional Wisdom

We think relatively few American schools have managed to sustain a simultaneous focus on students' social, ethical, and intellectual development. What will it take to achieve this on a much broader scale? First, it will take changes in thinking; the agenda we have proposed runs counter to much

When children see how the ideas and skills of school help them understand and act upon the world—how they are genuinely useful—they begin to practice these skills throughout their home and school lives.

current conventional wisdom in education.

Such changes cannot be expected to come quickly or easily. Because adults, too, are constructive learners, they need the same five conditions that children do. School improvement hinges on a sense of community and collaboration among teachers, conditions that enable teachers to risk changing practice and to admit and learn from mistakes.

At the schools participating in the Child Development Project, teachers spend up to 30 days over three years in staff development. The schools have worked consciously to build strong personal connections among staff members. They do this through social events, shared planning and reflection, and often by meeting regularly in "learning partnerships" of two to four teachers to discuss their efforts to reshape practice. In an era of tight budgets, such time for adult learning is difficult to obtain.

Finally, we need to recognize that community and learning are interdependent and must be pursued in context. This means that it is not enough to ask whether a new science curriculum increases students' mastery of important scientific concepts; we must also ask whether it fosters their capacity to work with fellow students, their intrinsic interest in science, and their recognition that science depends upon both collaboration and honesty. This is a big picture to keep in focus. Educators who have traditionally worked in isolation from one another—specialists in subject matter, pedagogy, school climate, motivation—must help one another to keep it in perspective.

References

Battistich, V., D. Solomon, D. Kim, M. Watson, and E. Schaps. (In press).

"Schools as Communities, Poverty Levels of Student Populations, and Students' Attitudes, Motives, and Performance." *American Education Research Journal.*

Brophy, J., and J. Alleman. (1991). "Activities as Instructional Tools: A Framework for Analysis and Evaluation." *Educational Researcher* 20, 4: 9–23.

Bryk, A. S., and M. E. Driscoll. (1988). *The School as Community: Theoretical Foundations, Contextual Influences, and Consequences for Students and Teachers.* Madison, Wisconsin: National Center on Effective Secondary Schools.

Hom, A., and V. Battistich. (April 1995). "Students' Sense of School Community as a Factor in Reducing Drug Use and Delinquency." Presentation to the 1995 American Educational Research Association Annual Meeting.

Hopfenberg, W. (1993). *The Accelerated Schools.* San Francisco: Jossey-Bass.

Kohn, A. (1993). *Punished by Rewards: The Trouble with Gold Stars, Incentive Plans, A's, Praise, and Other Bribes.* Boston: Houghton Mifflin.

Lepper, M. R., and D. Greene. (1978). *The Hidden Costs of Reward: New Perspectives on the Psychology of Human Motivation.* Hillsdale, N.J.: Lawrence Erlbaum Associates.

Nicholls, J. (1989). *The Competitive Ethos and Democratic Education.* Cambridge, Mass.: Harvard University Press.

Palmer, P. J. (1983). *To Know as We Are Known: A Spirituality of Education.* San Francisco: HarperCollins.

Solomon, D., M. Watson, V. Battistich, E. Schaps, and K. Delucchi. (1992). "Creating a Caring Community: A School-Based Program to Promote Children's Prosocial Development." In *Effective and Responsible Teaching: The New Synthesis,* edited by E. Oser, J. L. Patty, and A. Dick. San Francisco: Jossey-Bass.

Catherine C. Lewis is the Formative Research Director, **Eric Schaps** is President, and **Marilyn S. Watson** is Program Director, of the Developmental Studies Center, 2000 Embarcadero, Suite 305, Oakland, CA 94606-5300.

Herbert J. Walberg and Rebecca C. Greenberg

Using the Learning Environment Inventory

How do your students rate their classroom on its cohesion, absence of friction and favoritism, and other social and academic factors? The Learning Environment Inventory lets you find out.

Students' emotional development is tied to the social and emotional climate they experience as they grow up, particularly the amount of stimulation, respect, and care they derive from their families, peer groups, and—not least of all—schools. Well-being and academic achievement do not constitute an either-or proposition; each enhances the other.

In optimal environments, children and adolescents and adults as well enjoy themselves more and get more done (Moos 1991). Under less desirable conditions, they harbor resentments and ill will, their productivity declines, and their alienation prevents their energies from flowing into their work. In fact, research has shown that the classroom social environment is one of the chief psychological determinants of academic learning (Walberg 1984).

Further, students' feelings about their classes not only affect their interest and engagement in the subject matter but also help them acquire essential social skills. Even when the instruction is intensive and the students' abilities considerable, these factors count for little if students see their classmates as uncooperative or their teachers as unfair (Fraser 1991, Walberg 1991).

Taking Stock

What social qualities of your classroom promote learning and what qualities impede it? Researchers have found ways of measuring the social climate of classrooms, and their findings suggest specific steps that educators can take. For junior and senior high schools, the Learning Environment Inventory is a widely used measure.

Educators have used this scale to evaluate new curriculums, instructional methods, and programs for racial desegregation and violence prevention. The counterpart for elementary schools is the My Class Inventory (Fraser et al. 1991).

Figure 1 shows the 15 features of classroom groups that the Learning Environment Inventory measures. Each feature is accompanied by a sample statement. For example, for "Cohesiveness," the statement is "Students know one another very well." For "Favoritism," it is "Every student enjoys the same privileges." Students rate how well these statements describe their classroom on a five-point scale: strongly agree, agree, unsure, disagree, and strongly disagree.

The numbers show how many times each feature was investigated in our

© Susie Fitzhugh

FIGURE 1

Students Rate Their Classroom Environment

Environment Feature	Number of Comparisons	Percent Positive Influence on Learning	Description	Sample Item
Satisfaction	17	100	Enjoyment of work	There is considerable satisfaction with the classwork.
Challenge	16	87	Difficulty with work	Students tend to find the work hard to do.
Cohesiveness	17	86	Whether students know, help, and are friendly toward one another	Students know one another very well.
Physical Environment	15	85	Availability of adequate books, equipment, space, and lighting	Students can easily get the books and equipment they need or want in the classroom.
Democracy	14	85	Extent to which students share equally in class decision making	Class decisions tend to be made by all the students.
Goal direction	15	73	Clarity of goals	The class knows exactly what it has to get done.
Competition	9	67	Emphasis on competition	Students seldom compete with one another.
Formality	17	65	Extent to which formal rules guide behavior	The class is rather informal and few rules are imposed.
Speed	14	54	How quickly class work is covered	Students do not have to hurry to finish their work.
Diversity	14	31	Extent to which student interests differ and differences are provided for	Students have many different interests.
Apathy	15	14	Student affinity with class activities	Members of the class don't care what the class does.
Favoritism	13	10	Teacher favoritism	Every student enjoys the same privileges.
Cliquishness	13	8	Extent to which some students refuse to mix with others	Certain students work only with their close friends.
Disorganization	17	6	Extent to which activities are confusing and poorly organized	The class is well organized and efficient.
Friction	17	0	Tension and quarreling among students	Certain students instigate petty quarrels.

Adapted from the Learning Environment Inventory (Fraser et al. 1991).

research study and the percentage of times the feature resulted in positive influences on learning outcomes. For example, a classroom characterized as "challenging" influenced learning positively 87 percent, or 14 of the 16 times investigated. As we would expect, apathy and favoritism rarely showed positive influences on learning.

Tallying the Results

In general, students in highly-rated classes achieved more academically and had more positive attitudes toward the subject matter. These students also engaged more often in nonrequired activities related to the subject matter. In science classes, for example,

> **Affectionately remembered classes sustain interest in learning.**

students were more likely to read science articles in newspapers and to go to zoos and science museums.

In short, the study confirmed that students learn more when their classes are satisfying, challenging, and friendly and they have a voice in decision making. The study also showed, however, that students need structure, direction, and organization to make sense of their classes. When classes are unfriendly, cliquish, and fragmented, they leave students feeling rejected and therefore impede learning.

In designing the Learning Environment Inventory, we derived the state-

ments from questionnaires that businesses, military agencies, and other adult workplaces used in their research. Not surprisingly, the workplace research also showed that work groups with good morale enjoy their work and get more done.

Our findings demonstrate that we should select lessons and set the pace of learning so as to challenge students appropriately. We should clarify goals and organize lessons to help students make the most efficient use of their time.

As for the social climate of the classroom, allowing students to share their ideas through teams and cooperative groups is one way to promote democratic decision making and foster cohesiveness and satisfaction in the classroom. In addition, by helping students recognize that they all share certain ideas and feelings, a teacher can help prevent cliques from forming and generally reduce social friction. Activities such as role-playing exercises will help students gain insights into how others feel. In fact, educators themselves may need such exercises to help them avoid favoring some students over others.

Looking Beyond the Classroom

Though research on the social and emotional qualities of classrooms began a quarter century ago, it is especially pertinent today for several reasons. First, the social and political pressure for greater student achievement is accelerating. In addition, educators, like businesspeople and other professionals, are increasingly realizing the importance of satisfying their customers. In the case of educators, a satisfied customer—one whose

feelings are considered—is also a successful learner.

Though educators rightfully emphasize achievement, they should also think of motivating their students and awakening a love of learning for its own sake. Affectionately remembered classes sustain interest in learning in the workplace and over a lifetime.

Finally, well-organized, satisfying classrooms foster responsibility, humaneness, and mutual respect—the very social skills students need to participate productively in our civil society. ∎

Authors' note: The Learning Environment Inventory and My Class Inventory are available free of charge for local reproduction and use from Barry J. Fraser, Curtin University, Faculty of Education, Bentley, Australia WA6102.

References

Fraser, B.J. (1991). "Two Decades of Classroom Environment Research." In *Educational Environments: Evaluation, Antecedents, and Consequences,* edited by B.J. Fraser and H.J. Walberg. Oxford, England: Pergamon Press.

Fraser, B.J., G.J. Anderson, and H.J. Walberg. (1991). *Assessment of Learning Environments: Manual for Learning Environment Inventory (LEI) and My Class Inventory (MCI).* Perth, Western Australia: Curtin University of Technology, Science and Mathematics Education Center.

Moos, R.H. (1991). "Connections Between School, Work, and Family Settings." In *Educational Environments: Evaluation, Antecedents, and Consequences,* edited by B.J. Fraser and H.J. Walberg. Oxford, England: Pergamon Press.

Walberg, H.J. (1991). "Educational Productivity and Talent Development." In *Educational Environments: Evaluation, Antecedents, and Consequences,* edited by B.J. Fraser and H.J. Walberg. Oxford, England: Pergamon Press.

Walberg, H.J. (May 1984). "Improving the Productivity of America's Schools." *Educational Leadership* 41, 8: 19–27.

Herbert J. Walberg is Research Professor of Education and Psychology at the University of Illinois College of Education, Mail Code 147, 1040 W. Harrison St., Chicago, IL 60607 (e-mail: hwalberg @uic.edu). **Rebecca C. Greenberg** is a doctoral student in educational psychology at the university. She can be reached at 4502 N. Artesian, Apt. 3, Chicago, IL 60625 (e-mail: rgreen3 @uic.edu).

Blueprints
for Learning

Using Cognitive Frameworks for Understanding

Joseph R. Boyle
Noranne Yeager

■

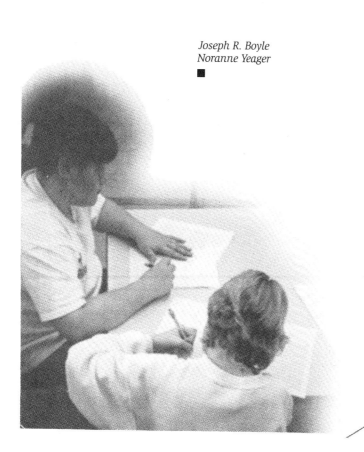

You have just finished teaching what you feel was a great lesson and you decide to check student comprehension of the material by asking a series of questions. To your astonishment, you find that students have difficulty answering even the most basic questions (i.e., literal comprehension questions), let alone higher-level questions.

From *Teaching Exceptional Children,* March/April 1997, pp. 26-31. © 1997 by The Council for Exceptional Children. Reprinted by permission.

You quietly ask yourself, "What happened?" You decide to reteach the lesson, but are uncertain how to assist students with the retention and retrieval of the information.

If this scenario sounds familiar, you are not alone. Every day in classrooms across the United States, teachers are presenting information to students with the assumption that learning is automatically occurring; but when teachers assess student knowledge, they are often surprised at the results. In fact, many students, particularly those at risk or with mild disabilities, do not respond to traditional teaching techniques used in general education (i.e., recitation, lecturing, rote memory, etc.), but instead need more cognitive support during the learning process to learn and remember information (Simmons & Kameenui, 1996).

Just as a house is constructed around a framework, so too is memory. Transferring and encoding information to long-term memory occurs best when information is personalized, organized, and developed around prior knowledge (Mann & Sabatino, 1985; Norman, 1982).

Teachers can help students transfer and retain information through teaching tools called *cognitive frameworks*. Cognitive frameworks support student learning by presenting component information in an organized manner and by linking related information together. More specifically, during academic activities cognitive frameworks aid students by highlighting the important points, visually displaying the relationships between ideas, and serving as guides for studying after the lesson.

Cognitive frameworks go by many names (e.g., story maps, critical thinking maps, webs, cognitive maps, semantic feature analyses, induction towers, flowcharts, study guides, and structured outlines). In this article, we focus on three types of frameworks—study guides, story/critical thinking maps, and cognitive organizers. Each can be used during the different stages of instruction—preinstruction, during instruction, and postinstruction—throughout the various steps of a lesson (model, guided practice, and independent practice), and in many content areas (e.g., science, history, social studies).

Study Guides

A study guide highlights the salient points of an academic activity. Study guides help students learn and retain information from textbooks or lectures by providing an organized framework developed around content using questions or keywords. These guides focus students' attention on the major points of the text, promoting active engagement in the task and organizing incoming information within a structured framework (Tierney, Readence, & Dishner, 1995).

Developing Study Guides

A study guide can take many formats, depending on its purpose (e.g., used as a review prior to the presentation of new information, used to engage students in fact-finding during a lesson, or used as notes for later study). When you develop a study guide, make sure it is comprehensive, including the following components:

- A description of the reading materials.
- Objectives and a rationale.
- Important vocabulary.

Figure 1

Study Guide for a Chapter on Health—4th Grade Level

Reading Assignment. The students will read the chapter in the text called "Nutrition and You."

Objectives. The students will apply the information about nutrients and the food pyramid to a sample diet for themselves for one day.

Rationale. Students need to apply food information in daily choices for their lives. Some students cook for themselves or for their family and can begin to apply their knowledge in better eating habits.

Primary Vocabulary:

nutrients
carbohydrates
fats
proteins
vitamins
minerals
water
basic food groups

Secondary Vocabulary:

glucose
digestion
enzyme
saliva
intestine
oxidized
calories
metabolism

Activities. Choose two activities to complete.

2   List foods eaten in one day to identify the percentages from the basic food groups.

1   List foods to be eaten in one day which will fulfill the balanced percentage from the basic food groups.

3   List a typical fast food meal and identify the percentages from the basic food groups.

3 or 1   Using the chart in your chapter, figure out how many calories are burned by three different activities for an hour.

Activities Key

1. Student does independently.
2. Student does with partner.
3. Students do in a cooperative group and report the results.

Questions Based on Bloom's Taxonomy

Knowledge: Name a basic food group.

Comprehension: Why does the body digest food?

Application: Plan a holiday meal and determine if there is balance among the food groups.

Analysis: Which organ provides the most to the process of digestion and why?

Synthesis: If a person needed to gain weight, what changes could he/she make to their diet?

Evaluation: The advertisement says that pizza is the perfect food! Do you agree or disagree and why?

- A description of activities used to meet the criteria of the objectives.
- Questions of varying comprehension levels.
- A method by which students can self-correct (Hudson, Ormsbee, & Myles, 1994).

Figure 1 shows a sample study guide developed for health.

Variations on Study Guides

You can also construct study guides around the K-W-L technique (Ogle, 1986). K-W-L consists of three basic steps to aid students during learning:

K—What We **K**now.
W—What We **W**ant to Find Out.
L—What Did We **L**earn?

Using this technique, you can create study guides by using K-W-L for the headings of each major topic. Next, before reading, you or your students fill in information under the "K" and "W" heading of the guide. During or after reading, students complete the guide by describing what they read and by recording that information under the "L" heading.

Another variation involves developing analogical study guides (Bean, Singer, & Cowen, 1985). Create these study guides by listing key terms (concepts or vocabulary) along with an analogous item. Because analogies are especially useful to help students understand complex or unfamiliar material, they are often ideal frameworks to use for study guides. For example, in a biology class, you could ask students to relate the functions of the different parts of a *cell* to an analogy of a *factory* (e.g., cell walls are similar to factory walls, the cell membrane is similar to the function of a security guard, etc.). After you review a few analogies with the students, it then becomes their turn to describe the function that would complete the analogy (i.e., the cell membrane acts like a security guard—in ways the text explains) (Bean et al.).

A Final Note on Study Guides

Finally, because study guides are meant to enhance the current curriculum, you should individualize them for students with varying learning abilities (i.e., learning disabilities, gifted, average learners, etc.). For example, when developing study guides for students with mild disabilities, you may want to do the following:

- Provide multiple written prompts (e.g., to answer this question, look on p. 12).
- Highlight the keywords or critical points.
- Use group activities to aid in the completion of the study guide.

Conversely, for students of higher ability, you may incorporate fewer prompts and require more elaboration of terms or concepts. Regardless of the modifications you make, make sure you design them so that *all* students can successfully and accurately complete them. In addition, Tierney et al. (1995) point out that they should always "be used within the context of a well planned lesson" and "students should be well prepared for the reading assignment through background development and a purpose-setting discussion" (p. 338).

Story and Critical Thinking Maps

Another type of cognitive framework that is gaining popularity is the story or critical thinking map (Idol, 1987; Idol & Croll, 1987). Story maps focus student attention to the story components (i.e., setting, problem, goal, action, and outcome) of narrative stories; critical thinking maps direct student attention to the critical points of textbook passages (important events/points, main idea, other viewpoints, reader's conclusion, and relevance to today).

Developing Story and Critical Thinking Maps

When preparing story maps, develop them around the following prompts (Idol, 1987; Idol & Croll, 1987):
- The setting (characters, time, place).
- The problem.
- The goal.
- The action.
- The outcome.

As students read a story aloud, instruct them to write responses directly on to the story-map outline that corresponds to each of the prompts.

Once students are familiar with the process of using the map, encourage them to work independently to complete the story maps.

transferring and encoding information to long-term memory occurs best when information is personalized, organized, and developed around prior knowledge.

A critical thinking map uses a format similar to the story map. You might prepare critical thinking maps around the following format:
- Important events.
- Main idea.
- Other views.
- Reader's conclusion.
- Relevance to today.

Again, as students read their textbook assignment, they should fill in the information in the space provided below each prompt.

Variations on Story and Critical Thinking Maps

Depending on the content area or purpose of your assignment, you can modify the written prompts and allotted space to enhance acquisition and retention of information. For elementary science, for example, you may want to tailor the critical thinking map to fit a lesson on the solar system, as follows:
- "Important events/points / steps" could be changed to "important astronomy concept being discussed" (i.e., changes that occurred in our galaxy over time).
- "Main idea/lesson" could be changed to "main point of solar system."
- "Other viewpoints/opinions" could be modified to read "different opinions about changes in the galaxy."
- "Relevance to today" could be changed to "relevance to the future".

In certain cases, you may use the prompts without making any modifications (i.e., "reader's conclusion").

A Final Note on Story and Critical Thinking Maps

To acquaint students to any new technique such as story mapping, first teach them to use it with familiar materials before proceeding on to more complex materials. In addition, during your introductory lessons, teach students to periodically pause from reading the passage to identify the main points of the text, particularly when these points are not explicit to the student. Teaching the "pause" may actually involve interjecting written cues (such as "stop here") on the reading passage. If students do not learn about pausing, many of them simply continue to read the entire assignment without ever incorporating any of the written prompts.

Cognitive Mapping

According to Darch and Eaves (1986), cognitive mapping involves the "use of lines, arrows, and spatial arrangements to describe text content, structure, and key conceptual relationships" (p. 310). Cognitive maps, also referred to as *cognitive organizers* or *visual displays,* allow students to visually arrange the component ideas and details from large amounts of information. Cognitive maps clearly display ideas and make explicit the implicit relationships between ideas.

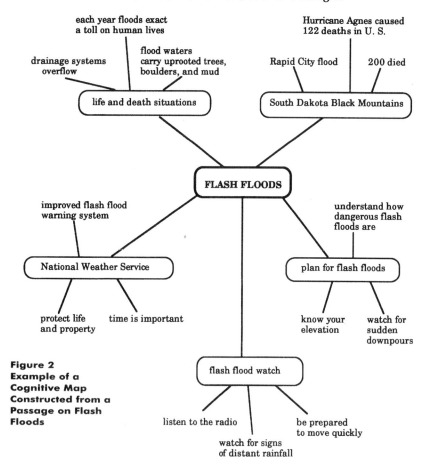

**Figure 2
Example of a
Cognitive Map
Constructed from a
Passage on Flash
Floods**

Developing Cognitive Maps

Generally used during lectures or reading assignments, cognitive maps provide anchors of knowledge around which students attach new information. You can develop cognitive maps before the lesson (Darch & Eaves, 1986), or students can develop them during the lesson (Boyle, 1996).

When you prepare a cognitive map, incorporate pictures with keywords (Darch & Carnine, 1986). Remember to keep sentences and details to a minimum. Use keywords, not complex sentences, and simple drawings, not elaborate pictures.

Boyle (1996) developed a useful strategy for students to use to generate their own cognitive maps. With this strategy, using the acronym *TRAVEL*, students refer to each step (i.e., letter) to construct maps from reading passages (Figure 2 shows a sample student-constructed map):

- *T-Topic:* Students write down the topic and circle it.
- *R-Read:* students carefully read the first paragraph.

- *A-Ask:* Students covertly ask themselves what the main idea and three details are and then write them down.
- *V-Verify:* Students verify the written main idea by placing a circle around it and then draw a line from the main idea to each detail, thereby physically linking the main idea of the paragraph with three details.
- *E-Examine:* Students repeat the *Read, Ask,* and *Verify* steps on each successive paragraph.
- *L-Link:* Students link together all of the main ideas that are related to one another.

During all the writing steps (i.e., *Topic* and *Ask* steps), encourage students to describe the topic, main idea, or details using as few words as possible (typically three to five words).

Variations on Cognitive Maps

Horton, Lovitt, and Bergerud (1990) developed a few variations of cognitive organizers that were used by students as they read social studies and science text-

book chapters. From their research, all the versions of organizers were found to be more effective than the control intervention (self-study). Here are three versions:

- The instructor prepared an organizer in which some information was missing, but provided students with a direction sheet that described how to develop the organizer to assist them at completing it.
- The teacher prepared the organizer with missing information, but provided students with a reference sheet (e.g., "see page 53") for finding the information.
- The teacher prepared the organizer with missing information and also provided the answer sheet for completing the cognitive organizer. The answer sheet contained all of the necessary information for completing the organizer, except that the answers were not in order.

A Final Note on Cognitive Maps

Here are some important hints for preparing cognitive organizers (Clarke, 1990):

- Introduce simple forms before using more complex forms.
- Review unfamiliar vocabulary words before incorporating them in the organizer.
- Use students' prior knowledge as starting points for developing the organizers.
- Focus on only the important topics and keywords.
- Follow logical relationships for linking up ideas/details.
- Leave sufficient space on the organizer so that students can record keywords or details.

Teaching Students How to Use Cognitive Frameworks During Learning

Teaching students to properly use cognitive frameworks requires explicit instruction. Because students with mild disabilities often fail to pick up on subtle academic behaviors, we have found that it is critical to teach and then monitor their use of cognitive frameworks during learning activities. When you initially introduce frameworks, use materials that you know students can use independently, or materials that are intentionally below their grade level. When they use such "easy" material, students can properly attend to the instructional cues for using the framework.

The most common instructional technique used to teach students how to use frameworks is direct instruction, as follows:

- Model the framework.
- Guide students through their construction of it.
- Assess performance during independent practice.

As you model the framework, "think aloud" so that students fully understand how you are constructing the framework. Next, allow students to practice using the framework with less challenging content. During this stage of the training, provide immediate feedback with reinforcement in an attempt to shape appropriate behavior.

Once students have mastered the use of the framework with these materials, incorporate the framework with grade-level content and materials. Periodically thereafter, monitor students' use of the framework to ensure that they are using it properly with new material.

Teaching the Independent Use of Cognitive Frameworks

Teaching students to use cognitive frameworks independently requires sufficient instruction so that students can apply them to new situations and utilize them independent of teacher prompts. Students with mild disabilities usually require explicit instruction in generalizing and maintaining frameworks in their mainstreamed classes. Wong (1994) has suggested two methods—mediating student mindfulness and engaging in transfer-promoting activities—that would promote the independent use of frameworks during academic activities, as follows:

Mediating student mindfulness during instruction involves helping the student to understand the underlying principles of framework that make it an effective technique. This understanding is important, in that it encourages students to modify the framework to fit novel materials and settings.

Engaging in transfer-promoting activities during the final stages of framework instruction increases the odds that students will continue to use the framework over time.

Retention, Recall, and Retrieval of Information

Cognitive frameworks are ideal teaching aids for students both with and without disabilities. Not only do they provide students with an opportunity to mediate and facilitate learning of basic content from text as it applies to their own knowledge base, but cognitive frameworks also have the potential to serve as an intermediate step in more complex learning situations (i.e., they can serve as a link between newly presented information and higher-level thought processes).

By using frameworks as blueprints for learning, students can construct knowledge in an organized and readily retrievable form. Cognitive frameworks can increase students' understanding and recall and can reduce confusion and retrieval problems.

References

Bean, T. W., Singer, H., & Cowen, S. (1985). Analogical study guides: Improving comprehension in science. *Journal of Reading, 29*, 246-250.

Boyle, J. R. (1996). The effects of a cognitive mapping strategy on the literal and inferential comprehension of students with mild disabilities. *Learning Disability Quarterly, 19*, 86-98.

Clark, J. H. (1990). *Patterns of thinking.* Boston: Allyn & Bacon.

Darch, C., & Carnine, D. (1986). Teaching content area material to learning disabled students. *Exceptional Children, 23*, 204-246.

Darch, C., & Eaves, R. (1986). Visual displays to increase comprehension of high school learning disabled students. *Exceptional Children, 20*, 309-318.

Horton, S., Lovitt, T., & Bergerud, D. (1990). The effectiveness of graphic organizers for three classifications of secondary students in content area classes. *Journal of Learning Disabilities, 23*, 12-29.

Hudson, F., Ormsbee, C. K., & Myles, B. (1994). Study guides: An instructional tool for equalizing student achievement. *Intervention in School and Clinic, 30*, 99-102.

Idol, L. (1987). A critical thinking map to improve content area comprehension of poor readers. *Remedial and Special Education, 8*, 28-40.

Idol, L., & Croll, V. J. (1987). Story mapping training as a means of improving reading comprehension. *Learning Disability Quarterly, 10*, 214-229.

Mann, L., & Sabatino, D. A. (1985). *Foundations of cognitive process in remedial and special education.* Rockville, MD: Aspen.

Norman, D. A. (1982). *Learning and memory.* New York: W. H. Freeman.

Ogle, D. M. (1986). K-W-L: A teaching model that develops active reading of expository text. *The Reading Teacher, 39*, 564-570.

Simmons, D. C., & Kameenui, E. J. (1996). A focus on curriculum design: When children fail. In E. L. Meyen, G. A. Vergason, & R. J. Whelan (Eds.), *Strategies for teaching exceptional children in inclusive settings.* Denver, CO: Love.

Additional Resources

Memory and Learning

Gagne, E. D. (1985). *The cognitive psychology of school learning.* Boston: Little, Brown.

Mann, L., & Sabatino, D. A. (1985). *Foundations of cognitive process in remedial and special education.* Rockville, MD: Aspen Systems Corporation.

Norman, D. A. (1982). *Learning and memory.* New York: W. H. Freeman.

Cognitive Organizers/Maps

Clarke, J. H. (1990). *Patterns of thinking: Integrating learning skills in content teaching.* Needham Heights, MA: Allyn & Bacon.

Novak, J. D., & Gowin, D. B. (1984). *Learning how to learn.* New York: Cambridge University Press.

Pehrsson, R. S., & Denner, P. R. (1989). *Semantic organizers: A study strategy for special needs learners.* Rockville, MD: Aspen Publishers.

Study Guides

Tierney, R. J., Readence, J. E., & Dishner, E. K. (1995). *Reading strategies and practices: A compendium (4th ed.).* Needham Heights, MA: Allyn & Bacon.

Tierney, R. J., Readence, J. E., & Dishner, E. K. (1995). *Reading strategies and practices.* Boston: Allyn & Bacon.

Wong, B. (1994). Instructional parameters promoting transfer of learned strategies in students with learning disabilities. *Learning Disability Quarterly, 17*, 110-120.

Joseph R. Boyle *is now an assistant professor at Virginia Commonwealth University, Dept. of Teacher Education, P.O. Box 842020, Richmond, VA 23284-2020;* **Noranne Yeager,** *(CEC Nebraska Federation), is Assistant Professor of Special Education, Chadron State College, Chadron, Nebraska.*

Virginia Commonwealth University, Department of Teacher Education, P.O. Box 842020, Richmond, VA 23284-2020.

Photographs by Joseph R. Boyle.

The authors would like to thank Jane Crawley, Jan Cryder, and Melissa Reed-Bipen for their assistance in the development of this article.

Kids, Computers, and Constructivism

David L. Brown

With the proliferation of computers in classrooms, educators must verify the effectiveness of computer-assisted instruction in early childhood education. This article focuses on research findings and the relationship between computer use in the classroom and constructivist education. Three ways of using computers emerged: computers as books or workbooks; computers for word processing; and computer programming of graphics. It was concluded that the word processing use of computers was the most compatible with constructivist education for young children.

The proliferation of computers in society and in schools has promoted investigations into the effects of computers on young children's learning. Some leaders in early childhood education are concerned about the efficacy and appropriateness of the early exposure of young children to computer instruction. Among them is David Elkind, a former president of the National Association for the Education of Young Children (NAEYC), and a former student of Jean Piaget. Elkind (1987) views the computer as a vehicle to accelerate children in their development, to put them at risk for negative attitudes and failure, and to prevent them from actively manipulating their environments. Another former president of the NAEYC, Lilian Katz (1990), expressed a similar concern at the spring 1990 Early Childhood Education Symposium of the Federation of North Texas Area Universities, when she stated, "Just because they [young children] can do it doesn't mean they *should* do it."

The concern for using computers in early childhood learning situations is rooted

Dr. David L. Brown, Associate Professor of Early Childhood Education, Texas A&M University, Commerce, Texas 75429.

Correspondence concerning this article should be addressed to Dr. David L. Brown, Associate Professor, Early Childhood Education, Texas A&M University, Commerce, Texas 75429.

in the findings of Piaget. The NAEYC defines early childhood as birth through eight years. Piaget defined a level of development—approximately eighteen months to eight years of age—which he called the intuitive or the preoperational level. Many educators are expressing the most concern about computer instruction during this developmental stage. Children at the preoperational stage of thinking need many opportunities to construct their own knowledge through hands-on activities, which by their very nature require opportunities for manipulation of three-dimensional, sensory-stimulating objects. These activities are regarded as important components of constructivist learning. Perhaps a major fear about young children's use of computers is the possibility of the computer program's being used as a workbook on a screen, much like the programmed instruction that was popular in the 1970s and 1980s (Elkind, 1987).

The constructivist classroom encourages the pupils to think and to develop their own perceptions of the world. Therefore, "constructivist teaching practices .. . help learners to internalize and reshape, or transform new information" (Brooks & Brooks, 1993, p. 15). The development of a constructivist classroom with appropriate instructional strategies and planning experiences for children "requires that we study children's process of learning and facilitate their process of construction instead of

From *Journal of Instructional Psychology*, September 1996, pp. 189-195. © 1996 by the Journal of Instructional Psychology. Reprinted by permission.

continuing to teach in ways that seem efficient for adults" (Kamii, Lewis, & Jones, 1991, p. 21).

Purpose of the Review

The following review of research concerning young children's use of computers seeks to determine the relationship between computer instruction and constructivist thinking. In surveying the research, three major categories of computer use emerged: (a) computers as books or workbooks; (b) computers for word processing; and (c) computer programming of graphics.

Computers as Books or Workbooks

Worden, Kee, and Ingle (1987) using the computer as a workbook compared parent-child interactions with an alphabet book and with a computer software program, "My First Alphabet." Twenty parents and their three-year-old children, average age of three years and five months, were engaged in both tasks. The researchers found that parents discussed more letters, repeated more letters, took more turns, and engaged in more conversational cycles with their children while using the book than when using the software. Both parents and children talked more with the book usage, and parents made more identifications and extraneous references when using the book than when using the software. The parents, however, gave more directions and more commands when using the software as compared with using the book. On the other hand, although the children made more identifications in the book, they produced more comments and more questions when using the software.

Using the computer as a book or workbook, Calvert, Watson, Brinkley, and Bordeaux (1989) tested children's free recall of words presented on the Apple IIe. They found that the children remembered significantly more words that had moving illustrations as compared to words with illustrations in still frames.

Grover (1986) studied the use of computers as workbooks in classrooms. Two types of software were used: (a) one type was designed according to cognitive-development principles; (b) the other did not incorporate such principles. One hundred thirty-four young children—eighteen preschool, eighty-two kindergarten, and thirty-four first-grade students—were randomly assigned to learn the two software programs and were later tested for correct responses.

Grover found that the preschool children and kindergarten students who used software designed in accordance with cognitive-development principles had significantly higher numbers of correct responses than those students who worked with software not incorporating such principles.

McCollister, Burts, Wright, and Hildreth (1986) studied the relationship between mathematics achievement and computer use of fifty-two kindergarten children. The researchers found that those students who were more mathematically able preferred to work with the computer program, "How Many Squares," which was designed to teach numerical recognition and cardinal counting. In addition, the students who were just beginning to recognize numerals showed a definite preference for working with the teacher rather than working with a computer.

In Amsterdam, in a word-recognition study using computers with six- and seven-year-old children, Spaai, Reitsma, and Ellermann (1987) conducted a four-day computer session using three groups of children. One group received no feedback from the computer regarding words that were identified from among three foils, and the second group received partial feedback as right and wrong responses were identified. Whereas, the third group received complete feedback; that is, not only were right answers acknowledged, and wrong answers identified, but in the case of a wrong answer, the target response was given. Reading scores for children who received some sort of feedback improved significantly. By the fourth day of the investigation, the third group of children who had received complete feedback was significantly improved over the second group of children who had only received partial feedback.

Computers for Word Processing

Although workbook-style computer programs may result in some improvement in the target responses, these programs are not suitable for constructivist-oriented learning situations. Computer programs that are designed for word processing are more likely to approach the goal of hands-on experiences for children. Even if children do not get a chance to practice grapho-motor skills during word processing activities, they should have the opportunity to do so at some other time during the school day. Specially designed word processing programs, such as those described by Block, Simpson, and Reid (1987), Pontecorvo and Zucchermaglio (1991), and Eimerl (1985), will enable children to overcome language barriers and to participate in cooperative learning. Word processing programs can enhance a constructivist classroom when they include a rich environment with opportunities for physical activity, experimentation, and investigation..

Block, Simpson, and Reid (1987) studied children's transfer skills from three preparatory programs using Logo word processing. They discovered that the KEY program, which taught keyboarding skills, resulted in students' being significantly better able to perform Logo's word processing tasks. The children using computer-assisted instruction (CAI) and Robot (ROB) programs had little transfer. The researchers also found that boys were significantly more adept than girls in using programming technology. The girls, however, were equal to the boys in the number of words used and the number of story-grammar elements used, particularly, settings, initiating events, internal responses, attempts, consequences, and reactions.

Pontecorvo and Zucchermaglio (1991) tested an experimental group of nineteen third-grade students and a Montessori-trained control group of the same age and number at a school in Rome. The students were trained in language comprehension and production, including using sentences and stories in a problem-solving setting. The examiners found that linguistic interactions increased for all groups of children after activity with software, that there was an increase in planning and restructuring processes, and that there was an increase in verbalized explanations.

Eimerl (1985) conducted a particularly interesting study using mostly lower-SES, non-French-speaking preschoolers attending a public school in Paris. Although no quantifying data were included in the study, the study is noteworthy. The subjects in the study included sixty children (twenty-six girls and thirty-four boys) with a mean age of five years, four months. The researcher and a participating observer were accepted by the children and were, therefore, able to record the children's social behaviors and academic productions. The children were taught some basic word-processing skills in groups of three to five children, using Logo's microworld "Sprite," chosen for its graphics, its colors, its animation, and its easy and motivating creation and manipulation of images. The children were allowed free exploration, with adult intervention provided mostly on request. The children progressed through sub-programs ("Shapes," "Letters," and "Sentences") arranged by difficulty.

As the children advanced through the program, the researcher noted that more efficient postures and key-striking behaviors were developing; children became more aware of classroom print; and students recognized letter from non letter. In addition, they became more word oriented, recognizing the part-to-whole relationship between letters and words; they saw the left-to-right progression of words and sentences; and they recognized the unchanging nature of the letters. The children also began to work together better, to become more goal oriented, and to show a reduction in negative comments to one another. In addition, the shy children talked more, and talkative children became more focused (Eimeral, 1985). The children seemed pleased to be able to manipulate their own commands, to create an illustrated sentence, and to write one long command. The immediate feedback of the image, related to the word or sentence typed, helped students progress more rapidly in their acquisition of the French language, indicating the development of an intrinsic motivation in the writing activity (Eimerl).

Upon completion of the program, 30% of the subjects went on to write short stories spontaneously. Continued use of the program allowed observance of behaviors that were advanced: (a) sustained attention of 20 to 30 minutes, (b) deep concentration; and (c) greater tolerance for delay. The students also seemed to have an awareness of their own memory and its reliability, as evidenced by their occasional checking of the posted sign of commands for rule verification (Eimerl, 1985).

As a result of the program's success, Eimerl (1985) recommended that the use of computers in the classroom become a part of a multi-disciplinary environment. Eimerl also stated that collaboration by teachers, designers, computer specialists, psychologists, and curriculum specialists was necessary for the success of any program using computers to enhance instruction.

Computer Programming of Graphics

Computer programming is another way of using computers in the classroom. Schaefer and Springle (1988) trained twenty preschoolers—ten boys and ten girls having an average age of four years, eight months—for three months in three competencies: (a) computer terminology, (b) computer programming, and (c) math concepts. The girls showed growth in learning computer terminology beyond that expected by maturation. Both sexes showed an increase in computer programming ability and math concepts, but there was no significant difference in performance between the two groups.

Degelman, Free, Scarlato, and Blackburn (1986) conducted a five-week computer study using fifteen children with an average age of five years and three months. They used two Apple IIe computers with the single-stroke Logo program. The children were taught simple programming skills in order to manipulate the turtle to create desired graphics. When checked on four problem solving tasks using graphics, the Logo-taught group scored significantly higher on two tasks, but showed no significant difference on the other two problems.

Campbell, Fein, and Schwartz (1991) studied the ability of children to perform an estimate of distance task on a computer screen. The subjects in the study were forty-eight first grade students—twenty-three first-graders were in the experimental group and twenty-five first-graders were in the control group. The experimental students were trained in Logo skills for one hour each week from October through April; the control group received no special training. After completing the Logo training, the students were tested on their ability to estimate the length of measure under the condition of changing unit size. Students trained in Logo were significantly more accurate in estimating distance, although both groups usually gave underestimations. Specifically, long distances were estimated by the Logo experimental group to an average of 90% of the actual length, whereas the control group guessed only to an average of 78% of the actual length. Short distances were guessed to 75% of the actual length by the Logo group, but to only 60% of the actual length by the control group. There was no significant difference in their ability to adjust estimates as required when distances were

changed. Line length interacted with a change in unit size across both groups.

Lehrer and Randle (1987) studied the effect of computer program training on the achievement of thirty-nine, first-grade students from low SES backgrounds in New York City Schools. The group consisted of twenty-three boys and sixteen girls, of whom thirty-two were African-American and seven were white. The students were assigned to three different groups: (a) programming training in Logo graphics, (b) programming training with another commercial software for language composition, and (c) a control group receiving no treatment. The students in the two computer groups received training over five months, twice a week for 20 to 25 minutes each session. Both the Logo and the composition groups showed significantly higher scores than the control group in problem solving skills. In metacognition tasks, Logo-fluent children scored significantly higher than the composition or the control group. There were no significant differences in performance of the writing tasks conducted among the three groups (Lehrer & Randle, 1987).

Kull (1988) conducted an interesting study involving children and computers in which there were no formal hypotheses stated because of a lack of empirical or theoretical evidence. The research team consisted of Kull, two teachers, and their participating classes (consisting of twenty-three students each), and two graduate assistants. The students worked in pairs for fifteen minutes, twice a week. Pre-Logo programming training was provided through the experiences of manipulating of a turtle and by typing some learned commands on a keyboard.

The team used a guided discovery approach, allowing students to work together to achieve various levels, or plateaus, and to revise old graphics as they learned new ones. Team members wrote down everything they heard and saw at the computer stations which they later shared with the others in the group at biweekly meetings. Observations included children's posing of graphic problems and their discussions of codes and findings. New Logo commands were posted regularly and assimilated as needed into the students' routines (Kull, 1988).

As a result of the observations, Kull (1988) concluded that Logo was a rich, well-structured, consistent medium in which increasingly difficult mathematics and graphics problems could be posed and solved. Kull also found that the medium allowed for the construction of mathematics ideas and metacognitive skills, and that Logo-generated ideas occurred only when the methods of transfer were modeled by adults. In other words, learning was not automatic and the medium when used in a cooperative learning setting promoted reflection of thought, revision of work, and construction of knowledge by the children.

Cohen (1987) observed the Logo programming skills taught to thirty second-grade students in one classroom with one teacher and one computer. The researcher worked from the premise that Logo was designed to allow for self-directed, discovery-oriented, Piagetian constructivist learning, especially since the medium provided concrete, immediate feedback. When examining the end-of the-school year assessment in Logo skills, Cohen discovered that children did not automatically learn to program Logo, even with prolonged contact, and that extensive adult intervention was necessary. The students, although excited and enthusiastic, experienced difficulty in trying to control the turtle, even after prolonged contact with the program. Cohen concluded that the children were not developmentally ready to cope with the skills involved and that they needed extensive guidance and tutorial support to learn to program Logo. Cohen suggested that Logo be redesigned to cater to the needs and abilities of young children.

Lehrer, Guckenberg, and Lee (1988) studied the impact of two different Logo Programs and a third problem solving software control (non-Logo) on the computer skills and knowledge of a group of forty-five, third-grade children. The students in the study were given twenty minutes of Logo programming training two to three times a week. The instruction was inquiry-based, and included both positive and negative examples of construct cases, comparison cases, and hypothetical cases. Students receiving the Logo training were found to solve planning tasks significantly more efficiently. Both Logo groups produced significantly more dynamic descriptions of geometric concepts than the control group, and the Logo-geometry group displayed a significantly increased mastery of metacognitive skills. In addition to these findings, some results were similar to Cohen's (1987). Even after prolonged exposure, children had less

than absolute mastery of some of the elementary forms of Logo's syntax, and long-term memory, rather than short-term memory, contributed to Logo mastery. The researchers concluded that, although Logo is not an educational panacea, it can be a tool for promoting cognitive evolution, particularly in geometry.

Conclusions

Research in young children's computer use reveals that computers can be, and have been, used to teach children in the form of books or workbooks, through word-processing formats, and by the imparting of programming skills, especially those for graphics programming. The use of computers as workbooks is not compatible with constructivist thinking because children are not allowed to manipulate and change the information, but simply have to choose the right answer. The teaching of computer programming skills can be valuable to some students in the development of metacognitive abilities, but the development and use of these skills seem to be far too advanced for the capabilities of most children at the intuitive level of thought. The use of the computer as a word processor, as demonstrated and supported by the research, was the most compatible with constructivist theory, allowing for flexibility according to ability; cooperation with others; and construction, as well as reconstruction, of a child's thoughts and experiences. Overall, the value of the computer in the classroom depended on two things: (a) the type and quality of the program used, and (b) the teacher's modeling behavior with the computer, including the teacher's knowledge of the program and willingness to integrate the computer into the classroom format.

The concern with computer presence and use in the classroom, and the worry about the seeming lack of concrete experiences with the medium may have been best addressed by Clements, Nastasi, and Swaminathan (1993), who, in their survey of research on young children and computers, cited a study in which the computer environment offered "equal, and sometimes greater, control and flexibility to young children" than a three-deminisiional, tangible object learning situation. They stated, "what is 'concrete' to the child may have more to do with what is meaningful and manipulable than with physical characteristics" (Clements,

Nastasi, & Swaminathan, p. 56). Keeping this is mind, early childhood teachers using computers for instructional purposes may be freer to utilize the valuable contributions that computers can make to constructivist classrooms.

References

Block, E. B., Simpson, D. L., & Reid, D. K. (1987). Teaching young children programming and word processing skills: The effects of three preparatory conditions. *Journal of Educational Computing Research, 3,* 435-442.

Brooks, J. & Brooks, M. (1993). *The case for constructivist classrooms.* Alexandria, VA: ASCD.

Calvert, S. L., Watson, J. A., Brinkley, V. M., & Bordeaux, B. (1989). Computer presentational features for young children's preferential selection and recall information. *Journal of Educational Computing Research, 5,* 35-49.

Campbell, P. F., Fein, G. G., & Schwartz, S. S. (1991). The effects of Logo experience on first-grade children's ability to estimate distance. *Journal of Educational Computing Research, 7,* 331-349.

Clements, D. H., Nastasi, B. K., & Swaminathan, S. (1993). Young children and computers: Crossroads and directions from research. *Young Children, 48,* 56-64.

Cohen, R. (1987). Implementing Logo in the grade two classroom: Acquisition of basic programming concepts. *Journal of Computer-Based Instruction, 14,* 124-132.

Degelman, K., Free, J., Scarlato, M., & Blackburn, J. (1986). Concept learning in preschool children: Effects of a short-term Logo experience. *Journal of Educational Computing Research, 2,* 199-205.

Eimerl, K. (1985). Quelques competences acquises par Pendant dans l'exploration de l'ordinateur. *Enfance, 2-3,* 165-282.

Elkind, D. (1987). *Miseducation: Preschoolers at risk.* New York: Knopf.

Grover, S. (1986). A field study of the use of cognitive-developmental principles in microcomputer design for young children. *Journal of Educational Research, 79,* 325-332.

Kamii, C., Lewis, B., & Jones, S. (1991). Reform in primary mathematics education: A constructivist view. *Educational Horizons, 7,* 19-26.

Katz, L. (1990, April). Engaging young children's minds through a project approach. Symposium conducted at the meeting of the Federation of North Texas Area Universities, Dallas, TX.

Kull, J. A. (1988). Children learning Logo: A collaborative, qualitative study in first grade. *Journal of Research in Childhood Education, 3,* 55-75.

Lehrer, R., Guckenberg, T., & Lee, O. (1988). Comparative study of the cognitive consequences of inquiry-based Logo instruction. *Journal of Educational Psychology, 80,* 543-553.

Lehrer, R., & Randle, L. (1987). Problem solving, metacognition and composition: The effects of interactive software for first-grade children. *Journal of Educational Computing Research, 3,* 409-427.

McCollister, T. S., Burts, D. C., Wright, V. L., & Hildreth, G. J. (1986). Effects of computer-assisted instruction and teacher-aided instruction on arithmetic task achievement scores of kindergarten children. *Journal of Educational Research, 80,* 121-125.

Pontecorvo, C., & Zuccxhermaglio, C. (1991). Computer use in learning about language. *European Journal of Psychology of Education, 6,* 15-27.

Schaefer, L., & Springle, J. E. (1988). Gender differences in the use of the Logo programming language. *Journal of Educational Computing Research, 4,* 49-55.

Spaai, G. W. G., Reitsma, P., & Ellermann, H. H. (1987). Effects of several feedback methods for correcting reading errors by computer-assisted instruction. *L. P. O. Annual Progress Report, 22,* 87-96.

Worden, P. E., Kee, D. W., & Ingle, M. J. (1987). Parental teaching strategies with preschoolers: A comparison of mothers and fathers within different alphabet tasks. *Contemporary Educational Psychology, 12,* 95-109.

Motivation and Classroom Management

Motivation (Articles 30–32)
Classroom Management and Discipline (Articles 33–36)

The term *motivation* is used by educators to describe the processes of initiating, directing, and sustaining goal-oriented behavior. Motivation is a complex phenomenon, involving many factors that affect an individual's choice of action and perseverance in completing tasks. Furthermore, the reasons why people engage in particular behaviors can only be inferred; motivation cannot be directly measured.

Several theories of motivation, each highlighting different reasons for sustained goal-oriented behavior, have been proposed. We will discuss three of them: behavioral, humanistic, and cognitive. The behavioral theory of motivation suggests that an important reason for engaging in behavior is that reinforcement follows the action. If the reinforcement is controlled by someone else and is arbitrarily related to the behavior (such as money, a token, or a smile), then the motivation is extrinsic. In contrast, behavior may also be initiated and sustained for intrinsic reasons such as curiosity or mastery.

UNIT 5

Humanistic approaches to motivation are concerned with the social and psychological needs of individuals. Humans are motivated to engage in behavior to meet these needs. Abraham Maslow, a founder of humanistic psychology, proposes that there is a hierarchy of needs that directs behavior, beginning with physiological and safety needs and progressing to self-actualization. Some other important needs that influence motivation are affiliation and belonging with others, love, self-esteem, influence with others, recognition, status, competence, achievement, and autonomy.

The dominant view of motivation in the educational psychology literature is the cognitive approach. This set of theories proposes that our beliefs about our successes and failures affect our expectations and goals concerning future performance. Students who believe that their success is due to their abilities and efforts are motivated toward mastery of skills. Students who blame their failures on inadequate abilities have low self-efficacy and tend to set ability and performance goals that protect their self-image.

William Glasser, in the unit's first selection, argues that when teachers use coercive management techniques, students feel that teachers do not care about them and they become unmotivated. When choice theory is implemented, however, the student-teacher relationship is nurtured, and students want to learn. Next, Deborah Stipek echoes the importance of allowing children to set their own goals. She also discusses other techniques to encourage more effort on academic tasks. Then, Rachel Collopy and Theresa Green describe how one elementary school has changed in response to the dramatic findings of achievement goal theory. The school they created emphasizes learning rather than relative ability.

No matter how effectively students are motivated, teachers always need to exercise management of behavior in the classroom. Classroom management is more than controlling the behavior of students or disciplining them following misbehavior. Instead, teachers need to initiate and maintain a classroom environment that supports successful teaching and learning. The skills that effective teachers use include preplanning, deliberate introduction of rules and procedures, immediate assertiveness, continual monitoring, consistent feedback to students, and specific consequences.

The articles by Nancy Martin, Rheta DeVries, and Betty Zan in the next subsection describe the most current thinking about the new forms of classroom management that will be required to meet the needs of learner-centered classrooms. Martin argues that student-teacher relationships need to be nurtured in student-centered classrooms. Teacher-centered classroom management techniques conflict with the philosophy of student-centered instruction and can undermine its effectiveness. Practical principles that create a sociomoral atmosphere appropriate for a learner-centered elementary classroom are explained by DeVries and Zan.

Selections by Geoff Colvin, David Ainge, and Ron Nelson, and David Johnson and Roger Johnson address disciplinary issues facing educators today: confrontational students and violence in schools. Colvin, Ainge, and Nelson observe that even effective classroom managers are sometimes faced with confrontational students. The authors discuss diffusing tactics that can minimize the likelihood of escalating conflict. Finally, Johnson and Johnson argue that violence prevention needs to focus on helping students resolve conflicts in appropriate ways, such as using peer mediation. The adults in schools, too, need to model constructive ways to resolve conflicts by eliminating corporal punishment.

Looking Ahead: Challenge Questions

Discuss several ways to motivate both at-risk and typical students. What difference is there?

How are motivation and classroom management related?

How are classroom management and discipline different? Discuss whether discipline can be developed within students, or whether it must be imposed by teachers, supporting your argument with data derived from your reading.

A New Look at School Failure and School Success

BY WILLIAM GLASSER, M.D.

The cause of both school failure and marriage failure is that almost all people believe in and practice stimulus/response psychology, Dr. Glasser contends. He suggests a better alternative—CHOICE THEORY^{SM}—to nurture the warm, supportive human relationships that students need to succeed in school and that couples need to succeed in marriage.

JOHN IS 14 years old. He is capable of doing good work in school. Yet he reads and writes poorly, has not learned to do more than simple calculations, hates any work having to do with school, and shows up more to be with his friends than anything else. He failed the seventh grade last year and is well on his way to failing it again. Essentially, John chooses to do nothing in school that anyone would call educational. If any standards must be met, his chances of graduation are nonexistent.

We know from our experience at the Schwab Middle School, which I will describe shortly, that John also knows that giving up on school is a serious mistake. The problem is he doesn't believe that the school he attends will give him a chance to correct this mistake. And he is far from alone. There may be five million students between the ages of 6 and 16 who come regularly to school but are much the same as John. If they won't make the effort to become competent readers, writers, and problem solvers, their chances of leading even

minimally satisfying lives are over before they reach age 17.

Janet is 43 years old. She has been teaching math for 20 years and is one of the teachers who is struggling unsuccessfully with John. She considers herself a good teacher but admits that she does not know how to reach John. She blames him, his home, his past teachers, and herself for this failure. All who know her consider her a warm, competent person. But for all her warmth, five years ago, after 15 years of marriage, Janet divorced. She is doing an excellent job of caring for her three children, but, with only sporadic help from their father, her life is no picnic. If she and her husband had been able to stay together happily, it is almost certain that they and their children would be much better off than they are now.

Like many who divorce, Janet was aware that the marriage was in trouble long before the separation. But in the context of marriage as she knew it, she didn't know what to do. "I tried, but nothing I did seemed to help," she says. She is lonely and would like another marriage but, so far, hasn't been able to find anyone she would consider marrying. There may be more than a million men and women teaching school who, like Janet, seem capable of relationships but are either divorced or unhappily married. No one doubts that marriage failure is a huge problem. It leads to even more human misery than school failure.

William Glasser, M.D., is the founder and president of the William Glasser Institute in Chatsworth, Calif. In 1996 he changed the name of the theory he has been teaching since 1979 from "control theory" to CHOICE THEORY^{SM}. He is currently writing a new book on the subject. All his books are published by HarperCollins.

I bring up divorce in an article on reducing school failure because there is a much closer connection between these two problems than almost anyone realizes. So close, in fact, that I believe the cause of both these problems may be the same. As soon as I wrote those words, I began to fear that my readers would jump to the conclusion that I am blaming Janet for the failure of her marriage or for her inability to reach John. Nothing could be further from the truth. The fact that she doesn't know something that is almost universally unknown cannot be her fault.

If you doubt that the problems of John and Janet are similar, listen to what each of them has to say. John says, "I do so little in school because no one cares for me, no one listens to me, it's no fun, they try to make me do things I don't want to do, and they never try to find out what I want to do." Janet says, "My marriage failed because he didn't care enough for me, he never listened to me, each year it was less fun, he never wanted to do what I wanted, and he was always trying to make me do what he wanted." These almost identical complaints have led John to "divorce" school, and Janet, her husband.

Are these Greek tragedies? Are all these students and all these marriages doomed to failure no matter what we do? I contend they are not. *The cause of both school failure and marriage failure is that almost no one, including Janet, knows how he or she functions psychologically.* Almost all people believe in and practice an ancient, commonsense psychology called stimulus/response (SR) psychology. I am one of the leaders of a small group of people who believe that SR is completely wrongheaded and, when put into practice, is totally destructive to the warm, supportive human relationships that students need to succeed in school and that couples need to succeed in marriage. The solution is to give up SR theory and replace it with a new psychology: *choice theory.*

To persuade a teacher like Janet to give up what she implicitly believes to be correct is a monumental task. For this reason I have hit upon the idea of approaching her through her marriage failure as much as through her failure to reach students like John. I think she

> **To persuade a teacher like Janet to give up what she implicitly believes to be correct is a monumental task.**

will be more open to learning something that is so difficult to learn if she can use it in both her personal and her professional lives. From 20 years of experience teaching choice theory, I can also assure her that learning this theory can do absolutely no harm.

If John could go to a school where choice theory was practiced, he would start to work. That was conclusively proved at the Schwab Middle School. To explain such a change in behavior, John would say, "The teachers care about me, listen to what I have to say, don't try to make me do things I don't want to do, and ask me what I'd like to do once in a while. Besides, they make learning fun." If Janet and her husband had practiced choice theory while they still cared for each other, it is likely that they would still be married. They would have said, "We get along well because every day we make it a point to show each other we care. We listen to each other, and when we have differences we talk them out without blaming the other. We never let a week go by without having fun together, and we never try to make the other do what he or she doesn't want to do."

Where school improvement is concerned, I can cite hard data to back up this contention. I also have written two books that explain in detail all that my staff and I try to do to implement choice theory in schools. The books are *The Quality School* and *The Quality School Teacher.*[1] Where marriage failure is concerned, I have no hard data yet. But I have many positive responses from readers of my most recent book, *Staying Together,*[2] in which I apply choice theory to marriage.

The most difficult problems are human relationship problems. Technical problems, such as landing a man on the moon, are child's play compared to persuading all students like John to start working hard in school or helping all unhappily married couples to improve their marriages. Difficult as they may be to solve, however, relationship problems are surprisingly easy to understand. They are all some variation of "I don't like the way you treat me, and even though it may destroy my life, your life, or both our lives, this is what I am going to do about it."

READERS familiar with my work will have figured out by now that choice theory used to be called control theory because it teaches that the only person whose behavior we can control is our own. I find choice theory to be a better and more positive-sounding name. Accepting that you can control only your own behavior is the most difficult lesson that choice theory has to teach. It is so difficult that almost all people, even when they are given the opportunity, refuse to learn it. This is because the whole thrust of SR theory is that we do not control our own behavior, rather, our behavior is a response to a stimulus from outside ourselves. Thus we answer a phone in response to a ring.

Choice theory states that we never answer a phone because it rings, and we never will. We answer a phone—and do anything else—because it is the most satisfying choice for us at the time. If we have something better to do, we let it ring. Choice theory states that the ring of the phone is not a stimulus to do anything; it is merely *information.* In fact, all we can ever get from the outside world, which means all we can give one another, is information. But information, by itself, does not make us do anything. Janet can't make her husband do anything. Nor can she make John do anything. All she can give them is information, but she, like all SR believers, doesn't know this.

What she "knows" is that, if she is dissatisfied with someone, she should try to "stimulate" that person to change. And she wastes a great deal of time and energy trying to do this. When she discovers, as she almost always does, how hard it is to change another person, she begins to blame the person, herself, or someone else for the failure. And from blaming, it is a very short step to punishing. No one takes this short step more frequently and more thoroughly than husbands, wives, and teachers. As they attempt to change their mates, couples develop a whole repertoire of coercive behaviors aimed at punishing the other for being so obstinate. When teachers attempt to deal with students such as John, punishment—masquerading as "logical consequences"—rules the day in school.

Coercion in either of its two forms, reward or punishment, is the core of SR theory. Punishments arc by far the more common, but both are destructive to relationships. The difference is that rewards are more subtly destructive and generally less offensive. Coercion ranges from the passive behaviors of sulking and withdrawing to the active behaviors of abuse and violence. The most common and, because it is so common, the most destructive of coercive behaviors is criticizing—and nagging and complaining are not far behind.

Choice theory teaches that we are all driven by four psychological needs that are embedded in our genes: the need to belong, the need for power, the need for freedom, and the need for fun. We can no more ignore these psychological needs than we can ignore the food and shelter we must have if we are to satisfy the most obvious genetic need, the need for survival.

Whenever we are able to satisfy one or more of these needs, it feels very good. In fact, the biological purpose of pleasure is to tell us that a need is being satisfied. Pain, on the other hand, tells us that what we are doing is not satisfying a need that we very much want to satisfy. John suffers in school, and Janet suffers in marriage because neither is able to figure out how to satisfy these needs. If the pain of this failure continues, it is almost certain that in two years John will leave school, and of course Janet has already left her marriage.

If we are to help Janet help John, she needs to learn and to use the most important of all the concepts from choice theory, the idea of the *quality world.* This small, very specific, personal world is the core of our lives because in it are the people, things, and beliefs that we have discovered are most satisfying to our needs. Beginning at birth, as we find out what best satisfies our needs, we build this knowledge into the part of our memory that is our quality world and continue to build and adjust it throughout our lives. This world is best thought of as a group of pictures, stored in our brain, depicting with extreme precision the way we would like things to be—especially the way we want to be treated. The most important pictures are of people, including ourselves, because it is almost impossible to satisfy our needs without getting involved with other people.

Good examples of people who are almost always in our quality worlds are our parents and our children—and, if our marriages are happy, our husbands or wives. These pictures are very specific. Wives and husbands want to hear certain words, to be touched in certain ways, to go to certain places, and to do specific activities together. We also have special things in our quality world. For example, the new computer I am typing this article on is very much the computer I wanted. I also have a strong picture of myself teaching choice theory, something I believe in so strongly that I spend most of my life doing it.

When we put people into our quality worlds, it is because we care for them, and they care for us. We see them as people with whom we can satisfy our needs. John has long since taken pictures of Janet and of most other teachers—as well as a picture of himself doing competent schoolwork—out of his quality world. As soon as he did this, neither Janet nor any other SR teacher could reach him. As much as they coerce, they cannot make him learn. This way of teaching is called "bossing." Bosses use coercion freely to try to make the people they boss do what they want.

To be effective with John, Janet must give up bossing and turn to "leading." Leaders never coerce. We follow them because we believe that they have our best interests at heart. In school, if he senses that Janet is now caring, listening, encouraging, and laughing, John will begin to consider putting her into his quality world. Of course, John knows nothing about choice theory or about the notion of a quality world. But he can be taught and, in a Quality School, this is what we do. We have evidence to show that the more students know about why they are behaving as they do, the more effectively they will behave.

Sometime before her divorce, Janet, her ex, or both of them took the other out of their quality worlds. When this happened, the marriage was over. If they had known choice theory and known how important it is to try to preserve the picture of a spouse in one's quality world, they could have made a greater effort than they did to care, listen, encourage, and laugh with each other. They certainly would have been aware of how destructive bossing is and would have tried their best to avoid this destructive behavior.

As I stated at the outset, I am not assigning blame for the failure of Janet's marriage. I am saying that, as soon as one or the other or both partners became dissatisfied, the only hope was to care, listen, encourage, and laugh and to completely stop criticizing, nagging, and complaining. Obviously, Janet and her ex-

husband would have been much more likely to have done this if they had known that the only behavior you can control is your own.

When Janet, as an SR teacher, teaches successfully, she succeeds with students because her students have put her or the math she teaches (or both) into their quality worlds. If both she and the math are in their quality worlds, the students will be a joy to teach. She may also succeed with a student who does not particularly want to learn math, but who, like many students, is open to learning math if she gives him a little attention.

John, however, is hard core. He is more than uninterested; he is disdainful, even disruptive at times. To get him interested will require a real show of interest on her part. But Janet resents any suggestion that she should give John what he needs. Why should she? He's 14 years old. It's his job to show interest. She has a whole classroom full of students, and she hasn't got the time to give him special attention. Because of this resentment, all she can think of is punishment.

> **When Janet punishes John, she gives him more reasons to keep her and math out of his quality world.**

When Janet punishes John, she gives him more reasons to keep her and math out of his quality world. Now he can blame her; from his standpoint, his failure is no longer his fault. Thus the low grades and threats of failure have exactly the opposite effect from the one she intends. That is why she has been so puzzled by students like John for so many years. She did the "right thing," and, even though she can see John getting more and more turned off, she doesn't know what else to do. She no more knows why she can't reach John than she knows why she and her husband found it harder and harder to reach each other when their marriage started to fail.

FROM THE beginning to the end of the 1994–95 school year, my wife Carleen and I worked to introduce Quality School concepts into the Schwab Middle School, a seventh- and eighth-grade school that is part of the Cincinnati Public School System. (Carleen actually began training many staff members in choice theory during the second semester of the 1993–94 school year.) This school of 600 regularly attending students (750 enrolled) has at least 300 students like John, who come to school almost every day. With the help of the principal, who was named best principal in Ohio in 1996, and a very good staff, we turned this school around.

By the end of the year, most of the regularly attending students who were capable of doing passable schoolwork were doing it.[3] Indeed, some of the work was much better than passable. None of the students like John were doing it when we arrived. Discipline problems that had led to 1,500 suspensions in the previous year slowly came under control and ceased to be a significant concern by the end of the school year.

By mid-February, after four months of preparation, we were able to start a special program in which we enrolled all the students (170) who had failed at least one grade and who also regularly attended school. Most had failed more than one grade, and some, now close to 17 years of age, had failed four times. Teachers from the regular school staff volunteered for this program. Our special program continued through summer school, by the end of which 147 of these 170 students were promoted to high school. The predicted number of students who would go to high school from this group had been near zero. Getting these students out of the "on-age" classes where they had been disruptive freed the regular teachers to teach more effectively, and almost all the "on-age" students began to learn. The "on-age" seventh-graders at Schwab had a 20% increase in their math test scores, another positive outcome of the program.

We were able to achieve these results because we taught almost all the teachers in the school enough choice theory to understand how students need to be treated if they are to put us into their quality worlds. Using these concepts, the teachers stopped almost all coercion—an approach that was radically different from the way most of these students had been treated since kindergarten. When we asked the students why they were no longer disruptive and why they were beginning to work in school, over and over they said, "You care about us." And sometimes they added, "And now you give us choices and work that we like to do."

What did we do that they liked so much? With the district's permission, we threw out the regular curriculum and allowed the students to work at their own pace. We assigned lessons that, when successfully completed, proved that the students were ready for high school. The seven teachers in the special program (called the Cambridge Program)—spurred on by the challenge that this was their school and that they could do anything they believed necessary—worked day and night for almost two months to devise these lessons, in which the students had to demonstrate that they could read, write, solve problems, and learn the basics of social studies and science.

We told the students that they could not fail but that it was up to them to do the work. We said that we would help them learn as much as we could, and teachers from the "on-age" classes volunteered their free periods to help. Some of the students began to help one another. The fear began to dissipate as the staff saw the students begin to work. What we did was not so difficult that any school staff, with the leadership of its principal, could not do it as well. Because we had so little time, Carleen and I were co-leaders with the principal. A little extra money (about $20,000) from a state grant was also spent to equip the room for the Cambridge Program with furniture, carpeting, and computers, but it was not more than any school could raise if it could promise the results we achieved.

THESE Quality School ideas have also been put to work for several years in Huntington Woods Elementary School in Wyoming, Michigan. This nearly 300-student K–5 school is located in a small middle-class town and is the first school to be designated a Quality School. There were very few Johns in this school to begin with, so the task was much easier than at Schwab. Nonetheless, the outcomes at Huntington Woods have been impressive.

- All students are doing competent schoolwork, as measured by the Michigan Education Assessment Program (MEAP). The percentages of Huntington Woods students who score satisfactorily as measured against a state standard are 88% in reading and 85% in math (compared to state averages of 49% in reading and 60% in math).
- As measured by both themselves and their teachers, all students are doing some quality work, and many are doing a great deal of quality work.

- While there are occasional discipline incidents, there are no longer any discipline problems.
- The regular staff works very successfully with all students without labeling them learning disabled or emotionally impaired.
- Even more important than these measurable outcomes, the school is a source of joy for students, teachers, and parents.

I emphasize that no extra money was spent by the district to achieve these results. The school, however, did some fund raising to pay for staff training.

I CITE Schwab and Huntington Woods because I have worked in one of these schools myself and have had a great deal of contact with the other. They are both using the ideas in my books. Huntington Woods has changed from an SR-driven system, and Schwab has made a strong start toward doing so. Moreover, Schwab's start has produced the results described above. And more than 200 other schools are now working with me in an effort to become Quality Schools.

So far only Huntington Woods has evaluated itself and declared itself a Quality School. Even Schwab, as improved as it is, is far from being a Quality School. But, in terms of actual progress made from where we found it, what Schwab has achieved is proportionally greater than what Huntington Woods has achieved.

While many schools have shown interest in what has been achieved at Huntington Woods and at Schwab, very few of them have accepted the core idea: change the system from SR theory to choice theory. Indeed, there are many successful SR schools around the country that are not trying to change the fundamental system in which they operate, and I believe their success is based on two things.

First, for a school to be successful, the principal is the key. When an SR school succeeds, as many do, it is led by a principal whose charisma has inspired the staff and students to work harder than they would ordinarily work. This kind of success will last only as long as the principal remains. I am not saying that some charismatic principals do not embrace many of the ideas of the Quality School, or that the principal doesn't have to lead the systemic change that choice theory makes possible. However, once the system has been changed, it can sustain itself (with the principal's support, of course, but without a charismatic leader).

Second, the SR schools that are working well have strong parental support for good education and few Johns among their students. Where such support is already present or can be created by hard-working teachers and principals, schools have a very good chance of being successful without changing their core system. After all, it is these schools that have traditionally made the SR system seem to work. In such schools, Janet would be a very successful teacher.

While Huntington Woods had the kind of support that would have made it a good school without changing the system, the staff wanted it to become a Quality School and set about changing the system from the outset. With the backing of the superintendent, the staff members were given an empty building and the opportunity to recruit new staff members, all of whom were anxious to learn the choice theory needed to change the system. The fact that Huntington Woods has a charismatic leader is certainly a plus, but it is her dedication to the ideas of choice theory that has led to the school's great success. With very high test scores, no discipline problems, and no need for special programs, Huntington Woods has gone far beyond what I believe the typical SR school could achieve. Many educators who have visited the school have said that it is "a very different kind of school."[4]

Schwab today is also very different from the school it was. And what has been accomplished at Schwab has been done with almost no active parental support. The largest number of parents we could get to attend any meeting—even when we served food and told them to bring the whole family—was 20, and some of them were parents of the few students who live in the middle-class neighborhood where the school is located. Almost all the Schwab students who are like John are bused in from low-income communities far from the school, a fact that makes parents' participation more difficult.

At Schwab an effort was made to teach all the teachers choice theory. Then Carleen and I reminded them continually to use the theory as they worked to improve the school. At Huntington Woods, not only were the teachers and principal taught choice theory in much more depth than at Schwab and over much more time than we had at Schwab, but all the students and many parents were also involved in learning this theory and beginning to use it in theirlives.

Unfortunately, Janet has never taught in a school that uses choice theory. When she brings up her problems with John in the teachers' lounge, she is the beneficiary of a lot of SR advice: "Get tough!" "Show him right away who's boss." "Don't let him get away with anything." "Call his mother, and demand she do something about his behavior." "Send him to the principal." Similarly, like almost everyone whose marriage is in trouble, Janet has been the beneficiary of a lot of well-intended SR advice from family and friends—some of which, unfortunately, she took.

Her other serious problem is that she works in an SR system that is perfectly willing to settle for educating only those students who want to learn. The system's credo says, "It's a tough world out there. If they don't make an effort, they have to suffer the consequences." Since Janet is herself a successful product of such a system, she supports it. In doing so, she believes it is right to give students low grades for failing to do what she asks them to do. She further believes it is right to refuse to let them make up a low grade if they don't have a very good attitude—and sometimes even if they do.

In her personal life, she and her husband had seen so much marriage failure that, when they started to have trouble, it was easy for them to think of divorce as almost inevitable. This is bad information. It discourages both partners from doing the hard work necessary to learn what is needed to put their marriage back together. Life is hard enough without the continuing harangues of the doomsayers. In a world that uses choice theory, people would be more optimistic.

There has been no punishment in the Huntington Woods School for years. There is no such thing as a low grade that cannot be improved. Every student has access to a teacher or another student if he or she needs personal attention. Some students will always do better than others, but, as the MEAP scores show, all can do well. This is a Quality system, with an emphasis on continual improvement, and there is no settling for good enough.

Unfortunately for them, many Schwab students who experience success in school for the first time will fail in high school. The SR system in use there will kill them off educationally, just as certainly as if we shot them with a gun. They didn't have enough time with us and were too fragile when we sent them on. However, if by some miracle the high school pays attention to what we did at Schwab, many will succeed. There was some central office support for our efforts, and there is some indication that this support will continue.

The Huntington Woods students are less fragile. They will have had a good enough start with choice theory so that, given the much stronger psychological and financial support of their parents, they will probably do well in middle school. Indeed, data from the first semester of 1995–96 confirm that they are doing very well.

It is my hope that educators, none of whom are immune to marriage failure, will see the value of choice theory in their personal lives. If this happens, there is no doubt in my mind that they will begin to use it with their students.

---

1. William Glasser, *The Quality School* (New York: HarperCollins, 1990); and idem, *The Quality School Teacher* (New York: HarperCollins, 1994).
2. William Glasser, *Staying Together* (New York: HarperCollins, 1995).
3. The school also had about four classes of special education students who were in a special program led by capable teachers and were learning as much as they were capable of learning.
4. See Dave Winans, "This School Has Everything," *NEA Today,* December 1995, pp. 4–5.

Motivating Underachievers:
Make them *want* to try

DEBORAH STIPEK

Deborah Stipek was an associate professor of education at UCLA when she wrote this article.

SOONER OR LATER, AN UNDER-achiever will challenge your teaching skill – and your patience – with unfinished assignments, complaints, and excuses. Maybe you'll try to coax the child into working harder. Maybe you'll enlist the aid of parents. Maybe you'll search for special projects to pique the child's interest. And maybe none of these tactics will succeed.

Laziness, boredom, and apathy don't explain the behavior of all underachieving students. For many smart kids who fail, *not* trying simply makes more sense than the alternative. Take Melanie and Jeff, for example.

Melanie, an intelligent 2nd grader, rarely hands in homework. And when given an in-class assignment, she invariably whines, "That's too hard" or "I can't do this" until her teacher comes to help. On tests, Melanie often "consults" her classmates' papers.

Jeff, on the other hand, would never cheat on a test or seek help from a teacher or classmate. But the 6th grader is often conspicuously inattentive in class. And "bad luck" keeps him from completing a surprising number of tasks, particularly ones dealing with new material. He leaves books necessary for doing homework at school. He loses assignments on the bus. Sometimes during a test his pen runs out of ink, and he wastes valuable time rummaging through his desk to find another.

Why try?
Both Jeff and Melanie pay a price for their lack of effort: bad grades, reprimands from their teachers, detentions. Yet both persist in their behavior. Why? The answer is deceptively simple: These kids see the benefits of not trying as outweighing the costs.

Melanie is sure she *can't* do the assigned work, regardless of how hard she tries. Since effort or apathy will lead to the same end – failure – putting forth the least effort possible is perfectly logical. So Melanie continues to rely on teachers and classmates to get her through.

Unlike Melanie, Jeff isn't convinced that he can't do his schoolwork. But he has serious doubts. Since Jeff desperately wants to believe that he's intelligent and competent, and wants others to believe this too, he's afraid to try hard and fail. So for Jeff also, *not* trying – and flaunting his lack of effort – makes sense. It allows him to hold on to a self-image of competence.

Stubborn beliefs
For students like Jeff and Melanie, beliefs about personal ability and the costs and benefits of

effort can be difficult to change. For example, when Melanie *does* do well on an assignment or test, she's likely to attribute her success to the teacher's help, an easy task, or good luck. So occasional successes won't necessarily bolster her self-confidence. What really needs to be changed is her belief that no amount of effort will improve her chances of succeeding. Similarly, Jeff needs to be persuaded that making mistakes isn't a sign of stupidity or incompetence, but a natural part of the learning process. Only then will trying make sense.

Encouraging effort

The following guidelines will help you make sure that the benefits of trying outweigh those of not trying—for *all* your students.

1. Make sure that assigned tasks are realistic, so that all students can complete them if they really try. When your class contains kids with vastly different skill levels, this isn't easy. But you can use such techniques as teaching in small, flexible groups; creating cooperative work groups or setting up a peer teaching program; and preparing different assignments for different skill levels. To alleviate the additional burden this places on you, have your students check some of their own or one another's assignments. This also gives students a sense of responsibility for their own learning.

2. Focus students' attention on their own progress, not on their classmates' performance. When students measure their success by their peers' performance, those who don't do as well are bound to feel like failures. Base grades and rewards on mastery or improvement, not on relative performance. Reward the child who reduced his spelling errors from 50 percent to 20 percent just as enthusiastically as you reward the child who invariably gets all the words right. Put papers that show improvement, not just the best papers, on the bulletin board. Consider marking workbook exercises with a check mark if they're correct but making no mark if they're not. Have the student continue to work on the exercises until all have received a check mark. This allows kids many opportunities to improve their performance without any negative evaluation.

3. Reward effort, whatever the outcome. Tell your students that in learning, as in any endeavor, setbacks are inevitable. But effort and perseverance *do* pay off. Praise kids when they make progress, not just when they get everything right. If only success is praised, some students may become demoralized when their efforts don't lead to immediate mastery—which is a likely outcome when they're studying new material. And when a student does immediately master a new skill, take care not to be overly enthusiastic. Otherwise, you'll risk sending the message that you really do value brilliance rather than diligence, and slower kids may become discouraged.

4. Give every student opportunities to demonstrate competence in class. Consider setting aside a few minutes each week for kids to demonstrate an unusual—and nonacademic—skill. For example, ask your teeny Houdini to show off some sleight of hand, or your fledgling "Bird" to play a saxophone solo. This way, even academically weak students will get a good dose of self-confidence.

5. Allow students to set their own goals. (Of course, you need to make sure that these goals are realistic but challenging.) For example, encourage a child who consistently fails the weekly math quiz to set a goal for next week's quiz (say, getting two more problems correct). Have the child record the goal and his actual performance on a chart. This will give the child a concrete picture of his own progress and will foster personal responsibility. It will also reinforce the importance of perseverance.

Using Motivational Theory with At-Risk Children

Rawsonville Elementary used achievement goal theory to create a learner-centered school, where success is measured not by relative ability but by individual accomplishment.

Rachel Buck Collopy
and Theresa Green

Rachel Buck Collopy is a doctoral student, Combined Program in Education and Psychology, 1400 School of Education, University of Michigan, Ann Arbor, MI 48109. **Theresa Green** is Principal, Rawsonville Elementary School, 3110 Grove Rd., Ypsilanti, MI 48198.

Rawsonville Elementary is a neighborhood school near Detroit, where the automotive industry is the major employer. Recent layoffs have affected many families in the area, and more than half of the school's 480 students receive reduced or free lunch. Of the district's six elementary schools, Rawsonville has been identified as most in need of Chapter 1 services. For years, the school improvement team had worked hard to improve student motivation and learning. Yet, something was still missing. The number of at-risk and underachieving students entering the school continued to increase.

At the same time, a group of researchers at the University of Michigan had been testing a theory of student motivation known as achievement goal theory (see Maehr and Midgley 1991, Maehr and Pintrich 1991). Their work confirmed what other studies had indicated: The goals that students pursue have a powerful influence on the quality of their learning. Schools, through their policies and practices, give strong messages to students about how success is defined within their walls. As collaborative partners, the faculty at Rawsonville Elementary and the researchers at the University of Michigan aimed to create a school where the emphasis was on learning rather than on relative ability.

Emphasizing Achievement, Not Ability

Often in schools where students adopt ability goals, students come to believe that success is defined in terms of how they do in comparison to others. Implicit in the comparative definition of success is the belief that some students are smart, some are average, and some are dumb. The goal becomes trying to look smart—or at least not to look dumb. Mistakes and failure, because they indicate lack of ability, are threats to a child's self-esteem (Covington 1984). Students who adopt ability goals are more likely to avoid challenging tasks and to give up in the face of difficulty (Elliott and Dweck 1988).

In contrast, learning goals define success in terms of developing skills, expanding knowledge, and gaining understanding. Success means being able to do something you could not do before. When students adopt learning goals, they take on more challenging tasks, persist longer, are less debilitated by mistakes and failure, and use higher-level thinking skills than when they focus on ability goals (See Ames 1992 for a review of research).

As partners in a three-year collaboration, we aimed to make Rawsonville a school where the emphasis was on learning rather than on relative ability. Achievement goal theory does not mandate policies and practices. Rather, practitioners use it as a framework to develop consistent, integrated policies and practices that are appropriate to the needs and strengths of their students, staffs, and communities. The issues of most urgent concern to teachers were our starting point.

Creating Learning-Focused Classrooms

Having heard a lot about the long-term negative effects of retaining students, Rawsonville's teachers were eager to find alternatives to retention. Their early discussions focused on add-ons of financial, human, and material resources. Then, two teachers suggested fundamentally changing the structure of the classroom. If several grades were taught together, they proposed, children would focus on their own improvement and progress at their own developmental pace.

A flood of questions followed.

From *Educational Leadership,* September 1995, pp. 37-40. © 1995 by Rachel Buck Collopy and Theresa Green. Reprinted by permission.

FIGURE 1

Rawsonville Elementary School's Principles of Recognition

1. Recognize individual student effort, accomplishment, and improvement.

2. Give all students opportunities to be recognized.

3. Give recognition privately whenever possible.

4. Avoid using "most" or "best" for recognizing or rewarding, as in "best project" or "most improved." These words usually convey comparisons with others.

5. Avoid recognizing on the basis of absence of mistakes. For example, avoid giving awards for students who get "fewer than five words wrong on a spelling test."

6. Avoid using the same criteria for all students. For example, avoid giving an award to "all students who get an *A* on the science test, or all students who do four out of five projects."

7. Recognize students for taking on challenging work or for stretching their own abilities (even if they make mistakes).

8. Recognize students for coming up with different and unusual ways to solve a problem or approach a task.

9. Try to involve students in the recognition process. What is of value to them? How much effort do they feel they put in? Where do they feel they need improvement? How do they know when they have reached their goals?

10. It's OK to recognize students in various domains (behavior, athletics, attendance), but every student should have the opportunity to be recognized *academically*.

11. Try to recognize the quality of students' work rather than the quantity. For example, recognizing students for reading a lot of books could encourage them to read easy books.

12. Avoid recognizing grades and test scores. This takes the emphasis away from learning and problem solving.

13. Recognition must be real. Do not recognize students for accomplishing something they have not really accomplished, for improving if they have not improved, or for trying hard if that is not the case.

Copyright © 1993 by Carol Midgley and Timothy Urdan, *Middle School Journal*. Reprinted with permission.

More than just the ages of students would be different in these classrooms. All areas of schooling—from curriculum, materials, and scheduling to teaching methods, classroom management, and evaluation—needed to be reconsidered. Together, we gathered information from experts in other schools and universities. We discussed the obstacles to change. Most important, we confronted our assumptions about the way learning and schooling had to be conducted and began to dream about how it could be.

As the learning-focused, multi-age classrooms began to take shape, it became clear that high- as well as low-achieving students would benefit from the proposed changes:

■ Students would stay with the same teacher for at least two years.

■ The approach to instruction would be interdisciplinary and thematic.

■ Students would progress at their own speed—focusing on meeting learning objectives, not following a lockstep curriculum.

■ The learning-focused classrooms would take advantage of the variety of skill levels through peer tutoring, cooperative learning, and inter-age cooperation.

■ Report cards would reflect progress and mastery rather than emphasizing comparative performance with letter grades.

Four teachers decided to pilot the classrooms during 1990–91. At the beginning, they were understandably anxious about possible student failures. By the end of the first year, however, they reported that students were more willing to participate in learning activities, more enthusiastic about learning, and showed greater concern for the learning of classmates. Now, half of Rawsonville's classrooms contain children of two or three grade levels.

Developing a learning-focused environment for children did not stop at the doorway of multi-age classrooms. The theoretical framework of achievement goal theory can be used to redesign single-age classrooms, too. Since Rawsonville's self-renewal began five years ago, the teachers of single-age classrooms have also moved toward an emphasis on improvement, understanding, and effort. Teachers now share methods and techniques that encourage students to adopt learning goals across all classrooms.

School change, of course, is about more than just changing classrooms. Classrooms exist within schools and are affected by the policies and practices of the wider school culture. The efforts of an individual teacher to emphasize learning goals can be undermined by school policies that emphasize relative ability and comparative performance.

Abandoning the Honor Roll

As her understanding of achievement goal theory increased, Rawsonville's principal realized that the traditional honor roll defined the goal of learning as outperforming others, not improving regardless of relative performance. Each term, only a small group of students received honor roll certificates. In addition to serving as a disincentive for the children who never received the certificates, the honor roll also discouraged high-achieving children from trying challenging tasks.

The principal's decision to eliminate the honor roll started a firestorm of controversy. Many teachers felt that they had lost a carrot to urge students to try hard; they also pointed out that many parents took pride in the honor roll certificates. As they searched for ways to recognize children in a learning-focused manner, teachers came up with Rawsonville's Principles of Recognition. Instead of dictating uniform recognition policies and practices, these principles serve as guidelines that respect the professionalism, creativity, and personal style of teachers.

Other schoolwide recognition policies were also guided by the new principles. As an alternative to making the honor roll, every upper elementary student now receives a certificate recognizing him or her for an area of improvement, accomplishment, and effort. Similarly, at the 5th grade awards ceremony, every graduate is applauded for an accomplishment. In the past, only a handful of students were recognized for their achievements—and often these students received several awards. By the fifth or sixth time a student went up to collect an award, other students would groan instead of applaud.

The faculty at Rawsonville Elementary have also redesigned other schoolwide policies and practices in line with a more learning-focused environment. Rather than emphasizing rewards and punishments, discipline procedures now focus on teaching children to become problem solvers. The use of mini-lessons on conflict resolution and peer mediation, for example, has lessened discipline problems more than rewarding the "good" and punishing the "bad" ever did.

After the three-year collaboration with the University of Michigan formally ended, Rawsonville sought out a second collaborative relationship with another nearby university with the goal of increasing students' computer literacy. Staff have implemented classroom computer use within the framework of achievement goal theory. Teachers now view computers as a way to help all children—not just slow learners or gifted students—learn problem-solving and reasoning skills.

Continuing the Effort

Rawsonville Elementary's approach is but one example of how to put achievement goal theory into practice. Other schools may decide to focus on other pressing issues or design solutions that are theoretically consistent with, but superficially different from, Rawsonville's. What is important is the theoretical perspective, the philosophical underpinnings, that these changes in practice exemplify.

Today, because a large proportion of children entering Rawsonsville is still considered at risk, the faculty's commitment to the course they have set has become more important than ever. At the beginning of each school year, the principal and teachers review the changes they made and discuss the rationale behind them. Teachers have taken over the researchers' role of questioning: Will every child benefit from this experience? What message will this give about the goal of learning? What does this say about what is valued at this school?

Now that we know that achievement goal theory can be put into practice, what difference has it made? Teachers have reported improved attendance, increased enthusiasm for learning, and decreased discipline problems. As one teacher said, "I could never go back to teaching the way I did before." Referring to students' improved attitude toward learning, a 20-year veteran wrote:

> Some students became so interested in some aspect of classwork that they did correlating activities on their own at home. Children brought in books, magazines, newspapers, and artifacts that pertained to areas of study. They wrote plays, drew pictures, and made dioramas.... During our study of Japan, one little boy got so interested in haiku that he borrowed my books on it and began writing it—in school and at home. His mom reported that he was driving them "cuckoo" with his "haiku."

Parents are very supportive of these efforts to change. Through formal and informal feedback, they report that their children have become more confident, more willing to take on challenges, more excited about school, and better at working independently and with others. About her son, one parent wrote on a survey that she saw "great improvement in all areas—from a student who was failing and had low self-esteem to an interested, highly motivated *learner*!"

One clear example stands out of the extent to which the school community has embraced the changes brought about by achievement goal theory. At a recent PTO meeting, two parents suggested adding competitive rewards to an annual school event. Other parents told them that Rawsonville is not about winning and losing. It is about every child having access to the same enriching and educational experiences. It is about *learning*.

References

Ames, C. (1992). "Classrooms: Goals, Structures, and Student Motivation." *Journal of Educational Psychology* 84, 3: 261–271.

Covington, M. V. (1984). "The Self-Worth Theory of Achievement Motivation: Findings and Implications." *Elementary School Journal* 85: 5–20.

Elliott, E. S., and C. S. Dweck. (1988). "Goals: An Approach to Motivation and Achievement." *Journal of Personality and Social Psychology* 54: 5–12.

Maehr, M. L., and C. Midgley. (1991). "Enhancing Student Motivation: A Schoolwide Approach." *Educational Psychologist* 26, 3 & 4: 399–427.

Maehr, M. L., and P. R. Pintrich. (1991). *Advances in Motivation and Achievement, Vol. 7.* Greenwich, Conn.: JAI Press.

Authors' note: An earlier version of this paper was presented at the annual meeting of the American Educational Research Association, Atlanta, 1993. This work was supported in part by grants from the Office of Educational Research and Improvement. The opinions expressed, however, are those of the authors and do not represent OERI policy.

This collaboration would not have been possible without Carol Midgley and Martin Maehr of the University of Michigan and the teachers of Rawsonville Elementary School.

HOW TO DEFUSE

CONFRONTATIONS

DEFIANCE · THREATS · CHALLENGES

The T-shirt attention getter...
Prohibited cookies on the bus...
Profanity in class...
Outright refusal to do classwork...
Chair-throwing...

A comprehensive system of behavior management has three critical components: prevention, defusion, and follow-up.

Do some of your students engage in confrontational behavior like this? Here's a litany of such behavior: attention-getting, defiance, challenges, disrespect, limit testing, verbal abuse, blatant rule violations, threats, and intimidation. Some students test the patience of teachers who have what they thought was an effective behavior-management system. This article presents teacher-tested ways to *defuse* such behavior and allow the students to learn and participate in positive ways.

Special education teachers have always had the task of managing students who display seriously disturbing behavior. More recently, these teachers are expected to provide support and consultation to general education teachers who need assistance on managing the behavior of all students in inclusive classrooms. Special education teachers can assist other educators in a comprehensive system of behavior management composed of three critical components: prevention, defusion, and follow-up (see box, "Three Approaches to Behavior Management").

We focus here particularly on *defusion,* an approach that is helpful with students who are continually confrontational. Such behavior not only leads to class disruption, but also can readily escalate to more serious behavior—and threats to the safety of both staff and stu-

Geoff Colvin
David Ainge
Ron Nelson
■

dents. Let's look at some examples of confrontational behavior and then explore how we can deal with it.

Three Confrontational Students

● Joe steps onto the school bus holding a monster cookie in his hand. Above his head is a large sign that reads, "No food on the bus." Joe looks at the driver, takes a huge bite of the cookie, and takes another step on the bus. The bus driver points to the sign and says quite emphatically, "Look, no food on the bus. You'll have to give me that cookie." Joe says equally emphatically, "No," and takes another bite. The driver looks him right in the eye and says, "If you don't give me the cookie, you will not ride the bus." Joe says, "So," takes another bite of the cookie, and begins to move toward his seat. The driver calls transportation to have the student removed from the bus.

● Sarah walks into the classroom wearing a T-shirt displaying a toilet bowl with an arrow coming up out of the bowl and a written statement underneath, "Up your AZ." Some students giggle, and another asks, "Where did you get that?" The teacher comes over and says, "Sarah, that shirt is not acceptable in a public school. You had better go to the restroom and turn it inside out." Sarah looks at the teacher and says, "I'm not gonna do that. My dad gave it to me and you can't make me turn it inside out." The teacher says that if she does not cooperate, she will be sent to the office. Sarah throws her book down and heads to the back of the room.

From *Teaching Exceptional Children,* July/August 1997, pp. 47-51. © 1997 by The Council for Exceptional Children. Reprinted by permission.

- Jamie is sitting at his desk, arms folded, shoulders rounded, feet firmly planted on the floor, and staring at the floor with a scowl on his face, while the rest of the class is working on an independent math assignment. The teacher eventually approaches Jamie and prompts him to start on his math. He scowls and says in a harsh tone that he can't do it. So the teacher offers to help him. He says he still can't do it. The teacher provides more detail with the explanation and directs him to make a start. He says he hates math. The teacher tells him that he needs to start or he will have to do his math during the break. He utters a profanity and storms out of the room.

What Happened?

In each case, the supervising staff person reacts to a problem behavior in a direct manner. There is a high likelihood that the student *expects* a response. In fact, the student not only expects a response, but he or she expects a *particular* response.

For all practical purposes, the staff person is *already set up for confrontation*. In other words, the student displays engaging behavior that is highly likely to elicit a predictable response from staff that includes a clear direction. The student refuses to follow the direction, which engages staff further, leading to ultimatums and additional problem behavior.

Moreover, if the staff person becomes confrontational at this point, there is a strong likelihood that the student will react with more serious behavior. In effect, we can see a pattern—a cycle—of successive interactions beginning with problem behavior leading to more serious behavior, such as throwing a book (Sarah), continuing to disregard requests (Joe), or profanity (Jamie). These vignettes have five common features:

1. The student displays defiant, challenging, or inappropriate behavior.
2. The supervising staff person reacts to the problem behavior and provides a direction in opposition to the student's behavior.
3. The student challenges the direction by not complying and by displaying other inappropriate behavior.
4. The staff person reacts to the non-compliance and presents an ultimatum.
5. The student takes up the challenge of the ultimatum with further defiance and exhibits hostile and explosive behavior.

What Strategies Can Help?

When students exhibit confrontational behavior, you need approaches that are likely to defuse the problem behavior, rather than lead to more serious behavior. Defusing strategies minimize the likelihood that interactions between you and the student will escalate the confrontation. We have found five defusing strategies that work—in order of least intrusive student behavior to more serious confrontational behavior. These strategies range from ignoring the behavior to delaying a response and allowing the student to calm down.

Focus on the Task to Defuse Minor Attention-Getting Behavior

Students often display minor problem behavior to secure attention: talking out in class, moving out of their seats, starting work slowly, and pencil tapping. Once you respond to such behavior, the student may exhibit more attention-getting behavior. The basic approach for managing this level of problem behavior is to use a *continuum* of steps based on the level of attention you provide:

- Attend to the students exhibiting expected behavior, and ignore the students displaying the problem behavior.
- Redirect the student to the task at hand. Do not respond to or draw attention to the problem behavior.
- Present a choice between the expected behavior and a small negative consequence (such as a loss of privilege).

For example, Michael is out of his seat wandering around the room while other students are seated and engaged in a class activity. The teacher moves among the students who are on task, acknowledges their good work and ignores Michael. Michael continues to move around the class. The teacher approaches him and says privately, "Michael, listen, it's math time. Let's go." and points to his seat. Michael still does not return to his seat. The teacher secures his attention and says calmly and firmly, "Michael, you have been asked to sit down and start work or you will have to do the work in recess. You decide." The teacher follows through on whatever Michael chooses to do.

Present Options Privately in the Context of a Rule Violation

Sometimes students will break a rule to challenge you. They know you will react and give a direction. The student will then refuse to follow the direction. In this way, a confrontation scene is established. For example, in the cases of Joe and Sarah, the staff member gave the students a direction that the students refused to follow—the cookie was not turned in to the driver, the T-shirt was not turned inside out. Here are steps to follow in such cases:

- State the rule or expectation.
- Request explicitly for the student to "take care of the problem."
- Present options for the student on how to take care of the problem.

In this way, you lessen the chance of confrontation when you present options and focus how the student might decide to take care of the problem, rather than whether the student follows a specific direction.

For example, the bus driver might have quietly said something like this to Joe: "Look, there is no food on the bus, thank you. You had better take care of that. You can eat it before you get on or leave it here and collect it later." Note the options the bus driver might have provided.

Or, to deal with Sarah's offensive T-shirt, the teacher might take Sarah aside and say, "Sarah, that shirt is not OK in a public school. It has a rude message. You can turn it inside out, get a shirt from the gym, or wear a jacket."

Reduce Agitation in a Demand Situation

Sometimes students are already agitated when they enter a situation. When you or other people place demands on them, their behavior will likely escalate.

For example, Jamie's body posture and tone of voice suggest he is upset.

*F*irst, communicate concern to the student. Then allow the student time and space. Give the student some choices or options.

When the teacher tries to prompt him to work, even in a very reasonable manner, his behavior escalates to storming out of the room. Here, the teacher might have used agitation-reduction techniques.

Signs of Agitation. Students show agitation by either increasing distracting behavior or decreasing active, engaged behavior (Colvin, 1992). Here are common signs of increases in *distracting behavior*:

- Darting eyes
- Nonconversational language
- Busy hands
- Moving in and out of groups
- Frequent off-task and on-task behavior
- Starting and stopping activities
- Moving around the room

Paradoxically, sometimes agitation doesn't seem to live up to its name. Some students can be agitated and not show it. Watch for the following *decreases in behavior* and a lack of engagement in class activities:

- Staring into space
- Subdued language
- Contained hands
- Lack of interaction and involvement in activities
- Withdrawal from groups and activities
- Lack of responding in general
- Avoidance of eye contact

Techniques for Reducing Agitation. Once you recognize that the student's behavior is agitated, your primary goal is to use strategies to calm the student down and assist him or her to become engaged in the present classroom activity. Because these strategies are supportive in nature, you need to use them *before* the behavior becomes serious; otherwise, you risk reinforcing the seemingly endless chain of inappropriate behavior. The critical issue is *timing*. Use the following techniques at the *earliest* indications of agitation:

Teacher support: Communicate concern to the student.

Space: Provide the student with an opportunity to have some isolation from the rest of the class.

Choices: Give the student some choices or options.

Preferred activities: Allow the student to engage in a preferred activity for a short period of time to help regain focus.

Teacher proximity: Move near or stand near the student.

Independent activities: Engage the student in independent activities to provide isolation.

Movement activities: Use activities and tasks that require movement, such as errands, cleaning the chalkboard, and distributing papers.

Involvement of the student: Where possible, involve the student in the plan. In this way, there is more chance of ownership and generalization to other settings.

Relaxation activities: Use audiotapes, drawing activities, breathing and relaxation techniques.

Now let's replay Jamie's situation. This time, the teacher determines that Jamie seems to be agitated—he shows a *decrease* in behavior. The teacher says, as privately as possible, "Jamie, it's time for math. Are you doing OK? Do you need some time before you start?" In this way, the teacher is recognizing the agitation, communicating concern to Jamie, and giving him time to regain his focus.

Preteach and Present Choices to Establish Limits and Defuse Noncompliance

Use this strategy to establish limits and to defuse sustained noncompliance. Essentially, the student is refusing to follow the teacher's directions.

For example, suppose that Scott has been off task and distracting other students for several minutes. The teacher has tried to provide assistance, redirect

Three Approaches to Behavior Management

Prevention. The teacher places a strong focus on teaching desirable behavior and orchestrating effective learning activities. These proactive strategies are designed to establish a positive classroom structure and climate for students to engage in productive, prosocial behavior.

Defusion. Teachers use strategies designed to address problem behavior after the behavior has commenced. The goal here is to arrest the behavior before it escalates to more serious behavior and to assist the student to resume class activities in an appropriate manner.

Follow-up. A teacher or an administrator may provide consequences for the problem behavior and endeavors to assist the student to terminate the problem behavior and to engage in appropriate behavior in the future.

The goal of these approaches is to provide information to the student on the limits of behavior and to use problem-solving strategies to enable the student to exhibit alternative appropriate behavior in subsequent events (Biggs & Moore, 1993; Colvin & Lazar, 1997; Kameenui & Darch, 1995; Myers & Myers, 1993; Sprick, Sprick & Garrison, 1993; Sugai & Tindal, 1993; Walker, Colvin, & Ramsey, 1995).

him, and give a formal direction to begin work. Scott refuses to cooperate. At this point, the teacher wants to communicate to him that "enough is enough," and to establish some classroom limits. When the teacher tries to establish limits, however, Scott may become more hostile and aggressive.

The following steps in the preteaching strategy can establish limits without escalating the behavior. Role-playing

*T*he most important thing to remember is that your responses can change things.

---

these steps can help students learn how to use self-control.

Preteach the procedures: Carefully rehearse the procedures with the student, give explanations, model the steps, and describe the consequences. Do preteaching at a neutral time when the student is relatively calm and cooperative.

Deliver the information to the students without being confrontational:

1. Present the expected behavior and the negative consequence as a decision; place responsibility on the student.

2. Allow a few seconds for the student to decide. This small amount of time helps the student calm down, enables face saving in front of peers, enables you to pull away from the conflict, and leaves the student with the decision.

3. Withdraw from the student and attend to other students. You thus help the student focus on the decision, not attend to you.

Follow through: If the student chooses the expected behavior, briefly acknowledge the choice and continue with the lesson or activity. If the student has not chosen the expected behavior, deliver the negative consequence. Debrief with the student and problem solve.

For example, if Sarah refused to take care of the T-shirt problem, the teacher could say. "Sarah, you have been asked to take care of the shirt (expected behavior), or I will have to make an office referral (negative consequence). You have a few seconds to decide." The teacher moves away from Sarah and addresses some other students or tasks. The teacher follows through on the choice made by the student.

Disengage and Delay Responding in the Presence of Serious Threatening Behavior

Students may escalate to a point of serious confrontational behavior involving threats or intimidation. For example, the teacher may have presented options, given the student time, and provided a consequence: "Eric, you are asked to start work or you will have to stay after school. You have a few seconds to decide." Eric walks over to the teacher and says, "I know where you live."

Suppose a more serious situation occurs, such as this real incident: An administrator told a student to go to the in-school suspension area or he would call his probation officer. The student picked up a cup of coffee from the secretary's desk, moved to the administrator, held the coffee in his face, and said, "You call my P.O. and I will throw this in your f_____ face."

In each of these cases, there is a direct threat to a staff member and the danger that the student's behavior may escalate. Whether the student's behavior becomes more serious *depends on the staff member's initial response to the threat*. The primary intent of this strategy is to avoid responding directly to the student's behavior and to disengage momentarily and then to redirect the student.

We are *not* suggesting that this strategy is all you need to do. Rather, the primary purpose of this strategy is to defuse a crisis situation. Once the crisis has been avoided, you should follow up and address the previous threatening behavior so that such behavior does not arise again. Here are steps to use in disengaging and delaying:

Break the cycle of successive interactions by delaying responding: This pattern consists of successive hostile or inflammatory interactions between you and the student—the student challenges you to respond. The first step is to *delay responding*, because the student is expecting an immediate response. To delay responding, very briefly look at the student, look at the floor, look detached, and pause.

Prevent explosive behavior by making a disengaging response: Do not leave the

student waiting too long; otherwise, an "extinction burst" may occur. That is, if events do not go the way the student expects them to, he or she may exhibit explosive behavior, such as throwing a chair at the wall (or staff, or another student), or throwing the coffee cup. To prevent this burst, disengage swiftly and engage in something neutral or unrelated (Lerman & Iwata, 1995). For example, say to the student, "Just a minute," and move and pick up something on your desk.

Return to the student, redirect, and withdraw: If the student has not exhibited further problem behavior and is waiting, simply return to the student and present the original choice.

For example, approach the student and say, "You still have a moment or two to decide what you wish to do," and withdraw. If the student engages in more serious behavior, implement emergency procedures and policies established by the school or district.

Follow through: If the student chooses the expected behavior, acknowledge the choice briefly and debrief later. If the student does not choose the expected behavior, deliver consequences and debrief later.

Debrief: The debriefing activity is designed to help the student problem solve by reviewing the incident and events leading up to the incident, identifying the triggers, and examining alternatives. The debriefing finishes with a focus or agreement on what the student will try to do next time that would be an appropriate response to the situation (Sugai & Colvin, in press).

Now Let's Debrief

How many Sarahs and Jamies and Erics do you know? Are you tired of throwing up your hands and sending these stu-

---

*D*efusing strategies minimizes the likelihood that interactions between you and the student will escalate the confrontation.

Sometimes students will break a rule to challenge you; others are already agitated when you try to correct them.

dents to the office, or facing hostility and muttered challenges—or even threats to your own safety? Are you equally concerned that these students (and other students in your class) may be missing out on learning opportunities?

The most important thing to remember is that *your responses can change things.* Go back to the section on "Disengage and Delay Responding" and memorize it. Then follow the steps in "Preteaching," and you are on your way to helping students control their own be-

havior and create a better environment for learning.

References

Biggs, J. B., & Moore, P. J. (1993). *The process of learning.* New York: Prentice Hall.

Colvin, G. (1992). *Video program: Managing acting-out behavior.* Eugene, OR: Behavior Associates.

Colvin, G., & Lazar, M. (1997). *The effective elementary classroom: Managing for success.* Longmont, CO: Sopris West.

Kameenui, E. J., & Darch, C. B. (1995). *Instructional classroom management: A proactive approach to behavior management.* White Plains, NY: Longman.

Lerman, D., & Iwata, B. (1995). Prevalence of the extinction burst and its attenuation during treatment. *Journal of Applied Behavior Analysis, 28*, 93-94.

Myers, C. B., & Myers, L. K. (1993). *An introduction to teaching and schools.* Fort Worth, TX: Rinehart and Winston.

Sprick, R., Sprick, M., & Garrison, M. (1993). *Interventions: Collaborative planning for students at risk.* Longmont, CO: Sopris West.

Sugai, G., & Colvin, G. (in press). Debriefing: A proactive addition to negative consequences for problem behavior. *Education and Treatment of Children.*

Sugai, G., & Tindal, G. (1993). *Effective school consultation: An interactive approach.* Pacific Grove, CA: Brooks/Cole.

Walker, H., Colvin, G., & Ramsey, E. (1995). *Antisocial behavior in school: Strategies and best practices.* Pacific Grove, CA: Brooks/Cole.

Geoff Colvin *(Oregon Federation), Research Associate, Special Education and Community Resources, University of Oregon, Eugene.* **David Ainge,** *Senior Lecturer, Special Education Department, James Cook University, Queensland, Australia.* **Ron Nelson** *(CEC Chapter #374), Associate Professor, Applied Psychology Department, Eastern Washington University, Spokane.*

Address correspondence to Geoff Colvin, Special Education and Community Resources, University of Oregon, Eugene, OR 97405 (e-mail: geoff_colvin@ccmail.uoregon.edu).

Connecting Instruction and Management in a Student-Centered Classroom

Nancy K. Martin

M s. Thompson's seventh grade students have been studying the solar system and are busily working in cooperative learning groups. Each group has been assigned one planet and their objective is to create a description of a being that could live on "their" planet. Because Ms. Thompson has done a good job of orchestrating positive interdependence, students are relying on their groups to achieve their objective while the teacher serves as a facilitator (Johnson, Johnson, Holubec, & Roy, 1988). The noise level here is slightly higher than in the typical classroom as students interact with each other and fulfill their assigned roles. The teacher explained the rules for behavior to the students prior to beginning the project: "Keep hands, feet, and objects to yourself," "Let others have a chance to speak," and "Contribute to your group." She has predetermined consequences for both appropriate and inappropriate behavior and shared those with the class.

Ray and Bill have been having trouble getting along together and today does not seem to be an exception as they continue to "pick on" each other. Even though a warning has been issued to both students, there is yet another altercation between them. Ms. Thompson explains, "Boys, this means detention for both of you." Ray turns pale and looks upset. Bill continues poking Ray with his pencil and says, "Detention's no big deal. I don't care." Ms. Thompson explains to Bill that a call to his parents will be made.

The classroom environment promoted by this teacher is typical of many middle school teachers. The instruction was creative and student centered, but the classroom management techniques were expedient and teacher centered. There can be little doubt that an interesting, well-organized lesson is the single best means to prevent off-task behavior. Still, when coupled with teacher-centered behavior management methods, the subtle but unmistakably clear message students receive is: "It's 'us' against 'them.'"

Classroom atmosphere is an important consideration for educators at all levels. However, it is especially important for teachers at the middle level because of the many developmental changes their students experience simultaneously. In addition to physical, social, and cognitive changes, young adolescents also encounter new academic demands and are required to make the adjustment from a small self-contained classroom with one teacher to a larger, possibly less personal school structure (Santrock, 1987). The purpose of this article is to consider the elements of a student-centered learning environment and the connection between the teacher's instructional methods and his or her approach to classroom management.

Historically classrooms have been teacher-centered. Instructors were accepted as experts conveying the subject matter. The focus in this type of classroom was on the teacher's needs (e.g. the content to be covered and student obedience). Student activity was limited and students were, at best, passive learners. They spoke when recognized by the teacher and were typically not allowed to interact with each other during lessons. Although rote learning may have flourished in the teacher-centered classroom, active learning (problem-solving and critical thinking) was unlikely to emerge. As we prepare to enter the 21st century, this type of learning environment is no longer favorable. If the classroom is to be the center of "intellectual inquiry, students and teachers must feel free

Nancy K. Martin teaches at the University of Texas at San Antonio.

From *Middle School Journal*, March 1997, pp. 3-9. © 1997 by the National Middle School Association (NMSA). Reprinted by permission.

to pursue ideas and make mistakes" (Prawat, 1992, p. 10). Recently, student-centered instruction has gained new advocacy (Aaronsohn, 1993).

Unlike classrooms of the past, student-centered classrooms focus on student "interaction with meaningful content, with each other, and with the teacher as facilitator of that independence" (Aaronsohn, 1993, p. 3).

Today quality instruction is characterized by developmentally appropriate methods that consider the intrinsic needs of students. Students' decision-making skills are fostered and opinions are validated by focusing on creativity and critical thinking rather than rote learning.

Although often considered separately, classroom management and instruction cannot be isolated from each other because they work together to create a classroom atmosphere (Martin & Baldwin, 1994). Yet many schools across the country encourage and use student-focused instructional methods while simultaneously adopting packaged approaches to classroom management, even though these approaches may not be designed to support student-centered instruction. Without student-centered instruction and classroom management, a truly learner-focused environment cannot exist. Still, when I try to convey this connection to teachers, I am frequently met with skepticism: "Can't I be student centered in my instruction and teacher centered in my classroom management?" The answer is no; you are trying to mix oil with water.

The student-centered classroom is an outgrowth of a philosophy sensitive to the whole child. Therefore, by definition it must focus on the psychological and emotional aspects of the child as well as on the cognitive and intellectual domains. As Wilson (1994) explains, "teachers who view their students simply as academic learners fail to consider the impact of each student's affective state on achievement in the middle school. ... Teachers

who appear too busy to respond to significant social/affective related needs of young adolescents assure an incomplete learning ethos in their classrooms, counter-productive to excellence in scholarship" (p. 53).

The Goal of Classroom Management

This brings to light important questions. First, what is the overall goal of classroom management? In the teacher-centered classroom, control is key to being able to "cover" the material. Keeping pupils still and quiet in the most expedient fashion possible is the primary objective. Traditional, teacher-centered classroom management techniques usually require appropriate behavior in response to some type of reward. Therefore, the teacher must be present to view the behavior and dispense the reinforcer. By utilizing systems such as these, we run the risk of creating a situation in which students behave only for what they "get" and the teacher's absence implies permission to misbehave.

One of the most widely used teacher-centered paradigms is Canter's (1992) *Assertive Discipline*. More than 750,000 teachers have been trained in the use of this model which advocates the use of incentive systems and punishment and focuses on teacher control and student obedience (Hill, 1990). Canter (1992) defines the assertive teacher as, "One who clearly and firmly communicates her expectations to her students, and is prepared to reinforce her words with appropriate actions. She responds in a manner which maximizes her potential to get her needs to teach met, but in no way violates the best interest of the students" (p. 14). This model consists of a set of rules and a hierarchy of predetermined rewards and consequences. When the child misbehaves, he or she is allowed one warning before the predetermined consequence is automatically doled out without consideration of the individual child or the motivation of the misbehavior.

Consider the following scenario typical of the assertive discipline classroom. As Mr. Martinez is presenting his lesson, he sees Emily turn and whisper to Jason. "Emily, that's a warning."

"But, Mr. Martinez, I . . ."

"No 'buts', Emily. You know the rules. Next time, you go to detention. " The classroom belongs only to Mr. Martinez; there is no sense of community here. Emily is likely to become resentful and other students may be upset or angry by observing similar interactions.

In the student-centered classroom, however, Mr. Martinez's response would be very different. Here, the teacher might simply ask, "Emily, is there something I can help you with?"

"What page are we on, Mr. Martinez? I didn't hear you say."

"Page 53, Emily, but remember that the assignment is always written on the board so your can look there in the future." In this simple exchange, the teacher has first tried to be pro-active by putting information on the board. But when Emily did not remember or notice, she was still given the benefit of the doubt. She was listened to and respected. In this scenario, we see reciprocal interaction; not a one-way or topdown exchange.

Assertive Discipline, on the other hand, treats all students the same. But being fair means not treating all children the same. When a physician has a waiting room full of patients with different illnesses, he or she does not come out and say: "Today is aspirin day; all patients will be treated equally and given aspirin to solve their ailments" (Mendler, 1993, p. 5). In the student-centered classroom, misbehavior is considered a golden opportunity to foster self-discipline and responsibility. To that end, consequences are tailored to individual students and their needs. The consequences for appropriate and inappropriate behavior should not be predetermined but, instead, considered on an individual basis. Unlike the physician who gives all patients aspirin or the teacher who doles out the same consequences to all students, one should consider the specific situation and tailor the response to fit the needs and motives of the "patient."

Student-centered classrooms are characterized by the teacher's consideration of the student's developmental tasks, needs, motives, and feelings. As middle school students struggle with the development of a personal identity and greater social independence, the student-centered environment fosters the development of an internalized moral code (Alexander, 1965/1995). Student input, discussion, and compromise are important parts of this teacher's classroom management plan so self-discipline and responsibility are encouraged. Therefore, classroom rules and policies could be the objective for a cooperative learning assignment at the beginning of the year. To foster a student-centered environment, students could brainstorm ideas, discuss, and possibly vote on how the classroom community should function within the broader school context.

Student-Centered Classroom Management Sounds Good, But...

Another important questions is this: Why are teachers reluctant to implement student-centered theories of classroom management that encourage self-discipline and responsibility? In my work with teachers, I have found six frequently expressed reasons.

1. What will others think if . . . ? Teachers often feel pressured to create a quiet and orderly classroom environment so material can be "covered" and/or because of concern about the opinions of others (e.g., administrators, colleagues, or parents). Aaronsohn (1993) quotes a student teacher who said, " [My cooperating teacher] evaluated me on how I controlled the class—on who was off task.... How am I going to make the school people happy?" (p. 26). Indeed, the piece of advice probably most often given to new teachers is, "Go in there, take control and don't smile until Christmas."

"Can't I be student centered in my instruction and teacher centered in my classroom management?" The answer is no; you are trying to mix oil with water.

On the other hand, student-centered, intrinsic classroom management strategies focus on the whole child, his or her needs and motives. A consequence for inappropriate behavior is only successful if it results in students realizing the repercussions of their actions, envisioning other behavioral choices, and making a sincere plan to use those choices in the future. The student-centered classroom may be lively with active learners but intrinsic classroom management techniques are also needed for students to become self-disciplined, independent learners.

The importance of administrative and collegial encouragement is paramount in overcoming the "what will people think" obstacle. Without such support, it is unlikely that a student-focused atmosphere will materialize. School administrators and fellow teachers must provide the moral support and professional development opportunities necessary if student-centered classroom management practices are to predominate.

2. Forget classroom management theory. If it works, use it. This is the "fly-by-the-seat-of-the-pants" approach to classroom management. Teachers have been using it for decades. Aaronsohn (1993) explains, "'the way it is' is a powerful model ... since 'it's always been that way'" (p. 7). Traditionally educators have learned how to manage classrooms from each other where the focus is on practice rather than theory. When classroom management is taught and learned in this manner we run the risk of making the same mistakes year after year without realizing why.

When a physician has a waiting room full of patients with different illnesses, he or she does not come out and say: "Today is aspirin day; all patients will be treated equally and given aspirin to solve their ailments."

Theory is important because it provides us with an explanation of observations. We may all see and experience the same things but our explanation for the underlying causes of these events can be very different. A consistent theoretical perspective lends the teacher a coherent base from which to draw. Without it, we are left with a mere "bag of tricks" and are often at a loss for alternatives when a particular discipline method inevitably fails. Dismissing theory as unimportant is analogous to walking a tightrope without a net.

The teacher's transition to a student-centered classroom environment is a gradual process that involves a great deal of introspection and cannot be accomplished overnight. It is not unusual to see practicing teachers who want to hang on to the old, comfortable classroom management techniques because they "work," even though they may not be appropriate. Many things work; this does not mean they are necessarily appropriate. Extra work given as punishment, writing "lines," and teacher sarcasm are all examples of interventions that may "work" in that they temporarily stop the behavior but are never appropriate.

No one wants to develop a pool of techniques that does not work; that would be silly. At the same time, educators have a responsibility to critically evaluate classroom management techniques. Are these techniques accomplishing what we think they are and, if so, how well? When a student misbehaves, we typically use a discipline technique, see its immediate impact, and think it is effective. Claiming it "works," we prepeatedly use it. If it really worked, we would not need it again. Even worse, at times educators embarrass and humiliate students into compliance. Strategies such as these can leave deep emotional scars and have long-term negative effects. Both teacher-centered and student-centered models of classroom management can be used effectively for short-term control of children's classroom behavior. However, it is dangerous to value discipline for its own sake "without regard for the effects of these programs on the overall learning and development of children" (Benshoff, Poidevant, & Cashwell, 1994, p. 166). It is imperative that we consider what happens later. What happens to the student's self-esteem, motivation for

learning, or dignity (Mendler, 1993)? Any interaction that diminishes these is inappropriate, even though it may stop the misbehavior.

3. My philosophy is "eclectic." I use a combination of models and classroom management techniques. Without student-centered classroom management techniques, there can be no student-centered classroom. Altering curriculum and instruction is of little use if the overall classroom atmosphere is still teacher-centered. This is a difficult change to make as it usually requires letting go of some of the teacher implemented rules and requirements. As a result, teachers have a tendency to combine conflicting models that sound good with ones that "feel" right to them as traditional teachers (e.g., Canter's (1992) *Assertive Discipline* with Glasser's (1986) *Control Theory* or Ginott's (1972) ideas with behavior modification). In theory as well as in practice, this is impossible. It cannot be done. When the teacher "combines" a teacher-centered model of classroom management with a student-centered model, at least one of them is bastardized—usually the student-centered one.

The teacher-student relationship is at the heart of student-centered classroom management. Mutual respect and trust are prerequisite to success. When teachers try to combine conflicting models, students learn that they are only listened to when they agree with the teacher. One experienced teacher explained his professional transition as follows:

> In the past, I have combined many different ideas. Many of those ideas send conflicting signals to students. I want trust in a classroom but I also want students to do what I say when I say. I want to meet the needs of students but I also want students to sit down and shut up. I want to talk to students when I want to talk to students. When I look at all that is happening in my classroom, I realize that what I do is a major part of behavior problems. I have to let go. I have to free myself from past experiences and provide an environment that meets the needs of my students instead of meeting only my needs.

Traditionally, classroom management techniques were likely drawn from no particular theoretical base at all or from theories such as behaviorism where the focus is on extrinsic control via reinforcements. Classic behavior modification does not recognize students as active participants in the learning process but instead views them as passive learners who simply respond to the environment. Behaviorally based models of classroom management such as Canter's (1992) *Assertive Discipline* or

Jones's (1987) model cannot co-exist with a student-centered curriculum.

Others present very different theories and models for classroom management that focus on the individual and advocate free will rather than determinism (e.g., Dreikurs, Grunwald, & Pepper, 1982; Glasser, 1986; Ginott, 1972; Gordon, 1974). Glasser (1986) described all behavior as a choice and believes that, "None of what we do is caused by any situation outside of ourselves" (p. 17). A good teacher is one who considers his or her role as one of a modern manager who shares power, rather than the traditional, teacher-centered manager who does not (Glasser, 1986).

Similarly, Dreikurs, Grunwald, and Pepper (1982) maintained that humans are social beings and all behavior is enacted with some purpose in mind. Specifically, humans attempt to find their place in the group in which they function such as the family or class. Again, the focus is on the individual and the origin of behaviors. In other words, both Glasser and Dreikurs addressed the underlying cause for the behaviors of both the teacher and the student. Control—and therefore, responsibility—lies within each individual. Likewise, Ginott (1972) and Gordon (1974) encouraged teachers to invite students' cooperation and encouraged the use of "I-messages," realizing that students make their own decisions and choices regarding behavior.

4. How can we teach students respect for authority if we give them too much control? I answer this question with another question. How can we teach students respect for anyone if we do not show them the respect all people deserve? Teaching respect begins by giving respect. Teacher-centered models of classroom management are focused on the teacher and, therefore, by definition disregard students' needs.

In addition, the idea that control is ours to give is an illusion. Any "control" one has over another exists only because the recipient allows it. As an individual, I can influence others, but I cannot actually control anyone except myself—and sometimes even that is difficult. Because students may be used to teacher-centered classrooms, they may not be aware that they are the ones who control their behavior. As a result, they may be giving others more power over their lives than they should. Student-centered classroom management models teach students that they—not others—are responsible for their behavior.

If students are out of control today, it is partly because their sense of personal control has been taken away from them. They have felt disregarded and disempowered by traditional, teacher-centered—sometimes

authoritarian—school systems. A sense of validation can go a long way to facilitate some of the developmental struggles associated with young adolescence.

Unfortunately, not all authority figures have children's best interests in mind. Because we have seen an increase in drug use, gang activity, reported cases of child abuse and molestation, students today should be encouraged to differentiate between those who do and do not deserve their trust and respect. It is a dangerous proposition to teach our children otherwise.

5. Some classroom management theories are not appropriate for the type of student I teach. Younger (older, "typical," exceptional) students need more teacher control. Simultaneously, other teachers say, "I should use a less controlling (student-centered) classroom management model because my students are younger (older, typical, exceptional)." Neither age nor exceptionality is the issue. If the classroom management theory is appropriate for one group, it is appropriate for another. Although this may seem to conflict with the previous "aspirin" analogy, it does not. A theory is an umbrella that encompasses a collection of techniques. In the student-focused classroom, interventions are designed with the particular students and specific situations in mind. Although the manner in which the theory is implemented in specific instances may differ, the theoretical base does not.

As an individual, I can influence others, but I cannot actually control anyone except myself—and sometimes even that is difficult.

6. I like the sound of this theory but I do not see how to actually use it. It looks good on paper but may be too idealistic. Teachers often see the merit of a student-centered classroom management theory or model and want to put it into practice but do not see how to bridge the all-important gap between theory and application. Attending workshops or university classes pertaining to classroom management and instruction is an important first step. Exposure to ideas must occur before change can happen. However, an equally important issue surrounds what happens after teachers return to their classrooms. After educators have been exposed to new theories and techniques, do they actually translate them into practice? There is a temptation to try the new techniques learned and, if they do not work the way the teacher thinks they should or do not show "results" in a short time period, discard them as not practical for the real classroom.

Old habits are hard to break. Fortunately, there are several student-centered "packages" of classroom management that provide clear guidelines for implementation and can serve as "training wheels" for the teacher until student-centered classroom management comes naturally. Based on student-focused, intrinsic theories, Albert (1989), Gathercoal (1990), and Dinkmeyer, McKay, and Dinkmeyer (1980) present student-focused models of classroom management.

To illustrate how a student-centered model might look in practice, return to the classroom scenario with Ms. Thompson, Ray, and Bill. Using a teacher-centered classroom management model, Ms. Thompson assigned the predetermined consequence to both boys. However, a more student-centered Ms. Thompson would take a holistic perspective and consider all she knows about both students before she acts. As Ray and Bill "pick on" each other, Ms. Thompson notes, "You two seem to have a problem. In a little while, I would like to discuss what I can do to help you solve it but in the meantime, I want you two to move away from each other." Bill says, "I ain't going anywhere 'cause I wasn't doing anything!" Ray moves a few seats away from Bill, seems to calm down, and is on task the rest of the class period.

Bill, on the other hand, is a much tougher customer to deal with because of the emotion his defiance is likely to evoke. Automatic detention may only serve to make him more angry—not a lasting solution to the problem. He is lashing out at the teacher and, although tempted to respond in a similar manner, Ms. Thompson explains, "Bill, solving this problem is more important than punishing you for your misbehavior. I'd like to help you do that. Fill out this card and we will visit in a few minutes." Bill is given a card with the following four questions on it (Charles, 1992, p. 121):

1. What were you doing when the problem started?
2. Was it against the rules?
3. Can we work things out so it won't happen again?
4. What could you and I do to keep it from happening?

When Ms. Thompson finds a few spare minutes, the answers are used to structure a conversation between her and Bill.

Based on Glasser's intrinsic theory of motivation, the objectives of the conference are three fold: to point out the connection between Bill's behavior and its results, to obtain a sincere commitment from Bill to do better, and to plan a strategy more likely to be successful for Bill in the future (Charles, 1992). Ms. Thompson also

explains to Bill that he is the only one who can truly control his behavior. His behavior is his choice and under his control. In pointing this out to Bill, she is not losing control; she is only acknowledging something he already has. Such acknowledgment will only lead to validation of his self-worth and decrease the likelihood that the misbehavior will re-occur.

Since Ray and Bill control their own behavior but can be influenced by others, their parents may be involved to work as partners with the teacher and their child—but this would be a last resort. This is a very different perspective than the teacher-centered approach of calling the parent and charging them with "fixing" their child. No one can be "fixed" without their cooperation and input.

Summary & Conclusion

If learning is fostered by a student-centered environment, then quality instruction requires the creation of a "learning community" within the classroom. In such a community, students feel psychologically and intellectually safe to explore, to try, to make mistakes, and explore again. Their needs are acknowledged and validated. In order for such an environment to exist, all components of it must be addressed and in place.

As knowledge is dynamic and changing, so is society. If our schools are to be effective in the next century, we must respond to this evolution. "Simple" changes in curriculum and instruction techniques are not enough to create a student-centered environment; classroom management theory and models must also follow suit in order for a truly student-focused learning environment to exist. This is especially important when dealing with young adolescents who are in the midst of myriad developmental changes. As they seek to develop a clear sense of self, they may try on a number of personas. Student-focused classroom environments facilitate the development of a healthy identity and an internalized moral structure.

Both student- and teacher-centered approaches to classroom management can create orderly environments, provide structure, and set limits. Still, no matter how expedient, teacher-centered models do not address students' emotional needs or long-term concerns regarding self-discipline, responsibility, or critical reasoning. They do not touch the students' humanness. Teacher-centered, obedience models of classroom management many appear to allow us the opportunity to cover more material and teach more facts, but at what cost? The irony is that the more control we take the more control we loose. When the focus is on controlling others, there is little freedom left for us. Comprehensive student-focused classroom communities are necessary to develop independent, self-disciplined, life-long learners. Communities such as these only come about when both the instruction and the classroom management center on the students.

References

Aaronsohn, E. (1993, April). *Supporting student-centered teaching: Reconceptualizing the roles of teacher and teacher educator.* Paper presented at the annual meeting of the American Educational Research Association, Atlanta, GA.

Albert, L. (1989). *A teacher's guide to cooperative discipline: How to manage your classroom and promote self-esteem.* Circle Pines, MN: AGS.

Alexander, W. M. (1995). The junior high school: A changing view. *Middle School Journal, 26*(3), 21-24. (Reprinted from *Readings in Curriculum*, pp. 418-425, by G. Hass & K. Wiles, Eds., 1965, Boston: Allyn and Bacon)

Benshoff, J. M., Poidevant, J. M., & Cashwell, C. S. (1994). School discipline programs: Issues and implications for school counselors. *Elementary School Guidance and Counseling, 17*, 163-169.

Canter, L. (1992). *Assertive discipline: Positive behavior management for today's classroom.* Santa Monica, CA: Lee Canter & Associates.

Charles, C.M. (1992). *Building classroom discipline* (4th ed.). White Plains, NY: Longman.

Dinkmeyer, D., McKay, G. D., & Dinkmeyer, D. (1980). *STET: Systematic training for effective teaching.* Circle Pines, MN: AGS.

Dreikurs, R., Grunwald, B. B., & Pepper, F. C. (1982). *Maintaining sanity in the classroom* (2nd ed.). New York: Harper & Row.

Gathercoal, F. (1990). *Judicious discipline.* Davis, CA: Caddo Gap Press.

Ginott, H. (1972). *Teacher and child.* New York: Avon Books.

Glasser, W. (1986). *Control theory in the classroom.* New York: Harper & Row.

Gordon, T. (1974). *Teacher effectiveness training.* New York: Wyden.

Hill, D. (1990). Order in the classroom. *Teacher, 1*(7), 70-77.

Johnson, D.W., Johnson, R.T., Holubec, E.J., Roy, P. (1988). *Circles of learning: Cooperation in the classroom.* Reston, VA: Association for Supervision and Curriculum Development.

Jones, F. (1987). *Positive classroom discipline.* New York: McGraw-Hill.

Martin, N. K., & Baldwin, B. (1994, January). *Beliefs regarding classroom management style: Differences between novice and experienced teachers.* Paper presented at the annual meeting of the Southwest Educational Research Association, San Antonio, TX.

Mendler, A. N. (1993). Discipline with dignity in the classroom: Seven principles. In F. Schultz (Ed.), *Education 94/95.* (pp. 110-112). Guilford, CT: The Dushkin Publishing Group.

Prawat, R. S. (1992). From individual differences to learning communities: Our changing focus. *Educational Leadership, 49*(7), 9-13.

Santrock, J. W. (1987). *Adolescence* (4th ed.). Dubuque, IA: Wm. C. Brown Publishers.

Wilson, J. H. (1994). An open letter to middle level educators: A parent's concern. *Middle School Journal, 26*(1), 53.

Creating a Constructivist Classroom Atmosphere

Rheta DeVries and Betty Zan

E very classroom has a sociomoral atmosphere that either hinders or promotes children's development. Consider the following transcripts from classrooms in which the teachers promote very different attitudes toward rules and create very different classroom atmospheres.

We present these two very different approaches to helping children remember rules as reflecting very different sociomoral atmospheres that influence children's development in different ways.

Rheta DeVries, Ph.D., is director of the Regents' Center for Early Developmental Education and professor of curriculum and instruction at the University of Northern Iowa. A former teacher, Rheta DeVries is the author of numerous books and articles on constructivist education and regularly conducts workshops for teachers.

Betty Zan, M.A., is a research fellow at the Regents' Center for Early Developmental Education at the University of Northern Iowa. A doctoral candidate in developmental psychology at the University of Houston, she has written and conducted numerous workshops on constructivist education with Rheta DeVries.

Classroom 1 (kindergarten):

The teacher is across the room talking to an adult who has come to the door. The children are sitting in a semicircle, waiting for her to return. Some children are engaged in skirmishes with each other—hitting, kicking, and yelling at each other—while other children are telling them to stop. One child gets up to tell the teacher. The teacher returns.

Teacher: OK, scoot back. Salisha? Leanne, would you sit down? Everybody's eyes up here. *(Raises voice.)* Eyes up here, right now!

Jamal *(to another child):* Move.

Teacher: No! You sit right where you are. Legs crossed. And if you want to pout, Jamal, that's fine, you just go ahead and pout. *(Glares at Jamal.)* Now, I am not, *at all*—Odetta, up here *(meaning, "Look at me")*—happy with the behavior you have had today. I'm not happy.

When I turn my back to talk to another teacher, you know what you're supposed to be doing, and you know what you're not supposed to be doing. Shondra, you, for one, are not supposed to be back there. *(Glares at Shondra.)* You're never allowed in that back row. You get here next to Linda. You're not supposed to be talking when I'm talking to someone else. You're not supposed to be talking when I'm talking, Shondra. You are *never* supposed to touch anyone.

We're going over these rules, again. *(Points to bulletin board with rules.)* "Number 1: Use your quiet voice." *(Uses an accusing tone.)* You all were talking out loud. You're supposed to use your quiet voice at all times. When you're at your seats, when you're answering me, when I tell you in the lunch room that you can talk to each other, you use your quiet voice.

Jamal, if you're pouting, you had better turn around and face me when you pout. Turn around, unless you want to go in where David was *(to the principal's office, to be disciplined).*

"Number 2: Raise your hand to talk." Did I see any hands in the air? Did I? No. There wasn't one hand in the air. "Number 3: Keep your hands, feet, and objects to yourself." I've seen more tapping and more hitting and more kicking going on today than I ever want to see the rest of the year. Sarah, what's the problem?

Sarah *(complaining):* Nicole keeps on scooting . . . *(unintelligible).*

Teacher: Nicole, you scoot over and you don't move. You pretend you're a statue. You don't move. You don't touch her, your elbow doesn't touch her. Scoot it over. That way everybody is happy. *(To another child),* What's the matter with you?

Jason: Can I read rule 4?

Teacher: No. I will read rule 4, thank you. "Number 4 is, Work quietly." That also means sit quietly. That means when I'm talking, we're quiet. Now, the rest of the day we're going to practice these rules *perfectly.* I don't want to hear one person talk without her hand up. I don't want to see one person touch another person. Now, get your eyes on me.

Jamal, you're through pouting now, get your eyes on me and have your legs Indian style. Now, more on our farm unit. *(The teacher continues with the lesson that had been interrupted.)*

Classroom 2 (prekindergarten):

The teacher and children have gathered in a circle for morning grouptime. The teacher has a list of rules that the children had dictated to her the week before.

Teacher: Before we get started with morning circle, do you remember what these are about? These rules?

Carter: No.

Teacher: These are rules that you guys told me to write. You told me the words, and I wrote your words down. They talk about how we want to be treated in our classroom. Do you remember that? Because some people were doing some hurting of feelings and of bodies, and we wrote these words so that people would know how to be friends in class. Do you remember what these are about?

Nan: The rules [are] about so we can make happy children, and some kids are not following them.

Teacher: That is exactly it. Let's read them again so you can remember what they are. *(Points to the written rules.)* This one is "Call them their name. Don't call them 'naughty girl' or 'naughty boy'."

Greg: That's Nan's *(meaning Nan suggested the rule).*

Teacher: So people want to be called their own name. OK.

Nan: Zina didn't call me my name.

Teacher: "Use their words. And if the words don't work, go get the teacher." If the words don't work, can you pinch and then go tell the teacher?

Children: No!

Teacher: If your words don't work, can you hit them and then go get the teacher?

Children: No!

Teacher: Donald, if your words don't work and somebody kicks you, can you kick them back?

Donald: No, I don't kick back.

Teacher: What do you do?

Hank: Go tell the teacher.

Donald: You know what happened outside today? Ben throwed sand in my mouth.

Teacher: Really? What did you do?

Donald: I told the teacher.

Teacher: Did the teacher help you to talk to Ben?

Donald: Yes.

Teacher: That's important. This one says, "Friendly hands and friendly words." So we want to use friendly hands and friendly words. Hey, you know what we could do? We could practice friendly hands.

Greg: What is that?

Teacher: You cross your hands over. *(Demonstrates.)* Now hold the hand of the person next to you. *(They all join hands in a circle.)* Now shake. Just a gentle shake. That's the biggest handshake. That's friendly hands, huh?

Aaron: Marcus doesn't have his hands crossed.

Teacher: That's OK. Now this one says, "No hitting."

Wally: I did that *(meaning he suggested that rule).*

Teacher: Do you guys remember those rules?

Children: Yeah!

Teacher: What do you think? Do you think we can remember them during outside time and during activity time?

Children: Yeah!

What do we mean by sociomoral atmosphere?

By *sociomoral atmosphere* we refer to the entire network of interpersonal relations in a classroom. This includes the child's relationship with the teacher, with other children, with academics, and with rules. In our recent book, *Moral Classrooms, Moral Children* (DeVries & Zan 1994), we describe the constructivist approach to social and moral education, exemplified by the transcript of the second teacher.

Constructivist education is a developmentally appropriate approach to early education, inspired by Piaget's theory that the child constructs knowledge, intelligence, personality, and social and moral values. This approach has been defined in terms of activities that appeal to children's interests, encourage experimentation in the physical world, and foster perspective taking and cooperation in the social world (DeVries & Kohlberg 1990). However, constructivist education is not just a set of activities. Implementing constructivist education in its most essential aspect involves more than activities, materials, and classroom organization.

The first principle of constructivist education is that a sociomoral atmosphere must be cultivated in which respect for others is continually practiced. In this sense, constructivist education is an approach to moral as well as intellectual education. Some people believe that the school should not be concerned with moral education but should focus on teaching academics or promoting intellectual development.

The problem with this view is that schools *do* influence moral development, whether they intend to or not. Teachers cannot avoid communicating moral messages as they take stands on rules and behavior and provide information about what is good and bad, right and wrong. The challenge is to relate to children and engage them in activities in which they construct their own moral convictions about relations with others.

In this article we point out the unavoidable moral aspect of schooling and describe the teacher–child relationship in a constructivist classroom. Then we specifically address how the constructivist teacher creates a cooperative sociomoral atmosphere in conducting grouptime, using cooperative alternatives to discipline, dealing with conflict, providing for activity time, engaging children in clean up, and promoting academics.

The teacher–child relationship

Constructivist classrooms are characterized by mutual, or two-way, respect between teacher and children. This philosophy contrasts with that found in most classrooms, in which respect is one-way only—children are expected to respect the teacher. Mutual respect can be discussed in terms of a particular type of teacher–child relationship that is essential to a constructivist classroom.

Our guide to the constructivist teacher–child relationship comes from Piaget's (1932) distinction between two types of morality, corresponding to two types of adult-child relationships, one that promotes children's development and one that retards it.

1. The first type of morality is a morality of obedience.

Piaget called this "heteronomous" morality, because it means following rules made by others. Therefore, the individual who is heteronomously moral follows moral rules given by others out of obedience to authority—simply ac-

cepting, conforming to, and following external rules without question.

2. The second type of morality is "autonomous."

By autonomy, Piaget did not mean simple independence in doing things for oneself without help. Rather, the individual who is autonomously moral follows moral rules of the self, rules that emerge out of internal feelings of necessity about how to treat others.

Certainly most developmentally oriented educators would not support a goal of purely obedience-based morality for children but rather want children to believe with personal conviction in such basic moral values as respect for others. Without beliefs that arise from personal conviction, children will not be likely to follow moral rules—especially in the absence of authority. Nevertheless, educators often manage children in ways that promote obedience rather than autonomy. In many schools the sociomoral atmosphere requires children to be submissive and conforming, at the expense of initiative, autonomy, and reflecting thinking.

Constructivist teachers respect children by upholding children's rights to their feelings, ideas, and opinions. These teachers use their authority selectively and refrain from using power unnecessarily. In this way they give children the opportunity to develop personalities characterized by self-confidence, respect for self and others, and active, inquiring, creative minds.

Grouptime

For many teachers, grouptime may be the most challenging time of the day. When it goes well, everyone feels as if they are a part of a caring community. Children participate in class rituals; share their feelings, discoveries, and accomplishments with each other;

and make decisions that affect their life in the classroom. The teacher must exercise subtle leadership to guide this process. Without leadership, grouptime can quickly deteriorate into chaos. With too much leadership, grouptime becomes teacher-directed instruction. The teacher must strike a delicate balance.

Rule making and decision making

A unique characteristic of constructivist education is that responsibility for decision making is shared by everyone in the class community. The teacher turns over to the children much of the power to decide how to run the class. Inviting children to make rules and decisions is one way the teacher can reduce adult authority and promote children's self-regulation.

Children also practice expressing their ideas in a clear and acceptable way so that everyone can understand and decide whether to agree. Children have the possibility of taking the perspective of the group as a whole community.

Rules are an ever-present part of every child's experience in school. Whether explicit and written or implicit and verbal, rules are a necessary part of life in a classroom. If children's experiences with rules are to contribute to their moral and social development, the teacher must consider carefully how to work with children in relation to rules.

The two examples at the beginning of this article deal with classroom rules. The first example came from videotape data collected as a part of a comparison study of sociomoral atmosphere and children's sociomoral development in classrooms reflecting different theories of learning and development (see DeVries, Haney, & Zan 1991 for a fuller description of the study). In this classroom the rules pertain mostly to behaviors, and the teacher does not discuss the reasons for these rules.

Every classroom has a sociomoral atmosphere that either hinders or promotes children's development.

The second example was taken from videotape data collected at the Human Development Laboratory School at the University of Houston. In this classroom the teacher's focus is on the reasons for the rules, based on consideration for others' feelings. In the first classroom the teacher wrote all of the rules at the beginning of the year and presented them to the children. In the second classroom the children made the rules in response to problems with hitting and name calling.

As we try to illustrate with the second example, it is not necessary to give children ready-made rules. With the teacher's careful guidance, children can suggest rules, although the rules may not take the form the teacher would have given them. Occasions for rule making may include the need for guidelines to make the classroom a happy place and the need for solving a particular classroom problem (for example, when some children think it is unfair when other children do not help with clean up).

In discussions about rules, the teacher can emphasize the reasons for the rules. When children make the rules themselves in response to problems they experience in the classroom, they are more likely to take ownership of the rules. They are also more likely to feel the necessity of following the rules and to share in the responsibility for enforcing the rules with each other.

Children's rules—in their own words and, when possible, in their own handwriting—should be available in some written form (a rule book illustrated by children, a list posted on the wall, etc.) in the classroom. Then, when break-downs do occur (and they will), the constructivist teacher can refer to the rules *that the children have made* and emphasize that the moral authority of the classroom comes not from the teacher but from the children themselves.

When teachers offer children opportunities to make certain (carefully selected) decisions about what happens in their classroom (for example, which of two books to read, where to go on an upcoming field trip, or what foods to serve at a class party), children feel a sense of community and shared responsibility for what takes place in their classroom.

Voting

When children have differing opinions about classroom decisions, teachers can introduce children to voting. Voting offers excellent opportunities for children to exchange and defend points of view, listen to others' points of view, and decide issues fairly. (The astute teacher will see in voting numerous opportunities for lessons in oral and written language and math, as well.) Through many experiences of voting, even 4-year-olds can eventually construct the idea of equality as they see each person's opinion valued and given equal weight in the decision-making process.

Voting may be conducted in various ways, but we advise against asking young children to raise hands. This method presents numerous problems. Often children tire of holding up their hands, so hands droop and the teacher must exhort children to keep their hands raised until he or she can count them all. Many children who do not fully understand the process may vote for every option, provoking other children to complain that it is not fair for some children to vote twice.

Finally, when the teacher counts the hands, children may not be sure that *their* hands were seen and counted. In short, children have difficulty following the process, and much of the value of voting is lost. The teacher should choose a voting process that children can follow and understand, such as polling children by going systematically around the circle and writing each child's name under the choice, or allowing children to cast ballots.

Social and moral dilemma discussions

Grouptime offers opportunities for the teacher to engage children's moral reasoning by conducting social and moral discussions. Everyday life in the classroom often provides material for these discussions, such as when something happens that children believe is not fair.

Children's literature also can provide material for discussing social and moral dilemmas. For example, in *Dr. DeSoto* by William Steig (1982), the mouse dentist (Dr. DeSoto) takes pity on a fox with a toothache, even though his policy is not to treat cats and other animals dangerous to mice. The fox clearly plans to eat Dr.

Perhaps the most distinguishing characteristic of a constructivist approach to academics is the teacher's respect for children's errors.

The first principle of constructivist education is that a sociomoral atmosphere must be cultivated in which respect for others is continually practiced.

DeSoto and his wife, but the clever mice trick him by using a "secret formula" (glue) on his teeth that they say will prevent further toothaches. In discussing this situation, the teacher can raise the question of whether it is OK for the mice to trick the fox by gluing his mouth closed.

When conducting moral discussions of this story with 4- and 5-year-olds, we observed that most children defend the mice. However, one child took the perspective of the fox and worried that, with his mouth glued shut, the fox would starve. One very advanced 4-year-old took the perspective of the entire town and argued that it is OK to glue the fox's teeth shut because if the fox ate the mice, there would be no one to fix teeth! These experiences of perspective taking contribute especially to children's construction of moral judgment.

Cooperative alternatives to discipline

The constructivist approach to "discipline" does not consist of controlling and punishing children in order to socialize them. Rather, we work *with* children as they gradually figure out how to relate to others in mutually satisfying ways. This does not mean that teachers are permissive and children run wild. On the contrary! Constructivist teachers are quite active in their search for alternatives to discipline that emphasize the natural and logical consequences of the misdeed and the resulting break in the social bond. When an object is broken, other people are deprived of its use and may be angry or sad. Whenever

possible, the person who broke the object is given an opportunity to make restitution by repairing or replacing the object. When someone lies, others may feel that they no longer can trust the one who told the lie. The rift in the social bond then requires repair.

It goes without saying that children must value these social bonds in order to want to repair them. This makes close, caring relationships between children, as well as between teacher and child, an integral component of the constructivist sociomoral atmosphere.

Conflict and its resolution

Conflicts are inevitable in any classroom where children interact freely. Rather than trying to prevent conflicts, the constructivist teacher uses conflicts between children in the interactive classroom as opportunities to help children recognize the perspectives of others and learn how to develop solutions that are acceptable to all parties. Teachers can support children's conflict resolution by stating the problem in terms the children can understand, helping children verbalize feelings and desires to each other and to listen to each other, and inviting children to suggest solutions. These principles are illustrated in the boxed example above.

We recognize that conflict resolution is not unique to constructivist education. However, the constructivist perspective may be unique in welcoming conflict and its resolution as important parts of the curriculum and not just

viewing conflict as a problem to be managed. Piaget's work leads to the recognition that conflict resolution is not just a skill but that it undergoes developmental change involving coming to recognize and figure out how to reconcile different points of view.

Activity time

Activity time (or center time) is perhaps the most important period of the day in a constructivist classroom. The objective of activity time in a constructivist classroom is that children will be intellectually, socially, and morally active and more and more self-regulating. For example, in a sinking-and-floating activity, the constructivist teacher asks children to reflect on why some objects sink and some objects float, encourages children to consider contradictory opinions, and supports the search for knowledge drawn from observation and experimentation.

In the course of acting on objects and discussing results, children "read" the results of an experiment and have the opportunity to accept these results even if they predicted something different. The teacher also asks children to reflect on how to take turns with an activity, helps them become conscious that many children want this privilege at the same time, and suggests that they try to figure out ways to satisfy everyone. When constructivist teachers refuse to be all-knowing or all-powerful, they open the way for children to struggle with issues themselves and not rely solely on adults for guidance.

Classroom activities long associated with the child development approach in early education include pretend play, block building and other construction activities, art, and reading and writing. Other activities unique to constructivist education are group games (Kamii & DeVries 1980)

We Can Help Children Solve Social Problems

Hector has placed a small ladder across the hole of the box serving as the beanbag target. Marcel does not want the ladder there.

Teacher: I'm sorry. I can't hear your words. Can you tell me again?

Hector: *(Inaudible.)*

Teacher: Oh, then to make it more exciting, you put that there? Is it harder to throw in there, or easier?

Hector: *(Inaudible.)*

Teacher: Well, Marcel, do you think that would be a fun way to play with it?

Marcel: *(Inaudible.)*

Teacher: Oh, Hector says it makes it fun for him.

Marcel: It makes it bad.

Teacher: Well, why don't you tell Hector about that? What would you like to tell him about it?

Marcel: I don't know.

Teacher: Well, what do you think we should do, because Hector likes to play with it that way?

Marcel: *(Shrugs shoulders, says something inaudible.)*

Teacher: Hector, Hector, you know what? *(Sits on floor be-side Hector.)* I see that we have a problem. You know what the problem is? *(Hector continues to play with ladder and does not seem to be listening.)* Hector, can you hear my words? I see that you would like to play with this. *(Takes ladder.)* Marcel says that he would *not* like to play with this. So what should you guys do?

Hector: I want him to play . . . *(inaudible).*

Teacher: Marcel, can you hear his idea? What is your idea, Hector?

Marcel: *(Inaudible.)*

Teacher: Did you hear his idea?

Marcel: Um hmm. After we put it away . . . *(inaudible).*

Teacher: Hector, can you hear Marcel's idea?

Hector: Yeah.

Teacher: Let's listen to it. What is your idea, Marcel?

Marcel: I said . . . .

Hector: *(Throws beanbag; seems not to be listening.)*

Teacher: Hector, let's listen to Marcel's idea because I heard that he had an idea. *(Teacher takes beanbag.)* Hector, we'll take just a minute out from play-ing with the beanbags so that we can hear the other idea. What was that other idea, Marcel?

Marcel: After you put it away, then you could get it out again.

Teacher: Oh, does that sound like a good idea?

Hector: No, I want to do it like this.

Teacher: Hector wants to do it right now.

Marcel: Well, he may play for two more seconds with that red thing *(points to ladder)*, and then I'll . . . *(points to hole and ladder)*. Well, maybe we could share, I don't know.

Teacher: Maybe you could share? Do you think you could share, Hector? Marcel said that would work.

Hector: *(Inaudible.)*

Teacher: OK! You know what, when you guys give it a try, let me know if you need any help, but I'll bet you can figure it out. *(Upon observing a cooperative attitude, and thinking the boys can work it out, she leaves.)*

Hector and Marcel succeed in playing together, tossing the bean-bag at the hole. Marcel accepts the ladder propped across the hole.

---

and physical-knowledge activities (Kamii & DeVries 1978/1993). In constructivist classrooms, activi-ties are planned with children's interests in mind, and children are regularly consulted about what they want to know and do. New opportunities can be intro-duced at grouptime, with sugges-tions about possible purposes children might want to pursue. "Remember that you said you wanted to learn about bubbles? I put some pipe cleaners and soapy water in the messy center so you can experiment and figure out how to make wands that form good bubbles."

The constructivist teacher al-lows children to choose freely their activities and playmates. In-tervening sparingly while allow-ing children to exercise initiative, the teacher assesses children's reasoning and engages with chil-dren to encourage them to test out their ideas. "What kind of shape do you think your square wand will make?" Some children expect the square wand to make a square bubble and spontane-ously announce this prediction.

Peer interaction is encouraged by referring children to other children for help, supporting ne-gotiation when tensions arise, and promoting friendly, shared experiences.

Clean-up time

Some early childhood teachers regard clean-up time as one of the most difficult times of the day and solve clean-up problems by doing all the cleaning in their classrooms themselves. How-ever, constructivist teachers use clean-up time to promote the de-

Constructivist teachers respect children by upholding children's rights to their feelings, ideas, and opinions. These teachers use their authority selectively and refrain from using power unnecessarily. In this way they give children the opportunity to develop personalities characterized by self-confidence, respect for self and others, and active, inquiring, creative minds.

velopment of children's feelings of responsibility. Care for the classroom is moral when it is motivated by consideration and fairness toward everyone in the classroom community.

By encouraging children to take responsibility for the care of their classroom, teachers turn the moral authority over to children, thereby promoting the development of children's self-regulation. Problems with clean up inevitably provide opportunities for teachers to lead discussions that help children reflect on the practical and moral reasons for clean up. "Did anybody notice that some children were just walking around during clean-up time? Does anybody have any ideas about what we should do about clean-up time?"

Academics

A misconception about constructivist education is that because it includes play, it does not include academics. In fact, constructivist teachers are serious-minded about children's construction of knowledge about literacy, numeracy, science, social studies, and fine arts. We want to emphasize that academic learning in a constructivist classroom occurs in the context of the sociomoral atmosphere we describe here. It is not possible to understand the constructivist approach to academics without first understanding the constructivist sociomoral atmosphere.

The problem for the constructivist teacher in approaching any academic content is to distinguish what must be *constructed* from what must be *instructed.* Piaget's distinction among three kinds of knowledge aids the teacher in making this distinction. When a topic involves knowledge of physical objects (for example, which objects float and sink), the teacher encourages children to act on objects and reflect on the reactions. When a topic is arbitrary or conventional in nature (such as that Christmas is on December 25 and that the letter *A* is called "a"), the teacher does not hesitate to inform children. Because all content involves logico-mathematical knowledge, the teacher encourages children to put things into relationships (for example, that heavy objects seem to sink and light objects seem to float—but not always), make comparisons and generalizations, and test their hypotheses.

Perhaps the most distinguishing characteristic of a constructivist approach to academics is the teacher's respect for children's errors. This respect results in children feeling free to express their honest reasoning without fear of being wrong. The constructivist teacher accepts children's incorrect or partially correct ideas as necessary to the constructive process that ends eventually (but by no means immediately) in correct knowledge. For example, when a 4- or 5-year-old insists that the dots on a die will be visible in its shadow, the teacher knows that the child will not be convinced by be-

ing told otherwise. The teacher thus refrains from correcting the child, instead creating opportunities for the child to experiment and find out by observing the die's shadow.

Similarly, the teacher may observe a child making a logical error when counting spaces in a board game. That is, the child rolls the die and counts as "1" the space occupied (on which he or she landed on the previous turn) rather than moving to the next space. Recognizing that the child is convinced of the correctness of this strategy (due to not having separated ordinality from cardinality, to not having integrated zero in the ordinal sequence, and to not linking the turns of play), the teacher refrains from correcting the child's counting. Rather, the constructivist teacher provides a die with only ones and twos, so that the child will count "1" and go nowhere! Feelings of contradiction will lead children eventually to correct their own logic.

Creating active situations

The constructivist integration of academics involves the creation of active situations in which children pursue their own interests and purposes. As Dewey ([1913] 1975) pointed out almost a century ago (and as probably most people can attest to in their everyday lives), people always invest more time, energy, and attention in what interests them. When a child's purpose is to play a certain path game, interest in reading rules, counting, and writing words and numerals is spontaneous. When children want to cook, they are inspired to try to figure out what the recipe says.

Young children are more mentally active when they are physically active in trying to figure out how to do something. Physical-knowledge activities involving the movement of objects (elementary physics) and changes in objects (elementary chemistry) inspire children to construct knowledge about the physical world. Using a ball on a string (as a pendulum bob) to knock down a target inspires children to construct knowledge about spatial and causal relations. "Do you think you can knock over the target if I put it here (out of the range of the pendulum)?" Experimenting with using different amounts of flour, water, and oil to make playdough inspires children to construct knowledge about the influence of each substance on the playdough's consistency: "What can you add to make your playdough less gooey?"

Fostering social interaction

The constructivist approach to academics also involves fostering social interaction around specific academic content. Social life is filled with communication needs. Writing and reading numerals, counting, and calculating are necessary in a variety of activities. Children can write the names and prices of items on a menu for a pretend restaurant, add numbers when keeping score in group games such as bowling, and learn to write others' names to address valentines.

Emphasizing self-regulation and reflection

The constructivist approach to academics emphasizes self-regulation and reflection that leads to understanding, self-confidence, and an attitude of questioning

The only way for us to live together successfully as a human species is to figure out how to deal with diversities of all sorts.

and critical evaluation. It motivates children to think about causes, implications, and explanations of physical and logical phenomena as well as social and moral phenomena. We therefore see the development of morality and intelligence as interconnected and argue that life in a moral classroom also promotes children's intellectual development. We caution, however, that it is possible to establish a cooperative sociomoral atmosphere with inadequate attention to academics. The best teaching of academics is laid on a foundation of understanding how children construct knowledge.

Conclusion

The practical principles of teaching discussed in this article rest on a foundation laid by John Dewey and other pioneers in progressive education. While some of our sociomoral activities are not entirely new, constructivist education provides new rationales and practices rooted in research-based theory. With this theoretical framework, old activities are enriched and new possibilities emerge.

The kind of sociomoral attitudes that we discuss can develop very early. Children's evident capacities suggest that educators should build on these attitudes at least from age 4. Our research demonstrates that children from classrooms characterized by a constructivist sociomoral atmosphere are more advanced in their sociomoral development, resolve more of their conflicts, and enjoy more friendly interactions with their peers than do children from more authoritarian classroom atmospheres (DeVries, Haney, & Zan 1991; DeVries,

Reese-Learned, & Morgan 1991).

The only way for us to live together successfully as a human species is to figure out how to deal with diversities of all sorts. If young children learn to do this in their small classroom group, perhaps they will be able to expand it to larger groups in society. By giving children at an early age opportunities to develop sociomoral competence, we may avoid their development into adults who know only how to mindlessly submit to or rebel against the rules of people in power. By fostering early sociomoral development of children, we may put them on the path to becoming the kinds of adults who can take up the responsibilities of democratic citizenship and work toward equity in human relationships.

References

DeVries, R., J. Haney, & B. Zan. 1991. Sociomoral atmosphere in direct-instruction, eclectic, and constructivist kindergartens: A study of teachers' enacted interpersonal understanding. *Early Childhood Research Quarterly* 6: 449–71.

DeVries, R., & L. Kohlberg. 1987/1990. *Constructivist early education: Overview and comparison with other programs.* White Plains, NY: Longman, 1987. Reprint, Washington, DC: NAEYC.

DeVries, R., H. Reese-Learned, & P. Morgan. 1991. Sociomoral development in direct-instruction, eclectic, and constructivist kindergartens: A study of children's enacted interpersonal understanding. *Early Childhood Research Quarterly* 6: 473–517.

DeVries, R., & B. Zan. 1994. *Moral classrooms, moral children: Creating a constructivist atmosphere in early education.* New York: Teachers College Press.

Dewey, J. [1913] 1975. *Interest and effort in education.* Edwardsville, IL: Southern Illinois University Press.

Kamii, C., & R. DeVries. 1978/1993. *Physical knowledge in preschool education: Implications of Piaget's theory.* New York: Teachers College Press.

Kamii, C., & R. DeVries. 1980. *Group games in early education: Implications of Piaget's theory.* Washington, DC: NAEYC.

Piaget, J. [1932] 1965. *Moral judgment of the child.* London: Free Press.

Steig, W. 1982. *Doctor DeSoto.* New York: Farrar, Straw & Giroux, A Sunburst Book.

Why Violence Prevention Programs Don't Work—and What Does

David W. Johnson and Roger T. Johnson

David W. Johnson is Professor of Educational Psychology, and **Roger T. Johnson** is Professor of Curriculum and Instruction, University of Minnesota, Cooperative Learning Center, 202 Pattee Hall, 150 Pillsbury Drive, S.E., Minneapolis, MN 55455-0298.

The best school programs in conflict resolution tend to follow six key principles.

"Joshua was chasing Octavia. He pushed her down, and she kicked him."

"Danielle is going to beat up Amber after school. They were spitting in each other's faces and calling each other names."

"Tom shoved Cameron up against the lockers and threatened him. Cameron said he's going to bring a knife to school tomorrow to get even."

Schools are filled with conflicts. The frequency of clashes among students and the increasing severity of the ensuing violence make managing such incidents very costly in terms of time lost to instructional, administrative, and learning efforts.

If schools are to be orderly and peaceful places in which high-quality education can take place, students must learn to manage conflicts constructively without physical or verbal violence. The following six principles may be helpful to schools that are trying to accomplish this goal.

1. Go beyond violence prevention to conflict resolution training.

To curb violence among students, many schools have implemented violence prevention programs. Some schools focus on anger management and general social skills. Others invite guest speakers (for example, police officers) to school, employ metal detectors, or ask police to patrol the school. Still others show videotapes of violent encounters and structure discussions around how fights start and alternative ways to manage aggression.

The proliferation of such programs raises the question: Do they work? In a review of three popular violence prevention curriculums—Violence Prevention Curriculum for Adolescents, Washington [D.C.] Community Violence Prevention Program, and Positive Adolescent Choices Training—Webster (1993) found no evidence that they produce long-term changes in violent behavior or decrease the risk of victimization. The main function of such programs, Webster argues, is to provide political cover for school officials and politicians.

In their survey of 51 violence prevention programs, Wilson-Brewer and colleagues (1991) found that fewer than half of the programs even claimed to have reduced levels of violence, and few had any data to back up their claims. Tolan and Guerra (in press), after reviewing the existing research on violence prevention, concluded that (1) many schools are engaged in well-intentioned efforts without any evidence that the programs will work, and (2) some programs actually influence relatively nonviolent students to be more violence-prone.

Why don't violence prevention programs work? Here are a few possible reasons.

1. Many programs are poorly targeted. First, they lump together a broad range of violent behaviors and people, ignoring the fact that different people turn to violence for different reasons. Second, few programs focus on the relatively small group of children and adolescents who commit most of the acts of serious violence. In our studies of a peer mediation program in inner-city schools, for example, we found that less than 5 percent of students accounted for more than one-third of the violent incidents in the school (Johnson and Johnson 1994a).

2. The programs provide materials

Few violence prevention programs focus on the relatively small group of children and adolescents who commit most of the acts of serious violence.

but don't focus on program implementation. Many programs assume that (a) a few hours of an educational intervention can "fix" students who engage in violent behavior, (b) a few hours of training can prepare teachers to conduct the program, and (c) no follow-up is needed to maintain the quality of the program. In other words, the programs ignore the literature on successful innovation within schools (Johnson and Johnson, in press) and, therefore, are often poorly implemented.

3. Proponents of violence prevention programs confuse methods that work in neighborhoods with those that work in schools. Conflicts on the street often involve macho posturing, competition for status, access to drugs, significant amounts of money, and individuals who have short-term interactions with one another. The school, on the other hand, is a cooperative setting in which conflicts involve working together, sharing resources, making decisions, and solving problems among students who are in long-term relationships. Different conflict resolution procedures are required in each setting. Street tactics should not be brought into the school, and it is naive and dangerous to assume that school tactics should be used on the street.

4. Many programs are unrealistic about the strength of the social forces that impel children toward violence. To change the social norms controlling street behavior requires a broad-based effort that involves families, neighbors, the mass media, employers, health care officials, schools, and government. Schools do not have the resources to guarantee health care, housing, food, parental love, and hope for the future for each child. Educators cannot eliminate the availability of guns (especially semi-automatic handguns), change the economics of the

drug trade (and other types of crime), or even reduce the dangers of walking to and from school. Because there is a limit to what schools can do in reducing violence among children and adolescents outside of school, violence prevention programs should be realistic and not promise too much.

Initiating a violence prevention program will not reduce the frequency of violence in schools and in society as a whole. While violence does need to be prevented, programs that focus exclusively on violence prevention may generally be ineffective. Schools must go beyond violence prevention to conflict resolution training.

2. Don't attempt to eliminate all conflicts.

The elimination of violence does not mean the elimination of conflict. Some conflicts can have positive outcomes (Johnson and Johnson 1991, 1992). They can increase achievement, motivation to learn, higher-level reasoning, long-term retention, healthy social and cognitive development, and the fun students have in school. Conflicts can also enrich relationships, clarify personal identity, increase ego strength, promote resilience in the face of adversity, and clarify how one needs to change.

It is not the presence of conflict that is to be feared but, rather, its destructive management. Attempts to deny, suppress, repress, and ignore conflicts may, in fact, be a major contributor to the occurrence of violence in schools. Given the many positive outcomes of conflict, schools need to teach students how to manage conflicts constructively.

3. Create a cooperative context.

The best conflict resolution programs seek to do more than change individual students. Instead, they try to transform

the total school environment into a learning community in which students live by a credo of nonviolence.

Two contexts for conflict are possible: cooperative and competitive (Deutsch 1973, Johnson and Johnson 1989). In a competitive context, individuals strive to win while ensuring their opponents lose. Those few who perform the best receive the rewards. In this context, competitors often misperceive one another's positions and motivations, avoid communicating with one another, are suspicious of one another, and see the situation from only their own perspective.

In a cooperative context, conflicts tend to be resolved constructively. Students have clear perceptions of one another's positions and motivation, communicate accurately and completely, trust one another, and define conflicts as mutual problems to be solved. Cooperators typically have a long-term time orientation and focus their energies both on achieving mutual goals and on maintaining good working relationships with others.

Students cannot learn to manage conflicts constructively when their school experience is competitive and individualistic. In such a context, constructive conflict resolution procedures are often ineffective and, in fact, may make the students who use them vulnerable to exploitation. Instead, schools should seek to create a cooperative context for conflict management, which is easier to do when the majority of learning situations are cooperative (Johnson and Johnson 1989, Johnson et al. 1993).

4. Decrease in-school risk factors.

Three factors place children and adolescents at risk for violent behavior. The first is academic failure. One way that schools can promote higher achievement and greater competence in using higher-level reasoning by students is to emphasize cooperative learning more than competitive or individualistic learning (Johnson and Johnson 1989). The more students know and the greater their ability to analyze situations and think through decisions, the better able they will be to envision the consequences of their actions, respect differing viewpoints, conceive of a variety of strategies for dealing with conflict, and engage in creative problem solving.

A second factor that puts children and adolescents at risk for violent and destructive behavior is alienation from schoolmates. In order to create an infrastructure of personal and academic support, schools need to encourage long-term caring and committed relationships. Two procedures for doing so are (1) using cooperative base groups that last for a number of years (Johnson et al. 1992, 1993); and (2) assigning teams of teachers to follow cohorts of students through several grades, instead of changing teachers every year (Johnson and Johnson 1994a).

Third, children and adolescents who have high levels of psychological pathology are more at risk for violent and destructive behavior than students who are psychologically well adjusted. David Hamburg, the president of Carnegie Corporation, states that reversing the trend of violence among the young depends on teaching children how to share, work cooperatively with others, and help others. The more children and adolescents work in cooperative learning groups, the greater will be their psychological health, self-esteem, social competencies, and resilience in the face of adversity and stress (Johnson and Johnson 1989).

In summary, schools must not overlook the in-school factors that place students at risk for engaging in violence and other destructive ways of managing conflicts. Anything that allows students to fail, remain apart from classmates, and be socially inept and have low self-esteem, increases the probability that students will use destructive conflict strategies.

5. Use academic controversy to increase learning.

To show students that conflicts can have positive results, schools should make academic controversies an inherent and daily part of learning

situations. It is unclear whether cognitive, social, and moral development can take place in the absence of conflict. Academic *controversy* exists when one student's ideas, information, conclusions, theories, and opinions are incompatible with those of another, and the two seek to reach an agreement (Johnson and Johnson 1992).

For example, teachers can assign students to cooperative learning groups of four, divided into two pairs. One pair is assigned a pro position on an issue and the other pair, the con position. Each pair prepares a persuasive presentation (consisting of a thesis statement, rationale, and conclusion) to convince the other side of the position's validity. The two pairs then meet, and each side presents the best case possible for its position. Afterward, during an open discussion, students refute the opposing position (by discrediting the information and/or the inductive and deductive logic used) while rebutting criticisms of their position. At the same time, they try to persuade the other pair to change their minds. Next, a perspective reversal occurs in which each pair presents the best case possible for the opposing position. Finally, after trying to view the issue from both perspectives simultaneously, the students drop all advocacy and come to a consensus about their "best reasoned judgment" based on a synthesis of the two positions.

Over the past 25 years, we have conducted numerous studies on academic controversy. Similar to cooperative learning, academic controversy results in increased student achievement, critical thinking, higher-level reasoning, intrinsic motivation to learn, perspective-taking, and a number of other important educational outcomes (Johnson and Johnson 1979, 1992).

6. Teach all students how to resolve conflicts constructively.

Most of the diverse conflict resolution programs present in schools are either cadre or total student body programs. In the *cadre approach,* a small number of students are trained to serve as peer mediators for the entire school. While

this approach is relatively easy and inexpensive to implement, having a few peer mediators with limited training is not likely to decrease the severity and frequency of conflicts in a school.

In the *total student body approach,* every student learns how to manage conflicts constructively by negotiating agreements and mediating their schoolmates' conflicts. The responsibility for peer mediation is rotated throughout the entire student body (or class) so that every student gains experience as a mediator. A disadvantage of this approach is the time and commitment required by the faculty. The more students who are trained how to negotiate and mediate, however, the greater the number of conflicts that will be managed constructively in the school.

An example of the total student body approach is the *Teaching Students to Be Peacemakers Program,* which we have implemented in several countries (Johnson and Johnson 1991). We conceive the training as a 12-year spiral curriculum in which each year students learn increasingly sophisticated negotiation and mediation procedures.

The negotiation procedure consists of six steps. Students in conflict: (1) define what they want, (2) describe their feelings, and (3) explain the reasons underlying those wants and feelings. Then the students: (4) reverse perspectives in order to view the conflict from both sides, (5) generate at least three optional agreements with maximum benefits for both parties, and (6) agree on the wisest course of action.

The mediation procedure consists of four steps: (1) stop the hostilities, (2) ensure that the disputants are committed to the mediation process, (3) facilitate negotiations between the disputants, and (4) formalize the agreement.

Once the students complete negotiation and mediation training, the school (or teacher) implements the Peacemakers Program by selecting two students as mediators each day. It is the actual experience of being a mediator that best teaches students how to negotiate and resolve conflicts. In addition to using the procedures, students receive additional training twice a week for the rest of the school year to expand and refine their skills.

Until recently, very little research validating the effectiveness of conflict resolution training programs in schools has existed. Over the past five years, we have conducted seven studies in six different schools in both suburban and urban settings and in two different countries (Johnson and Johnson 1994b). Students in 1st through 9th grades were involved in the studies. We found that before training, most students had daily conflicts, used destructive strategies that tended to escalate the conflict, referred the majority of their conflicts to the teacher, and did not know how to negotiate. After training, students could apply the negotiation and mediation procedures to actual conflict situations, as well as transfer them to nonclassroom and nonschool settings, such as the playground, the lunchroom, and at home. Further, they maintained their knowledge and skills throughout the school year.

Given the choice of using a "win-lose" or a "problem-solving" negotiation strategy, virtually all untrained students used the former, while trained students primarily chose the problem-solving approach. In addition, students who were taught the negotiation procedure while studying a novel during an English literature unit not only learned how to negotiate, but performed higher on an achievement test on the novel than did students in a control group, who spent their entire time studying the novel. This study represents a model of how to integrate conflict resolution training into an academic class.

After their training, students generally managed their conflicts without involving adults. The frequency of student-student conflicts teachers had to manage dropped 80 percent, and the number of conflicts referred to the principal was reduced by 95 percent. Such a dramatic reduction of referrals of conflicts to adults changed the school discipline program from arbitrating conflicts to maintaining and supporting the peer mediation process.

Knowing how to negotiate agreements and mediate schoolmates' conflicts empowers students to regulate their own behavior. Self-regulation is a central and significant hallmark of cognitive and social development. Using competencies in resolving conflicts constructively also increases a child's ability to build and maintain high-quality relationships with peers and to cope with stress and adversity.

In short, training only a small cadre of students to manage conflicts constructively and to be peer mediators will not change the way other students manage their conflicts. For this reason, schools must teach all students skills in negotiation and mediation.

Making the Future a Better Place
Every student needs to learn how to manage conflicts constructively. Without training, many students may never learn how to do so. Teaching every student how to negotiate and mediate will ensure that future generations are prepared to manage conflicts constructively in career, family, community, national, and international settings.

There is no reason to expect, however, that the process will be easy or quick. It took 30 years to reduce smoking in America. It took 20 years to reduce drunk driving. It may take even longer to ensure that children and adolescents can manage conflicts constructively. The more years that students spend learning and practicing the skills of peer mediation and conflict resolution, the more likely they will be to actually use those skills both in the classroom and beyond the school door.

References
Deutsch, M. (1973). *The Resolution of Conflict*. New Haven, Conn.: Yale University Press.

Johnson, D. W., and R. Johnson. (1979). "Conflict in the Classroom: Controversy and Learning." *Review of Educational Research* 49, 1: 51–61.

Johnson, D. W., and R. Johnson. (1989). *Cooperation and Competition: Theory and Research*. Edina, Minn.: Interaction Book Company.

Johnson, D. W., and R. Johnson. (1991). *Teaching Students to Be Peacemakers*. Edina, Minn.: Interaction Book Company.

Johnson, D. W., and R. Johnson. (1992). *Creative Controversy: Intellectual Challenge in the Classroom*. Edina, Minn.: Interaction Book Company.

Johnson, D. W., and R. Johnson. (1994a). *Leading the Cooperative School*. 2nd ed. Edina, Minn.: Interaction Book Company.

Johnson, D. W., and R. Johnson. (1994b). *Teaching Students to Be Peacemakers: Results of Five Years of Research*. Minneapolis: University of Minnesota, Cooperative Learning Center.

Johnson, D. W., and R. Johnson. (In press). "Implementing Cooperative Learning: Training Sessions, Transfer to the Classroom, and Maintaining Long-Term Use." In *Staff Development for Cooperative Learning: Issues and Approaches*, edited by N. Davidson, C. Brody, and C. Cooper. New York: Teachers College Press.

Johnson, D. W., R. Johnson, and E. Holubec. (1992). *Advanced Cooperative Learning*. 2nd ed. Edina, Minn.: Interaction Book Company.

Johnson, D. W., R. Johnson, and E. Holubec. (1993). *Cooperation in the Classroom*. 6th ed. Edina, Minn.: Interaction Book Company.

Tolan, P., and N. Guerra. (In press). *What Works in Reducing Adolescent Violence: An Empirical Review of the Field*. Denver: Center for the Study of Prevention of Violence, University of Colorado.

Webster, D. (1993). "The Unconvincing Case for School-Based Conflict Resolution Programs for Adolescents." *Health Affairs* 12, 4: 126–140.

Wilson-Brewer, R., S. Cohen, L. O'Donnell, and I. Goodman. (1991). "Violence Prevention for Young Adolescents: A Survey of the State of the Art." Eric Clearinghouse, ED356442, 800-443-3742.

Assessment

In which reading group does Jon belong? How do I construct tests? How do I know when my students have mastered the course objectives? How can I explain test results to Mary's parents? Teachers answer these questions, and many more, by applying principles of assessment. Assessment refers to procedures for measuring and recording student performance and constructing grades that communicate to other levels of proficiency or relative standing. Assessment principles constitute a set of concepts that are integral to the teaching-learning process. Indeed, a significant amount of teacher time is spent in assessment activities, and with more accountability has come a greater emphasis on assessment.

Assessment provides a foundation for making sound evaluative judgments about students' learning and achievement. Teachers need to use fair and unbiased criteria in order to assess student learning objectively and accurately and to make appropriate decisions about student placement. For example, in assigning Jon to a reading group, the teacher will use his test scores as an indication of his skill level. Are the inferences from the test results valid for the school's reading program? Are his test scores consistent over several months or years? Are they consistent with his performance in class? The teacher should ask and then answer these questions so that he or she can make intelligent decisions about Jon. On the other hand, will knowledge of the test scores affect the teacher's perception of classroom performance and create a self-fulfilling prophecy? Teachers also evaluate students in order to assign grades, and the challenge is to balance "objective" test scores with more subjective, informally gathered information. Both kinds of evaluative information are necessary, but both can be inaccurate and are frequently misused.

The first article in this unit examines assessment principles in the context of large-scale and classroom assessment of young children. Further discussion of standardized

testing is presented in "Taking Aim at Testing." The next two authors discuss performance-based, "authentic" assessment. This form of assessment has great potential to integrate measurement procedures with instructional methods more effectively and to focus student learning on the application of thinking and problem-solving skills in real-life contexts.

In the last article, teachers' grading practices and procedures that benefit student learning and lead to accurate conclusions and reporting are reviewed.

Looking Ahead: Challenge Questions

What are some important principles for assessing young children? How is the purpose of the assessment related to these principles?

Many educators believe that schools should identify the brightest, most capable students. What are the assessment implications of this philosophy? How would low-achieving students be affected?

What are both the advantages and disadvantages of alternative assessments that may be labeled "authentic" or "performance-based"?

What principles of assessment should teachers adopt for their own classroom testing? Is it necessary or feasible to develop a table of specifications for each test? How do we know if the tests that teachers make are reliable and if valid inferences are drawn from the results?

How can teachers grade thinking skills such as analysis, application, and reasoning? How should objectives for student learning and grading be integrated? What are some grading practices to avoid? Why?

What are appropriate teacher uses of standardized test scores? What common mistakes do teachers make when interpreting these scores?

The Challenges of Assessing Young Children Appropriately

In the past decade, testing of 4-, 5-, and 6-year-olds has been excessive and inappropriate. Given this history of misuse, Ms. Shepard maintains, the burden of proof must rest with assessment advocates to demonstrate the usefulness of assessment and to ensure that abuses will not recur.

Lorrie A. Shepard

LORRIE A. SHEPARD is a professor of education at the University of Colorado, Boulder. She is past president of the National Council on Measurement in Education, past vice president of the American Educational Research Association, and a member of the National Academy of Education. She wishes to thank Sharon Lynn Kagan, M. Elizabeth Graue, and Scott F. Marion for their thoughtful suggestions on drafts of this article.

PROPOSALS to "assess" young children are likely to be met with outrage or enthusiasm, depending on one's prior experience and one's image of the testing involved. Will an inappropriate paper-and-pencil test be used to keep some 5-year-olds out of school? Or will the assessment, implemented as an ordinary part of good instruction, help children learn? A governor advocating a test for every preschooler in the nation may have in mind the charts depicting normal growth in the pediatrician's office. Why shouldn't parents have access to similar measures to monitor their child's cognitive and academic progress? Middle-class parents, sanguine about the use of test scores to make college-selection decisions, may be eager to have similar tests determine their child's entrance into preschool or kindergarten. Early childhood experts, however, are more likely to respond with alarm because they are more familiar with the complexities of defining and measuring

development and learning in young children and because they are more aware of the widespread abuses of readiness testing that occurred in the 1980s.

Given a history of misuse, it is impossible to make positive recommendations about how assessments could be used to monitor the progress of individual children or to evaluate the quality of educational programs without offering assurances that the abuses will not recur. In what follows, I summarize the negative history of standardized testing of young children in order to highlight the transformation needed in both the substance and purposes of early childhood assessment. Then I explain from a measurement perspective how the features of an assessment must be tailored to match the purpose of the assessment. Finally, I describe differences in what assessments might look like when they are used for purposes of screening for handicapping conditions, supporting instruction, or monitoring state and national trends.

Note that I use the term *test* when referring to traditional, standardized developmental and pre-academic measures and the term *assessment* when referring to more developmentally appropriate procedures for observing and evaluating young children. This is a semantic trick that plays on the different connotations of the two terms. Technically, they mean the same thing. Tests, as defined by the *Stan-*

dards for Educational and Psychological Testing, have always included systematic observations of behavior, but our experience is with tests as more formal, one-right-answer instruments used to rank and sort individuals. As we shall see, assessments might be standardized, involve paper-and-pencil responses, and so on, but in contrast to traditional testing, "assessment" implies a substantive focus on student learning for the purpose of effective intervention. While *test* and *assessment* cannot be reliably distinguished technically, the difference between these two terms as they have grown up in common parlance is of symbolic importance. Using the term *assessment* presents an opportunity to step away from past practices and ask why we should try to measure what young children know and can do. If there are legitimate purposes for gathering such data, then we can seek the appropriate content and form of assessment to align with those purposes.

Negative History of Testing Young Children

In order to understand the negative history of the standardized testing of young children in the past decade, we need to understand some larger shifts in curriculum and teaching practices. The distortion of the curriculum of the early grades during the 1980s is now a familiar and well-documented story. Indeed, negative effects persist in many school districts today.

Although rarely the result of conscious policy decisions, a variety of indirect pressures — such as older kindergartners, extensive preschooling for children from affluent families, parental demands for the teaching of reading in kindergarten, and accountability testing in higher grades — produced a skill-driven kindergarten curriculum. Because what once were first-grade expectations were shoved down to kindergarten, these shifts in practice were referred to as the "escalation of curriculum" or "academic trickle-down." The result of these changes was an aversive learning environment inconsistent with the learning needs of young children. Developmentally inappropriate instructional practices, characterized by long periods of seatwork, high levels of stress, and a plethora of fill-in-the-blank worksheets, placed many children at risk by setting standards for attention span, social maturity, and academic productivity that could not be met by many normal 5-year-olds.

Teachers and school administrators responded to the problem of a kindergarten environment that was increasingly hostile to young children with several ill-considered policies: raising the entrance age for school, instituting readiness screening to hold some children out of school for a year, increasing retentions in kindergarten, and creating two-year programs with an extra grade either before or after kindergarten. These policies and practices had a benign intent: to protect children from stress and school failure. However, they were ill-considered because they were implemented without contemplating the possibility of negative side effects and without awareness that retaining some children and excluding others only exacerbated the problems by creating an older and older population of kindergartners.[1] The more reasonable corrective for a skill-driven curriculum at earlier and earlier ages would have been curriculum reform of the kind exemplified by the recommendations for developmentally appropriate practices issued by the National Association for the Education of Young Children (NAEYC), the nation's largest professional association of early childhood educators.[2]

The first response of many schools, however, was not to fix the problem of inappropriate curriculum but to exclude those children who could not keep up or who might be harmed. Readiness testing was the chief means of implementing policies aimed at removing young children from inappropriate instructional programs. Thus the use of readiness testing increased dramatically during the 1980s and continues today in many school districts.[3]

Two different kinds of tests are used: developmental screening measures, originally intended as the first step in the evaluation of children for potential handicaps; and pre-academic skills tests, intended for use in planning classroom instruction.[4] The technical and conceptual problems with these tests are numerous.[5] Tests are being used for purposes for which they were never designed or validated. Waiting a year or being placed in a two-year program represents a dramatic disruption in a child's life, yet not one of the existing readiness measures has sufficient reliability or predictive validity to warrant making such decisions.

Developmental and pre-academic skills tests are based on outmoded theories of aptitude and learning that originated in the 1930s. The excessive use of these tests and the negative consequences of being judged unready focused a spotlight on the tests' substantive inadequacies. The widely used Gesell Test is made up of items from old I.Q. tests and is indistinguishable statistically from a measure of I.Q.; the same is true for developmental measures that are really short-form I.Q. tests. Assigning children to different instructional opportunities on the basis of such tests carries forward nativist assumptions popular in the 1930s and

Illustration by Kay Salem

1940s. At that time, it was believed that I.Q. tests could accurately measure innate ability, unconfounded by prior learning experiences. Because these measured "capacities" were thought to be fixed and unalterable, those who scored poorly were given low-level training consistent with their supposedly limited potential. Tests of academic content might have the promise of being more instructionally relevant than disguised I.Q. tests, but, as Anne Stallman and David Pearson have shown, the decomposed and decontextualized prereading skills measured by traditional readiness tests are not compatible with current research on early literacy.[6]

Readiness testing also raises serious equity concerns. Because all the readiness measures in use are influenced by past opportunity to learn, a disproportionate number of poor and minority children are identified as unready and are excluded from school when they most need it. Thus children without preschool experience and without extensive literacy experiences at home are sent back to the very environments that caused them to score poorly on readiness measures in the first place. Or, if poor and minority children who do not pass the readiness tests are admitted to the school but made to spend an extra year in kindergarten, they suffer disproportionately the stigma and negative effects of retention.

The last straw in this negative account of testing young children is the evidence that fallible tests are often followed by ineffective programs. A review of controlled studies has shown no academic benefits from retention in kindergarten or from extra-year programs, whether developmental kindergartens or transitional first grades. When extra-year children finally get to first grade, they do not do better on average than equally "unready" children who go directly on to first grade.[7] However, a majority of children placed in these extra-year programs do experience some short- or long-term trauma, as reported by their parents.[8] Contrary to popular belief that kindergarten children are "too young to notice" retention, most of them know that they are not making "normal" progress, and many continue to make reference to the decision years later. "If I hadn't spent an extra year in kindergarten, I would be in __ grade now." In the face of such evidence, there is little wonder that many early childhood educators ask why we test young children at all.

Principles for Assessment And Testing

The NAEYC and the National Association of Early Childhood Specialists in State Departments of Education have played key roles in informing educators about the harm of developmentally inappropriate instructional practices and the misuse of tests. In 1991 NAEYC published "Guidelines for Appropriate Curriculum Content and Assessment in Programs Serving Children Ages 3 Through 8."[9] Although the detailed recommendations are too numerous to be repeated here, a guiding principle is that *assessments should bring about benefits for children, or data should not be collected at all.* Specifically, assessments "should not be used to recommend that children stay out of a program, be retained in grade, or be assigned to a segregated group based on ability or developmental maturity."[10] Instead, NAEYC acknowledges three legitimate purposes for assessment: 1) to plan instruction and communicate with parents, 2) to identify children with special needs, and 3) to evaluate programs.

Although NAEYC used *assessment* in its "Guidelines," as I do, to avoid associations with inappropriate uses of tests, both the general principle and the specific guidelines are equally applicable to formal testing. In other words, tests should not be used if they do not bring about benefits for children. In what follows I summarize some additional principles that can ensure that assessments (and tests) are beneficial and not harmful. Then, in later sections, I consider each of NAEYC's recommended uses for assessment, including national, state, and local needs for program evaluation and accountability data.

I propose a second guiding principle for assessment that is consistent with the NAEYC perspective. *The content of assessments should reflect and model progress toward important learning goals.* Conceptions of what is important to learn should take into account both physical and social/emotional development as well as cognitive learning. For most assessment purposes in the cognitive domain, content should be congruent with subject matter in emergent literacy and numeracy. In the past, developmental measures were made as "curriculum free" or "culture free" as possible in an effort to tap biology and avoid the confounding effects of past opportunity to learn. Of course, this was an impossible task because a child's ability to "draw a triangle"

or "point to the ball on top of the table" depends on prior experiences as well as on biological readiness. However, if the purpose of assessment is no longer to sort students into programs on the basis of a one-time measure of ability, then it is possible to have assessment content mirror what we want children to learn.

A third guiding principle can be inferred from several of the NAEYC guidelines. *The methods of assessment must be appropriate to the development and experiences of young children.* This means that — along with written products — observation, oral readings, and interviews should be used for purposes of assessment. Even for large-scale purposes, assessment should not be an artificial and decontextualized event; instead, the demands of data collection should be consistent with children's prior experiences in classrooms and at home. Assessment practices should recognize the diversity of learners and must be in accord with children's language development — both in English and in the native languages of those whose home language is not English.

A fourth guiding principle can be drawn from the psychometric literature on test validity. *Assessments should be tailored to a specific purpose.* Although not stated explicitly in the NAEYC document, this principle is implied by the recommendation of three sets of guidelines for three separate assessment purposes.

Matching the Why and How Of Assessment

The reason for any assessment — i.e., how the assessment information will be used — affects the substance and form of

> *The intended use of an assessment will determine the need for normative information or other means to support the interpretation of results.*

the assessment in several ways. First, the degree of technical accuracy required depends on use. For example, the identification of children for special education has critical implications for individuals. Failure to be identified could mean the denial of needed services, but being identified as in need of special services may also mean removal from normal classrooms (at least part of the time) and a potentially stigmatizing label. A great deal is at stake in such assessment, so the multi-faceted evaluation employed must have a high degree of reliability and validity. Ordinary classroom assessments also affect individual children, but the consequences of these decisions are not nearly so great. An inaccurate assessment on a given day may lead a teacher to make a poor grouping or instructional decision, but such an error can be corrected as more information becomes available about what an individual child "really knows."

Group assessment refers to uses, such as program evaluation or school accountability, in which the focus is on group performance rather than on individual scores. Although group assessments may need to meet very high standards for technical accuracy, because of the high stakes associated with the results, the individual scores that contribute to the group information do not have to be so reliable and do not have to be directly comparable, so long as individual results are not reported. When only group results are desired, it is possible to use the technical advantages of matrix sampling — a technique in which each participant takes only a small portion of the assessment — to provide a rich, in-depth assessment of the intended content domain without overburdening any of the children sampled. When the "group" is very large, such as all the fourth-graders in a state or in the nation, then assessing a representative sample will produce essentially the same results for the group average as if every student had been assessed.

Purpose must also determine the content of assessment. When trying to diagnose potential learning handicaps, we still rely on aptitude-like measures designed to be as content-free as possible. We do so in order to avoid confusing lack of opportunity to learn with inability to learn. When the purpose of assessment is to measure actual learning, then content must naturally be tied to learning outcomes. However, even among achievement tests, there is considerable variability in the degree of alignment to a specific curriculum. Although to the lay person "math is math" and "reading is reading," measurement specialists are aware that tiny changes in test format can make a large difference in student performance. For example, a high proportion of students may be able to add numbers when they are presented in vertical format, but many will be unable to do the same problems presented horizontally. If manipulatives are used in some elementary classrooms but not in all, including the use of manipulatives in a mathematics assessment will disadvantage some children, while excluding their use will disadvantage others.

Assessments that are used to guide instruction in a given classroom should be integrally tied to the curriculum of that classroom. However, for large-scale assessments at the state and national level, the issues of curriculum match and the effect of assessment content on future instruction become much more problematic. For example, in a state with an agreed-upon curriculum, including geometry assessment in the early grades may be appropriate, but it would be problematic in states with strong local control of curriculum and so with much more curricular diversity.

Large-scale assessments, such as the National Assessment of Educational Progress, must include instructionally relevant content, but they must do so without conforming too closely to any single curriculum. In the past, this requirement has led to the problem of achievement tests that are limited to the "lowest common denominator." Should the instrument used for program evaluation include only the content that is common to all curricula? Or should it include everything that is in any program's goals? Although the common core approach can lead to a narrowing of curriculum when assessment results are associated with high stakes, including everything can be equally troublesome if it leads to superficial teaching in pursuit of too many different goals.

Finally, the intended use of an assessment will determine the need for normative information or other means to support the interpretation of assessment results. Identifying children with special needs requires normative data to distinguish serious physical, emotional, or learning problems from the wide range of normal development. When reporting to parents, teachers also need some idea of what constitutes grade-level performance, but such "norms" can be in the form of benchmark performances — evidence that children are working at grade level — rather than statistical percentiles.

To prevent the abuses of the past, the purposes and substance of early childhood assessments must be transformed. Assessments should be conducted only if they serve a beneficial purpose: to gain services for children with special needs, to inform instruction by building on what students already know, to improve programs, or to provide evidence nationally or in the states about programmatic needs. The form, substance, and technical features of assessment should be appropriate for the use intended for assessment data. Moreover, the methods of assessment must be compatible with the developmental level and experiences of young children. Below, I consider the implications of these principles for three different categories of assessment purposes.

Identifying Children with Special Needs

I discuss identification for special education first because this is the type of assessment that most resembles past uses of developmental screening measures. However, there is no need for wholesale administration of such tests to all incoming kindergartners. If we take the precepts of developmentally appropriate practices seriously, then at each age level a very broad range of abilities and performance levels is to be expected and tolerated. If potential handicaps are understood to be relatively rare and extreme, then it is not necessary to screen all children for "hidden" disabilities. By definition, serious learning problems should be apparent. Although it is possible to miss hearing or vision problems (at least mild ones) without systematic screening, referral for evaluation of a possible learning handicap should occur only when parents or teachers notice that a child is not progressing normally in comparison to age-appropriate expectations. In-depth assessments should then be conducted to verify the severity of the problem and to rule out a variety of other explanations for poor performance.

For this type of assessment, developmental measures, including I.Q. tests, continue to be useful. Clinicians attempt to make normative evaluations using relatively curriculum-free tasks, but today they are more likely to acknowledge the fallibility of such efforts. For such difficult assessments, clinicians must have specialized training in both diagnostic assessment and child development.

When identifying children with special needs, evaluators should use two general strategies in order to avoid confounding the ability to learn with past opportunity to learn. First, as recommended by the National Academy Panel on Selection and Placement of Students in Programs for the Mentally Retarded,[11] a child's learning environment should be evaluated to rule out poor instruction as the possible cause of a child's lack of learning. Although seldom carried out in practice, this evaluation should include trying out other methods to support learning and possibly trying a different teacher before concluding that a child can't learn from ordinary classroom instruction. A second important strategy is to observe a child's functioning in multiple contexts. Often children who appear to be impaired in school function well at home or with peers. Observation outside of school is critical for children from diverse cultural backgrounds and for those whose home language is not English. The NAEYC stresses that "screening should never be used to identify second language learners as 'handicapped,' solely on the basis of their limited abilities in English."[12]

In-depth developmental assessments are needed to ensure that children with disabilities receive appropriate services. However, the diagnostic model of special education should not be generalized to a larger population of below-average learners, or the result will be the reinstitution of tracking. Elizabeth Graue and I analyzed recent efforts to create "at-risk" kindergartens and found that these practices are especially likely to occur when resources for extended-day programs are available only for the children most in need.[13] The result of such programs is often to segregate children from low socioeconomic backgrounds into classrooms where time is spent drilling on low-level prereading skills like those found on readiness tests. The consequences of dumbed-down instruction in kindergarten are just as pernicious as the effects of tracking at higher grade levels, especially when the at-risk kindergarten group is kept together for first grade. If resources for extended-day kindergarten are scarce, one alternative would be to group children heterogeneously for half the day and then, for the other half, to provide extra enrichment activities for children with limited literacy experiences.

Classroom Assessments

Unlike traditional readiness tests that are intended to predict learning, classroom assessments should support instruction by modeling the dimensions of learning. Although we must allow considerable latitude for children to construct their own understandings, teachers must nonetheless have knowledge of normal development if they are to support children's extensions and next steps. Ordinary classroom tasks can then be used to assess a child's progress in relation to a developmental continuum. An example of a developmental continuum would be that of emergent writing, beginning with scribbles, then moving on to pictures and random letters, and then proceeding to some letter/word correspondences. These continua are not rigid, however, and several dimensions running in parallel may be necessary to describe growth in a single content area. For example, a second dimension of early writing — a child's ability to invent increasingly elaborated stories when dictating to an adult — is not dependent on mastery of writing letters, just as listening comprehension, making predictions about books, and story retellings should be developed in parallel to, not after, mastery of letter sounds.

Although there is a rich research literature documenting patterns of emergent literacy and numeracy, corresponding assessment materials are not so readily available. In the next few years, national interest in developing alternative, performance-based measures should generate more materials and resources. Specifically, new Chapter 1 legislation is likely to support the development of reading assessments that are more authentic and instructionally relevant.

For example, classroom-embedded reading assessments were created from ordinary instructional materials by a group of third-grade teachers in conjunction with researchers at the Center for Research on Evaluation, Standards, and Student Testing.[14] The teachers elected to focus on fluency and making meaning as reading goals; running records and story summaries were selected as the methods of assessment.

But how should student progress be evaluated? In keeping with the idea of representing a continuum of proficiency, third-grade teachers took all the chapter books in their classrooms and sorted them into grade-level stacks, 1-1 (first grade, first semester), 1-2, 2-1, and so on up to fifth grade. Then they identified representative or marker books in each category to use for assessment. Once the books had been sorted by difficulty, it became possible to document that children were reading increasingly difficult texts with understanding. Photocopied pages from the marker books also helped parents see what teachers considered to be grade-level materials and provided them with concrete evidence of their child's progress. Given mandates for student-level reporting under Chapter 1, state departments of education or test publishers could help develop similar systems of this type with sufficient standardization to ensure comparability across districts.

In the meantime, classroom teachers — or preferably teams of teachers — are left to invent their own assessments for classroom use. In many schools, teachers are already working with portfolios and developing scoring criteria. The best procedure appears to be having grade-level teams and then cross-grade teams meet to discuss expectations and evaluation criteria. These conversations will be more productive if, for each dimension to be assessed, teachers collect student work and use marker papers to illustrate continua of performance. Several papers might be used at each stage to reflect the tremendous variety in children's responses, even when following the same general progression.

Benchmark papers can also be an effective means of communicating with parents. For example, imagine using sample papers from grades K-3 to illustrate expectations regarding "invented spelling." Invented spelling or "temporary spelling" is the source of a great deal of parental dissatisfaction with reform curricula. Yet most parents who attack invented spelling have never been given a rationale for its use. That is, no one has explained it in such a way that the explanation builds on the parents' own willingness to allow successive approximations in their child's early language development. They have never been shown a connection between writing expectations and grade-level spelling lists or been informed about differences in rules for first drafts and final drafts. Sample papers could be selected to illustrate the increasing mastery of grade-appropriate words, while allowing for misspellings of advanced words on first drafts. Communicating criteria is helpful to parents, and, as we have seen in the literature on performance assessment, it also helps children to understand what is expected and to become better at assessing their own work.

Monitoring National and State Trends

In 1989, when the President and the nation's governors announced "readiness for school" as the first education goal, many early childhood experts feared the creation of a national test for school entry. Indeed, given the negative history of readiness testing, the first thing the Goal 1 Technical Planning Subgroup did was to issue caveats about what an early childhood assessment must *not* be. It should not be a one-dimensional, reductionist measure of a child's knowledge and abilities; it should not be called a measure of "readiness" as if some children were not ready to learn; and it should not be used to "label, stigmatize, or classify any individual child or group of children."[15]

However, with this fearsome idea set aside, the Technical Planning Subgroup endorsed the idea of an early childhood assessment system that would periodically gather data on the condition of young children as they enter school. The purpose of the assessment would be to inform public policy and especially to help "in charting progress toward achievement of the National Education Goals,

Beginning in 1998-99, a representative sample of 23,000 kindergarten students will be assessed and then followed through grade 5.

and for informing the development, expansion, and/or modification of policies and programs that affect young children and their families."[16] Assuming that certain safeguards are built in, such data could be a powerful force in focusing national attention and resources on the needs of young children.

Unlike past testing practices aimed at evaluating individual children in comparison with normative expectations, a large-scale, nationally representative assessment would be used to monitor national trends. The purpose of such an assessment would be analogous to the use of the National Assessment of Educational Progress (NAEP) to measure major shifts in achievement patterns. For example, NAEP results have demonstrated gains in the achievement of black students in the South as a result of desegregation, and NAEP achievement measures showed gains during the 1980s in basic skills and declines in higher-order thinking skills and problem solving. Similar data are not now available for preschoolers or for children in the primary grades. If an early childhood assessment were conducted periodically, it would be possible to demonstrate the relationship between health services and early learning and to evaluate the impact of such programs as Head Start.

In keeping with the precept that methods of assessment should follow from the purpose of assessment, the Technical Planning Subgroup recommended that sampling of both children and assessment items be used to collect national data. Sampling would allow a broad assessment of a more multifaceted content domain and would preclude the misuse of individual scores to place or stigmatize individual children. A national early childhood assessment should also serve as a model of important content. As a means to shape public understanding of the full range of abilities and experiences that influence early learning and development, the Technical Planning Subgroup identified five dimensions to be assessed: 1) physical well-being and motor development, 2) social and emotional development, 3) approaches toward learning, 4) language usage, and 5) cognition and general knowledge.

Responding to the need for national data to document the condition of children as they enter school and to measure progress on Goal 1, the U.S. Department of Education has commissioned the Early Childhood Longitudinal Study: Kindergarten Cohort. Beginning in the 1998-99 school year, a representative sample of 23,000 kindergarten students will be assessed and then followed through grade 5. The content of the assessments used will correspond closely to the dimensions recommended by the Technical Planning Subgroup. In addition, data will be collected on each child's family, communi-

ty, and school/program. Large-scale studies of this type serve both program evaluation purposes (How effective are preschool services for children?) and research purposes (What is the relationship between children's kindergarten experiences and their academic success throughout elementary school?).

National needs for early childhood data and local needs for program evaluation information are similar in some respects and dissimilar in others. Both uses require group data. However, a critical distinction that affects the methods of evaluation is whether or not local programs share a

Fearing that "assessment" is just a euphemism for more bad testing, many early childhood professionals have asked, Why test at all?

common curriculum. If local programs, such as all the kindergartens in a school district, have agreed on the same curriculum, it is possible to build program evaluation assessments from an aggregation of the measures used for classroom purposes. Note that the entire state of Kentucky is attempting to develop such a system by scoring classroom portfolios for state reporting.

If programs being evaluated do not have the same specific curricula, as is the case with a national assessment and with some state assessments, then the assessment measures must reflect broad, agreed-upon goals without privileging any specific curriculum. This is a tall order, more easily said than done. For this reason, the Technical Planning Subgroup recommended that validity studies be built into the procedures for data collection. For example, pilot studies should verify that what children can do in one-on-one assessment settings is consistent with what they can do in their classrooms, and assessment methods should always allow children more than one way to show what they know.

Conclusion

In the past decade, testing of 4-, 5-, and 6-year-olds has been excessive and inappropriate. Under a variety of different names, leftover I.Q. tests have been used to track children into ineffective programs or to deny them school entry. Prereading tests held over from the 1930s have encouraged the teaching of decontextualized skills. In response, fearing that "assessment" is just a euphemism for more bad testing, many early childhood professionals have asked, Why test at all? Indeed, given a history of misuse, the burden of proof must rest with assessment advocates to demonstrate the usefulness of assessment and to ensure that abuses will not recur. Key principles that support responsible use of assessment information follow.

• No testing of young children should occur unless it can be shown to lead to beneficial results.

• Methods of assessment, especially the language used, must be appropriate to the development and experiences of young children.

• Features of assessment — content, form, evidence of validity, and standards for interpretation — must be tailored to the specific purpose of an assessment.

• Identifying children for special education is a legitimate purpose for assessment and still requires the use of curriculum-free, aptitude-like measures and normative comparisons. However, handicapping conditions are rare; the diagnostic model used by special education should not be generalized to a larger population of below-average learners.

• For both classroom instructional purposes and purposes of public policy making, the content of assessments should embody the important dimensions of early learning and development. The tasks and skills children are asked to perform should reflect and model progress toward important learning goals.

In the past, local newspapers have published readiness checklists that suggested that children should stay home from kindergarten if they couldn't cut with scissors. In the future, national and local assessments should demonstrate the richness of what children do know and should foster instruction that builds on their strengths. Telling a story in conjunction with scribbles is a meaningful stage in literacy development. Reading a story in English and retelling it in Spanish is evidence of reading comprehension. Evidence of important learning in beginning mathematics should not be counting to 100 instead of to 10. It should be extending patterns; solving arithmetic problems with blocks and explaining how you got your answer; constructing graphs to show how many children come to school by bus, by walking, by car; and demonstrating understanding of patterns and quantities in a variety of ways.

In classrooms, we need new forms of assessment so that teachers can support children's physical, social, and cognitive development. And at the level of public policy, we need new forms of assessment so that programs will be judged on the basis of worthwhile educational goals.

1. Lorrie A. Shepard and Mary Lee Smith, "Escalating Academic Demand in Kindergarten: Counterproductive Policies," *Elementary School Journal,* vol. 89, 1988, pp. 135-45.

2. Sue Bredekamp, ed., *Developmentally Appropriate Practice in Early Childhood Programs Serving Children from Birth Through Age 8,* exp. ed. (Washington, D.C.: National Association for the Education of Young Children, 1987).

3. M. Therese Gnezda and Rosemary Bolig, *A National Survey of Public School Testing of Pre-Kindergarten and Kindergarten Children* (Washington, D.C.: National Forum on the Future of Children and Families, National Research Council, 1988).

4. Samuel J. Meisels, "Uses and Abuses of Developmental Screening and School Readiness Testing," *Young Children,* vol. 42, 1987, pp. 4-6, 68-73.

5. Lorrie A. Shepard and M. Elizabeth Graue, "The Morass of School Readiness Screening: Research on Test Use and Test Validity," in Bernard Spodek, ed., *Handbook of Research on the Education of Young Children* (New York: Macmillan, 1993), pp. 293-305.

6. Anne C. Stallman and P. David Pearson, "Formal Measures of Early Literacy," in Lesley Mandel Morrow and Jeffrey K. Smith, eds., *Assessment for Instruction in Early Literacy* (Englewood Cliffs, N.J.: Prentice-Hall, 1990), pp. 7-44.

7. Lorrie A. Shepard, "A Review of Research on Kindergarten Retention," in Lorrie A. Shepard and Mary Lee Smith, eds., *Flunking Grades: Research and Policies on Retention* (London: Falmer Press, 1989), pp. 64-78.

8. Lorrie A. Shepard and Mary Lee Smith, "Academic and Emotional Effects of Kindergarten Retention in One School District," in idem, pp. 79-107.

9. "Guidelines for Appropriate Curriculum Content and Assessment in Programs Serving Children Ages 3 Through 8," *Young Children*, vol. 46, 1991, pp. 21-38.

10. Ibid., p. 32.

11. Kirby A. Heller, Wayne H. Holtzman, and Samuel Messick, eds., *Placing Children in Special Education* (Washington, D.C.: National Academy Press, 1982).

12. "Guidelines," p. 33.

13. Shepard and Graue, op. cit.

14. The Center for Research on Evaluation, Standards, and Student Testing is located on the campuses of the University of California, Los Angeles, and the University of Colorado, Boulder.

15. *Goal 1: Technical Planning Subgroup Report on School Readiness* (Washington, D.C.: National Education Goals Panel, September 1991).

16. Ibid., p. 6.

Taking Aim At Testing

A veteran education writer says it's time to draw a bead on our over-reliance on standardized testing

BY ROBERT ROTHMAN

Some *41 million schoolchildren take as many as 127 million tests annually—and some of them, no doubt, attend schools in your district. But in recent years, criticism of standardized testing has mounted—and calls for alternative assessments have increased. What are the limits of standardized testing? In the following excerpt from* Measuring Up: Standards, Assessment, and School Reform, *Robert Rothman, senior associate at the National Alliance for Restructuring Education, points out the limits of norm-referenced tests and discusses the pitfalls of making testing a high-stakes enterprise. One drawback: The emphasis on standardized testing, and the push for school districts to score well, often has an inordinate—and detrimental—effect on minority and at-risk youth.*

. . . John Jacob Cannell was practicing family medicine in the small town of Beaver, W. Va., in 1987 when he began noticing something strange. The children he was seeing in his clinic appeared deeply troubled, yet when he asked their schools about them, he was told that they were all performing "above average."

Checking further, Cannell learned that the school district overall was above average, a finding that to him did not make sense: If this poor Appalachian town was above average, he asked himself, what place could possibly be below average? To find out, he surveyed the states

Robert Rothman, a senior associate at the National Alliance for Restructuring Education, is the author of Measuring Up: Standards, Assessment, and School Reform, *from which this excerpt is taken. This excerpt is reprinted with the permission of Jossey-Bass Publishers.*

Roxana Villa/SIS

and large cities to learn their test scores. His results, published in a small pamphlet out of his house, catapulted the country doctor into the national spotlight and rocked the foundations of the testing enterprise in the United States.

Cannell found that, contrary to what appeared to be common sense, every state and most cities reported that the average test score of their elementary school students was "above the national average." This finding soon became known as the "Lake Wobegon effect," after the humorist Garrison Keillor's fictional town, where "all the women are strong, all the men are good-looking, and all the children are above average."

Though Cannell's methods were flawed and he overstated his case, his study helped expose many of the problems brought on by the explosion of high-stakes testing in schools and cast a

TEACHERS SAY THEY SELDOM FIND
NORM-REFERENCED TESTS USEFUL FOR
DIAGNOSING STUDENTS' STRENGTHS AND WEAKNESSES

heavy shadow of doubt on the tests and the way they were used. Like the boy in the story who dared to reveal that the emperor had no clothes, the West Virginia physician showed that tests did not do what they were supposed to do: inform people about the state of student achievement.

To the general public, Cannell's finding appeared to defy logic, and it led many people to wonder whether school officials were misleading them in reporting test scores. To those familiar with testing, the finding—confirmed by a federally sponsored study by leading experts—pointed up many of the problems brought on by reliance on high-stakes testing. In any event, Cannell's small, crude study helped fuel a mounting criticism of the enterprise.

Criticism of tests is nothing new, of course. Almost from the outset, tests have come under fire for misjudging people's abilities and acting as inappropriate "gate-keepers" to advancement. As Stephen Jay Gould writes in *The Mismeasure of Man,* measures of human intelligence have always reached the same conclusion: that those doing the testing are superior to those from other, less privileged racial and ethnic groups. And the disadvantaged groups have suffered in the process.

But while a few writers . . . raised their voices in protest against increased testing as it advanced, they were not able to stem the testing tide . . . .

The phenomenon Cannell identified in his report came about because of a little-known but key feature of the way standardized tests are designed. Contrary to many parents' assumptions, a child's score on a test—whether "above the national average" or "in the 75th percentile"—is not based on a comparison with the other students who took the test that year. If that were the case, then only half the test-takers could indeed be above average. Rather, the test scores are based on comparisons with a "norm group" of children—a group that may have taken the test as many as seven years before.

When test publishers produce a new version of a test, they first administer it to a representative sample of students across the nation. Their scores become the "national norms" against which all subsequent scores are compared. Publishers also produce norms for different groups of students (such as urban students and those who attend independent schools) for schools that wish to compare their students' performance with that of students from like schools. . . .

Norming is an important feature of testing. As H.D. Hoover, the director of the Iowa Basic Skills Testing Program, explains, norms place test scores in context much the way they place information about size in context. Without norms, the statement, "He is six feet tall and weighs 100 pounds" is meaningless for comparison; knowing roughly what the average weight for someone that tall is, however, we can say, "He is thin."

But despite that advantage, norming also poses a number of problems. For one thing, norm-referenced scores provide a very limited view of what students know and can do. Presenting a student's performance only in comparison to that of other students says little about the skills and knowledge a student has attained. A score does not indicate which questions a student answered correctly and which she answered incorrectly; indeed, because students need only *choose* an answer, not construct it, we do not know whether they possess the knowledge and skills the question was designed to tap or simply guessed well.

This problem is made worse by the fact that conventional tests are kept secret. In order to prevent students from seeing the questions in advance, test publishers and schools have devised elaborate security procedures. But the effect of these measures is to hide from students and their parents the knowledge and skills the students are expected to demonstrate and to hide from students and teachers their corrected work. . . .

As a result of this limitation, teachers say they seldom find norm-referenced tests useful for diagnosing students' strengths and weaknesses. In a study conducted by Pennsylvania, for example, teachers said tests only *supplement* what they already know about their students. If classroom performance and test scores diverge, teachers give their own observations more credence.

A second problem with norm-referenced tests is related to the first. Even if a student performed in the 75th percentile—that is, better than three-fourths of the norm group—we do not know how good that is. What if the norm group consisted of poor performers? This problem becomes particularly serious when scores are reported in terms of grade levels, as they often are. If a student's score is at "3.2," for example, that means she performed at about the average of those in the second month of third grade. But this score is less informative than one might think. We do not know whether the third-graders are doing single-digit arithmetic or calculus. . . .

Even if schools set their own goals, they have no way to compare students against the goals; simply reviewing their students' scores on standardized tests is clearly not sufficient. Another problem with norm-referenced test scores is the problem that Cannell identified. Because most publishers set norms only about once every seven years—it is too costly to do it more often, they say—schools' test scores can rise each year while the norms stay the same. The result: Everybody can be above average. Although testing experts criticized Cannell for his methodology, a subsequent study by Robert L. Linn and his colleagues at the University of Colorado, Boulder, confirmed that almost all states and most school districts reported test results above the national average.

Test publishers, who reacted strongly to Cannell's charges, pointed out that this result may reflect genuine improvements in student achievement. In fact, evidence from the publishers' own norming studies and from other sources suggests that achievement did rise during the 1980s; thus student performance at the time of Cannell's

ANOTHER PROBLEM WITH TEACHING
TO THE TEST IS THAT IT CAN NARROW
THE CURRICULUM TO THE MATERIAL ON THE TEST

study *should* have been above that of the average of the norm group. . . .

Despite those findings, there is also considerable evidence that the test scores Cannell reported were inflated and showed greater improvement than in fact occurred. Moreover, this inflation was a direct result of the high stakes this country placed on the tests. We are faced with a paradox: States and school districts imposed testing mandates on schools and put consequences on the results to make sure that schools improved, but these actions only ensured that we could not see the true picture of student performance. . . .

Teaching to the test

More commonly, school administrators and teachers have sought to raise test scores through various practices known as "teaching to the test." Teaching to the test is often frowned upon in schools, but it is not necessarily a bad thing. Different tests measure different knowledge and skills, and administrators usually select the test that most closely matches a school's curriculum. They want their teachers to emphasize the skills and knowledge the test measures because those are the skills and knowledge they think are important. In a survey of officials in 40 states with high-stakes testing programs, Lorrie A. Shepard, a professor of education at the University of Colorado, Boulder, found near-unanimous agreement that teachers spend more time teaching skills and knowledge they know to be objectives of a required test than they spend teaching other skills and knowledge. As one official responded, "In fact, the presence of the test is forcing attention to the essential skills that had been identified."

Some educators have argued that this is an appropriate function of tests. Since teachers pay attention to tests, why not use tests to inspire improvements in instruction.

In practice, though, teaching to the test has distorted the information tests provide about what students know and the way teachers teach. And it has become more and more common as states and school districts have imposed testing mandates and used test scores to hold schools accountable for student performance.

As a number of researchers have noted, the term "teaching to the test" actually covers a range of activities, some of which are clearly unethical. On the unethical side of the spectrum are practices such as giving students actual test questions or answers. But other techniques teachers use to prepare students for tests are quite benign. For example, many schools hold pep rallies the day before tests to encourage students to do well. And one school in Pennsylvania tried to motivate students to do well on the tests by broadcasting over the loudspeaker this song, sung to the tune of "High Hopes":

We have worked and studied so long,
Hope we don't get anything wrong,
As you have probably guessed

On the test
We'll do our very best
'Cause we've got high hopes. . . .

In between those two extremes are a number of practices that raise questions about the tests and their influence on instruction. As Lorrie Shepard found in her survey of state officials, many schools use practice tests to familiarize students with the format and type of questions used on the test. This is reasonable; it would be unfair to spring a multiple-choice test on a youngster who had never answered that sort of question before. Some practice tests, though, include questions that are very similar to those used in commercially available standardized achievement tests. "One-time practice with test format, especially when these activities are consistent with standardized procedures, is not the cause of inflated test scores," Shepard writes. "However, repeated practice or instruction geared to the format of the test rather than the content domain can increase scores without increasing achievement."

One survey of math and science teachers suggests that such test preparation practices are more common in predominantly minority classrooms. Among classes where more than 60 percent of the students were members of minority groups, the survey found, about three-fourths of teachers reported teaching test-taking skills and beginning test preparation more than a month before the test. In classes with few minority students, by contrast, about 40 percent of teachers said they employed such practices. Likewise, a separate survey of upper-elementary teachers found that those with more disadvantaged students were twice as likely as those teaching wealthier students to report giving practice tests and practicing with old versions of mandated standardized tests.

Another problem with teaching to the test is that it can narrow the curriculum to the material on the test. There are only so many hours in a school day; teachers who choose to focus on what is tested must leave something else out. In some extreme cases, whole subject areas are left out, at least for part of the year. If the state tests students in reading and mathematics, for example, teachers may put off instruction in science and social studies until after the test.

One example of this practice comes from Maryland, where the state requires students to pass "functional" (or basic-skills) tests in reading, writing, mathematics, and citizenship in order to graduate from high school. The citizenship test, in particular, proved difficult for many students, who found the detailed questions about local, state, and federal governments daunting. As a result, teachers there spent time teaching about civics at the expense of other subjects. As one building administrator said, "We realize a kid is taken out of science every other day for citizenship and will fail science to maybe pass the citizenship test."

In other cases, schools resort to the absurd practice of "doubling up" the curriculum in order to teach both what is on the test and what they want to teach. The Pelham Road Elementary School in Greenville, S.C., for example, has automated its library and has begun to instruct students in how to scroll through computers to find the materials they need. Teachers there consider this an important skill, since many public and research libraries have also moved to computerized systems. But since the state testing program tests students on their ability to use traditional card catalogues, the school has also maintained its card catalogue and teaches students to use it as well, thus spending valuable curricular time on a skill the school has determined is outmoded.

More frequently, teaching the content tested means teaching a narrow segment of a subject area. As Lee Cronbach, one of the leading scholars in the field, noted three decades ago, no test can measure all of the knowledge and skills in a whole subject. As he stated, "Whenever it is critically important to master certain content, the knowledge that it will be tested produces a desirable concentration of effort. On the other hand, learning the answer to a set of questions is by no means the same as acquiring understanding of whatever topic that question represents."

As with the previously cited features of teaching to the test, narrowing instruction to the material on standardized tests has a disturbing characteristic: It appears to be more prevalent in low-income and minority classes than it does in schools that cater to more affluent students. According to one survey, disadvantaged students are less likely than their more affluent peers to receive instruction in science, art, thinking skills, and other areas not included on standardized tests. Thus tests drive instruction more for minorities, who tend to lag behind whites in test performance. Perhaps schools make more of a deliberate effort to teach to the tests with students who seem to be falling behind. Perhaps teachers in predominantly white schools feel they do not need to take special steps to raise scores, since their students perform well on the tests anyway.

But, in practice, the emphasis on raising test scores has thrown into doubt the meaning of the higher test scores. If test scores go up because schools have focused extensively on preparing students for the test at the expense of other material, what does the increase signify? To cite one commonly used analogy, placing all your energy on raising test scores is like prescribing massive doses of aspirin to lower the fever of a cancer patient. You may succeed in reducing her fever, but you have not addressed the underlying problem.

The quest for alternatives

. . . As alternatives to traditional tests, the reformers endorse methods that fall generally into three categories: performance-based assessments, projects, and portfolios. While these methods of measuring student performance are not completely new—they have been tried in classrooms and in research settings for many years—they do represent a substantial departure for most schools, particularly when applied to the external testing that has increasingly influenced instructional practice and the public's view of schooling. . . .

Their basic principles are as follows:

• Performance-based assessments are exercises that ask students to demonstrate their knowledge and skills by undertaking some type of performance, such as writing an essay or conducting a science experiment. Such requirements are common in athletics and the arts. Divers, for example, demonstrate their abilities by diving, not by answering written questions about techniques. Similarly, pianists are judged on their ability to play a Chopin étude.

• In contrast to performance, which can be relatively short in duration, *projects* are extended exercises that ask students to generate problems, come up with solutions, and then demonstrate their findings. One analogy is the type of activity Boy and Girl Scouts undertake to earn merit badges. Scouts on a camping trip, for example, must show that they can plan and execute the trip as well as deal with all of the unexpected situations that arise.

• *Portfolios* are long-term records of a student's performances. These are commonly used by artists and photographers to show gallery owners and editors the range of their work and their development over time.

All of these types of assessments share features that researchers and educators have advocated to counteract some of the negative aspects of conventional tests. Unlike the traditional tests, the new assessments match the type of instruction that cognitive scientists say enhances learning. For one thing, in place of abstract exercises cooked up just for the test, the new assessments demand work in a real-world context. For this reason, alternative assessments are often called *authentic* assessments. In carrying out a project—for example, preparing a videotape on the origins of the Civil War—a student must act like a documentary producer. He must gather information, sift through it, formulate a thesis, weigh the evidence for and against the thesis, write a script, and present his videotape. He is actively constructing his knowledge and skills, not receiving knowledge passively and in abstract form, the way students do when they hear lectures on the Civil War and then answer test questions based on the lectures. At the same time, if the videotape project is more meaningful to the student than a lecture-based test, he may find himself more motivated to do well on the assessment.

The new forms of assessment also allow students to demonstrate complex thinking, not just isolated skills. The student preparing the videotape must analyze and weigh facts, not just recall them. He must write something that marshals evidence in support of a conclusion. These assessments also challenge the view, implicit in multiple-choice tests, that there is only one right answer to every question and that the goal is to find it and to find it quickly. There may be more than one way to interpret a poem or a historical event. And, as in real life, the most important goal may be coming up with ways to find answers. Moreover, these assessments teach students that it takes time to solve complex problems. Students trained to answer long series of multiple-choice questions come to believe that if they cannot solve a problem within a few minutes, they will be unable to solve it at all. We want them to use their creativity and hard work to solve problems, just as we want them to on the job and in life.

What Happens

Between

Not only assessment needs to change. Curriculums and instructional strategies, too, must reflect a *performance* orientation. Here are seven principles for performance-based instruction.

Jay McTighe

Growing concern over the inadequacy of conventional tests has spurred interest in performance assessments, such as performance tasks, projects, and exhibitions. To many supporters, these performance assessments are better suited than traditional tests to measure what really counts: whether students can apply their knowledge, skills, and understanding in important, real-world contexts. More teachers are using performance assessments in their classrooms, and such assessments are beginning to influence district- and state-level testing programs as well.

Increasing the use of performance assessments—in and of itself—will not significantly improve student performance, however. To borrow the old farm adage: "You don't fatten the cattle by weighing them." If we expect students to improve their performance on these new, more authentic measures, we need to engage in "performance-based instruction" on a regular basis.

But what does it really mean to teach for performance? Working the past six years with hundreds of teachers using performance assessments, I have seen how the development of assessment tasks and evaluative criteria can influence instruction. Based on this experience, I offer seven principles of performance-based instruction, illustrated by vignettes from classrooms in which these principles are being applied.

Establish Clear Performance Targets

As part of a unit on nutrition, a middle school health teacher presents her students with the following performance task.

> You are having six of your friends over for your birthday party. You are preparing the food for the party, but your mother has just read a book on nutrition and tells you that you can't serve anything containing artificial sweeteners or lots of salt, sugar, or saturated fats. Plan a menu that will make your friends happy and still meet your mother's expectations. Explain why your menu is both tasty and healthy. Use the USDA Food Pyramid guidelines and the Nutrition Facts on food labels to support your menu selection.[1]

To teach effectively, we need to be clear about what we expect students to know, understand, and be able to do as a result of our instruction. But performance-based instruction calls for more. We also need to determine *how* students will demonstrate the intended knowledge, understanding, and proficiency. When establishing performance targets, consider Gardner's (1991) contention that developing students' *understanding* is a primary goal of teaching. He defines understanding as the ability to apply facts, concepts, and skills appropriately in new situations.

The principle of *establishing clear performance targets* and the goal of *teaching for understanding* fit together as a powerful means of linking curriculum, instruction, and assessment. A performance-based orientation requires that we think about curriculum not simply as content to be covered but in terms of desired *performances of understanding*. Thus, performance-oriented teachers consider assessment up front by conceptualizing their learning goals and objectives as performance applications calling for students to demonstrate their understanding. Performance assessments, then, become targets for teaching and learning, as well as serving as a source of evidence that students understand, and are able to apply, what we have taught.

Establishing clear performance targets is important for several reasons. Teachers who establish and

Assessments?

From *Educational Leadership*, December 1996–January 1997, pp. 6-12. © 1996 by the Association for Supervision and Curriculum Development. All rights reserved. Reprinted by permission.

communicate clear performance targets to their students reflect what we know about effective teaching, which supports the importance of instructional clarity. These teachers also recognize that students' attitudes and perceptions toward learning are influenced by the degree to which they understand what is expected of them and what the rationale is for various instructional activities. Finally, the process of establishing performance targets helps identify curriculum priorities, enabling us to focus on the essential and enduring knowledge in a crowded field.

Strive for Authenticity in Products and Performances

Fifth graders conduct a survey to gather data about community attitudes toward a proposal that public school students wear uniforms. The students organize the data and then choose an appropriate graphic display for communicating their findings. Finally, students write letters to the editor of the local paper to present their data and their personal views on the proposal. A direct link to the larger world is established when two student letters are published in the newspaper.

Leading reformers recommend that schools involve their students in authentic work. Performance tasks should call upon students to demonstrate their knowledge and skills in a manner that reflects the world outside the classroom. Although diagramming sentences may help students understand sentence structures and parts of speech, this is not really an authentic activity, because few people outside of school diagram sentences. When students engage in purposeful writing (for example, to persuade an identified audience), however, they are using their knowledge and skills in ways much more congruent with the demands of real life.

As in the larger world, authentic work in schools calls for students to apply their knowledge and skills, with the result typically being a tangible product (written, visual, or three-dimensional) or a performance. These products and performances have an

> When students have opportunities to examine their work in light of known criteria and performance standards, they begin to shift their orientation from "What did I get?" to "Now I know what I need to do to improve."

explicit *purpose* (for example, to explain, to entertain, or to solve a problem) and are directed toward an identified *audience*. Because real-world issues and problems are rarely limited to a single content area, authentic work often provides opportunities for making interdisciplinary connections.

Emphasizing authentic work does not lessen the importance of helping students develop basic skills. On the contrary, basic knowledge and skills provide an essential foundation for meaningful application. The "basics" are not ends in themselves, however; they serve a larger goal: to enable students to thoughtfully apply knowledge and skills within a meaningful, authentic context.

Research and experience confirm that when learners perceive classroom activities as meaningful and relevant, they are more likely to have a positive attitude toward them (McCombs 1984, Schunk 1990). In addition, many teachers have observed that when given the opportunity to produce a tangible product or demonstrate something to a real audience (for example, peers, parents, younger or older students, community members), students often seem more willing to put forth the effort required to do quality work.

Remember that what we assess sends

a strong signal to students about what is important for them to learn. When authentic performance tasks play a key role in teaching and assessing, students will know that we expect them to apply knowledge in ways valued in the world beyond the classroom.

Publicize Criteria and Performance Standards

Before beginning a laboratory experiment, a high school science teacher reviews the Science Department's performance list for a lab report with her students. The list, containing the criteria for a thorough report, clearly conveys the teacher's expectations while serving as a guide to the students as they prepare their reports. Before she collects the reports, the teacher allows students to exchange papers with their lab partners, give feedback to one another based on the performance list criteria, and make needed revisions.

Like the problems and issues we confront in the real world, authentic classroom performance tasks rarely have a single, correct answer. Therefore, our evaluation of student products and performances must be based upon judgment and guided by criteria. The criteria are typically incorporated into one of several types of scoring tools: a rubric, a rating scale, or a performance list. With all of these tools, the criteria help to spell out the qualities that we consider to be most significant or important in student work.

Teachers at elementary schools in Anne Arundel County, Maryland, use a "Writing to Persuade" rubric to help students learn the qualities of effective persuasive writing. A large poster of the rubric, containing the criteria in the form of questions, is prominently displayed in the front of the classroom to provide an easy reference for teachers and students. For example: "Did I clearly identify my position?" "Did I fully support my position with facts or personal experiences?" "Did I effectively use persuasive language to convince my audience?"

Evaluative criteria clearly are essential for summative evaluations, but teachers also are recognizing their role in *improving* performance. By sharing the criteria with students, we begin to remove the mystery of how work will be evaluated, while highlighting the elements of quality and standards of performance toward which students should strive. Teachers also can help students internalize these elements of quality by having them use scoring tools themselves to evaluate their own work or that of their peers. When students have opportunities to examine their work in light of known criteria and performance standards, they begin to shift their orientation from "What did I get?" to "Now I know what I need to do to improve."

Provide Models of Excellence

A middle school art teacher displays five examples of well-constructed papier-maché sculptures of "figures in action." The examples illustrate the criteria by which the sculptures will be evaluated: composition (figure showing action), strength and stability of armature (underlying structure), surface construction (application of papier-maché), finishing techniques (texture, color, details), and overall effect. The teacher notes that the quality of her students' sculptures has markedly improved since she began sharing and discussing actual models of excellence.

Providing students with lists of criteria or scoring rubrics is a necessary piece of performance-based instruction—but it isn't always sufficient. Not every student will immediately understand the criteria or how to apply them to their own work ("What do you mean by well organized?"). Wiggins (1993) suggests that if we expect students to do excellent work, they need to know what excellent work looks like. Following his idea, performance-based instruction calls for providing students with models and demonstrations that illustrate excellence in products or performances.

This approach, of course, is not unknown in schools. Effective coaches and sponsors of extracurricular activities often involve their club or team members in analyzing award-winning school newspapers or yearbooks, or reviewing videotapes of excellent athletic or dramatic performances. But providing models of quality work is also an essential piece of performance-based instruction in classrooms.

Teachers can use examples of excellent work during instruction to help students understand the desired elements of quality. Some teachers also present students with examples of mediocre and excellent work, asking them to analyze the differences and identify the characteristics that distinguish the excellent examples from the rest. In this way, students learn the criteria of quality through tangible models and concrete examples. In some classrooms, students actually help to construct the scoring tools (rubric, rating scale, or performance list), based on their growing knowledge of the topic and the criteria they have identified in the examples. (The potential benefits of providing students with tangible examples underscore the value of saving examples of student work from performance tasks for use as models in future years!)

Some teachers are wary of providing models of quality, fearing that students may simply copy or imitate the examples. This is a real danger with activities for which there is a single correct answer (or one "best" way of accomplishing the task). With more open-

ended performance tasks and projects, however, we can minimize this problem by presenting students with multiple models. In this way, students are shown several different ways to satisfy the desired criteria, thus discouraging a cookie-cutter approach.

By providing students with criteria *and* models of excellence, teachers are often rewarded with higher quality products and performances. In addition, they are helping students become more self-directed; students able to distinguish between poor and high-quality performance are more likely to be able to evaluate and improve their own work, guided by a clear conception of excellence.

Teach Strategies Explicitly

An elementary teacher introduces his students to two strategies—summarizing and predicting—to enhance their comprehension of text materials. He describes each strategy and models its use by thinking aloud while applying it to a challenging text. During the lesson, the teacher refers to large posters spelling out a written procedure and visual symbol for each strategy. Following the lesson, he distributes bookmark versions of the posters. Over the next two weeks, each student works with a reading buddy to practice using the strategies with both fiction and nonfiction texts while the teacher monitors their progress and provides guidance.

In every field of endeavor, effective performers use specific techniques and strategies to boost their performance. Olympic athletes visualize flawless performances, writers seek feedback from "critical friends," law students form study groups, coaches share tips at coaching clinics, busy executives practice time management techniques.

Students also benefit from specific strategies that can improve their performance on academic tasks. For example, webbing and mapping techniques help students see connections, cognitive reading strategies boost comprehension (Palinscar and Brown 1984; Haller, Child, and Walberg 1988), brainstorming techniques enhance idea generation, and mnemonics assists retention and recall.

Few students spontaneously generate and use strategies on their own, however, so we need to explicitly teach these thinking and learning strategies. One straightforward approach is to use the direct instruction model, in which teachers

1. introduce and explain the purpose of the strategy;

2. demonstrate and model its use;

3. provide guided practice for students to apply the strategy with feedback;

4. allow students to apply the strategy independently and in teams; and

5. regularly reflect on the appropriate uses of the strategy and its effectiveness.

In addition to direct instruction, many teachers find it helpful to incorporate thinking and learning strategies into tangible products, such as posters, bookmarks, visual symbols, or cue cards (McTighe and Lyman 1988). For example, students in a middle school mathematics class I am familiar with have constructed desktop spinners depicting six problem-solving strategies they have been taught. When working on open-ended problems, the students use the spinners to indicate the strategy they are using. Their teacher circulates around the room, asking students to think aloud by explaining their reasoning and problem-solving strategies. Later, she leads a class discussion of solutions and the effectiveness of the strategies used. The spinners provide students with a tangible reminder of the value of using strategies during problem solving. These and other cognitive tools offer students practical and concrete support as they acquire and internalize performance-enhancing strategies.

Use Ongoing Assessments for Feedback and Adjustment

A middle school social studies teacher notes that the quality of her students' research reports has markedly improved since he began using the writing process approach of brainstorming, drafting, reviewing feedback, and revising. Through the use of teacher and peer reviews of draft reports, students are given specific feedback on strengths, as well as on aspects of their reports that may be unclear, inaccurate, or incomplete. They appreciate the opportunity to make necessary revisions before turning in their final copy.

The Japanese concept of *Kaizen* suggests that quality is achieved through constant, incremental improvement. According to J. Edwards Deming, guru of the Total Quality Management movement, quality in manufacturing is not achieved through end-of-line inspections; by then, it is too late. Rather, quality is the result of regular inspections (assessments) *along the way*, followed by needed adjustments based on the information gleaned from the inspections.

How do these ideas apply in an academic setting? We know that students will rarely perform at high levels on challenging learning tasks on the first attempt. Deep understanding or high levels of proficiency are achieved only as a result of trial, practice, adjustments based on feedback, and more practice. Performance-based instruction underscores the importance of using assessments to provide information to guide improvement throughout the learning process, instead of waiting to give feedback at the end of instruction.

Once again, effective coaches and sponsors of clubs often use this principle as they involve their students in scrimmages, dress rehearsals, and reviews of bluelines. Such activities serve to identify problems and weaknesses, followed by more coaching and opportunities to practice or revise.

The ongoing interplay between assessment and instruction so common in the arts and athletics is also evident in classrooms using practices such as nongraded quizzes and practice tests, the writing process, formative performance tasks, review of drafts, and peer response groups. The teachers in such classrooms recognize that ongoing assessments provide the feedback that enhances their instruction and guides student revision. *Kaizen,* in the context of schools, means ensuring that assessment enhances performance, not simply measures it.

Document and Celebrate Progress

Early in the school year, a middle school physical education teacher has her students analyze their current fitness levels based on a series of measures of strength, endurance, and flexibility. The initial results are charted and used to establish personal fitness goals. The teacher then guides students in preparing individualized fitness plans to achieve their goals. Subsequent fitness tests at the middle and end of the year enable the teacher and her students to document their progress and, if necessary, establish new goals. The teacher believes that the focus on improvement based on a personal benchmark allows every student to achieve a measure of success while cultivating the habits necessary for lifelong fitness.

Perhaps one of the greatest challenges in this current era of school reform is the gap between our goal of higher standards of performance for all and the realization that some students are functioning well below these lofty standards. Many educators struggle daily with this tension: How do we preserve students' self-esteem without lowering our standards? How do we encourage

> Performance-based instruction underscores the importance of using assessments to guide improvement throughout the learning process, instead of waiting to give feedback at the end of instruction.

their efforts without conveying a false sense of accomplishment? Perceptive teachers also recognize that students' own beliefs about their ability to be successful in new learning situations are a critical variable. Confronted with rigorous performance standards, some students may well believe that the target is beyond their grasp and may not, as a result, put forth needed effort.

There are no easy solutions to this dilemma. But reflect for a moment on the natural inclination displayed by parents and grandparents of toddlers and preschoolers. They regularly support new performance by encouraging small steps ("C'mon, you can do it!"), celebrating incremental achievements ("Listen, everyone! She said, 'dada'!"), and documenting growth (witness the refrigerator displays ranging from scribbles of color to identifiable pictures). These celebrations encourage children to keep trying and to strive for greater competence. They focus on what youngsters *can do* and how they have *improved* as a means of spurring continued growth.

Performance-based instruction demands a similar tack. Acknowledging the limitations of one-shot assessments, such as tests and quizzes, as the primary measures of important learning goals, some educators are moving toward creating collections of student work over time. One manifestation of this is the growing interest in and use of portfolios. Consider an analogy with photography. If a test or quiz represents a snapshot (a picture of learning at a specific moment) then a portfolio is more like a photo album—a collection of pictures showing growth and change over time.

Just as portfolios can be extremely useful as a means of documenting student progress, they also provide a tangible way to display and celebrate student work. Grade-level teams at North Frederick Elementary School in Frederick, Maryland, for example, sponsor a "portfolio party" each fall and spring. Parents, grandparents, school board members, central office

Performance tasks should call upon students to demonstrate their knowledge and skills in a manner that reflects the world outside the classroom.

staff, business partners, and others are invited to review student work collected in portfolios. Before the party, teachers guide students in selecting examples from their portfolios that illustrate progress in key learning areas. During the party, students present their portfolios to the guests, describe their work during the year, highlight the progress they have made, and identify related goals for future improvement.

Principal Carolyn Strum says the school's portfolio program has had at least four benefits: (1) the systematic collection of student work throughout the year helps document student progress and achievement; (2) student work serves as a lens through which the faculty can reflect on their successes and adjust their instructional strategies; (3) school-to-home communication is enhanced as students present and explain their work to their parents and other adults; and (4) students assume greater ownership of their learning and display obvious pride when involved in selecting and showing off their accomplishments and growth.

Developing content standards, creating more authentic performance assessments, and establishing rigorous student performance standards will not—in and of themselves—substantially boost student achievement. But the seven principles above reflect

promising ways that teachers and schools are beginning to rethink their curriculum and instructional strategies to ensure that *performance* is more than something measured at the end of a unit.

[1]This performance task was developed in 1994 by R. Marzano and D. Pickering, Mid-Continent Regional Educational Laboratory Institute, Aurora, Colorado.

[2]For a detailed discussion and examples of classroom performance lists, see M. Hibbard and colleagues, (1996), *Performance-Based Learning and Assessment*, (Alexandria, Va.: Association for Supervision and Curriculum Development).

References

Haller, E., D. Child, and H. Walberg. (1988). "Can Comprehension Be Taught: A Qualitative Synthesis." *Educational Researcher* 17, 9: 5–8.

Gardner, H. (1991). *The Unschooled Mind.* New York: Basic Books.

McCombs, B. (1984). "Processes and Skills Underlying Intrinsic Motivation to Learn: Toward a Definition of Motivational Skills Training Intervention." *Educational Psychologist* 19: 197–218.

McTighe, J., and F. Lyman. (1988). "Cueing Thinking in the Classroom: The Promise of Theory-Embedded Tools." *Educational Leadership* 45, 7: 18–24.

Palinscar, A., and A. Brown. (1984). "Reciprocal Teaching of Comprehension Fostering and Comprehension Monitoring Activities." *Cognition and Instruction* 1: 117–176.

Schunk, D. (1990). "Goal Setting and Self-Efficacy During Self-Regulated Learning." *Educational Psychologist* 25, 1: 71–86.

Wiggins, G. (1993). *Assessing Student Performance: Exploring the Limits and Purposes of Testing.* San Francisco, Calif.: Jossey-Bass.

Jay McTighe is Director of the Maryland Assessment Consortium, c/o Urbana High School, 3471 Campus Dr., Ijarnsville, MD 21754 (e-mail: jmctighe@aol.com).

Practicing What We Preach in

Designing Authentic

Designing credible performance tasks and assessments is not easy—but we can improve our efforts by using standards and peer review.

Grant Wiggins

W hat if a student asked for a good grade merely for handing the paper in? What if student divers and gymnasts were able to judge and score their own performances in meets, and did so based on effort and intent? Naive ideas, of course—yet this is just what happens in schools every day when *faculty* submit new curricular frameworks or design new assessments.

Most faculty products are assessed, if at all, merely on whether we worked hard: Did we hand in a lengthy report, based on lots of discussion? Did we provide students with a test that we happen to like? Only rarely do we demand formal self- or peer-assessment of our design work, against standards and criteria. This not only leads to less rigorous reports and designs but also seems a bit hypocritical: We ask students to do this all the time. We need to better practice what we preach.

But how do we ensure that ongoing design and reform work is more rigorous and credible? At the Center on Learning, Assessment, and School Structure (CLASS) in Princeton, New Jersey, we use design standards and a workable peer review process for critiquing and improving all proposed new curricular frameworks, tests, and performance assessments. At the heart of the work is making adult work standards-based, not process-based or merely guided by good intentions. Using such standards can go a long way in helping parents, students, and the community have faith in locally designed systems.

Standard-Based vs. Process-Based Reform Work

Many new curriculum frameworks and assessment systems produce a significant (and often understandable) backlash. A major reason is that the work is typically produced without reference to specific standards for the proposals and final product.

Think of a typical districtwide curriculum reform project. Twelve teachers and supervisors hold meetings all school year to develop a new mathematics curriculum. Their work culminates in a report produced over a three-week period in the summer, at district behest and with district financial support, resulting in a new local mathematics curriculum framework. They follow a time-tested *process* of scanning national reports, searching for consensus about themes and topics and logical progressions, and summarizing their findings and recommendations. But against what standards is their *product* (as opposed to their process) to be judged? The usual answer is: no legitimate standards at all, other than the implicit one that when the authors deem their work finished, the report is complete.

By contrast, what if all report-writers had to answer these questions: Is the report useful to readers? Does it engage and inform the readers? Does it anticipate the reactions of its critics? Does it meet professional standards of curriculum design or measurement? Does it meet the purposes laid out in a charge to the committee? Most important: *Did the writers regularly self-assess and revise their work in progress against such criteria and standards? Did they regularly seek feedback from faculty affected en route?*—the same writing process questions we properly put to students. Their report would have far greater impact if they addressed such questions. By contrast,

© Susie Fitzhugh

From *Educational Leadership*, December 1996–January 1997, pp. 18–25. © 1996 by Grant Wiggins. Reprinted by permission.

Assessments

with no self-assessment and self-adjustment along the way, the work is predictably ineffective in getting other faculty to change practice or in helping skeptical parents understand the need to do so.

Similarly with new assessments. Almost every teacher designs tests under the most naive premise: "If I designed it and gave it, it must be valid and reliable." Yet we know from research, our own observations, and the process of peer review that few teacher-designed tests and assessments meet the most basic standards for tech-

> **The purpose of assessment is to find out what each student is able to do, with knowledge, in context.**

© Susie Fitzhugh

nical credibility, intellectual defensibility, coherence with system goals, and fairness to students.

When we practice what we preach about self-assessment and adjustment against standards, we can *ensure* more rigorous and effective local teacher products, greater collegiality, and better student performance.

In standards-based reform projects, in short, we must seek a disinterested review of products against standards all along the way—not just follow a process in the hope that our work turns out well. The challenge for school reformers is to ensure that their work has *impact*, like any other performance. Desired effects must be *designed in*; they must inform all our

work from the beginning.[1] As with student performances, then, we will meet standards only by "backwards design"—making self-assessment and peer review against performance standards central to the process of writing and revision—*before* it is too late.

Rather than teaching a lock-step

process of design, we at CLASS teach faculties to see that design is always *iterative*. We constantly rethink our designs, using feedback based on clear design standards. We will likely never revisit our original designs if we lack powerful criteria and a review process with the implicit obligation to critique

> **Complex performance tasks focus on understanding as an educational goal, as opposed to mere textbook knowledge.**

all work against the criteria. We are often satisfied with (and misled by) our effort and good intentions.

Assessment Design Standards

Standards-based reform work begins with clear standards for eventual products. At CLASS, we instruct faculties involved in performance-based assessment reform in the use of a design template, a design process, and a self-assessment and peer review process based on ultimate-product standards. In addition, we work with leaders to make such standards-based design work more routine in and central to local faculty life (linked to job descriptions, department meetings, and performance appraisal systems, as well as individual and team design work). The template is also the database structure for assessment tasks and rubrics on our World Wide Web site, http://www.classnj.org.

The standards guide all design decisions. The three main criteria for judging emerging tasks are *credibility, user-friendliness,* and *feasibility.* The standards are fixed by specific models that serve to anchor the self-assessment and peer review process (just as in the assessment of student writing). Each criterion is broken down further into subcriteria: Under credibility, for example, the designer (in self-assessing) and the peers (in peer reviewing) ask such questions as:

■ Does it measure what it says it measures? Is this a valid assessment of the intended achievement?
■ Are the scoring criteria and rubrics clear, descriptive, and explicitly related to district goals and standards?
■ Is the scoring system based on genuine standards and criteria, derived from analysis of credible models?
■ Does the task require a sophisticated understanding of required content?

■ Does the task require a high degree of intellectual skill and performance quality?
■ Does the task simulate or replicate authentic, messy, real-world challenges, contexts, and constraints faced by adult professionals, consumers, or citizens?
■ Does the scoring system enable a reliable yet adequately fine discrimination of degrees of work quality?
■ Is the task worthy of the time and energy required to complete it?
■ Is the task challenging—an appropriate stretch for students?

Naturally, in parallel to what we ask of students, there are rubrics for self-and peer-assessment of these questions.

Anticipating Key Design Difficulties

We ask designers to pay particular attention to three crucial, ever-present problems in local assessment design: whether a sophisticated understanding of core content is required by the task, whether the criteria and rubrics used are authentic and appropriate for such a task and target, and whether the tasks really measure the targeted achievement. This last problem can be stated as a single injunction that must be constantly invoked: Beware the temptation of confusing a neat instructional activity with an appropriate performance task.

1. Validity in design. Validity is essential. The purpose of assessment is to find out what each student is able to do, with knowledge, in context. But we must sample from a large domain. In asking students to do a *few* tasks well, we believe we are on solid ground because we view the tasks as apt—at the heart of the subject, and able to

yield more general inferences about achievement in a subject.

When we worry about validity in design, we are thinking backwards from the evidence we need. The task must yield the right kind of information and must enable us to elicit and observe the most salient performance, given the (more general) achievements we seek to measure.

In instruction, our worries are different. We typically try to develop activities that give rise to an educational experience and ask questions that differ from those that apply to assessment design: Will the students be engaged? Will we accommodate different styles, levels, and interests? Will the activity give rise to thinking and learning at the heart of my goal for the unit? Such questions are essential to teaching, but unlikely to ensure that we will have adequate assessment evidence for *each* student when the activity is over.

Easy to say, but what to do? That's where the peer review process comes in. We are now forced to *justify* our design in a nonconfrontational way. In peer review, we often discover that the design does not yet work as a sound assessment. (Eventually, our self-assessment becomes so skilled that we can foresee these kinds of problems without much peer review.)

These are the questions we use in peer review for validity:
■ Does the task evoke the right kind of evidence, given the target? Does the task evoke sufficient evidence?
■ Can a student master the task for the "right" reasons only? Or does the task unwittingly assess for a different outcome than intended by the designer?

> Yes, it measures what it's supposed to if the task can only be done well if students are in control of the key achievements.

> No, it doesn't measure what it should if students (1) can perform the task well without achieving the intended result or (2) fail to perform the task well for inappropriate reasons, that is, abilities or knowledge unrelated to the target.

■ Are the criteria apt? That is, given the achievements to be assessed and the nature of the task, are these the right traits of performance to assess and the right descriptions of differences in work quality?

■ Is the weighting of the different criteria appropriate, given the nature and purpose of such performance?

■ Do the scoring rubrics discriminate levels of quality appropriately and not arbitrarily?

■ Does the task imply a rich and appropriate understanding of the intended target? Or is the task implicitly based on a questionable or inappropriate definition of the achievement?

■ Do the rubrics honor the criteria and achievement? Or are they implicitly based on questionable or inappropriate definitions of exemplary performance?

2. Assessment for understanding. Because any complex performance tends to focus on fairly general academic skills, performance tasks often unwittingly lack sufficient intellectual rigor and credibility.[2] Many tasks simply reveal whether students can "communicate" or "problem solve"—and often allow great leeway in subject-matter content. Consider the specific knowledge required to perform these complex tasks developed by teachers in North Carolina:

> *Birds and Soldiers.* Wildlife officials and politicians are at odds because of the rare red-cockade woodpecker on the Fort Bragg military base. Fort Bragg officials have to limit military training exercises because of the protection required for the birds under the Endangered Species Act. The Act states that an endangered bird's environment cannot be tampered with. Almost half the

---

Peer review can yield a profound result: the beginning of a truly professional relationship with colleagues.

---

known red-cockade woodpecker population is located on the base. Your task is to propose a workable solution to the problem, based on a careful review of the military's needs and the relevant law. You will write a report and make a speech to a simulated EPA review board.

Federation/Confederation. This task involves three parts: a) the student is asked to assume the role of a resident of North Carolina on the eve of secession and deliver a speech from that person's perspective on whether or not North Carolina should secede from the Union, b) the student then synthesizes the points from all speeches given and writes a letter to the editor of the local newspaper reflecting this person's re-examined point of view, and c) writes a reflective piece in the person's journal, 15 years later, re-examining the wisdom of the earlier stands.

It's Your Choice: Health Insurance. Co-payment? Pretreatment estimate? Deductible? Is health care language a foreign language for you? Students take on the role of a financial analyst and must communicate to each of three different families, in a convincing manner, the best choice of coverage for their needs and budget.

FIGURE 1

What Does Understanding Mean?

Complete the following sentence to help construct an authentic, credible performance assessment in any subject matter:

The students *really* understand (the idea, issue, theory, event being assessed) only when they can...

■ provide credible theories, models, or interpretations to explain ...
■ avoid such common misunderstandings as ...
■ make such fine, subtle distinctions as ...
■ effectively interpret such ambiguous situations or language as ...
■ explain the value or importance of ...
■ critique ...
■ see the plausibility of the "odd" view that ...
■ empathize with ...
■ critically question the commonly held view that ...
■ invent ...
■ recognize the prejudice within that ...
■ question such strong personal but unexamined beliefs as ...
■ accurately self-assess ...

These tasks focus on *understanding* as an educational goal, as opposed to mere textbook knowledge. We at CLASS have developed a complex schema for teaching and assessing understanding, drawing not only on our own research of the past decade but also the fine work of Howard Gardner (1992), David Perkins (1992), and their Project Zero colleagues. As we see it, to assess for understanding means to assess for five related capacities: sophistication of explanations and interpretations; insight gained from perspective; empathy; contextual know-how in knowledge application; and self-knowledge based on knowing our talents, limits, and prejudices.

What is the evidence we need to gather? At CLASS, we use the exercise in Figure 1 as a reminder. As a prompt, we ask teachers to brainstorm ways to complete the sentence stem that reads, "The students understand the idea only when they can..." Then we integrate the brainstormed ideas by building a rubric of sophisticated understanding on a novice-to-expert continuum. For example, take key events in history: What is a novice versus a sophisticated understanding of the Civil War? What sorts of judgments and discriminations is an expert likely to make that a novice student is unlikely to make? Such questions force us to predict how students are likely to perform.

The most exciting effect of this exercise is to realize that we must be able to predict students' inevitable misunderstandings. Of all the assessment strategies we have used, this is the one that causes the most "Aha!" responses. To teach and assess *mindful of misunderstanding* requires not only rubrics for levels of understanding and misunderstanding, but a new perspective on teaching: If you can now predict student misunderstandings, what are you doing to avoid or aggressively compensate for them in your curriculum and instruction?[3]

3. Critique and revision of rubrics and criteria. The designer of assessments *always* has a blind spot about something. Peers can discover and help to remedy oversights. The following represent typical errors with most rubrics:

■ Turning a quality into a quantity. Thus, students improperly get a higher score for "more" library sources or footnotes, as opposed to "more apt" sources.

■ Using comparative or evaluative language alone, such as "6" or "excellent" and "5" or "good," and so forth, when observable traits of performance are more meaningful.

■ A lack of continuity in the "distance" between score points. Thus, in the descriptors for a 6, 5, and 4, the differences may be slight. Suddenly, a 3 is just awful and not passing, so the score points are bunched at one end and spread out at another, causing misleading results.

Other pitfalls to watch for include combining traits, such as "creative" and "organized," in the same descriptor, and confusing a criterion with its indicators. For example, "asking questions" is an indicator of *good listening,* but silence in church doesn't mean that people aren't listening. Inappropriate questions don't indicate good listening, either. In addition, most rubrics overemphasize content and form of the

work and underemphasize or ignore the *impact* of performance—criteria at the heart of what we mean by "performance."

Most of us make these mistakes when we begin writing rubrics. Peer review, based on design standards, ensures that rubrics are debugged of common mistakes.

Peer Review

Besides improving the process of developing performance assessments, peer review can yield a profound result: the beginning of a truly professional relationship with colleagues. In CLASS projects, teachers have termed peer review one of the most satisfying (if initially scary) experiences in their careers. As a 32-year veteran teacher put it, "This is the kind of conversation I entered the profession to have, yet never had. I'm rejuvenated. I'm optimistic."

Peer reviewers serve as consultants to the designer, not glib judges. The process itself is evaluated against a basic criterion in support of that goal: *The designer must feel that the design was understood and improved by the process, and the reviewers must feel that the process was insightful and team building.* As the following guidelines reveal, the reviewers give specific, focused, and useful feedback:

Stage 1: Peers review task without designer present.[4] The designer states issues he or she wishes highlighted, self-assesses (optional), and then leaves. The peers read the materials, referring to the *assessment design criteria.* Working individually, the peers summarize the work's strengths and weaknesses and then report to the group. The group fills out a sheet summarizing the key feedback and guidance, thus rehearsing the oral report to follow. Reviewers rate the task against the task rubric, if appropriate.

Stage 2: Peers discuss review with designer. Appointing a timekeeper/facilitator is crucial. The facilitator's job is to gently but firmly ensure that the designer listens (instead of defending). First, the designer clarifies technical or logistical issues (without elaboration)— *the design must stand by itself as*

much as possible. Second, the peers give oral feedback and guidance. Third, the group and the designer discuss the feedback; the designer takes notes and asks questions. Finally, the group decides what issues should be presented to the faculty as a whole—lessons learned and problems evoked.

Criteria for peer review:

1. The core of the discussion involves considering: To what extent is the "targeted achievement" well assessed? To what extent do the task and rubric meet the design criteria? What would make the assessment more valid, reliable, authentic, engaging, rigorous, fair, and feasible?

2. The reviewers should be friendly, honest consultants. The designer's intent should be treated as a given (unless the unit's goal and means are unclear or lack rigor). *The aim is to improve the designer's idea, not substitute it with the reviewers' aesthetic judgments, intellectual priorities, or pet designs.*

3. The designer asks for focused feedback in relation to specific design criteria, goals, or problems.

4. The designer's job in the second session is primarily to listen, not explain, defend, or justify design decisions.

5. The reviewers' job is first to give useful *feedback* (did the effect match the intent?), and only then, useful *guidance.*

Note that we distinguish here between feedback and guidance. The best feedback is highly specific and descriptive of how the performance met standards. Recall how often a music teacher or tennis coach provides a steady flow of feedback (Wiggins 1993). Feedback is *not* praise and blame or mere encouragement. Try becoming better at any performance if all you hear is "Nice effort!" or "You can do better" or "We didn't like it." Whatever the role or value of praise and dislike, they are not feedback: The information provided does not help **you improve. In feedback and guidance,** *what matters is judging the design against criteria related to sound assessment.* **Peer reviewers are free to** offer concrete guidance—suggestions on how the design might be improved—assuming the designer grasps and accepts the feedback.[5]

Assessment System Criteria

Beyond reviewing specific performance tasks and rubrics, we need to evaluate entire assessment systems. For such systemic assessments, a more complex set of criteria includes credibility, technical soundness, usefulness, honesty, intellectual rigor, and fairness (Wiggins 1996).

Again, a key to credibility is *disinterested* judging—using known and intellectually defensible tasks and criteria—whether we are talking about student or faculty work. A psychometrician may well find a local assessment system not up to a rigid technical standard; but such a system can still be credible and effective within the real-world constraints of school time, talent, and budgets.

Credibility is a concern of the whole school community. We need other feedback—not just from peer reviewers, teacher-designers, or psychometricians, but from parents, school boards, college admissions officers, and legislators. Alas, what one group finds credible, another often doesn't. Clients for our information have differing needs and interests in the data; if we fail to consider these clients, our local assessment systems may be inadequate and provincial. But if we improperly mimic large-scale, audit testing methods in an effort to meet psychometric standards for local assessment design, we often develop assessment systems that are neither authentic nor effective as feedback.

Peer review should always consider the possible customers for the assessment information, to determine whether both the task and the reporting of results are apt and adequate (Wiggins 1996). The primary customer is always the student.

Principles Underlying the Standards and Criteria

When proposing standards and criteria for performance assessments, we need to remember—and clearly state—the

> Consider the possible customers for the assessment information, to determine whether both the task and the reporting of results are apt and adequate.

underlying values of our proposals. Assessment is not merely a blind set of techniques, after all, but a means to some valued end. Effective and appropriate school assessment is based on five principles:

1. Reform focuses on the purpose, not merely the techniques, of assessment. Too many reform projects tamper with the technology of assessment without reconnecting with the purposes of assessment. Assessment must recapture essential educational aims: to help the student learn and to help the teacher instruct. All other needs, such as accountability testing and program evaluation, come second. Merely shifting from multiple-choice questions to performance testing changes nothing if we still rely on the rituals of year-end, secure, one-shot testing.

2. Students and teachers are entitled to a more instructional and user-friendly assessment system than provided by current systems and psychometric criteria. A deliberately instructional assessment makes sure that tests enlighten students about real-world intellectual tasks, criteria, context, and standards; and such an assessment is built to ensure user-friendly, powerful feedback. Conventional tests often prevent students from fully understanding and meeting their intellectual obligations. And teachers are entitled to an accountability system that facilitates better teaching

3. Assessment is central, not peripheral, to instruction. We must design curriculums backwards from complex and exemplary challenges. A performance-based system integrates curriculum and assessment design,

thereby making the sequence of work more coherent and meaningful from the learner's point of view.

4. Authentic tasks must anchor the assessment process, so that typical test questions play a properly subordinate role. Students must see what adults really do with their knowledge; and all students must learn what athletes already know—that performance is more than just the drill work that develops discrete knowledge and skill. Genuine tasks demand challenges that require good judgment, adaptiveness, and the habits of mind—such as craftsmanship and tolerance for ambiguity— never tested by simplistic test items.

5. In assessment, local is better. Site-level assessments must be of higher intellectual quality—more tightly linked to instruction—than superficial standardized tests can ever be. No externally run assessment can build the kind of local capacity for and interest in high-quality assessment at the heart of all genuine local improvement. But local assessment must be credible—and that means inviting disinterested assessment by people other than the student's teachers, and including oversight of the entire assessment design and implementation system (for case studies in assessment reform, see CLASS 1996).

By keeping these principles in mind, we can continually improve our reform work. Process-driven improvement efforts can become rigid and noncreative; we resort to following the letter of the law only. The real power of standards-based reform is that we are free to innovate and divert from process—if we see a better way to approach the standards and better honor our principles. Thus, our reform efforts, not just our designs, also demand constant self-assessment and self-adjustment, based on comparing emerging work against our principles.[6]

Professionalism depends on standards-based work and peer review. Despite the long-standing habits of schools where teachers are left alone to design assessments, we believe that such practices are counterproductive to both local credibility and professional development. Every school and district ought to require peer review of major assessments, based on sound and agreed-upon standards and criteria of design and use.

[1]For student performance tasks, too, rubric and task writers should emphasize impact-related criteria so that students know the purpose of the task. Thus, instead of just scoring for organization, clarity, and accuracy in essay writing, we should include criteria related to how persuasive and engaging the piece is.

[2]Bob Marzano believes that performance assessment is ill-suited for assessing understanding of subject matter. I disagree: Intellectual understanding is demonstrated by doing well at certain types of performance, but designing such tasks is indeed difficult.

[3]A full development of this schema of understanding will appear in 1997 in a new ASCD book and training program, co-authored by Jay McTighe and myself, and tentatively titled *Understanding by Design*.

[4]Some may wonder about the utility or ethics of discussing the work in the designer's absence. We have found that this first stage gives the peers freedom to express vague concerns and complete criticisms. When the designer is always present, we find that the session bogs down as the designer justifies and explains all decisions.

[5]Video and print material on the peer review process is available from CLASS.

[6]Fairtest (1995) has developed standards and indicators for assessment processes and systems. Contact Fairtest at National Center for Fair & Open Testing, 342 Broadway, Cambridge, MA 02139. Phone: (617) 864-4810; fax: (617) 497-2224; e-mail: FairTest@aol.com.

References

Center on Learning, Assessment, and School Structure (CLASS). (1996). *Measuring What Matters: The Case for Assessment Reform* (video). Princeton, N.J.: CLASS.

Fairtest: National Center for Fair and Open Testing. (1995). *Principles and Indicators for Student Assessment Systems.* Cambridge, Mass.: Fairtest.

Gardner, H. (1992) *The Unschooled Mind.* New York: Basic Books.

Perkins, D. (1992). *Smart Schools: Better Thinking and Learning in Every Child.* New York: Free Press.

Wiggins, G. (1993). *Assessing Student Performance: Exploring the Purpose and Limits of Testing.* San Francisco: Jossey-Bass.

Wiggins, G. (1996). "Honesty and Fairness: Toward Better Grading and Reporting," in *Communicating Student Learning,* edited by T. Guskey. 1996 ASCD Yearbook. Alexandria, Va.: ASCD.

Grant Wiggins is President of the Center on Learning, Assessment, and School Structure (CLASS), 648 The Great Road, Princeton, NJ 08540. He can be reached by e-mail at gpw@classnj.org.

Grades: The Final Frontier in Assessment Reform

By Gregory J. Cizek

The task of reforming educational assessment has just begun. New forms of assessment cannot provide clearer or more complete information about student achievement unless the ways in which achievement is communicated are refined. The real challenge for assessment reform will be to bring assessment and grading practices into the fold.

Assessment reform has become a centerpiece of efforts to improve U.S. education (Stiggins, 1988; Wolf, LeMahieu, and Eresh, 1992). The list of innovations is familiar: Students are preparing portfolios of their work to demonstrate complex characteristics like employability skills. Teachers are gathering and synthesizing more information about students involving a greater diversity of valuable educational outcomes. Administrators are evaluating the use of new forms of assessment. Districts are rethinking promotion and retention policies and the measures used to inform those decisions. Professional associations are promulgating new standards for both content and assessment. Test publishers are incorporating a wider variety of alternative assessment formats into their products. Nationally, the importance of assessment can be seen in the Goals 2000 legislation and other federal initiatives.

Gregory J. Cizek is associate professor of educational research and measurement, University of Toledo, Ohio; readers may continue the dialogue on the Internet at **gcizek@utnet.utoledo.edu.**

One might conclude that assessment reform efforts are making great strides toward a common goal: improving the range and quality of information about educational performance available to students, teachers, parents, administrators, and the public. But, maybe not.

How Performance Is Communicated

Despite all the other changes, a student's educational performance is still primarily reported using grades. Actually, the older term "marks" might be more accurate than grades, because the way achievement is reported does not always involve the use of grades. Instead, the marks *might* be in the form of letters (A, B, C, D, F); numbers (percent correct); symbols (S = Satisfactory, N = Needs Improvement, U = Unsatisfactory); descriptors (Emerging, Developing, Maturing); or other systems.

Regardless of the kinds of marks, however, at the local level, where an individual student's performance matters most to the student, parents, teachers, and others intimately involved in the student's education, grades continue to be relied upon to communicate important information about performance and progress. But they probably don't.

What's Wrong with Grades?

Grades in whatever form are primitive tools for doing the job they are asked to accomplish. As communication devices, they are more like two tin cans and a length of string than a cellular phone. It's an interesting con-

> **Despite all the other changes, a student's educational performance is still primarily reported using grades.**

trast: As bubble sheets whiz through a scanner in a district testing office, a teacher mulls a pile of papers with stickers and happy faces on them, concluding that this student's work merits an A for the marking period.

In a recent study, teachers from midwestern schools were asked about their assessment and grading practices. The findings revealed great differences in what teachers do, and great uncertainty about what they *should* do. For example, teachers were asked

to indicate what factors they consider when assigning marks to assignments and tests. A clear majority (83 percent) indicated they considered the percent or number correct on the assignment; from one-third to one-half the teachers, however, also said they considered the difficulty of the assignment, how the class performed overall, the individual students' ability levels, and the effort a student put into the work.

It appears that nearly *everything* is considered when assigning a mark. There are probably two reasons for this. First, educators want to consider all relevant aspects of a student's classroom experience when assigning a mark. At the same time, there is apparently no clear consensus about which factors *are* relevant to assigning a grade.

What about final grades? To this question, teachers responded that they combined the marks they had assigned to individual assignments and tests—that uncertain mix described above—with three other kinds of information:

• Formal achievement-related measures (attendance, class participation)

• Informal achievement-related measures (answers in class, one-on-one discussions)

• Other informal information (impressions of effort, conduct, teamwork, leadership, and so on).

Unfortunately, this mix of factors is difficult to disentangle. In an attempt to clear things up, teachers were asked to explain how they combine these diverse factors into a single mark. The interviews led to other revealing perspectives on classroom assessment practice.

Deciding on a Grade

Many teachers expressed a clear preference for non-cognitive outcomes. As one elementary teacher said, "Getting the child through the level with a positive attitude and good memories is more important than a raw number grade . . . Shaping the kids' minds through group interaction, effort, and participation is more important than averaging tests and quiz scores."

Another teacher reported that "assignments, quizzes, and tests are not crucial in [her] grading policies." This teacher "stresses group interaction and uses several other subjective methods combined with intuition to formulate a final grade." Attendance and participation were also highly valued by the teachers in the study, and these factors were also considered in assigning a final grade.

It was particularly interesting to learn how teachers reported combining the divergent sources of information into the final grade. Although many teachers did not provide much detail regarding how the composite was formed, one teacher said she "considers attendance, participation, effort, conduct,

and teamwork, and adds to this things such as tests and quizzes."

Another teacher was more specific about details. She designs the test she uses herself, and uses "an average of 16–20 grades during the grading period in calculating the final

> **Attendance and participation were also highly valued by the teachers in the study, and these factors were also considered in assigning a final grade.**

grade. However, the lower grades are not factored into the average." To this mix, she adds her "overall impressions of effort and how the class performed."

The practice described by this teacher is apparently not uncommon. Several teachers reported similar practices, throwing out the worst quiz score for each student, considering class performance as a whole, and considering impressions of a student's effort and ability.

The practice of "throwing out" one or more poor scores on formal assessments is apparently quite widespread. Ostensibly, teachers use the practice so that a single low score does not inappropriately affect a student's grade. No teacher, however, reported throwing out a single high score that might inappropriately inflate a student's final grade.

Finally, several teachers made specific mention of taking "extra credit" into account when assigning the final grade.

What Do These Practices Tell Us?

Taken together, these practices point to what might be called a *success orientation* in assigning marks. While educators consider a variety of factors in assigning a final grade, they combine the information in idiosyncratic ways: Not only do different teachers use different factors, they also combine the elements in different proportions within classrooms. The factors considered in arriving at a final grade are weighted in ways that are most advantageous for each student.

In math class, for example, a student who has not mastered fractions may still be awarded a B+ for maintaining a positive attitude, regularly participating in class discussions, and trying hard. On the other hand, an A student who has mastered fractions would usually not be downgraded for being pessimistic, silent during discussions, and "coasting."

Teachers seem to follow the advice our parents gave us: "If you can't say something nice about someone, don't say anything at all." In most cases, they are able to find something good to say.

Although our parents may be happy that we are following their advice, the parents of the students may not be so happy. They assume grades indicate achievement or content mastery. Students themselves are unlikely to be sophisticated enough to understand that their grades are complex composites. Instead, they probably assume—as nearly everyone else does—that their A's and B's mean they have successfully mastered rigorous academic work.

Perhaps the innovations accompanying assessment reform have prompted teachers to gather a more diverse array of information about student performance. The new problems, though, are "What should be done with all this information?" or "How should grades be assigned?" Unfortunately, these are questions that educators are currently not well-prepared to answer. Today many teachers are simply not comfortable with the task of assigning grades.

At least two factors contribute to the problem:

First, little training in educational assessment is available at undergraduate and graduate levels of teacher training, and competence in assessment is not always a prerequisite to licensure.[1]

The research paints an even grimmer picture about the training and experience of administrators with respect to assessment. A recent study sponsored by the National Association of Elementary School Principals (NAESP), the American Association of School Administrators (AASA), and the National Association of Secondary School Principals (NASSP) illustrates the need for educational leaders to become more "assessment literate" (Stiggins, 1991; Impara, 1993).

Second, many educators simply lack an interest in testing and grading (Hills, 1991).

Grades and Report Cards: What Can Be Done?

The lack of knowledge and interest in grading translates into a serious information breakdown in education. A recent study of how the content of report cards facilitates or

The lack of knowledge and interest in grading translates into a serious information breakdown in education.

hinders parents' understanding of the information they provide was not optimistic. The authors concluded that report cards are not successfully transmitting teachers' intended meaning to parents (Waltman and Frisbie, 1994).

The reform of classroom assessment and grading practices must become a top priority if educational improvement is to be effective. New forms of assessment are welcome, but there will be no educational advantage if the meaning of these measures remains murky. Assessment reforms have introduced a wealth of information to teachers, parents, and students. Our ability to *use* this information, however, has remained essentially unchanged.

At least eight initiatives are warranted; the effort should include all who are interested in reform.

1. All educators must make a commitment to professional development.

Professional development in assessment should become a top priority. There may be different focuses for these efforts: Teachers may be more interested in classroom assessment issues and administrators may be more in need of developing a vision for integrated, planned assessment systems.

2. Training in assessment must be relevant to classrooms.

Even when teachers and administrators receive formal training in assessment, university coursework often focuses on aspects of testing and grading that may not be applicable to those who actually *do* these things. College coursework should be redesigned to provide more relevant training.

3. Professional organizations must promote sound assessment practice.

Professional organizations have become active in this area,[2] although more work is necessary to highlight the need for assessment competence and the benefits of sound assessment practices for both teachers and students.

4. Educational leaders must develop an "assessment vision."

Considering the increasing attention to assessment and all the diverse purposes it serves, it is fair to say the big picture in educational assessment is sometimes chaotic, and is perhaps the most neglected issue in assessment reform. Educational leaders should promote a clear, coordinated conception about the varieties of assessment in classrooms and the purposes and uses they serve.[3] To be effective in promoting reforms, this vision must be communicated to teachers, parents, community members, and students.

5. Grading policies must be developed and applied consistently.

Administrators, parents, and teachers must work together to develop, disseminate, and maintain consistent grading policies. To maximize the utility of grades, developmental efforts should work to build consensus on the policies, listening closely to the information needs of parents, students, employers, and universities. A beginning effort might include discussions about what current policies reveal about the need for assessment reform: for example, many policies simply list percentage ranges for A's, B's, C's, D's, and F's and give teachers little additional guidance about sound evaluation practices.

6. End isolation.

Poor assessment practices flourish in schools where teachers are isolated and do not benefit from interaction about difficult assessment issues. Teachers must take the initiative to collaborate and cooperate on testing and grading practices. Administrators must facilitate collaboration and encourage consistency in grading practices.

7. Students must be initiated into a new grading culture.

Students often see grades and learning as separate, or value grades more than education. A significant educational reform will help students see the link between mastery of knowledge, skills, and abilities, and the grades they receive. We should teach students to value real learning.

8. Assessment experts must lend a hand.

New methods of assessment promise more and better information about student performance, but proliferation of innovative assessment formats has outstripped the development of ways to interpret and report this information. Experts in testing should explore new ways of synthesizing and communicating the information provided by alternative assessments to take full advantage of the innovations.

As the list of challenges implies, the task of assessment reform has just begun. New forms of assessment such as portfolios or

---

1. These problems have been well-documented for several years. See, for example, Ward (1980), Gullickson (1986), Schafer and Lissitz (1987), O'Sullivan and Chalnick (1991), and Wise, Lukin, and Roos (1991).
2. For one example, see the Standards for Teacher Competence in Educational Assessment of Students, developed by the American Federation of Teachers, National Council on Measurement in Education, and National Education Association, Washington, D.C., 1990.
3. See Cizek and Rachor (1994) for a more detailed description about what such a vision might entail—what the authors refer to as "planned assessment systems."

performance assessments cannot provide clearer or more complete information about student achievement unless the ways achievement is communicated are refined. The real challenge for assessment will be to make assessment and grading practices part of the reform effort.

References

American Federation of Teachers, National Council on Measurement in Education, National Education Association. *Standards for Teacher Competence in Educational Assessment of Students.* Washington, D.C.: National Council on Measurement in Education, 1990.

Cizek, G. J., and Rachor, R. E. "The Real Testing Bias: The Role of Values in Educational Assessment." *NASSP Bulletin,* March 1994.

Gullickson, A. R. "Teacher Education and Teacher-Perceived Needs in Educational Measurement and Evaluation." *Journal of Educational Measurement* 23(1986): 347–54.

Hills, J. R. "Apathy Concerning Testing and Grading." *Phi Delta Kappan* 72(1991): 540–45.

Impara, J. C. "Joint Committee on Competency Standards in Student Assessment for Educational Administrators Update: Assessment Survey Results." Presented at the Annual Meeting of the National Council on Measurement, New Orleans, La., April 1993.

O'Sullivan, R. G., and Chalnick, M. K. "Measurement-Related Course Work Requirements for Teacher Certification and Recertification." *Educational Measurement: Issues and Practice* 10(1991): 17–19, 23.

Schafer, W. D., and Lissitz, R. W. "Measurement Training for School Personnel: Recommendations and Reality." *Journal of Teacher Education* 38(1987): 57–63.

Stiggins, R. J. "Assessment Literacy." *Phi Delta Kappan* 72(1991): 534–39.

_____. "Revitalizing Classroom Assessment: The Highest Instructional Priority." *Phi Delta Kappan* 69(1988): 363–68.

Waltman, K. K., and Frisbie, D. A. "Parents' Understanding of Their Children's Report Card Grades." *Applied Measurement in Education* 7(1994): 223–40.

Ward, J. G. "Teachers and Testing: A Survey of Knowledge and Attitudes." In *Testing in Our Schools,* edited by L. M. Rudner. Washington, D.C.: National Institute of Education, 1980.

Wise, S. L.; Lukin, L. E.; and Roos, L. L. "Teacher Beliefs About Training in Testing and Measurement." *Journal of Teacher Education* 42(1991): 37–42.

Wolf, D. P.; LeMahieu, P. G.; and Eresh, J. "Good Measure: Assessment as a Tool for Educational Reform." *Educational Leadership* 49(1992): 8–13.

Acknowledgment: The author is grateful for the support of this work provided by the University of Toledo College of Education and Allied Professions.

Index

Credits/Acknowledgments

Cover design by Charles Vitelli

1. Perspectives on Teaching
Facing overview—© 1998 by Cleo Freelance Photography.

2. Development
Facing overview—© 1998 by Cleo Freelance Photography.

3. Exceptional and Culturally Diverse Students
Facing overview—© 1998 by PhotoDisc, Inc.

4. Learning and Instruction
Facing overview—© 1998 by Cleo Freelance Photography.

5. Motivation and Classroom Management
Facing overview—Dushkin/McGraw-Hill photo.

6. Assessment
Facing overview—© 1998 by Cleo Freelance Photography.

ANNUAL EDITIONS ARTICLE REVIEW FORM

NAME: _____ DATE: _____

TITLE AND NUMBER OF ARTICLE: _____

BRIEFLY STATE THE MAIN IDEA OF THIS ARTICLE: _____

_____

LIST THREE IMPORTANT FACTS THAT THE AUTHOR USES TO SUPPORT THE MAIN IDEA:

_____

_____

_____

_____

WHAT INFORMATION OR IDEAS DISCUSSED IN THIS ARTICLE ARE ALSO DISCUSSED IN YOUR TEXTBOOK OR OTHER READINGS THAT YOU HAVE DONE? LIST THE TEXTBOOK CHAPTERS AND PAGE NUMBERS:

_____

_____

_____

_____

_____

LIST ANY EXAMPLES OF BIAS OR FAULTY REASONING THAT YOU FOUND IN THE ARTICLE:

_____

_____

_____

_____

LIST ANY NEW TERMS/CONCEPTS THAT WERE DISCUSSED IN THE ARTICLE, AND WRITE A SHORT DEFINITION:

_____

_____

_____

_____

*Your instructor may require you to use this ANNUAL EDITIONS Article Review Form in any number of ways: for articles that are assigned, for extra credit, as a tool to assist in developing assigned papers, or simply for your own reference. Even if it is not required, we encourage you to photocopy and use this page; you will find that reflecting on the articles will greatly enhance the information from your text.

We Want Your Advice

ANNUAL EDITIONS revisions depend on two major opinion sources: one is our Advisory Board, listed in the front of this volume, which works with us in scanning the thousands of articles published in the public press each year; the other is you—the person actually using the book. Please help us and the users of the next edition by completing the prepaid article rating form on this page and returning it to us. Thank you for your help!

ANNUAL EDITIONS: EDUCATIONAL PSYCHOLOGY 98/99
Article Rating Form

Here is an opportunity for you to have direct input into the next revision of this volume. We would like you to rate each of the 41 articles listed below, using the following scale:

1. **Excellent: should definitely be retained**
2. **Above average: should probably be retained**
3. **Below average: should probably be deleted**
4. **Poor: should definitely be deleted**

Your ratings will play a vital part in the next revision. So please mail this prepaid form to us just as soon as you complete it.
Thanks for your help!

Rating   **Article**

1. A Piece of Cake
2. How Novice Teachers Can Succeed with Adolescents
3. Using Action Research to Assess Instruction
4. The Public's View of Public Schools
5. New Brain Development Research—A Wonderful Window of Opportunity to Build Public Support for Early Childhood Education!
6. The Moral Child
7. Early Childhood Programs That Work for Children from Economically Disadvantaged Families
8. Helping Children Become More Prosocial: Ideas for Classrooms, Families, Schools, and Communities
9. Developmental Tasks of Early Adolescence: How Adult Awareness Can Reduce At-Risk Behavior
10. Cooperative Learning in Middle and Secondary Schools
11. Where to Educate Rachel Holland? Does Least Restrictive Environment Mean No Restrictions?
12. A Holistic Approach to Attention Deficit Disorder
13. Is It Acceleration or Simply Appropriate Instruction for Precocious Youth?
14. Meeting the Needs of Young Gifted Students
15. The Creative Personality
16. The Goals and Track Record of Multicultural Education
17. "All Kids Can Learn": Masking Diversity in Middle School
18. Multiculturalism: Practical Considerations for Curricular Change
19. Making Information Memorable: Enhanced Knowledge Retention and Recall through the Elaboration Process

Rating   **Article**

20. The First Seven . . . and the Eighth
21. Styles of Thinking, Abilities, and Academic Performance
22. The Rewards of Learning
23. Rewards versus Learning: A Response to Paul Chance
24. Sticking Up for Rewards
25. The Tyranny of Self-Oriented Self-Esteem
26. The Caring Classroom's Academic Edge
27. Using the Learning Environment Inventory
28. Blueprints for Learning: Using Cognitive Frameworks for Understanding
29. Kids, Computers, and Constructivism
30. A New Look at School Failure and School Success
31. Motivating Underachievers: Make Them *Want* to Try
32. Using Motivational Theory with At-Risk Children
33. How to Defuse Defiance, Threats, Challenges, Confrontations . . .
34. Connecting Instruction and Management in a Student-Centered Classroom
35. Creating a Constructivist Classroom Atmosphere
36. Why Violence Prevention Programs Don't Work—and What Does
37. The Challenges of Assessing Young Children Appropriately
38. Taking Aim at Testing
39. What Happens between Assessments?
40. Practicing What We Preach in Designing Authentic Assessments
41. Grades: The Final Frontier in Assessment Reform

(Continued on next page)

ABOUT YOU

Name _____ Date _____

Are you a teacher? ❏ Or a student? ❏

Your school name _____

Department _____

Address _____

City _____ State _____ Zip _____

School telephone # _____

YOUR COMMENTS ARE IMPORTANT TO US!

Please fill in the following information:

For which course did you use this book? _____

Did you use a text with this *ANNUAL EDITION*? ❏ yes ❏ no

What was the title of the text? _____

What are your general reactions to the *Annual Editions* concept?

Have you read any particular articles recently that you think should be included in the next edition?

Are there any articles you feel should be replaced in the next edition? Why?

Are there any World Wide Web sites you feel should be included in the next edition? Please annotate.

May we contact you for editorial input?

May we quote your comments?

CONTENTS